AF496469

The AUSTRALIAN GARDEN

The AUSTRALIAN GARDEN

JANE EDMANSON
&
LORRIE LAWRENCE

VIKING O'NEIL

To our mothers – both great gardeners

Viking O'Neil
Penguin Books Australia Ltd
487 Maroondah Highway, PO Box 257
Ringwood, Victoria 3134, Australia
Penguin Books Ltd
Harmondsworth, Middlesex, England
Viking Penguin, A Division of Penguin Books USA Inc.
375 Hudson Street, New York, New York 10014, USA
Penguin Books Canada Limited
10 Alcorn Avenue, Toronto, Ontario, Canada M4V 3B2
Penguin Books (N.Z.) Ltd
182–190 Wairau Road, Auckland 10, New Zealand

First published by Penguin Books Australia Ltd 1992

10 9 8 7 6 5 4 3 2 1

Produced by Viking O'Neil
56 Claremont Street, South Yarra, Victoria 3141, Australia
A Division of Penguin Books Australia Ltd

Designed by Leonie Stott
Illustrated by Cathy Larsen
Typeset in Garamond by Bookset, Melbourne
Printed in Australia by Griffin Press, Adelaide

National Library of Australia
Cataloguing-in-Publication data

Edmanson, Jane.
The Australian garden.

Bibliography.
Includes index.
ISBN 0 670 90433 3.

1. Gardening – Australia. I. Lawrence, Lorrie. II. Title.

635.0994

CONTENTS

INTRODUCTION

How exhilarating it is to walk through a beautiful garden, with paths, flowers, trees and lawns seemingly arranged so that there are no unused or useless spaces. Just remember that it wasn't always like that. People have made the garden, probably over some years. It may have taken immense effort, although, with gardens, given time, most things are possible. Of course, there has to be some understanding of the nature of things – of the particular soil, the way the land slopes, the movement of the sun and how the wind blows. Perfect gardens usually result from careful planning and attention to detail. And someone, private or professional, needs to do a lot of work. But it doesn't have to be done all at once.

Gardens are for everyone. This book is designed to help you as a gardener or would-be gardener to assess your outdoor needs; to show you how to go about planning and making a garden relevant to those needs, and how to enjoy, care for and maintain your garden over the years. In it we suggest a range of options and components appropriate to various garden styles. There are ideas about ways of creating garden moods and pictures, and suggestions about how to integrate outdoor requirements without compromising beauty.

We have tried to create a book that is a harmonious mixture of inspiring colour photographs and illustrations and practical information about garden making. Often landscaping books address the home handyperson and are somewhat dull, while the large, glossy garden books are descriptive rather than analytical. Our book will help you to explore the ways in which gardens become beautiful and show you how to go about making lovely gardens – from rough site and soil, if you are starting from scratch, to plantings and ornaments. We have aimed at providing practical solutions, common sense and an enthusiasm for the pleasures of gardening in the wide range of conditions that Australia offers. We hope that our ideas offer something for everyone in Australia in terms of garden size and budget.

On the practical side, you will learn how paths are made and drives laid; the importance of drainage; ways of retaining earth; and when and how to make steps. There is a section on understanding soil and making it work for you and your plants. The book takes the mystery out of how things happen by looking at the fundamentals of growing; the effects of climate and aspect; and plant selection, planting, tending and pruning. It also describes methods of pest and weed control in keeping with the environment-conscious 1990s.

As well as practical care, the mood and individuality of a garden need to be nurtured and preserved. Gardens are not just passive things to be altered and manipulated. They grow their own beauty – and sometimes problems. Plants get crowded, need shaping and pruning, come and go at their own pace. Pests arrive – and depart. In time drainage fails, wood rots and mortar crumbles. The transient nature of gardens requires continuing watchfulness and care on your part if your garden is to retain its pleasing form. *The Australian Garden* will help you maintain a lovely garden.

In the 1980s Australians developed an awareness of the natural environment. There is now a greater appreciation of nature's ways, beauty and methods, and the idea of the natural garden – nature harnessed for domestic pleasure – is appealing to more and more people. There has been, too, a revival of Victorian and Edwardian gardens, teamed with renovated period houses. People are delving into history to recreate gardens of the past. Others, however, do not wish to follow one period style, but rather to develop a more individual look. Often they wish to use indigenous materials: local rocks and gravel, and Australian native plants. Sometimes elements of grand gardens are applied to small domestic settings – dignity and proportion are readily transferable. There are also people who want gardens with a focus on leisure, in which paved sitting places, swimming pools, trampolines and tennis courts are made part of the garden setting.

In *The Australian Garden* we recognise that Australians today are interested in many styles of garden, and tell you how to design and develop them. There are plant-centred gardens, including Australian native gardens and cottage gardens; there are gardens in the sun, the tropics, the shade and along the coast; there are gardens for balcony and courtyard; there are gardens of classical proportions, incorporating styles of other ages and other cultures; and there are gardens within gardens – rose gardens, herb gardens, vegetable gardens, children's gardens and gardens for cut flowers.

Keep in mind that the garden for you need not be elaborate. Small touches of care, soft plantings, flowers growing in pots, and some simple stepping stones may impart more charm than an expensive parterre.

So where do you begin? Throughout the book we try to guide you around the pitfalls and obstacles of garden making with the objective of getting things right. If you already live gardens, may you find fresh ideas, insight and enjoyment in this book; if you are a newcomer, may you be left with ideas and inspirations about the garden that is for you.

1/ Know yourself, know your garden

Beneath a lovely and practical garden lies more than fertile soil. Sound planning centred on the twin objectives of beauty and function is the essence of good garden design. A garden should be handsome, but it must also make sense.

The most important place for your garden plan is in your mind. Don't go in cold and start digging. Instead wander about the site and get it into your blood so that you have some sense of the where and the how, and a thrill of anticipation.

Whether you have to work with a paddock, a house that sits on a bare block or a garden already made, ideas and dreams are the stuff to begin your improvements with. You may have a sudden flight of imagination that transforms that bare site, or a quick vision, as you look from one of your windows, of a tree that could give you pleasure season by season. You may dream of a pond with around it a weeping bottlebrush, correas and ferns, or the arching rose 'Cornelia', mossy rocks, sedums and saxifrages. You may even have a secret plan for a rose garden in the children's play area when they have all grown up! Some people go about garden planning surreptitiously: they achieve one or two wonderful effects in their garden and pretend that all is complete, then lie low, harbouring schemes in their head, ready to spring on unsuspecting partners, families or landscape gardeners at a suitable moment.

On the other hand, your mind may be quite blank as you gaze at your land. Sometimes such blankness is the forerunner of a grand inspiration, so have patience. But even if no flash comes, don't despair. There are plenty of options for either revising your existing garden or starting from scratch. There is an array of acknowledged styles to entice, constrain or dictate to you: styles to match Victorian, Edwardian and Californian bungalow architecture; gardens associated with grand and less grand mountain properties; and designs inspired by Italian, Middle Eastern and oriental gardens. Nostalgic, cottagey gardens, rustic woodland styles and native gardens hold continuing appeal for Australian garden makers, and the restrained, rather formal gardens that often surround post-modern buildings have also established themselves as a garden style.

Look at other gardens in terms of their components – what makes them the way they are. Find the bones of each and try to understand how particular problems of the site were handled. Walk for a while in the boots of the people who planned and made the garden so that you understand what they were up against. Look at the way the slopes and changes in level were accommodated. Notice the width of the steps and the dimensions of risers and treads. Consider the paths and what they link, where they lead and why they are curved or straight. Are the sheds, clothesline and utility areas well hidden? Think of the problems that had to be overcome to achieve this. Think also about the way the trees, shrubs and hedges have been placed. They may have been grown for beauty alone or to screen an area from the sun, the prevailing wind or an unsightly view. Observe the leaf shapes, colours, textures and silhouettes of surrounding plants and the forms of their branches. All these impart character to a garden.

You will come to a point where your free-ranging ideas need to be reined in and related to that piece of land, with its particular resources and characteristics, that is to be your garden. Blank spots in your planning – for example, about what to do with the bare, dry, root-filled ground beneath an existing tree – will need more research. You may have to acknowledge that some notions, such as an informal pond and waterfall or a gazebo, are inappropriate for your garden space or style. Other constraints, such as aspect, prevailing wind and finances, will further the process of elimination and adjustment. Yet sometimes out of such disappointing moments of truth spring new options and happy compromises.

With all this, make sure that the garden you plan is one you will care about and want to be in; one that will suit the needs of you and your family. It should be beautiful and practical, but it must also feel as if it belongs to you.

This spring picture is the result of planning between neighbours. A low picket fence allows both gardens to enjoy a hedge of Mexican orange blossom and a flowering cherry.

KNOW YOUR SITE

It is important for you to come to grips with the limitations and possibilities of your land. If your house and garden already exist, you will probably know quite a lot about the site and how it works – if not, make sure you do. If you are still at the planning stage for both house and garden you will have a chance to think about the overall project; you can site your drive, garage, recreation areas, paths and garden spaces as you would like them, without the compromises that usually need to be made on a developed site. There are, however, likely to be some constraints – an ugly view that needs to be screened or a fine mature tree whose well-being and aesthetic contribution must be considered. Even so, many characteristics of a block, such as well-grown trees, rock outcrops, a creek or a small boggy spot, can be exploited to make an individual garden.

SIZE

Size, more than any other factor, will determine what can be done with your land. However, even if your block is small, careful planning can achieve space-saving economies and visual tricks that create an impression of greater space.

Key items you may need to allow for include car storage and a driveway, a sitting area, a lawn and lovely garden surroundings. As well you may want a children's play area and a swimming pool, and in all gardens some attention must be given to bin storage and other utility needs. Even at this early stage you should be roughing out, in your mind, where you could position the main components and noting how much room, broadly, they will require.

SOIL

To grow plants successfully you need to understand the soil on your site. Dig in it and study its qualities. Is it loose, sandy or a stiff clay that sticks to your spade? Is it hard and dry in summer or easy to dig at any time of the year? Notice what happens to it after rain: does water drain away quickly or slowly? The answers to these questions will enable you to assess what additions to the soil and what drainage measures are necessary, and Chapters 2 and 4 will help you to achieve good drainage and soil.

If your site is to be excavated by heavy machinery, arrange for your topsoil – the uppermost layer of soil, which contains nutrients necessary for healthy plant growth – to be stockpiled on a suitable part of your block. Otherwise it is likely that this precious soil will be covered by loads of clay or subsoil from deeper in the earth or will get inadvertently mixed up with rubbish and taken to the tip.

CLIMATIC INFLUENCES

To plan and garden successfully, you need to know how climatic factors affect your particular block. You need to know how much rain is received and during which seasons. You should have some idea of the annual temperature range: how hot the summers are likely to be and how cold the winters. As well, you should know from which direction the prevailing wind comes and which months are the windiest. This information will influence your choice of plants, drainage, use of windbreaks and siting of sitting areas and swimming pools.

Several other factors contribute to local climatic conditions.

Altitude and slope of the terrain

High land is likely to be cooler, with a shorter growing season, than land closer to sea level. A garden on a hill or mountain top is also much more exposed.

The way land slopes – whether it lies toward or away from the sun – makes quite a difference to the amount of heat received and hence to the growth rate of plants and even the varieties that will be successful.

OPPOSITE PAGE An abundant garden is the reward for sound soil preparation and careful plant selection to suit the aspect. In this garden with a north-eastern aspect, cottage flowers revel in the sun, while tree ferns and fuchsias enjoy a more protected position.

Proximity to hills and mountains

Hills and mountains provide shelter, although sometimes they also block out the sun. Hollows or valleys offer protection, but cold air can roll down the surrounding slopes on cold nights and settle against walls or buildings, causing frost.

Proximity to large buildings

Tall buildings can create shadows and block out the sun at various times of the day. On the other hand, when the sun shines directly on a wall or section of a building, that area absorbs and radiates heat, increasing the temperature of adjacent parts.

Wind, too, is affected by large buildings and walls. Where its path is obstructed, local gustiness results: an effect that is harmful to plants.

Proximity to the sea

The sea has a moderating effect on the weather, making coastal temperatures more even than inland ones. Inland gardens are more susceptible to a wide daily temperature range: while days may be quite hot, nights can be cool.

Direction of rain

Rain usually falls obliquely, blown by the prevailing breezes. This means that a patch of ground on one side of a building or large tree may be left comparatively unwatered.

The sun's movements

There is quite a difference between summer and winter in the way the sun moves around a garden. In summer the sun in Australia rises to the south of the eastern sky and soon sits high, reaching many parts of the garden, until it sets well to the south. In winter, the sun rises to the north of the eastern sky, and remains low in the north all day. So south-facing gardens will feel the sun's strong rays only in mid-summer.

LEFT Scarlet oriental poppies (*Papaver orientale*), in a mixed planting of annuals and perennials, benefit from an open site where they receive sun from the east, north and west.

OPPOSITE PAGE Not all plants need strong sun. Here apricot clivia, white impatiens and plants grown for their foliage flourish under a spreading tree.

ASPECT

The aspect of a site is the direction its frontage faces. A house on a suburban block is likely to have the same aspect as its site, but this may be varied. Houses are usually designed so that appropriate parts of the house take advantage of the aspect.

Aspect influences the nature of a garden and the sorts of plants that will grow in each part. However, structural features, such as walls, pergolas, high buildings and large trees, can modify conditions.

A northern aspect offers opportunities for a sunny, often even hot, front garden ideal for sun-loving plants and floweriness. If your garden is big enough, you may be glad of a tree to filter the sun's rays. A western aspect becomes extremely hot on summer afternoons and early evenings unless the garden is planted with a large tree or two or has some other means of shelter. A southern aspect receives hot sun in the late afternoon and early evening at the height of summer, although it is shaded throughout the rest of the year. A south-eastern aspect offers plenty of shelter from the harsh western sun and protection from the north, but in winter the low, reluctant sun will barely touch this area. Shade-loving plants do well here. There is not much winter sunlight in an eastern aspect, but in general it is a pleasant aspect for gardens because many things grow in its gentle light.

Obviously, then, there is no such thing as a best aspect. By understanding the aspect of your garden you will be able to use it or modify it to your best advantage. If you are building your own house, perhaps helped by an architect, your garden design as much as your house design should take aspect into consideration.

TOP A protected northern aspect and a white house wall turn a terrace garden into a suntrap. An ivy pelargonium and *Convolvulus mauritanicus* are ideal plantings.

BELOW Dainty variegated ivy provides a ground cover under a silver birch where shade and matted roots make lawn impossible.

MICROCLIMATES

Microclimates are special garden spots that have climatic characteristics untypical of the area or aspect as a whole. Microclimates can occur by north-facing walls, near ponds or beneath a large tree. Individual attention is needed to get the best from such spots, and it can take a year or more to become familiar with your garden and its special quirks. If you are a canny gardener, you will set about understanding your microclimates and ways of taking advantage of them to add depth and interest to your garden compositions, although some can present difficult challenges. Here are some examples of the sorts of microclimates you might find in your garden.

Shelter spots

Shelter spots occur under the eaves of houses, where the rain is prevented from reaching the soil. Unless some effort is made to keep the ground moist, most plants will die or fail to thrive in this microclimate.

Suntraps

In a sunny aspect, walls and paving create suntraps – areas that heat up quickly and retain their heat. Suntraps can occur in courtyards, terraces and sheltered parts of the garden receiving direct sunshine at particular times of the day, at any time of year.

You can actually create a suntrap with appropriate screening and paving, but first you must watch the sun's movements every day throughout the year, if possible, so that you know where to trap it! Given a particularly intense suntrap, tropical plants may even flourish in a temperate area if they have sufficient water. However, remember that although suntraps provide opportunities for sun-loving plants, they are not suitable for shade-loving or tender plants.

Shaded spots

Plants need to be specially chosen to grow under a shady tree. They need to be tough rooted to compete with large tree roots, a touch pushy and able to do without much water.

A high wall offers plants protection from the sun and wind, but also diverts rain. A shaded place like this, with rather still air, can be dry and spidery if it does not get special watering attention.

Windfunnels

Where the path of the wind is interrupted by tall buildings or thick tree plantings, a windfunnel is created. Compressed air rushes with astonishing force through the narrow area available to it, at times causing garden destruction. Even a light breeze becomes much more forceful under these conditions.

A slatted screen or a fence or brick wall with some open work allows air currents to pass through it, reducing their force. A similar result is achieved by planting shrubs in groups or clumps.

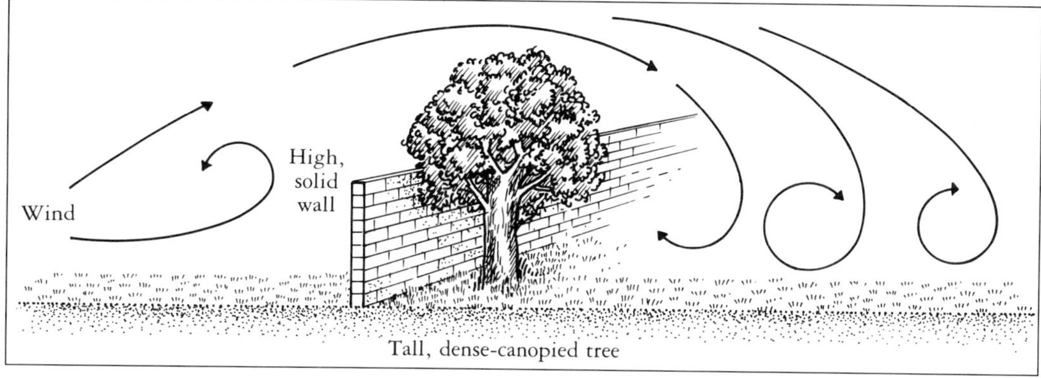

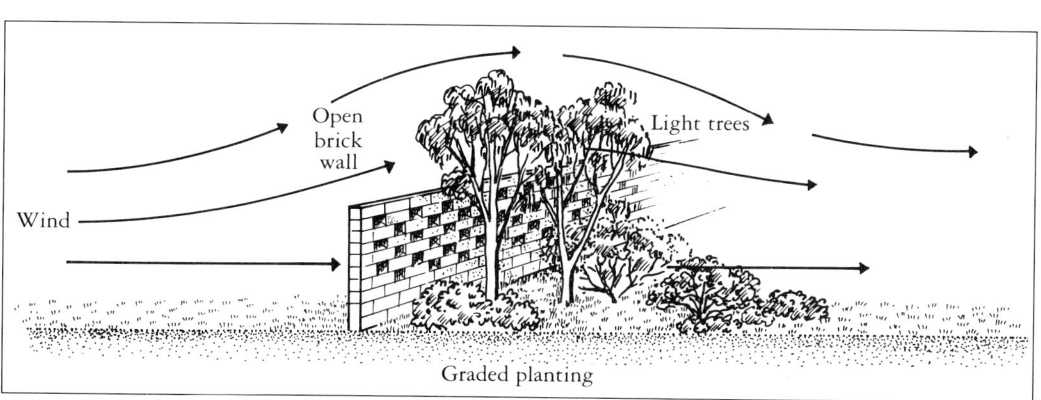

High walls and large trees don't block the wind: it simply hits the wall with full force, surges over and causes worse turbulence on the lee side. However, spaces left in a wall or fence, and a graduated planting of trees and shrubs, allow the wind to pass through and on, and reduce its force. The top illustration shows appropriate gaps left in the brickwork of a wall, and a planting of *Pittosporum tobira*, which is wind-fast and hardy.

KNOW YOUR NEEDS

Once you understand the physical characteristics of your site, make a detailed list of all the items that you want to include in your garden, adding to it as more ideas occur. Many of the same planning considerations apply whether a garden is small or large; the difference is in scale. Most properties will have open areas at the front and back and one or two side strips usually only sufficient for paths. Your list should include practical items, recreational features and your personal wishes for particular plants, plantings and ornament.

The early planning stage should be fun. Reach for the sky! You can soon tailor things to fit your space and your finances – most of us have to – but if you include one or two really special items, such as a pond and waterfall, stone steps or a silver-birch grove, at this stage, the notion may just linger and be allowed for in the reality of later on.

When you have made your list, go back to your site, walk around it and think some more about possibilities and priorities.

BELOW With good planning, a clothesline can be sited unobtrusively among plants, even in a small space.

BELOW RIGHT In this carport, space on one side has been used for a cupboard and a bin alcove.

ABOVE Detailed planning makes life easier in a garden. A wall arm provides neat storage for a hose.

LEFT Even an attractive garden shed is better partly concealed. Here a flowering crab apple (*Malus*) is underplanted with different daisies and diosma (*Coleonema*).

PLANNING A GARDEN: ITEMS TO CONSIDER

MAIN SPACES

Lawns
Garden areas
Courtyards

GARDEN BONES

Paths
Retaining walls
Steps or ramps
Driveways

RECREATION AREAS

Terraces or patios
Decks
Barbecue area
Children's play areas
Trampoline
Swimming pool, spa
Tennis court

STRUCTURAL FEATURES

Garage or carport
Walls, fences, gates, letter box
Pergolas
Screens
Sheds
Workshop or studio
Glasshouses, greenhouses, shadehouses

UTILITY AND STORAGE REQUIREMENTS FOR

Refuse heaps or compost bins
Potting table
Clothesline
Pots
Barrows and garden tools
Fuel
Rubbish bins
Bicycles, windsurfers, canoes, kayaks, boats and other leisure items

PLUMBING, ELECTRICAL WORK AND DRAINAGE

Taps (number, siting and height)
Sprinkler system
Agricultural and other drains
Gully traps
Pipes to, for example, a fountain
Outdoor lighting

PLACES FOR PETS

Dog kennel and run
Aviaries
Fowl yard

FAVOURITE PLANTS

SPECIAL PLACES

Places with special plantings of, for example, herbs, vegetables, fruit trees, roses
Places with a special style, such as a Japanese garden
Retreat
Secret garden
Fernery
Woodland walk

TREATS

Birdbath
Fountain
Sculptures
Pond
Seats
Gazebo

A rubbish bin can be made invisible, even without a screen. A carport provides a protected but airy place for a pull-out clothesline.

A FAMILY GARDEN ON AN IRREGULAR SITE

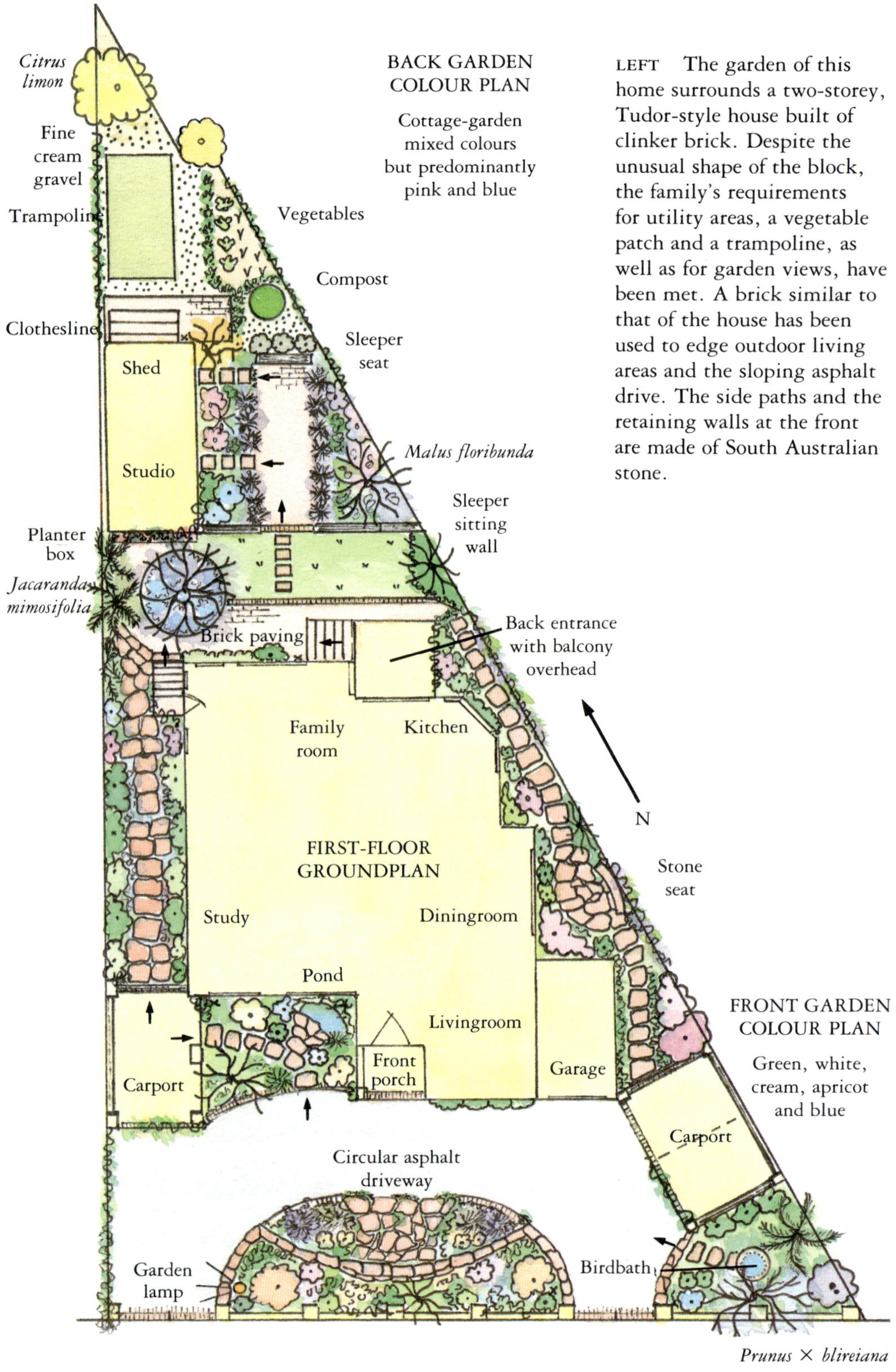

BACK GARDEN COLOUR PLAN

Cottage-garden mixed colours but predominantly pink and blue

Citrus limon

Fine cream gravel

Trampoline

Vegetables

Compost

Clothesline

Sleeper seat

Shed

Studio

Malus floribunda

Planter box

Sleeper sitting wall

Jacaranda mimosifolia

Brick paving

Back entrance with balcony overhead

Family room

Kitchen

N

FIRST-FLOOR GROUNDPLAN

Stone seat

Study

Diningroom

Pond

Livingroom

Front porch

Carport

Garage

FRONT GARDEN COLOUR PLAN

Green, white, cream, apricot and blue

Carport

Circular asphalt driveway

Garden lamp

Birdbath

Prunus × blireiana

LEFT The garden of this home surrounds a two-storey, Tudor-style house built of clinker brick. Despite the unusual shape of the block, the family's requirements for utility areas, a vegetable patch and a trampoline, as well as for garden views, have been met. A brick similar to that of the house has been used to edge outdoor living areas and the sloping asphalt drive. The side paths and the retaining walls at the front are made of South Australian stone.

ABOVE A step marks the transition from lawn to the central path and plantings in the back garden.

TOP, OPPOSITE PAGE The balcony overlooks the broad brick path and borders that lead through the back garden.

RIGHT A stone path leads from the asphalt drive to a curved stone seat in a retaining wall. Fairy fan flower (*Scaevola aemula*), white dianthus, alyssum of different colours and Westmoreland thyme (*Thymus serpyllum*) form the ground cover. Behind the seat and following its curve is a low hedge of English box (*Buxus sempervirens*), with white, cream and buff coloured roses beyond.

BELOW The broad back path leads to a simple sleeper seat that has a backdrop of *Pittosporum tenuifolium* 'James Stirling' screening the vegetable garden.

ABOVE A retaining wall of South Australian stone is complemented by overhanging blue *Convolvulus mauritanicus* and alyssum in mixed colours.

LEFT The small, stone-edged pond is seen from the front porch and a full-length window.

KNOW YOUR STYLE

As you plan your garden, you need to think about how you want it to look and the atmosphere you wish to evoke.

MOOD

Your selection of priority items, which largely reflects the relationship you want to have with your garden, will influence the appearance of your garden. You may want, for instance:

- a place to play in, where a range of leisure activities beckon from an attractive garden setting
- a neat, nice and orderly garden to complement your house
- a place to garden and spend many hours in, growing interesting plants and creating pictures season after season
- an easy-going garden, not needing much fussing over once it is 'done'
- a place to dream in, a place where you can sit quietly and read or reflect on the day.

Such aims automatically give character to gardens. However, each can be interpreted in different ways that will impart a particular feel or mood to the finished garden. For instance, sitting areas, a barbecue area, a swimming pool and play areas combined form a leisure-centred garden; nevertheless, if you choose to have rambling roses and lavenders around your sitting areas, a rustic stone barbecue in a setting of flowering cherry trees, and an informal pool paved about with irregular bluestone pieces and surrounded by lavenders, rosemary, plumbago and pink and white abutilon, with hydrangeas and ferns filling shady spots, your garden will exude a dreamy, old-world atmosphere. Yet the same leisure-centred garden could be given a predominantly Australian native setting, with bird-attracting trees and perhaps an emphasis on bright colours. The trees would mainly be small gums, such as *Eucalyptus leucoxylon* and *E. woodwardii*, callistemons, banksias, yellow-flowered native frangipani, rich gold and orange tecomas, azure agapanthus, and ginger plants for summer perfume. The mood would be

OPPOSITE PAGE In an extensive garden there is room for the grandeur of large trees. Wide steps match the garden's scale and style.

RIGHT Ivy and a camellia accentuate the graceful lines of a front porch.

ABOVE The informality of this garden meets the needs of both children and adults.

LEFT An oblong sandstone slab, set on South Australian stone supports, makes a seat, and at once a side path becomes a restful place.

bright and lively, reflecting the vigorous activities of the people who use the garden.

Even the neat, nice and orderly garden can have a special feel or mood. It will certainly have well-paved paths where no plant would ever dare to stray; however, this does not mean that the garden need be all concrete and shaven lawn. It may have clipped evergreen hedges and a well-placed statue – while yet working to a simple maintenance programme of seasonal clipping, feeding and regular sweeping and mowing. Alternatively, the neat, nice and orderly philosophy can be translated into a dense planting of well-behaved camellias and viburnums that require little care, set into pleasantly curving garden beds, with a few old-fashioned azaleas, such as 'Alba Magnifica', and hellebores and impatiens along the edges. The clipped garden will have a serene, constant quality, imparting a sense of peace. In the garden of camellias and viburnums there will be seasonal interest, with some autumn foliage and different flowers all year.

If you have not thought about the importance of mood to a garden before, put some time into analysing what appeals to you. (Of course, if you already have a garden and like its mood, make sure that you don't disturb this by introducing something too foreign in an effort to recharge its spirit.) There may be a garden you have admired from photographs in a magazine or book that you can keep in mind as you plan your garden. A walk in your local botanic gardens may suggest some aspect of garden design or mood that you could incorporate in your garden. As well, recall gardens that you have visited and how they felt to you. Was one like an exciting thoroughfare along which you passed en route to the house? Or in another did you wander happily off the path just to see more of it before you rang the doorbell? Maybe you enjoyed walking through that bush garden with the plants a little wild and the birds singing or the exuberance of the garden decked out with flowers and ornament that looked like a fashion parade?

Think of the elements that convey mood in the gardens you like: the way the garden is built or laid out, certainly; the careful concealment of unattractive but important practical items; the plants used; and the manner in which ornamental features are added.

Paths are important in establishing a garden's mood. It is largely from them that the garden is viewed and the basic layout felt and understood. In their width and the way they lie – straight and firm or soft and curving – they set the mood. Axial paths, often marked by formal plantings of shrubs and tight-clipped hedges and crossed at right-angles by clearly defined retaining walls that control slopes and set levels, are the essence of formality; although the regularly curved, sweeping paths often associated with large lawns and deep beds of azaleas and rhododendrons have a rhythmical symmetry that denotes formality, too. Such paths give you a polite invitation to enter the garden, tell you where you may go and where you ought not and almost guarantee your safe passage. In contrast, a path in a more frivolous mood will lead, seduce and surprise you – and give you a wonderful time in its garden. It will take you through woodland places, sometimes over irregular surfaces with flowery tufts growing in their cracks, and provide seats along the way, where you can rest or while away a pleasant hour.

Plants, too, have a great power to influence the mood of a garden. Notice the flowing beauty of naturally pendulous plants, such as *Callistemon viminalis* 'Hannah Ray' or weeping willows. In contrast, some banksias, such as *Banksia ericifolia*, and many conifers have an upright beauty. Standard camellias, azaleas and English box clipped into toffee-apples have superb decorative qualities. A wild beauty comes with rambling old-fashioned roses in flower. Daisy flowers of all kinds – gazanias, aurora daisies, marguerites, *Erigeron karvinskianus* and African daisies – give an abundant fullness to a garden. Flowering ivy pelargoniums overflow with cheerfulness.

STYLE

It will be becoming apparent that mood is closely linked to the style of a garden. Within the broad categories of formal and informal, there are many garden styles for you to choose from. A clearly defined style or modifications of a style will give your garden a pleasing coherence and structure as well as the mood you wish to convey.

The style of your garden needs to be appropriate to that of your house. Some kinds of gardens have been associated with particular house styles for hundreds of years. You need to be aware of your house's style and where it fits in the evolution of domestic architecture. If you do not know much about the garden styles associated with your house, find similar houses and work out which aspects of their gardens go well with that style and appeal to you.

You should be guided by the ethos of your house, as well as by the conventional styles that are appropriate. Your garden should be linked to the house by shared qualities, such as dignity, simplicity, charm and good, clean lines. Observe your house and picture how you expect the finished garden to look, then make sure that what you add is, in its way, in keeping.

Yet, with all these constraints, there is still room for individual expression in the choice of materials, plants, and degree of formality or informality. If, for example, the idea of a woodland glade appeals to you, but your house is rather formal, you can still have such a garden as long as it is some metres away, with a gradual transition provided. (No transition is needed, of course, if you have a small, informal house in a larger bushland environment.)

There are still more facets to garden style. The size of your plot and its physical characteristics need to be taken into account. If your block is small, you may decide that elaborate Italianate terraces would look overblown, whereas just one delightful statue and a simple symmetrical planting will achieve the effect you want. Significant existing features, such as mature trees and shrubs, contours and rocky outcrops, may well influence the style of garden you choose. You also need to be responsive to surrounding influences: to the character of your neighbourhood, the styles of nearby gardens and any large plantings to be seen along the boundaries.

Once you have decided on a style, interpret it faithfully. It can have changes of pace – stepping stones across the lawn instead of a solid path, or a quiet area where only leafy textures, not flowers, are important – but the whole garden must be integrated. When this wholeness is lacking, a garden can seem confusing or strangely restless. Ill-fitting decorative temptations, such as a Victorian wire arch in a bush garden or an informal, rustic waterfall in a formal courtyard, must be avoided. Self-restraint is an important quality to develop, if your garden is to keep its integrity over the years.

Fenceless front gardens provide scope for bold plantings of gazanias, shasta daisies (*Chrysanthemum maximum*), tall-plumed pride of Madeira (*Echium candicans*) and grey-leafed arctotis. The display can be enjoyed by owners, neighbours and passers-by.

KNOW YOUR COSTS, TIME AND ABILITIES

Lovely gardens need not be expensive. They can be, but there are usually less costly alternatives that you can consider before making expensive decisions. By keeping your garden style simple you will be keeping your expenses down – and ensuring an attractive garden, since simple designs usually look better than complicated ones.

Your concern may only be to revise part of your existing garden, and here dramatic improvements do not necessarily cost the earth. The greatest outlays are likely to occur when you are taming a paddock. Some earth-moving and major structural work is usually necessary, particularly if your site slopes. Swimming pools and tennis courts are expensive, but they are not really important or essential in gardens – they are optional extras that you can plan for at the start and install at a later date. Planning your own garden is time consuming but quite inexpensive and you can save money by working out your requirements carefully and getting them satisfactorily sited first up.

In working with a new site you must attend to its drainage requirements first. Undoing established gardens to install drainage schemes is much more expensive than doing the work initially, not to mention being destructive to your garden and your soul.

A garden needs a firm architectural element underlying the lovely and distracting plants clambering over it. In a rustic garden, where there is only a loose control of nature, this may come from a few well-set rocks here and there and the gravelly curve of a path. In a more complex garden, walls or fences, firm paths, retaining walls and steps, sitting ledges or benches, pergolas, screens and strong decorative elements, such as a well-placed arch, fountain or pond, are the structures that provide the architectural foundation for the living ingredients. Basic garden construction should be done well: by a professional if the work is complex or you are not a handyperson. Electrical conduits to garden lights, ponds and automatic gates that may come later, and water lines for proposed sprinkler systems and fountains, should be set under paving, edgings and walls. It is worth putting money into basic garden construction, even if you have to wait awhile for the garden to be complete. If you are unable to pay for paving work or cannot do it yourself at present, levels can be established and a bed of compacted crushed rock laid, making a reasonable walking surface until the next stage can be accomplished.

Plants can be expensive, but if you buy carefully you can save money. Remember that given reasonable care and suitable conditions all plants will grow. Don't rush to buy mature plants: buy young plants that will grow healthy, firm roots in your soil, and you will have the pleasure of watching them develop. It is essential to buy native plants young (usually in 10-centimetre pots) to ensure healthy growth. Ground covers and perennial plants bought small do well and will soon catch up to those from larger, dearer pots.

By choosing suitable plants for your local conditions you can save wasteful plant loss. It costs money to improve indigenous soil or bring in soil. Look around you at what seems to do well in the unimproved gardens of your area and try to plan a pretty garden using your creative skills and hardy, successful plants rather than temperamental performers. (Of course, you should still add compost to improve and maintain the soil's texture and keep up the supply of nutrients.)

Garden ornament is not an essential and should, in all cases, be used with restraint. One or two well-executed pieces – for instance, a birdbath and perhaps a special pot – should be quite enough for an average garden, and they can be treats that you look forward to choosing at a later date.

As your garden matures you will be able to propagate plants; you can also supplement your holdings with slips and cuttings from friends, trading some of your progeny. By propagating plants you are able to build grand effects into your garden, achieved by quantity and mass. For instance, from a couple of dwarf agapanthus plants you will soon have enough bulbs to plant small groups here and there along a long border. The hedge of rosemary or lavender that you want to enclose your vegetable garden can be propagated, too, from just one or two original plants.

You need to think about what time and effort you can put into managing your garden and trim your ideas to fit. Although many people are keen to increase their gardening, there are quite real limitations on the time that can be devoted to this most pleasant occupation. To discover how much of a gardener you want or are able to be, ask yourself these questions: do I have a gardening habit? Is gardening rather a chore? As I think about making my garden, am I already feeling inspired to be a more active gardener in the future? Can family or friends help? Can I afford to pay someone to do or share the work? Will I really become a better gardener once I understand more about it?

Modify your schemes according to your answers. Some styles and plants need much less care than others. Thoughtful design can save hours of work later: for instance, you can save time by ensuring your paths service all key areas efficiently and are made of serviceable, low-maintenance materials. Some labour-saving strategies are described in Chapter 7.

Most plants are not too demanding, but their particular needs must be understood and provided for. By understanding your garden's seasonal needs and its behavioural patterns throughout the year, you can plan and garden more effectively: for instance, you can prepare ahead for the times when you want your garden to look especially fine, such as mid-spring, Christmas or Easter. If you have regular holidays away, you will need to make provision for those times, particularly if they occur during the warmer weeks.

Australian plants, such as *Leptospermum juniperinum* 'Horizontalis' and ground-covering *Myoporum parvifolium*, thrive in a country garden that is large yet easy to maintain. Broad, sleeper-edged steps make a simple but grand approach to the house.

GARDEN SKETCHES – ON EARTH OR ON PAPER

Whether you are altering an existing garden or planning an entirely new garden, become comfortable with the project first by thinking about it on site and over time. When you are ready to translate your ideas into something more tangible, you can work directly in the garden, make rough sketches of varying accuracy or draw a plan to scale. If you have trouble visualising things even from drawn plans, mark out ideas on site with a long rope, a hose or two, some wooden stakes or a couple of tape measures.

If the job is quite straightforward and one you are going to do yourself – for instance, the re-forming of a few garden beds – mark your new curves with a hose and, if they look right, go ahead, digging out the curves to make a shallow channel. If the outline still looks good, dig up the whole area to form your bed.

For larger projects a quick sketch may be enough to help you work out where things should go. You can roughly measure the area by counting, for example, the spans between the posts of your boundary fences or you can use the time-honoured pacing method. On any plan, always mark in the direction of due north so that you are continually aware of aspect as you plan.

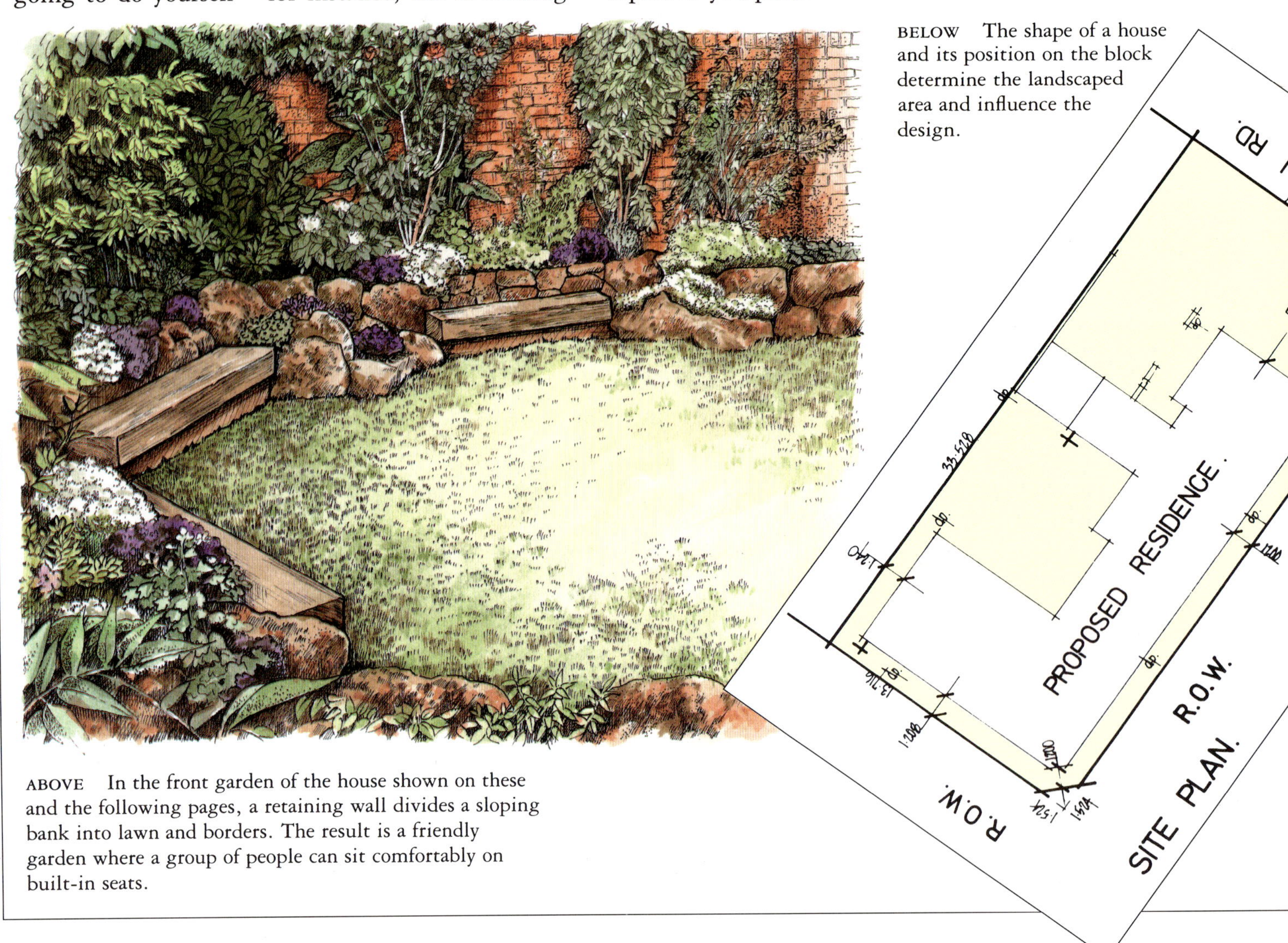

BELOW The shape of a house and its position on the block determine the landscaped area and influence the design.

ABOVE In the front garden of the house shown on these and the following pages, a retaining wall divides a sloping bank into lawn and borders. The result is a friendly garden where a group of people can sit comfortably on built-in seats.

Some layouts of gardens or parts of them, such as courtyards, are best drawn to scale in order to establish precise measurements and the relationships between proposed changes to the site. For instance, if you are revising an existing courtyard and hope to fit in a fountain, a sitting area and a tree, you will want to know exactly what space you have and how much space they require. An architect's or builder's plan, with the proposed or existing building marked on, makes a good basis for a scale drawing. If you do not have such a plan, you will have to measure the land and house boundaries before you start. A comfortable working scale frequently used by draftspeople is 1:100, meaning that every centimetre on the plan is equivalent to a metre on the site. Of course, for large properties you will need to use a smaller scale. If necessary, a site plan can be enlarged to a more workable size at a plan-printing office.

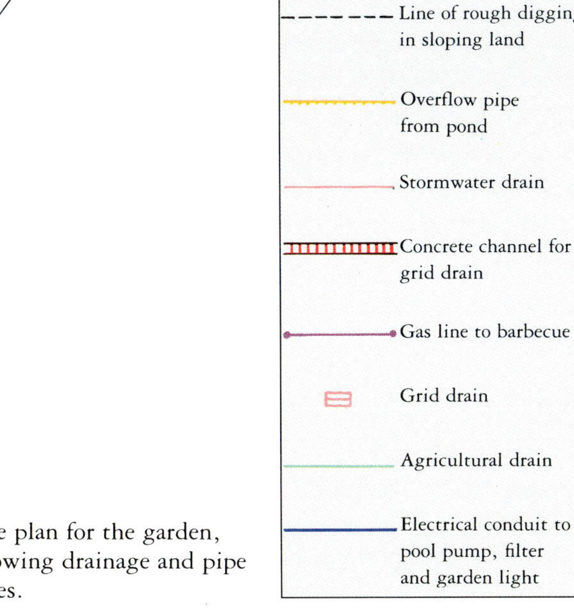

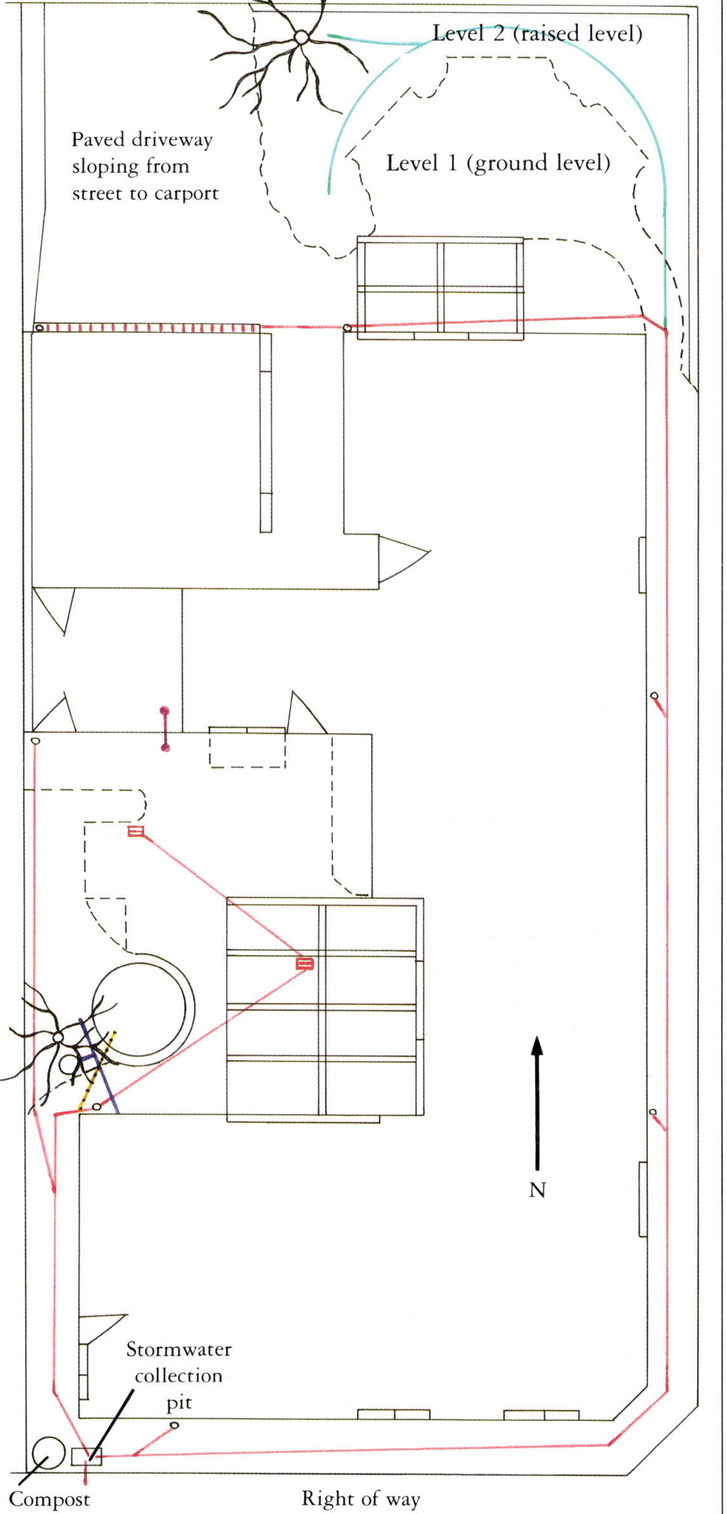

Site plan for the garden, showing drainage and pipe lines.

GARDEN SKETCHES – ON EARTH OR ON PAPER

Mark in, from house or municipal plans or from your own research, any easements, stormwater or agricultural drains, gas lines, sewage lines, water pipes and electric cables. If the drawing is likely to be too crowded, make a separate plan for this important information, referring to it as you make your garden plan and when work gets underway. If you have a contour plan you should refer to it, also, and mark on your garden plan retaining walls, steps and flat places correspondingly.

If you have trouble working out what you can fit in and where to put what, make scaled templates of the various parts or key items and try them in various places and combinations in relation to your house and its boundaries.

Remember that, even when you have planned every detail to scale, it is still essential to check the way the components look as they are being set out or built on site, and to modify them if the reality does not please you, rather than to feel bound by all aspects of the plan. It is far better to make corrections at this early stage than later on.

Mark in on the plan the major components of your garden, such as:

- the driveway, garage or carport, if needed
- retaining walls where soil must be shored up
- steps where there is a change in level
- paths linking and appropriate to the various parts of your garden
- walls or screens needed for windbreaks, blocking out ugly views, or privacy
- trees for shade or a major focus
- storage and utility areas
- recreation and play areas
- taps, lights and outside power points
- lawns
- beds and any special plantings, such as herb, rose and vegetable gardens
- microclimates, such as suntraps and dry, shaded areas, that will need special treatment
- decorative features, such as ponds, arches, rocky outcrops and seats.

OPPOSITE PAGE The plantings in the front garden have grown to make this picture in less than a year.

RIGHT In the final stage of planning, the two separate garden spaces allowed two colour schemes to be used.

BELOW A rockery gives the garden height and depth, overcoming the limitations of space.

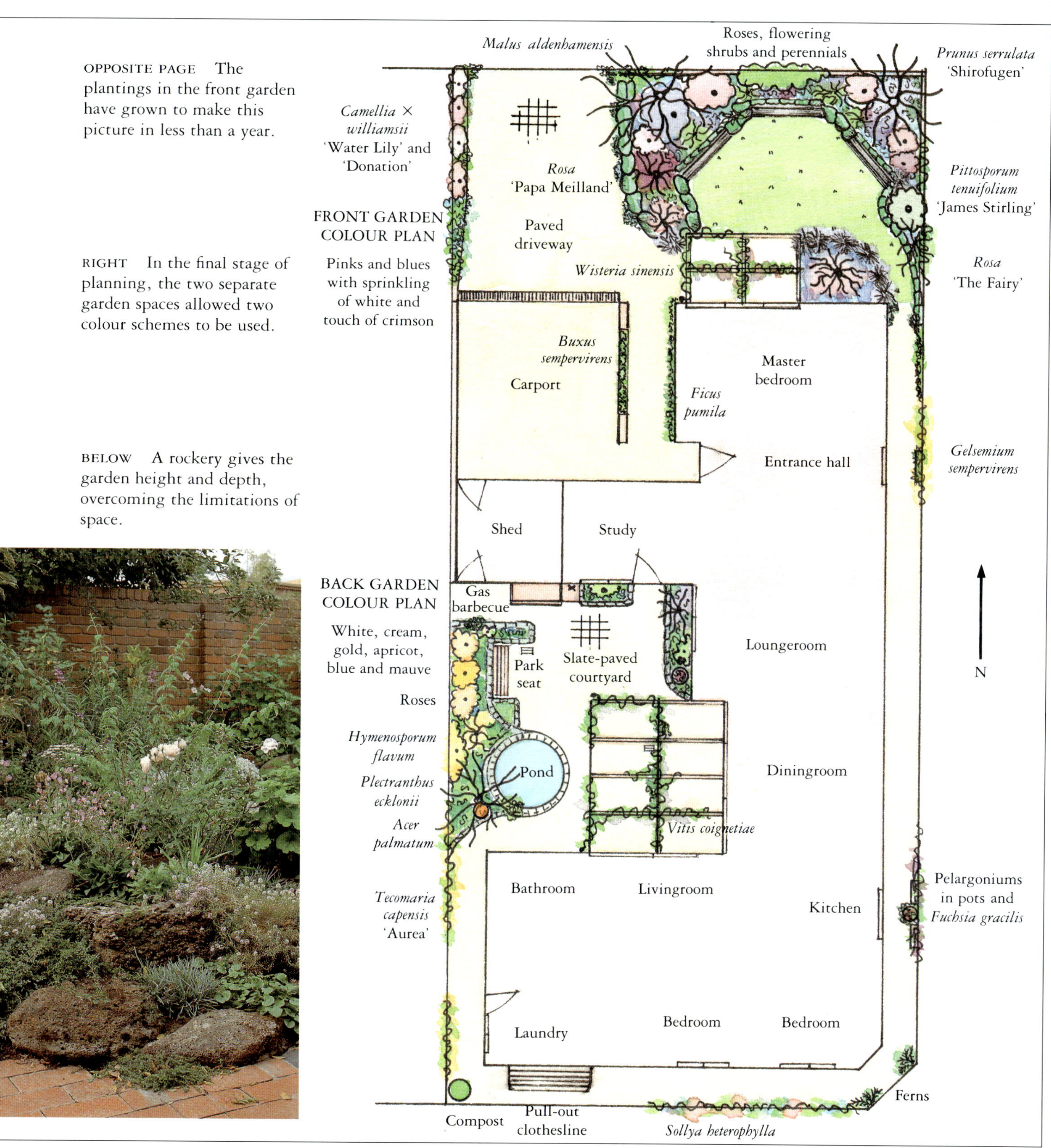

GARDEN SKETCHES – ON EARTH OR ON PAPER

In a small garden, the reward for careful planning is a compact, usable, yet attractive outdoor living area, as this view of the back garden shows.

Next, plan your plantings – trees, shrubs and low bushes, perennials, bulbs, annuals and ground covers – working to a colour scheme and design; Chapter 3 will help you. The details can be adjusted later, but it is important to be thinking about your sequence of seasonal garden pictures at this stage of planning. Key in the larger plantings by number from a plant list if you feel your plan will be overcrowded. Where distinct colour schemes are planned, indicate these on the plan so that you don't forget them.

Finally, mark on the materials – brick paving for the paths, rock for the retaining walls, slate for the steps and so on – that you have chosen to suit the style and mood of your garden. You may already have a clutch of materials that you wish to use in your garden.

A curving bed creates an alcove for a seat.

The plan will be looking quite exciting by this stage. Of course, some readers will have stopped drawing and be digging outside already! Some people, however, are by nature less adventurous than others, and, if you are one of these, you may prefer to live with a somewhat abstract plan for a while to convince yourself that it is the best way of meeting your needs.

2/ GARDEN BUILDING

As years have gone by roses have briared, weeds overtaken, branches died back and creepers crept. Lift off and cut back the neglect. There will still be the stone benches, purposeful paths and steps, terracing and well-set rocks. These are the structural elements that bind a garden together; things that endure.

A very pleasurable garden begins with beautiful bones. The bones are the essential structure you give to your garden to accommodate your planting and outdoor-living requirements. Garden building involves the adaptation and alteration of the natural surface of the site to meet your needs or the alteration of an existing garden as concepts and uses change.

Selecting landscaping materials is almost as complex a matter as selecting materials for the inside of houses. When you are making your decisions remember that the characteristics of your house materials and style, slope of land, and existing plantings, paths, steps, porches and terraces must be taken into account. And there are the very real considerations of aspect, and light variations through the day. For instance, bluestone or grey-toned slate and cement tiles can look rather dull or cold in a south or south-eastern aspect, whereas sandy colours add light and warmth to these aspects. Cut materials are more formal than rocks, and sleepers are at the other extreme – informal and rustic.

Basic structure will, to a large extent, determine the success of your garden, so at every stage of the project you must be concerned with both practicality and good looks.

GETTING ON WITH THE JOB

When you are ready to convert your garden plans into a real garden, there are some essentials to address. Your first move is to roughly mark out your plan on the ground with pegs or a hose.

Before you set to work on your site, remember to salvage any topsoil that might otherwise be lost under a mound of subsoil or deep clay as you dig. Put it in heaps, working by hand, with barrow and spade. Alternatively, you can use the skills of a bobcat and driver, but think carefully before you do so for a small area because these helpful machines can compact precious soil and consolidate the clay as they manoeuvre. In wet weather they can make an unbelievable mess. Make sure your bobcat operator knows about any underground pipes and lines. Ideally, you will by this stage have the whereabouts of electrical lines, water pipes, gas lines, telephone lines, sewage pipes, stormwater drains, easements and agricultural drains marked on a plan, to which you will need to refer as you work on your garden. Many are the underground traps awaiting inexperienced garden builders. If you lack information, excavate with care, even for small projects.

You may need to add to or alter your existing underground network of water pipes to provide taps at points that suit your garden design. As well, it is a wise idea to lay durable flexible hosing or PVC piping under potential paths, steps and retaining walls in case you wish to install sprinkler systems later on.

You may also need to lay electrical conduits to outdoor lighting sites, ponds or wall fountains that use pumps, automatic gates and barbecues. This is work for an electrician. Gas lines may be needed for gas barbecues. This is work for a plumber.

Additional drainage is likely to be needed to remove surplus moisture from the newly made or renovated garden areas. The installation of all the items mentioned and the setting of levels for different areas are vital preliminary steps in garden construction.

OPPOSITE PAGE AND LEFT
There is a timeless quality about this house, built in 1888, with its great peppercorn tree near the driveway. The surroundings have at times been neglected, but the present owners have sought to recapture the spirit of the original garden. Bluestone pitchers have been used for garden edges and seats.

GETTING THE DRAINAGE RIGHT

There should be more than fairies at the bottom of any garden. Good drainage is utterly essential to garden happiness. Drainage is the control of water on land – mainly water brought by rain, which has to go somewhere.

Some rain conveniently falls on reservoirs, creeks, rivers and seas. Puddles are made when rain fills depressions in hard surfaces, such as compacted clay, concrete and bitumen, or when water collects at low spots in bad paving. A lot of water goes into the soil and it moves, to varying degrees, downwards until it reaches the clay deposits; the water then tends to flow towards a low-lying place, such as a depression or valley, where it emerges as a wet patch, bog or swamp. Some water fills up garden beds and other earthy spaces, squelches in lawns and seems unable to get away. And of course rain falls on roofs of many shapes and sizes, enters the stormwater network via spoutings and downpipes and goes into the major drainage ways that run through vast tracts of land in closely settled areas.

Good drainage provisions should underlie all the structural work done in gardens. Drains are usually mandatory, sometimes optional but probably always advisable. At times they are rather like insurance policies against further troubles. One thing is sure: it is a lot easier to install adequate drainage initially, rather than later with hindsight and much expense. Since drainage problems rarely go away of their own accord, the best solution is to confront them. Knowing the options helps you to work out what is best for the job in hand. If you are uncertain about what is required or feel that the work required is too much for you, call in a professional landscaper or a plumber specialising in drainage.

STORMWATER DRAINS

Stormwater, grid and agricultural drains conduct water from downpipes and open gutters to a stormwater collection pit, which usually lies at a low point on any suburban block or in a street or lane nearby. Today stormwater drains are made of tough plastic piping.

When you are building a garden, it's important to know where any existing stormwater drains run so that excess garden water can be directed to them or the collection pit via additional pipes.

AGRICULTURAL DRAINS

Agricultural drains gather water from within the soil. They are pipes, laid underground, designed to gather water as they run through soil sloping gently towards a stormwater collection pit. There are a number of styles on the market, but a simple, successful one is a pipe of tough plastic with perforations. It can be bought in stiff lengths or as a coil handy for going around curves and corners.

Agricultural drains should be set within the soil on the clay bed or as near to it as feasible. Screenings or crushed scoria are piled around the pipe in the channel dug for it, creating a porous region through which

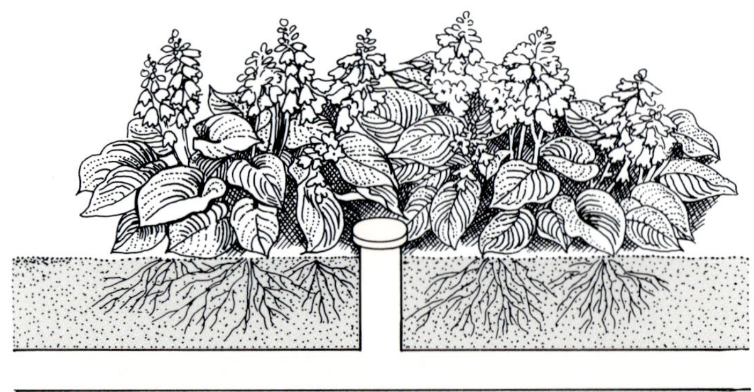

An inspection point in a stormwater or agricultural drain enables periodic checking for, and removal of, soil and litter.

water can filter into the pipe. The channel is filled with 2–3 centimetres of crushed scoria or screenings to about 10 centimetres from the soil's surface. If the stormwater pit is much higher than the clay bed the agricultural drains can be set at a compromise level so that they run into the pit. If an extreme build up of water exists, it may need to be pumped from the clay bed to the height of the stormwater drain.

If a large, open space is involved, a network of pipes about 2 metres apart can be laid, which drains into the stormwater outlet. Occasional inspection points in a stormwater or agricultural-drain system allow access for a hose or a flexible rod to keep drains free of litter. Vertical plastic pipes, fitted with plastic caps at surface level, are slotted into the horizontal drain pipes.

SPOON DRAINS

Spoon drains are small, open drains or gutters that are used to collect surface water that seeps from a slope or runs off the side of a paved area. They are often made of split terracotta pipes, but can be fashioned from a mortar mixture or concrete. They can be partially disguised with an overhang of paving material, such as tiles, slates or bricks, where this is appropriate.

GRID DRAINS

Grid drains gather surface water in a paved area. The paved surface is gently sloped to direct water into stormwater pipes set under the paving. The water enters the drain through neat, round or square metal grids, perhaps at two or three points depending on the size of the paved area. In a small paved area a sophisticated drainage system may not be necessary. The surface can just be sloped a little so that water runs off into the garden, provided the volume of water is not great.

BOX DRAINS

Box drains gather surface water. They are wide, oblong drains made of brick or concrete and covered with a fitted metal grid set flush with the ground. Where paving slopes directly towards the house or garage, a box drain can be set so that, even in heavy rain, water is captured and directed to a stormwater system. It is important to keep box drains free of leaves, grass clippings and other litter.

SOAKS

Soaks absorb water from within the soil. They are 1 metre by 1 metre deposits of crushed scoria that replace soil in an area prone to dampness. The water that gathers in the dug-out area is absorbed by the porous scoria initially, although it gradually seeps away into the surrounding drier soil. Soaks are particularly useful in areas, such as an internal courtyard, where access to a stormwater system is difficult.

WEEPHOLES

Weepholes are gaps left in the mortar joints at the base of masonry (concrete, brick or cut stone) retaining walls. They allow soil water to pass through, relieving the pressure of water that would otherwise build up on the filled-in side of the wall and eventually cause dampness and cracking.

While drains are being installed, it's a good idea to do a sketch of their position and make a few notes about what has been done when and how your drainage network operates. It is better than trusting your memory!

One or more drainage grids connected to a stormwater system can collect surface water from paving that has been gently sloped.

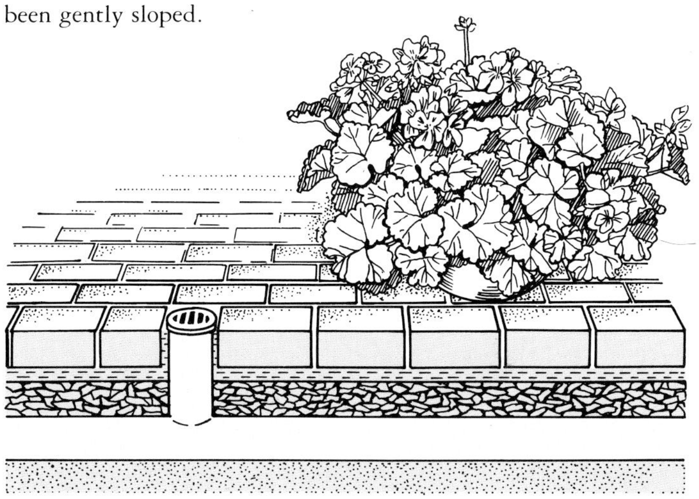

RETAINING WALLS

When a sloping site is being landscaped it is often necessary or desirable to build a retaining wall to hold the earth at a required level. Such walls are important landscape constructions and you should understand when to use them, the drainage needed and the range and appropriateness of materials available. Their construction is work for a landscaper or competent home handyperson.

OPPOSITE PAGE This huge liquidambar tree was planted in the 1930s behind a retaining wall. Beautiful though it is, a liquidambar or other large tree is a risky planting for such a position.

BELOW Retaining walls should be decorative as well as useful. Most ground-covering plants willingly tumble over wall edges and often seed on the level below.

PURPOSES

Retaining walls have two main functions.

1 They keep the soil from eroding or slipping down a slope, which is particularly likely to happen if the original ground cover of established grasses, shrubs or trees has been removed. The cavity behind the wall can be backfilled with soil to create more or less level ground, enabling new plantings to gain a firm foothold.
2 They hold the soil at specific levels, allowing the gardener to develop a new landscape feature – perhaps raised garden beds, a paved sitting area, a pool, a pond or a lawn.

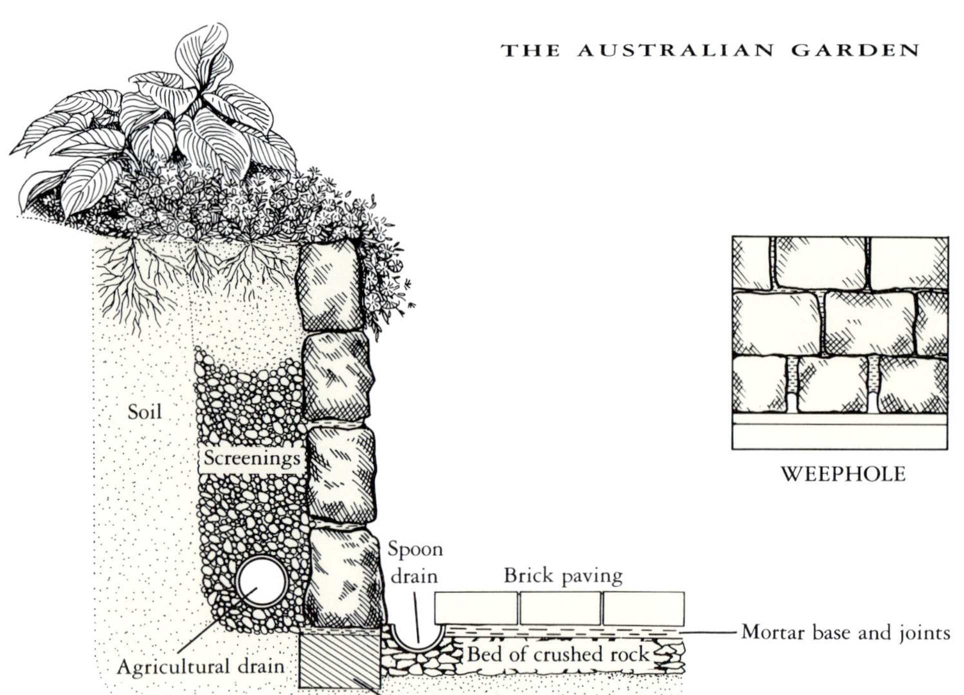

LEFT An agricultural drain should be laid behind a retaining wall to collect the soil water that would otherwise gather there. A spoon drain can collect surface water from gently sloping paving and soil water from weepholes, if necessary. Weepholes are made by leaving gaps in the mortar joints at the wall's base.

BELOW A retaining wall, such as this double-brick one, must have an agricultural drain behind it, plus weepholes, to remove soil water. A raised lawn should have a network of agricultural drains.

Retaining walls should be no more than 1.2 metres high. If the wall required must be higher than this, it is work for a landscape architect or engineer, computer and reinforced concrete. And, while two or three walls of up to 1.2 metres in height can be used to create a terraced effect on gently sloping land, this should not be attempted on steep sites.

DRAINAGE

There are plenty of hidden traps in landscaping, not the least of which is the drainage of retaining walls. Where natural slopes are cut into, the flow of water through the soil and from higher up is interrupted. The soil as a consequence is likely to ooze and drip, particularly during wet weather. If a retaining wall is then built, it will act as a dam wall, perhaps eventually collapsing under the pressure. To prevent this, agricultural drains, weepholes and spoon drains (see above) can be added.

Agricultural drains, sloping gently down to the nearest stormwater collection point, should be used behind and at the base of retaining walls. As discussed, masonry walls require weepholes. Excessive water will drain naturally through the earthy spaces between the sleepers or field rocks used in informal retaining work, but agricultural drains should still be used. If the volume of water from the retained area is considerable, spoon drains or gutters can be set in front of any type of retaining wall and directed to a stormwater system as a further safeguard.

It is advisable to put an agricultural drain behind a rocky outcrop that retains soil.

Baby's tears (*Erigeron karvinskianus*) is a useful plant for retaining walls and rock pockets.

BUILDING MATERIALS

You can choose from a range of materials for retaining walls, according to your tastes, style of house and the setting for your garden.

Stone

The stone used can be square-cut pitchers or rough quarried pieces called spalls. Bluestone or granite pitchers can be bought. The stones are best laid horizontally the way bricks are in a house wall. However, because the units are larger, retaining walls look especially attractive when some units are broken up into smaller portions or interspersed with small slate pieces of similar colour; but don't interfere with the horizontal course too much or you'll get a higgledy-piggledy look – quite a mistake with formal material. Rough quarried pieces of stone can be set with their flat surfaces flush and their shapes fitting together informally to produce a much freer effect.

No stonework is easy, and work done with unskilled hands is obvious to all but the most undiscerning! Bluestone work is not supposed to be a mortar mosaic held together by bluestone pieces: rather it is an art in which the beauty of the cut stone is shown to advantage and mortar plays a minor role, if any, on the front surface. Mortar stain is an additive introduced after Edwardian times and should be avoided in all Victorian or Edwardian restoration work and used at any time with discretion.

Sleepers

Sleepers are best supported by sleeper posts set in concrete. Sometimes a sleeper seat or a sleeper set flat to form a seat can be incorporated.

Bricks

Brick retaining walls must be strongly built of well-laid, double brick. Weepholes must be provided. Sometimes brick walls are rendered with mortar, bagged or used as a base for a veneer of tiles or slate.

Reinforced concrete

Walls of reinforced concrete are usually rendered with mortar, then bagged, and the surface can be painted in a colour to match boundary walls and the house. Weepholes must be provided. Alternatively, tiles or a veneer of slate may be added.

Field rocks

Field rocks are pieces of stone naturally occurring in the soil, which have weathered at the surface and often become coated with moss and lichen. The mossy ones should be handled with care and shown to advantage in rockwork. Natural-looking outcrops of rock can be created to form a retaining wall; the rocks are dug well into the soil, firmly locked together and cambered into the slope, with the larger ones at the base. The spaces behind the rock are backfilled with soil, making planting places for shrubs and smaller pockets for perennials, bulbs and tiny plants. The roots of the plants gradually bind the soil together, holding it in place in the low spots between the rocks.

A rock wall, like those sometimes seen along country roads, can be used for a more upright, stony effect. It may be a dry wall, or one using mortar, applied mainly behind the rocks. This wall must be sloped, or battered, back 2–5 centimetres (7 centimetres if no mortar is used) for every 30 centimetres gained in height.

PAVING

The intention to pave is really the intention to cover a designated area of ground with a hard suface. Paving should be both practical and attractive. It is important to think carefully about the shape and size of your paved areas, as well as about the aesthetic qualities, safety, maintenance and durability of the materials you wish to use. Paving will be with you for years to come. It is expensive and difficult to remove, so it is well worthwhile getting it right first up.

A path of concrete slabs laid on sand is bordered by strongly vertical plants.

There is a diverse range of materials available. Suppliers should be able to advise you on the most appropriate paving and method for the task and site, and they are often able to suggest tradespeople who could do the work for you should you so decide.

LAYING PAVING

Paving worth having must be well laid and well drained. Setting the paving surface at the appropriate level, from the viewpoint of aesthetics, drainage and common sense, is an important part of the work. Shortcuts are usually readily noticed. Working to the existing surface, throughout the area to be paved, soil is dug out to a depth of up to 13 centimetres, depending on the type of paving to be done. If the soil is of good quality, as much of it as possible should be spread in other parts of the garden or used in potting mixes and compost.

There are many methods of paving with the materials described below. Tradespeople and amateurs have their pet theories about materials and the way paving should be done. Some paving is not too difficult to do, particularly if you have a practical bent or some experience. Small areas, of course, are not as much of a challenge as large expanses. Paving on a bed of sand, with the units closely abutting, is not as complicated as paving on a bed of mortar, leaving 1-centimetre joints between the units. Paving with 600 × 600 millimetre concrete slabs, on a bed of sand, is straightforward, although the slabs are heavy to lift and place. Custom-cut materials can be more difficult, and some people prefer to have their slate or tiles laid by tradespeople.

Paved areas act as catchments for rain, hose water, any trickles through gaps in rocks and the downflow from steps and paths higher up. Something has to be done about this or the water will start causing problems. In the case of small areas of paving, surface water can be directed sideways to the garden – never towards a building. In larger spaces, grid drains are usually needed. Stormwater drains are laid underneath the paving to service one or two grid openings or more if needed. By adjustments to the paving levels, water is gently directed to these openings. A good paver knows whether grids are needed and where they should be positioned for minimum conspicuousness and maximum effect. Accidental hollows in paving, where water will sit, should be avoided.

If a path or paved space is to be laid in an area prone to dampness or seepage, agricultural drains should be laid to catch the water and conduct it away from the site, perhaps to a soak if the stormwater network is too far away. Agricultural drainage is particularly important for taking away the water that tends to collect in areas of porous gravel.

WHAT SORT OF PAVING?

Somehow local materials, such as stone or bricks made from the area's clay, almost invariably look right in landscaping. Even the gravel available to you will usually be of crushed local or nearby stone. You may feel that this is a little unimaginative. Well, if so, the fault probably lies not with the materials but with the way in which people have chosen to use them. It is up to us to use materials creatively. Patterns of brick incorporating local gravel can be really exciting, but of course the use of a free material, such as gravel, means that there will be more maintenance, and many of us are trying to minimise work in the first place by paving.

If local materials are not available or do not appeal to you, there is a huge range of paving materials to help you in your quest for attractive, functional paving. These materials include concrete, concrete blocks, bricks, stone and slate square cut or in random shapes, ceramic and terracotta tiles, bitumen, and gravel. There are also some imitations, such as mock slate and simulated stone, but for a lovely garden it's better to use materials that are not pretending to be something else.

Concrete

Concrete can be bagged, giving a roughened, more interesting finish, and tinted. A wide range of shades are available, including sandstone, mushroom, charcoal and light green.

Reinforced concrete has been widely used to make drives in the past. A concrete drive can be made very attractive if it is broken up every 3–4 metres with a seam of tilework, brick or bluestone – whatever is in keeping with the house and nearby paving.

A sleeper sitting wall and a large, circular paved area make a fine entertainment area. The problem of widening joints in the pattern has been solved by inserting wedges of trimmed brick in the outer circles.

Concrete blocks

Square-cut concrete slabs, plain or tinted, can be used in various combinations of squares and oblongs. You should work out a pattern unit, if you want to use slabs of various sizes, and repeat it. If you ad lib when you are laying the blocks the result is likely to look like 'a dog's breakfast'. If the blocks are 10 centimetres thick they can be laid on a bed of crushed rock topped with a layer of sand; it is otherwise advisable to lay them on a mortar base.

A drive of well-set concrete slabs, on a compacted bed of sand over crushed rock, is relatively inexpensive and uncomplicated. If a block develops a crack it is easily replaced, and, if you decide on a change the paving can be gathered up and sold or used elsewhere.

Brick

Conventional bricks or paving bricks, which are thinner, can be used; there is a host of colours and textures. Some sandstock bricks look quite like the handmade bricks found in very old buildings. Bricks with rougher surfaces provide more friction, making them safer to walk on.

Brick paving has an appealing quality. Well laid, using hard-surfaced bricks, it looks extremely formal, and yet set in a cottage garden it appears quite at home. In a cottage garden an irregularly shaped path of varying width will create an informal air; every now and then in a safe spot a brick can be left out, for a plant or two of alyssum or thyme. Brick paving works with most house styles, although great care needs to be taken to choose the right kind for a brick house; if you can't find one that matches or harmonises with the colour and texture of the house bricks, other materials should be considered.

Bricks or brick pavers are best laid on a bed of mortar, about 7.5 centimetres deep, over firmly compacted crushed rock, then joined with mortar. If you choose to lay bricks or brick pavers on sand use a 5-centimetre bed over crushed rock. It is not a good idea to use a sand base on a slope because the sand may wash away in time. Sand joints provide crevices for weeds to grow in, causing a lot of extra maintenance. Even bricks or brick pavers closely butted, with no joints, will still accommodate weeds in time. A brick drive should be laid on a 7-centimetre-thick slab of reinforced concrete; the bricks can be set in sand on this base or on mortar with mortar joints. A small drive can be paved in an interesting pattern, but a long drive looks best with a simple running bond or basket-weave pattern.

Sometimes brick paving looks more finished if it is given an edging of brick running end to end; or, if suitable, the bricks can be laid on their broad side, neatly side by side. Fitting the bricks within an edging requires additional cutting. Bricks on a sand base at the edge of the paving need to be mortared into position to prevent the paving spreading.

Stone and slate

Blocks of stone are expensive and heavy to handle. Local stone, such as bluestone, granite or sandstone, is usually available. Perhaps their best use is in edges and walls, but people sometimes favour these materials in driveways, particularly bluestone, reminiscent of the lanes of the Victorian era. Bluestone makes a sturdy drive. It is laid in blocks or pitchers on a crushed-rock base, set in about 5 centimetres of wet concrete, with a dry mortar mix to fill the joints – deep, raked joints look best.

Some sandstone and other light-coloured porous stones readily absorb oil and the marks remain visible.

These materials are thus best kept for paths and areas other than driveways and barbecues.

Autumn-coloured South Australian stone is being used increasingly for a range of purposes. It can be bought in pieces of various thickness. Ones less than about 7 centimetres are best laid on a reinforced concrete slab. Flat, irregularly sawn bluestone pieces can be laid in this way, also. Stronger slabs, 8 centimetres or more in thickness, can be laid on a wet concrete mix 5 centimetres thick, over crushed rock.

Indian Kota stone comes square cut in blue-grey or creamy green tonings. It is quite a strong material but is best laid in mortar over a reinforced concrete slab and with mortar joints. Handled in this way it is a suitable material for driveways.

People building in post-modern styles, in particular, have been attracted to square-cut stones or slates in soft pastel tonings, many of which are imported. Australian slate is usually rough cut and can be laid randomly for a more rustic effect. Some of the slates available can be quite slippery when wet; others are not so affected.

OPPOSITE PAGE A large reinforced concrete slab lies beneath the handsome slate paving of a courtyard.

RIGHT Gravel paths suit the softness of cottage garden plantings.

Rectangular or square cement tiles

Rectangular tiles, approximately 40 × 20 centimetres, and square tiles, approximately 20 × 20 centimetres, are yet other cement products suitable for paving. They come in a range of leafy and earth shades, with some blotched or shaded in a blend of colours. Cement tiles, or cobblestones as they are known, are often laid on a reinforced concrete slab for larger areas and always for driveways. For smaller spaces, the cement tiles can be laid on a layer of mortar over a 7.5-centimetre bed of compacted crushed rock and jointed with mortar or abutted.

Ceramic and terracotta tiles

Some people favour ceramic or terracotta tiles that give a Mediterranean look to a garden. Some tiles can be slippery when wet, so thoroughly research the product before deciding to use it in a landscape project.

Tiles should be set on a reinforced concrete slab and require a thinner mortar mix than usual, with an adhesive substance added. Tiles may even be laid on a reinforced concrete slab in driveways, but a caution about the tendency of porous terracotta to absorb oil must be added to the warning about slipperiness.

Gravel

Gravel is a viable alternative to paving. Smooth river pebbles of any size are not a good idea on paths because they provide an unstable surface into which people frequently sink, high heels and all! Crushed stones knit together to make a much more satisfactory surface. The gravel may be whatever is available locally – finely crushed stone or limestone toppings containing a proportion of fine particles that sink down to form a base.

People either like gravel or they don't. Some see it as a maintenance problem. It certainly needs raking at least every six to eight weeks and a vigilant eye kept on it for weeds. Others see only its natural, soft quality that complements their garden.

Gravel can look perfect with a simple cottage or a rural property; if allowed, little plants in adjoining beds will grow out across the edges. Yet the same material, set within edgings of mortared brick or stone and kept well raked, takes on quite a formal note. Because gravel is not set hard, it can be laid close to a large tree, or large trees can be planted near to it without fear of the roots cracking the surface.

Gravel is probably the most reasonably priced surface material for a driveway, although it is not ideal for a sloping drive because rain can wash the stones down the incline or make disfiguring rivulets during large downpours.

Gravel to a depth of 5 centimetres should be laid on an 8-centimetre-deep bed of compacted crushed rock.

Bitumen or asphalt

Bitumen or asphalt is available in a range of colours and, over a well-prepared, deep bed of stabilised compacted crushed rock, makes a good driving surface. It is suitable for sloping surfaces where gravel is impractical. Given a formal edging of brick or bluestone, it looks quite attractive.

A sound drive is made of a 10-centimetre bed of A-grade compacted crushed rock and a 5-centimetre layer of bitumen. The work is usually done by contractors.

Bituminous materials are not used much for paths these days, although asphalt paths, edged with red brick or terracotta tiles, were frequent in Victorian and Edwardian days.

PATHS

Paths are the essential link between various spaces and places in gardens – the unifying feature converting the parts to a whole. Though mostly their main purpose is to provide safe passage from one place to the other, they also provide valuable creative opportunities in terms of materials, width and shape.

In designing a path, its function must be taken into account. Essentially there are two categories: purposeful paths and paths for diversion.

Purposeful paths

Functional paths lead from the front door to the front gate or garage and, at the back, from the back door to clotheslines, sheds, service areas and barbecue. Such paths are very much task orientated and should be, as nearly as possible, the shortest distance between the two points or curved as the logic of the site demands. They cannot be too fiddly or people will disregard them and make sheep tracks through the lawn or garden beds to arrive more directly at their destination.

The width of such paths must be determined by the number of people likely to use them daily and the nature of any vehicular traffic, such as prams, a bin trolley, a wheelbarrow and bicycles. It is important that these paths have a safe, non-slippery surface and are well maintained.

Paths for diversion

Paths for diversion, such as informal or woodland paths, have a licence to exist more for beauty than function. As they leave the more civilised or formal areas, they should take on a look of abandonment, as if leading to a secret place. The secret place itself may turn out to be a sitting place in a cluster of shrubs – or the compost bin or tennis court! Such paths, with their special magic, can add greatly to the appeal of your garden. They may be just an earthy track, perhaps sprinkled with pine bark or gravel, or they may be made of a few stepping stones or rough-cut slate pieces, with little plants softening around them.

PAVED SITTING SPACES

Paved terraces and patios provide the main permanent sitting areas in gardens. Plan carefully to ensure that you have shelter and pleasant sitting-out conditions – largely determined by a good aspect, a generous allotment of space, protective screens and pergolas – for as much of the year as possible.

Often in these spaces garden decoration takes the form of attractive potted plants, though pockets for small plants may be left on larger terraces. The English idea of perennial plants, half a metre or so tall, growing among flagstones or slabs, seldom appeals to tidy-minded Australian gardeners, though the result is very pretty.

A sitting space can be created in a pleasant nook in the garden, and made more permanent and drier underfoot by the addition of paving. Especially in a small garden a paved sitting space can be charming, and if the garden is reduced to a few wall plants and pots, the outcome can be quite time saving for busy people.

PAVED COURTYARDS

Often the charm of a courtyard lies in the way paving has been used to delineate garden, walking and sitting spaces.

The paving can be formal, following a traditional symmetrical design in which clipped plants and paths are of equal importance. A post-modern courtyard often has tiling or square-cut slate used in a dramatic way as its central feature, with the plants playing a supportive design role. Irregular, randomly cut pieces of stone, gravel, Japanese maples and ferns create a gentle fantasy.

SPECIAL PAVED SPOTS

There are quite a few spots in gardens where paving can add a special touch. The paving may be a few stepping stones, set in mown grass, leading from one garden space to another, or heading off from a set of steps – not quite a path, but suggesting one. If you have a few flat pieces of stone you can lay them flush with the lawn on a bed of sand 2 to 3 centimetres deep, depending on the thickness of the pieces.

Just in front of a garden seat a small threshold of paving defines the area and can make mowing around the seat much easier. A little paving also sets off a garden ornament, statues, sculpture, birdbath or sundial.

Brick paving patterns.

PAVING, PATTERNS AND PANACHE

Australian paving has tended to be along conservative lines. Materials are mostly laid in a classic running bond or square pattern, or randomly if rough-cut pieces of stone or slate are involved. There has been a desperate little philosophy that paving, even in its ugliest bland concrete form, tidies up an area.

We just don't seem to be experimental enough yet, or perhaps we lack courage. Not that we should enter the tricky realms of kitsch. But striking patterns could be worked out with a little care – by treating bricks as mosaic pieces, for instance. Think of a simple mosaic of square-cut slates in two or three pastel colours, worked together with some cut diagonally, in a courtyard; or of square-cut Mintaro slate set here and there in sand-coloured brick paving. Smooth river pebbles set as seams in a brick or slate path or around centred concrete slabs may add interest to a path.

All these ideas are labour intensive, but more money spent on lovely and exciting paving work, and less on inappropriate and superficial garden 'features' such as fountains, lych gates and arches, is money well spent. After all, in this chapter we are talking about basic structure – bones – and of establishing the essential integrity of our gardens.

In designing paving thought should also be given to the type of planting that will suit it. If inspiration does not extend to supportive planting, paving will look, quite unfairly, out of place.

Basketweave brick paving.

Paving materials.

WHERE STRUCTURE IS EVERYTHING: A CITY GARDEN WITHOUT LAWN

ABOVE A split-level garden has a special appeal when viewed from inside the house.

BELOW Weathered timber furniture blends with the surroundings.

BELOW The strong structural elements of this small garden have great visual impact.

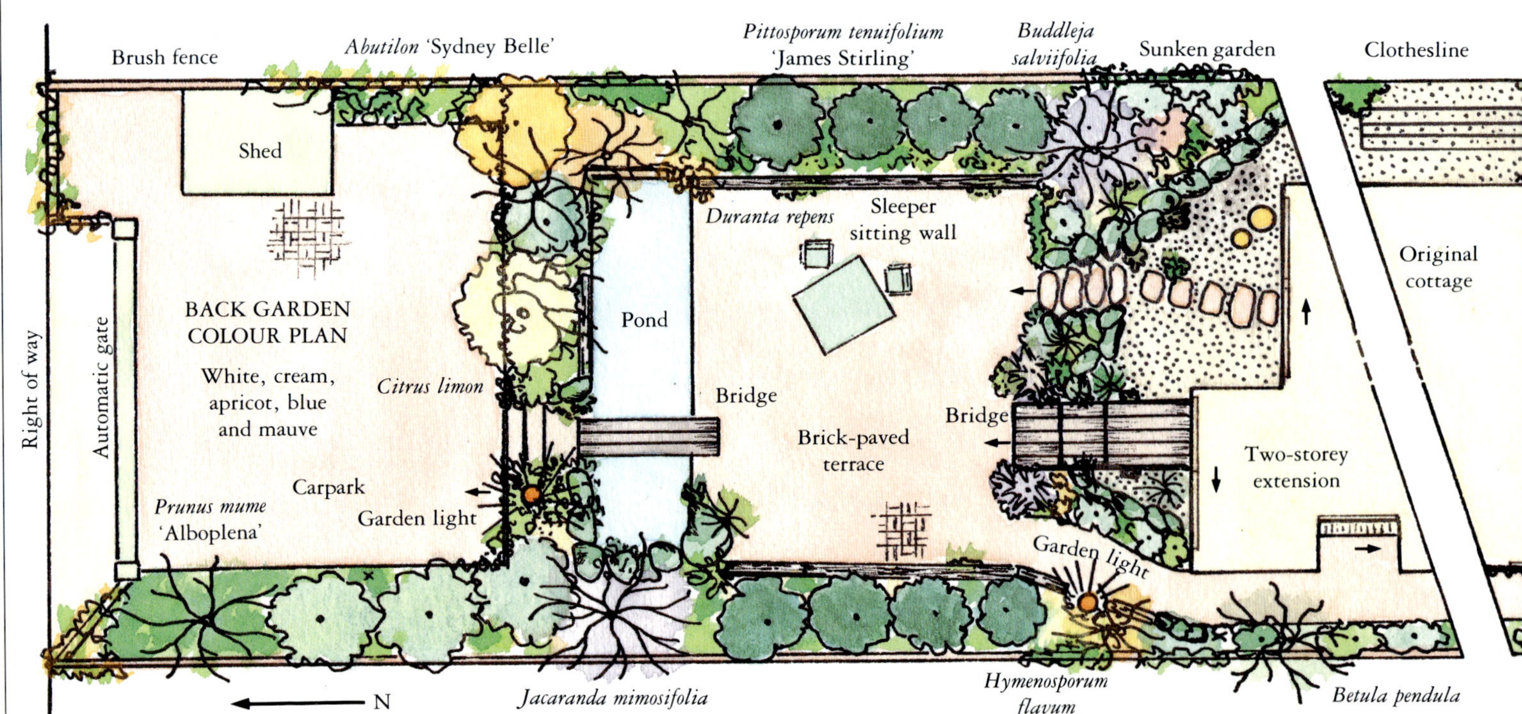

BELOW A large bay of glass lets the outside in.

FRONT GARDEN COLOUR PLAN

Cottage-garden mixed colours

ABOVE The simple but comprehensive design of the back garden is clearly seen from the balcony.

STEPS AND RAMPS

Steps and ramps are essential if there are different levels in the garden. There is something inviting about a well-built flight of steps offering access to places beyond. Slopes provide a perfect opportunity to introduce at least a step or two into a garden layout, with or without a retaining wall according to need. Changes of level add a vertical perspective to garden pictures.

GOOD DIMENSIONS MEAN GOOD-LOOKING STEPS

Perhaps it is the serenity of garden surroundings and the feeling they evoke that we have time to stroll leisurely – a different scale of space and time – that dictate the need for steps in gardens to have lower risers and deeper treads than those inside most buildings. To look their best in gardens, steps should each have a riser or height of not more than 13 centimetres, and the tread (top) should be at least 30 centimetres deep. A set of steps in domestic gardens is usually anything from 90 centimetres to 2 metres wide, depending on the situation and the degree of grandeur that is appropriate.

The Australian garden designer Edna Walling (1896–1973) had a great understanding of garden steps and how to use them. One of her concepts was a run of two shallow slate or brick steps going right across a lawn, creating two levels where previously the ground had just gently sloped. This achieved a great formality that was at once simple and grand.

DESIGNING WITH STEPS

Steps in a retaining wall may protrude from the wall or be recessed – whichever looks best for the space and garden style. If they are no more than 120 centimetres wide, they can also be set parallel to the wall, again either protruding or recessed. Where it suits the garden design and environment, steps can be angled or spoked a little, giving a slightly spiralled effect, or they can be bowed or curved in a convex or concave way.

If twelve or more steps are needed in a run it is best to have a break on the way up. This can be a landing or broader step with space for pausing – and perhaps a small seat or an ivy pelargonium in a large pot as a highlight. A flight of steps such as this can also have a change of direction after the landing or, if the garden is large, steps leading off to both the right and left.

BUILDING AND BLENDING MATERIALS FOR STEPS

Steps can be built from a variety of materials. It is usual to link the materials used with those of the adjoining pathways, though sometimes a harmonising stone can be used to give a substantial look to the steps when slate or brick is used in nearby paths. For instance, with square-cut, silver-grey slate paths, steps could be built of bluestone pitchers or long bluestone slabs.

A set of recessed steps usually begins with a lot of digging. Rough earth steps can be cut out, well under the finished dimensions, and concrete laid over a layer of crushed rock to form a firm bed for slate or brick. Stone steps can just be laid on the rough, stepped earth, with a bed of crushed rock and perhaps some mortar work for stability. The mortar can be concealed completely or the joints between the stones can be deeply raked.

When steps are to protrude from a wall, they must be built from scratch. They can be formed firstly in reinforced concrete or a brick structure can be made, with a central cavity that is filled with rubble and compacted. As with retaining walls, drainage must be attended to, though often the agricultural drains for the retaining wall will suffice. When a thin material, such as slate, cut stone or a concrete slab, is used, the steps can be veneered smoothly in slate or the treads can have a slight overhang, creating a shadow that emphasises the horizontal line of the steps. Sometimes

OPPOSITE PAGE Wide steps make a fitting approach to a large garden on different levels. The steps have South Australian stone risers overhung with a tread of Castlemaine slate pieces.

risers and treads are of two different materials. This adds interest and again emphasises the horizontal line. For instance, steps can have cut-rock or bluestone risers and slate or concrete slab treads, in either case overhung a touch.

Steps can be made of wooden sleepers or bridge timbers. It is important to know that these can grow moss in winter and, even just by being wet, become quite slippery. If timber steps are wanted for a main service area, they are best laid on their side to form risers and pegged from the back with nailed metal star-droppers, which must be set deeply and well hidden. The treads are then backfilled with gravel, brick or some other material. Such a combination of materials for the tread makes a safer step.

Where a gravel path leads to the steps, the risers can be of cut rock or rough-cut slate that also forms an edge to the treads, which are then backfilled with gravel. The sides of these steps are often informal rockwork that holds in the gravel and retains the surrounding soil.

Occasionally steps can just be cut into a grassy bank or slope. It is likely that you will also need, or feel happier with, a few small rocks set on either side of the steps to hold the earth back and to add to the natural effect. Usually wings are needed with more formal steps that are part of a retaining wall. Wings are normally made of the same material as the wall. They should be functional but inconspicuous, and may be overhung with soft plantings.

These steps are made of concrete with a slate veneer.

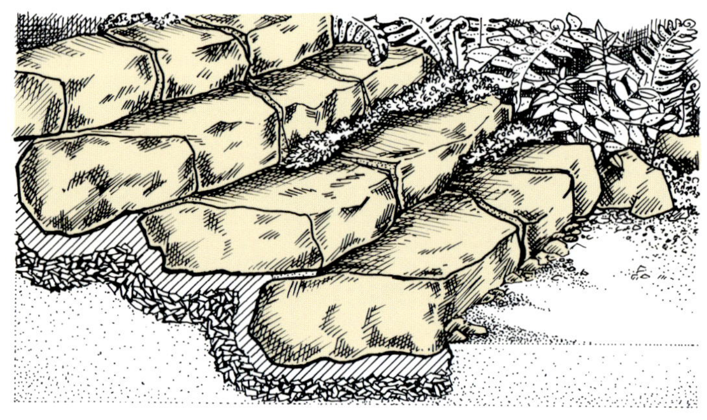

Steps made of stone blocks are laid in the earth on a bed of concrete and crushed rock.

OPPOSITE PAGE An unusual arrangement of Mintaro slate pieces and sleepers forms steps leading to a small, slate-paved courtyard.

LEFT Steps can be built into a grassy slope and softened with side plantings.

These steps have bluestone risers and slate treads.

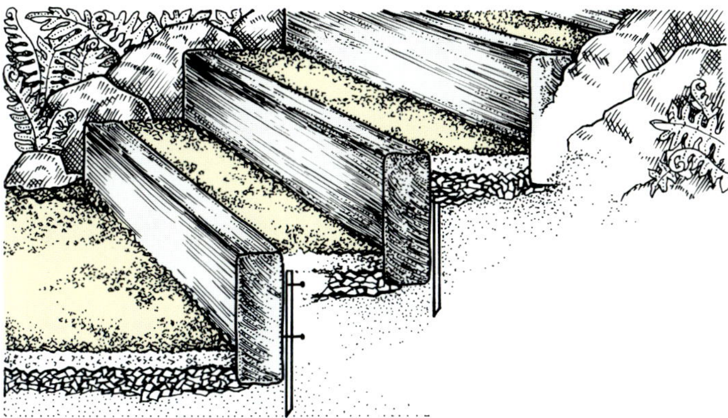

Railway-sleeper steps go well with a rock retaining wall or rocky outcrops.

To break the stark appearance of masonry steps, little plants can be encouraged in gaps at the sides and planting pockets can be left in safe places here and there towards the backs of the treads. Plants such as thyme, chamomile (*Anthemis*), ajuga, snow-in-summer (*Cerastium tomentosum*) and alyssum make pretty plantings for steps.

HANDRAILS

Sometimes it is necessary to have a handrail or banister on one or both sides of steps or ramps. It can be made of timber or wrought iron in an attractive and suitable design. You might think about having a handrail of wrought iron designed and made especially for you. Often it will not be much more expensive than a mass-produced one and will add to the beauty and interest of your garden.

RAMPS

Ramps are really sloping paths. They offer an alternative form of access to steps for elderly people, invalids and wheel chairs, babies and prams, wheelbarrows, lawnmowers and so on, but on the whole they lack the charm of garden steps. They should have a gentle, manageable slope; if not, steps are the only answer. Like steps, ramps may require handrails for safety (see above).

Ramps can be set parallel to a retaining wall rather than at right-angles and are less conspicuous this way. The exposed side may be stone, brick or timber, depending on the material used for the retaining wall, and softened with trailing plants. Slate can be slippery when wet, so it is not a good material for a ramp. Gravel is not very suitable either because people and vehicles can skid on the loose surface. However, it can be used if it surrounds centrally set concrete slabs; the two surfaces produce a friction, making the ramp safer to use. As long as the drainage is adequate, grass forms a useful and attractive surface.

When the change in level is small, a ramp to service wheeled traffic can be set inconspicuously at one end of a retaining wall. Traffic can also roll up and down steps with low risers and deep treads.

DRIVEWAYS

It would be wonderful if we could transfer the feeling of a woodland path to driveways, and where the style suits we should certainly try. But driveways are usually a far more complex matter. Nevertheless they, and accommodation for vehicles, boats and trailers, should be an integral part of any house plan and allowed for in the building budget. Unfortunately sometimes, even with quite expensive houses, the building may be complete and the swimming pool in, yet the owners are still wandering about, wondering where to put the drive and vehicles and how to pay for the work.

Historically, while the driveways might well have been at the side of the front garden or formed a circular sweep to the entrance of large houses, the horses, buggies and coaches were accommodated at the back. Sometimes just a service entrance led to the stables and sheds at the rear, and a rear lane provided access for vehicles.

In modern planning many people are constrained by limited space and funds and must make decisions based on family needs and lifestyle. Drives are expensive and take up a great deal of garden space. Any design faults will annoy you day in and day out. Careful planning will correspondingly reward you. This applies not only to a new site, but also to any redesigning or extension of existing vehicle access and accommodation.

Bear in mind that local councils have regulations about matters of crossovers, drives, carports and garages, which should be studied before your plans get underway.

LEFT A well-controlled front planting suits the clean-cut lines of the garage and façade of a modern house.

OPPOSITE PAGE Sloping driveways must be well constructed, durable and non-slippery. Stained concrete is a hardy, neutral material – and a foil for large, detailed plantings.

WHERE SHOULD THE DRIVE BE?

The site of a driveway usually depends on where the garage is or will be. The garage can be a free-standing building at the side of the house or elsewhere. Alternatively it can be part of your house structure, at basement or ground-floor level at the front, back or side, depending on your overall house plan and the slope of the land. If you are planning an attached garage, it is sensible for it to have an entry directly into the house, providing privacy and ease of loading and unloading. Such an entry is also a boon in inclement weather.

It is wise to be cautious about adding free-standing vehicle accommodation in a piecemeal fashion, especially where it interferes with the good looks of the front garden. Try to anticipate your future needs in your initial house-planning stages. If there is a choice between back and front entrances, weigh the alternatives carefully. Your decision should depend on what you have in mind for the back and front gardens and where your priorities lie.

A drive of local gravel, laid on a well-packed crushed-rock base and flanked by gums and wattles, harmonises with a rural setting.

Some properties are dominated by front driveways leading to large garages, designed to accommodate cars, a trailer and perhaps a boat. These driveways require a broad approach, or apron, in front of the garage entrance. On an ordinary block there is usually only one place with sufficient space to site such a complex, and the garden has to settle in around the drive. Sometimes a back entrance from a lane, street or right of way means that an adjacent garage or carport can be built and no driveway is needed.

SIZE AND SHAPE

A grand circular sweep, dominating the front, should always be well maintained, with perhaps softening overhead branches and tasteful plantings along its edges. If you do not have room for a grand circular sweep, keep your front drive as inconspicuous as possible. It is often best sited neatly along one side boundary of the property. Overhanging branches of nearby trees and shrubs, bold side plantings and trees further away can be employed to soften the expanse of paving. If space allows, it can be gently curved, enabling interesting planting on both sides.

A domestic drive should be 3 metres wide for comfortable use, with room allowed for people to get in and out of car doors on both sides. Doors must not knock against walls or get scratched by plants as they are opened. Consider the usage at key points of the drive and carport or garage. People getting in or out of cars at various points often carry armfuls of shopping, suitcases or portable cots. Clear access to the boot must also be provided.

If the garage or carport accommodates two or more vehicles abreast, there must be a wide approach for sensible access to each bay. Sometimes cars may need sufficient room for turning around, after backing out of the garage or carport.

3/ PICTURE MAKING

It's not the paint that makes a picture, but the brain and hand and heart of the man who uses it.

GERTRUDE JEKYLL

When you think of plants, you think of those you know best. However, when you think of gardens you should think of pictures rather than individual plants. In your mind you need to have an image of plant combinations, probably within a framework of paths and edges and often broken up by grassy spaces, with an occasional well-placed pot or two, a seat or a garden ornament.

The art of garden making is the arranging of plants according to their various attributes, site preferences and appearance within a spatial framework to create a succession of pictures. Garden pictures have a temporal dimension, too: they move, develop, flourish and fade through the seasons of the year. Each plant plays out its individual part – though some are more variable than others.

When people make gardens without this insight, the result, quite frequently, is a hotchpotch of plants, with little regard for height, leaf behaviour and the colour and appearance of flowers. Of course such garden makers have the odd success, but this luck will not last throughout the year. Front gardens often appear to have been planted without consideration for the style of the house. Often, appealing plants have been chosen at a nursery or from catalogues and quickly planted to fill spaces. All the favourites are there, but will they work as a group? Will they stand up to the test of seasonal change? And are they planted in the aspects and soil conditions that suit them? The awkward-looking garden where no one has been concerned with these questions can be spotted at a glance.

Still, there is hope. Most plants in their early stages are forgiving and come winter, when many are dormant and able to be shifted, plantings can be altered. At this time glaring colour gaffes can be corrected and plants arranged in more compatible groups. For instance, those wonderfully bright azaleas in various colours may now seem too disturbing planted in one group. The whites could go together and the purples and mauves in another patch. Crimsons and pinks, surprisingly enough, are a good combination, especially if there is plum-coloured foliage behind to tone down the brightness a little. Winter is also the time to thin out overcrowded spots and fatten up plantings where they are sparse.

Sometimes it can almost be worth having a bad start, just for the thrill of getting things right later. Given an open mind, anyone can be in the business of picture making.

LEFT A massed planting of just two well-chosen plants can have as much impact as a wide range of colourful plants.

OPPOSITE PAGE Nature's riotous ways are often the loveliest, particularly in spring.

WAYS AND MEANS

Some people look at plants in nurseries, or in the pages of garden books, and say 'I like that' or 'I don't care for this one'. Such arbitrary assessments made outside the garden context are too hasty to be wise. The plant has not had a chance to be judged fairly. It is important to evaluate such qualities as behaviour over time, ultimate height and shape and whether the plant offers a permanent evergreen structure or deciduous changes.

Evergreens are reliable; you know how they will grow and how they will look throughout the year. With deciduous trees, you have to see beyond their immature form and the bareness of winter. Honey locusts (*Gleditsia triacanthos*) and Manchurian pears (*Pyrus ussuriensis*) look like dead sticks early in life but take only a short time to build definite frameworks.

Hardiness should be taken into account. You may sniff a little at *Lantana montevidensis*, but this plant, with its pinky mauve, regular, clustered blooms, will flower and flower in a variety of aspects, soils and circumstances, from early spring to early winter. It looks enchanting when mixed with china-blue *Convolvulus mauritanicus* and the dainty, pale mauve Australian daisy *Brachyscome multifida*.

Plants must also be considered for their value in doing particular tasks. Though you may not care for plants with golden foliage, a shade-loving plant, such as *Aucuba japonica* 'Variegata', in a dark corner can bring a splash of light. The flowers of one plant or the leaf shapes of another may be insignificant, but, when autumn comes, the plant's inclusion in the garden may well be justified. By an off-white wall, a red-trunked maple (*Acer*) that is bare in winter or a japonica (*Chaenomeles japonica*), so vividly coloured in early spring, will look quite special. And, in a spot where nothing seems to grow, suddenly the boring-looking, but unbelievably hardy, shrubby germander (*Teucrium fruticans*) might be just the thing – and, when its pale blue-mauve, folded-butterfly-wing flowers come out, you might even become quite enthusiastic.

Sometimes a plant will look strange or inappropriate in a garden because it is not among visually compatible plants – a single palm tree, for instance, among a group of camellias – and needs to be removed to more congenial surroundings. A tree fern can look out of place if not supported by similar plants – even two are better, though a little contrived, while three become integrated in the most informal and acceptable way.

A number of plants of the same species planted in a row as a hedge or in groups can have a structural function: for instance, roses, camellias, cypresses, English box (*Buxus sempervirens*), silver birches (*Betula pendula*) if space allows, forest oaks (*Allocasuarina torulosa*) or medium shrubs, such as weigelas, in mixed colours.

Plants can be positioned to achieve various effects in a garden. In a small space a single plant, such as a crêpe myrtle (*Lagerstroemia indica*), set in a patch of ground cover, has much more visual impact than a more complex planting. In a suburban front or back garden a medium tree, such as a golden rain tree (*Koelreuteria paniculata*), with low shrubs planted along the boundary beyond, gives an impression of space because of the contrast within the picture.

SHAPES, SIZES AND SILHOUETTES

Vase, column, toffee apple and waterfall: generally speaking, these are the shapes of trees and shrubs, whether large or small. From this rich fund you can choose the shapes or combination of shapes that will form the backgrounds or special effects of your garden pictures, always bearing in mind variations of foliage and texture, seasonal characteristics and the nature of your site.

OPPOSITE PAGE Using seasonal variation in leaf colour is an important part of creative gardening.

The shapes of the trees you choose will probably be silhouetted against the sky. In the Southern Hemisphere you are best to plant conifers and other solid evergreens to the south, while lacy trees, whose beauty is in their intricate form or their autumn colour, should be planted to the north or the west so that the sun shines through them.

There are a host of shrub forms to consider. Classic deciduous shrubs, such as weigelas, abelias and viburnums, with their mix of old and new stems, branch out from close to the ground, while camellias and rhododendrons branch out from a single trunk. There are weeping forms, such as the weeping broom (*Genista monosperma*), *Melaleuca incana* and the pendulous roses 'Cornelia' and 'Buff Beauty'; and stiff bushes, such as the lavenders (*Lavandula*), the upright brooms (*Genista* and *Cytisus*), *Hebe* 'Autumn Gem', and *Raphiolepis* × *delacourii*. The low-growing conifers come in cones, pyramids and sprawling shapes.

In planning the framework of your garden pictures, be aware of the quite different effects you can achieve by using different configurations of trees and shrubs according to shape, mass and height. For instance, a pair of tall pencil pines gives balance and architectural strength planted 5 or so metres away from a two-storey house. A sweeping effect is achieved by grading planting from a medium-sized, spreading tree, such as the crab apple *Malus floribunda*, down to a tall, vase-shaped, pale pink weigela and the shrubby, pink-flowered rose 'Sarah van Fleet', and then to the rather low shrub *Spiraea* 'Anthony Waterer'; *Helleborus* and pink belladonna lilies (*Amaryllis belladonna*) can be planted under the tree, radiating out from a corner, with similar plantings for shrubs forming other spokes, the low shrubs interspersed with tall perennials.

GREEN LEAVES, TEXTURES AND SHADOW PLAY

Sometimes in a garden the most refreshing experience is just to be surrounded by green, the kindest of all colours. Think of the quiet beauty of the bush: green advancing and retreating; light and dark; broad, shiny leaves and lacy fern fronds. Leaf shapes and textures become all important, as do the movement and form of shadows.

In gardens we have the chance to create our own green space: a place where we can sit and think or just enjoy being there. That master of shadow play, the Japanese maple (*Acer palmatum*), could be planted there once a protective planting has grown up to shield it from the afternoon sun. A bird's nest fern (*Asplenium nidus*), planted so that its broad, pale leaves are lit from behind by the setting sun's rays, is quite lovely. Rocks in a green place might draw about them some of the shapely grasses, such as fountain grass (*Pennisetum alopecuroides*). Low, greenish ground-covering plants could suggest the presence of water in a garden.

LEFT Contrasting leaf shapes and colours add variety to a garden picture and offer a change from floral contrasts. Variegated flax (*Phormium tenax*), red and gold broom, and the fresh new growth of the loquat (*Eriobotrya japonica*) make an arresting combination.

OPPOSITE PAGE All the colours of the rainbow in varying intensities are brought together in a colour wheel.

However, you do not have to make a special green place to enjoy the textures and the play of shadows. Try to be aware of the possibilities of all plants. For instance, rugosa roses provide wonderfully textured, leathery leaves, and there is a fine mingling of colour and texture in the combination of mid-green, velvety peppermint geraniums (*Pelargonium tomentosum*) and the tiny, felt-leafed *Helichrysum petiolare* 'Limelight'. Watch the way the sun moves around your garden, see how the shadows fall and plant for shadow play.

COLOUR

If you are just a beginner you probably tend to be grateful if plants actually flower at all, whatever their colour! But after you gather some trust in nature and your ability to understand the needs of plants you can become choosier and try a colour strategy for lovely effects throughout the year.

In interior decoration and fashion, colour coordination is fundamental to success, and so it should be in gardens. If you want a particular plant it should be put into a section of your garden where it will fit in with the surrounding colours without compromising its requirements for growth. If a plant has flowers of a colour that won't work in your garden, do without it.

A colour wheel provides a useful way of studying the nature of colour. It consists of a circle divided into equal parts, showing all the colours of the rainbow, with the tones of each shading into the next – tones being the degrees of brightness or the strength of each hue. The wheel will help you to understand where each colour stands in relation to the other colours in terms of contrast and harmony. In planning garden colours you may choose to work with dark and light tones of hues quite close to each other to achieve tonal contrast, or you may use two strong, deep tones of colours quite distant on the colour wheel, for a rich harmonious feeling.

When you are working with colours, it is also helpful to understand that each colour has either blue or yellow as a factor in its basic make-up; for instance, the green leaves of a lemon tree contain yellow, while those of camellias usually contain blue. Among those plants with grey leaves – herbs, for example, such as rosemary or lavender – the majority are grey-blue or silvery blue. Only a few have a yellow component: Jerusalem sage (*Phlomis fruticosa*) is one. It's of some importance when you're setting out a garden to be conscious of these differences in foliage. Working up from a border of lavenders, you'll get a much better effect with shrubs or trees of a blue-green make-up. With predominantly orange and yellow flowers you'll appreciate the more harmonious look of yellow-green leaves in your supporting greenery.

You can study the blue–yellow factor in flowers with the help of the great rose family. In the mauve-lilac shades, the deep reds and crimsons and some of the rich and paler pinks you will become aware of a blue component; however, some of the red roses are scarlet, with a yellow component, and some pinks apricot, and there are oranges and vermilions, fleshy pinks and sunset shades of red, gold and yellow.

It's important to add to your understanding of hues and tonal variation this phenomenon of blue and yellow. See how they lie on opposite sides of the colour wheel, with a gradual transition from one to another. If you don't heed this, you may well grow a jangle of colours, but once you have grasped the principle you will find yourself applying it almost unconsciously. Consider the apricot shades. Some of them come from the blue side – that found in the rose 'Albertine', for instance. From the yellow side come orangy apricots, buff and flesh colours – think of the dainty roses 'Buff Beauty' and 'Goldfinch'. Both the blue and the yellow apricots are glorious, but, if you combine them, they don't work. Yet, having said all this, just a touch of pale blue can look quite special among the yellows, oranges and yellow-greens. In certain shades of blue, you see, there is a yellow component.

Here are a few tips that may be useful in your colour planning.

- White seems to bleach the richness out of colour. Use it sparingly or not at all in a mixed border where you are working with a tonal variation, such as pinks and crimsons.
- Silver foliage has a useful neutrality despite its blue or occasionally yellow make-up. You can use it to break up or delineate masses of colour without its interfering with their intensity.
- Too much colour contrast can be boring. Use a strong colour sparingly for dramatic highlights among groups of lighter-toned flowers of the same hue.
- Variegated plants in cream or gold with green – for example, *Aucuba japonica* 'Variegata' or variegated English box (*Buxus sempervirens* 'Variegata') – can create a look of dappled sunlight in semi-shady spots.
- Pale-toned flowers glow in reduced light, whereas dark or rich tones are swallowed up by the shadows; and, in the soft light of spring, pale colours make more impact throughout the day than they do in summer, for brighter colours are needed to match a harsh light.
- Bright, deep colours – the blues, purples and reds – fade in the evening glow, while pale or white flowers and the leaves of variegated plants show up and can be used well near paths and doorways.
- Pale flowers used against dark foliage create an impression of light: think of a wattle in bloom emerging from the dark foliage of surrounding trees.
- Silver plants usually hold their leaves in winter and can be used for a winter presence in a garden when perennials are underground and many shrubs and trees bare branched.
- Night flyers add another dimension to a garden. Evening primroses (*Oenothera*) are well known for their nocturnal beauty; they grow handsome, hollyhock-style flower stems in wonderful citrus-yellow shades.
- *Fuchsia corolle* by day or by night provides luminous, welcoming, pink-red flowers that do not readily disappear into the gloom – the exception to prove a rule.

PLANTS: THE LIVING INGREDIENTS

Good design cannot be over-stressed, but to most of us plants are the crowning glory. The more you learn about the multitude of plants available and their ways, the more you will understand the sorts of plants that are comfortable together in a garden and the many options open to you.

Every known plant in the world has a correct botanical name made up of two Latin words, sometimes followed by other words. The first part describes the plant's genus (subdivision within a family): for example, *Camellia* or *Eucalypt*. The second part denotes the species – the group within the genus – to which the plant belongs. The species name often describes a distinguishing feature of the plant. It might be its country of origin – for example, *Camellia japonica* (from Japan) – or the scent of its leaves: for example, *Eucalyptus citriodora* (lemon scented). From time to time a name within the international system may change as new plant discoveries are made and knowledge increases. In the wild there are naturally occurring variations of species, which are called varieties: for example *Camellia sinensis* var. *assamica*. Any variety that occurs in cultivation or is bred is called a cultivar: for example, *Camellia japonica* 'Magnoliiflora'. Hybrids are plants that result from cross-breeding two species: for example, *Raphiolepis* × *delacourii* is a cross between the two cultivars *R. umbellata* and *R. indica*.

As well as their botanical names, many plants have common names – simple names by which they are widely known. These can differ confusingly from country to country. To some people, baby's tears are the flat, tiny-leafed green *Soleirolia soleirolii*, to others the seaside daisy *Erigeron karvinskianus*. Although the botanical names can seem tedious, don't give up; being familiar with the system gives you a greater understanding of plants. You will have a better chance of finding what you want in nurseries, and you will have more fun.

TREES

A garden without trees or substantial shrubs will have a flat, incomplete look and remain a collection of plants from a nursery long after it should. At best the garden will appear dull. Trees provide a garden with height, natural overhead protection and interest.

You will notice that trees sometimes have the effect of dividing up the space around them. They can be used deliberately for this purpose in garden planning: for instance, as windbreaks, screens and in pleached rows and hedges. The sheer bulk of trees alone can exert a strong influence on the height, shape or breadth of the garden. They can screen out an unsightly view of, for example, a block of flats, or complement the garden style with their particular form of beauty. Leaf-clad trees provide shade and block out harsh sun, while deciduous trees allow sunlight through their branches when their leaves have fallen, letting warmth and light into houses and gardens in winter. Sometimes the most significant contribution a tree makes is the shelter and food it provides for birds that live in its branches.

TREES IN YOUR GARDEN PLAN

You can learn a great deal about trees by looking at them growing in other people's gardens and in parks. Most take up quite a lot of visual and underground space. Its growth from young plant to maturity must be understood when any tree is being considered for a garden site, for on its way to maturity it will contribute to a changing garden picture: at first it will be in intimate relationship with shrubs and herbaceous plants, but as it grows it will have a greater overhead

Once upon a time this quince tree (*Cydonia oblonga*) could barely be seen among the surrounding perennials. Now it has become the main feature of the space, giving delicate spring blossom, cool green in summer, golden autumn leaves and a strong, grey winter framework.

influence, reducing the light supply to the plants beneath, seasonally or year round. As well, the tree's extending root system will influence the garden picture by reducing the food and moisture available to nearby plants – which may struggle or die if not moved. The lawn under a tree may be poor (although a top dressing each autumn will help) or it may even die – perhaps to be replaced with mossy rocks and variegated ivy, which is tougher. Of course, at the cost of your original garden picture, you will have a magnificent mature tree, probably as you visualised it when you planted it out years ago. And, if your tree is deciduous, the winter light and rains will encourage winter and spring bulbs, such as daffodils (*Narcissus*) and bluebells (*Hyacinthoides*), that are dormant during the summer months when the ground is shaded and dry.

In using trees in your garden, you will often need to be quite firm with yourself: the number and type must suit the size of your garden, and, if you want a specimen tree in the lawn, there must always be adequate viewing space around it. One lovely, well-sited tree, such as a large-growing crab apple (*Malus*), a Chinese elm (*Ulmus parvifolia*) or an Irish strawberry tree (*Arbutus unedo*), may be your limit, but this will look far more pleasing than an overcrowded garden and will prevent the later heartbreak of having to remove a glorious liquidambar that is threatening your house and reducing your garden to a poorly grassed paddock. Even among the crab trees there is considerable variation in form and height. The well-loved *Malus ioensis* 'Plena' is a rather stiff candelabra when young; the purple crab *Malus aldenhamensis* is a flowery sprawl, with its amazingly firm but pendulous branch structure; *Malus floribunda* is a firm mop-top; while *Malus* 'Gorgeous' is a stiff, upright little tree.

Dainty trees or treelike shrubs, such as the lemon-scented tea tree (*Leptospermum petersonii*), the crêpe myrtle (*Lagerstroemia indica*), the tall lasiandra *Tibouchina urvilleana* 'Edwardsi', *Gordonia axillaris* or the wattle *Acacia spectabilis*, can give treelike structure to a small garden, working with nearby plantings of medium to low shrubs to form a scaled-down garden picture for a small garden or courtyard.

The manner in which trees are combined can create a sense of dignified orderliness or restful informality. Compare, for instance, the formal effect of a row of *Prunus cerasifera* 'Nigra' along a driveway or a planting of pleached plane trees (*Platanus*) in a large garden with the sense of freedom created by the informal groupings of trees in a woodland or Australian native garden.

If you inherit trees in your garden, carefully consider the qualities they offer. The first step is to identify the trees and learn about their seasonal behaviour. Mature trees can be significant shade givers and walls of colour and create a sense of timelessness and peace in a garden. A new garden can benefit enormously from the influence of existing trees, and valued old trees can well take on a new image. It should be noted, however, that all tree species have finite life spans: a diseased or mutilated tree should not be retained just because it is old. Again, if a tree is demanding light and space to the detriment of the rest of your garden, you may have to consider its removal.

OPPOSITE PAGE A mature flame tree (*Brachychiton acerifolius*) makes a splendid sight in a hot garden.

RIGHT Japanese flowering cherries (*Prunus serrulata*) are generally hardy and are covered with blossom in spring and russet leaves in autumn.

CHOOSING TREES COMPATIBLE WITH YOUR SITE

Although aesthetic considerations are vital, there are physical factors that must also be considered in tree selection.

Rate of growth

Some trees grow much faster than others and should be planted when quite small. Many Australian native plants, such as gums (*Eucalyptus*) and wattles (*Acacia*), are like this. Other plants grow more slowly and can be planted from containers when they are 1–2 metres tall. Advanced trees several metres high can be used for instant effect, although they are, of course, expensive and usually require two workers to handle and plant them. Large transplanted trees need special watering and mulching during the first year of their garden life. Some fast-growing trees, such as wattles, virgilias and albizias, are likely to flourish and fail in the space of ten to fifteen years. However, they serve some purpose in gardens where quick effects are needed: for instance, in a place where house renovations are planned for the future or to fill a gap in the top storey while slower-growing trees, such as the *Ginkgo biloba*, are taking shape.

Mature height and branch structure

You must consider height and structure before you include a particular tree in your garden. There is quite a difference between a forest giant of 30 metres and a tree, such as *Azara microphylla*, that ends up below the house eaves. Branch structures can interfere with the house roof spoutings or overhead electric wires. A suburban block can usually accommodate a few tidy fruit trees, such as a plum (*Prunus*) or pear (*Pyrus*), an apricot (*Prunus armeniaca*) and the small crab apple *Malus* 'Gorgeous', in the corners of its back garden. In the front garden there is often room for a couple of small trees, such as the crêpe myrtle and the spreading flowering cherry *Prunus serrulata* 'Mount Fuji', which grows to about 4 metres; or for a tall shrub, such as *Feijoa sellowiana*, that grows to the size of a small tree and gives a high, evergreen structure to the garden. Evergreen shrubs on the boundaries and one large, spreading tree in the centre, surrounded by lawn, also suit the space of a suburban garden. The deciduous, large-leafed Indian bean tree (*Catalpa bignonioides*), with its high canopy, allows room for a table and chairs beneath it, although it needs a clearance of at least 15 metres around it for it to relate comfortably to its surroundings.

Grouping

Some trees, such as wattles, Japanese maples (*Acer palmatum*) and silver birches (*Betula pendula*), lend themselves to planting in clumps of three or five. Planted this way, they control each other's growth. While they will not grow as tall as they would individually, they look lovely in such groupings.

RIGHT Magnolias come in many forms, all of them exquisite. Here *Magnolia denudata* thrusts its white, tuliplike flowers through the boughs of the smaller-growing *M. stellata*.

LEFT Appleblossom time, and time to rest on a rustic seat in a field of yellow *Moraea*.

Differences between species

You can't assume that because trees, such as maples (*Acer*) or crab apples, are often slight they are always so. Both examples have large as well as smaller species. It is sometimes useful to research other species of the genus to which the plant you are interested in belongs, because you may find a more suitable one.

Roots

No tree should be planted close to a house wall – either yours or a neighbour's. Light-rooted, small trees, such as crêpe myrtles, can be planted 3 metres away; larger trees should be at least 6 metres away, and some much more. Roots can also disrupt paving when trees are planted near drives, paths and terraces. There are many suitable shrubs for sites where the planting of trees would eventually cause disaster.

Trees such as the ash (*Fraxinus*), poplar (*Populus*), alder (*Alnus*), liquidambar and some species of *Melaleuca* have greedy, far-reaching, rather superficial roots that impoverish surface soil as they grow. For this reason they are not good lawn specimens. Poplars, willows (*Salix*) and large melaleucas crave water and are adept at discovering sewerage pipes. A poorly watered tree will send its roots further to seek water than one that receives regular deep soakings from its owners.

CHOOSING TREES TO ENHANCE YOUR GARDEN

A tree should be worthy of the space it occupies. Crab apple trees, for example, have charming changing habits throughout the year: beautiful spring blossom is followed by cool green or coppery purple summer leaves; then as the leaves turn to orange and gold, they produce their purple, golden or red fruit in splashes of colour before becoming bare, grey winter frames. Assess any tree you are considering for your garden in terms of the following attributes.

- Evergreen leaves give a constant backdrop for smaller plants and act as a screen. They come in a range of green, purple, bronze, gold and cream.
- A changing garden spectacle is provided by deciduous foliage. Young leaves form in spring, mature through summer and undergo an autumn colour

change. The leaves of many deciduous trees change to shining yellow-gold, burnished red or vibrant orange. But not all deciduous trees have wonderful autumn leaves; some leaves just wither and die in a rather ordinary way. The framework of the trees is entirely revealed in winter and can have a beauty of its own during those months.

- Most trees have flowers of some sort at one season or another. Some have large, striking flowers, like those of *Magnolia grandiflora*, while others, such as the Japanese maple, have tiny ones.
- Berries or fruit are the speciality of some trees. The Washington thorn (*Crataegus phaenopyrum*) has superb clusters of shiny, red, beadlike berries and reddish foliage in autumn. The lemon tree (*Citrus limon*) is handsome throughout the year, with scented blossom then fruit among its glossy evergreen leaves. The pomegranate (*Punica granatum*) flaunts its waxy, vermilion flowers in late summer and its shiny fruit throughout autumn and on its bare winter branches.
- Trunks can be striking. Those of the silver birch and crêpe myrtle are outstanding, but have you ever seen the trunks of Australia's angophoras? – or *Allocasuarina torulosa*, whose bark is as corky as that of the cork oak (*Quercus suber*)?
- Demeanour – the way a trunk is shaped and comes from the earth, the way branches leave the trunk and how they carry their twigs and leaves – is important. Some trees, such as the maple *Acer buergeranum*, look spunky and upright, while the Chinese elm (*Ulmus parvifolia*) has a special grace that goes deeper than its weeping form. Understanding this attribute will help you make your pictures. Pendulous trees, for example, look beautiful framing a path or arching over a pond, particularly with low, upright shrubs, such as *Rosmarinus officinalis* or English lavender (*Lavandula angustifolia*), nearby, adding strength and contrast.

TOP Ripe fruit, such as yellow crab apples, are important components of an autumn picture.

BOTTOM Trunks of lemon-scented gums (*Eucalyptus citriodora*) form elegant columns. The trunk colour varies slightly with the season.

TALL TREES (HEIGHT OVER 10 METRES)

TREE AND PLACE OF ORIGIN	LEAVES	HEIGHT (H), WIDTH (W) AND FORM	GROWTH RATE AND SPECIAL CHARACTERISTICS	PARTICULAR REQUIREMENTS AND HARDINESS
Acacia elata (cedar wattle) New South Wales, Queensland, Victoria	Evergreen; like pepper tree leaves	H: 24 m W: 9 m Erect, open textured	Fast Creamy blossom in summer	Prefers coastal climate; frost tender when young
Angophora costata (smooth-barked apple myrtle) Queensland	Evergreen; like gum tree leaves	H: 13–24 m W: 10 m Pyramidal, though spreading as matures	Moderate to fast Creamy white flowers, spring to early summer; distinctive, orange-red, peeling bark	Hardy in well-drained soil
Brachychiton acerifolius (flame tree) New South Wales, Queensland	Deciduous; attractive, maplelike; lost prior to flowering	H: 6–30 m W: 6 m Upright	Fast in ideal conditions Sprays of brilliant red bell flowers in summer; bottle-shaped trunk	Medium to deep soil; warm, protected position Frost tender
Callitris columellaris (Murray pine, white cypress pine) Mainland Australia	Evergreen conifer; fine, green or blue	H: 10–24 m W: 6 m Compact crown	Fast in ideal conditions Rich brown bark; useful combination of good form and foliage	Hardy, though dislikes heavy clays; withstands considerable exposure; moderately frost tender
Calodendrum capense (Cape chestnut) South Africa	Evergreen; oval, glossy green	H: 8–15 m W: 6 m Dense, compact crown	Slow Clusters of orchidlike, soft pink flowers in summer	Prefers well-drained soil and warm position; frost tender when young
Castanea sativa (Spanish chestnut) Mediterranean	Deciduous; long, elliptical, serrated	H: 15 m W: 8 m Large, spreading	Fast Small, creamy yellow flowers in spring; edible nuts in prickly cases; golden autumn leaves	Warm, well-drained soil; sun or semi-shade
Catalpa bignonioides (Indian bean tree) Southern United States of America	Deciduous; large, heart shaped	H: 12–15 m W: 8 m Strong, upright, with wide, high crown	Moderate Creamy, purple-spotted bell flowers in spring; golden autumn leaves	Best in cool climate and sheltered position; frost tender
Cedrus atlantica 'Glauca' (blue cedar) North Africa	Evergreen conifer; short, blue needles on stiff branches	H: 15–30 m W: 8 m Upright, triangular	Moderate Upright cones	Quite hardy, though does best in rich, deep soil; drought tender

TALL TREES				
TREE AND PLACE OF ORIGIN	**LEAVES**	**HEIGHT (H), WIDTH (W) AND FORM**	**GROWTH RATE AND SPECIAL CHARACTERISTICS**	**PARTICULAR REQUIREMENTS AND HARDINESS**
Cupressus sempervirens var. *stricta* (Italian cypress, pencil pine) Southern Europe, Western Asia	Evergreen conifer; mid-green	H: 6–20 m W: 1 m Columnar	Moderate Provides solid, narrow, vertical accent	Endures warm, dry conditions
Eucalyptus citriodora (lemon-scented gum) Tropical Queensland	Evergreen	H: 15–20 m W: 8–10 m Slender, upright, with lightly branched crown	Moderate Lemon-scented leaves; graceful white trunk	Hardy in well-drained soil; very frost tender when young
Eucalyptus ficifolia (Western Australian flowering gum) Western Australia	Evergreen; strong, dark green, yellow veined	H: 5–10 m W: 7 m Upright to sprawling	Fast in ideal conditions Immense branches of white, orange, pink or red blossom, usually in January and February	Prefers coastal climate; dislikes severe frost
Eucalyptus sideroxylon (red ironbark) New South Wales, Queensland, Victoria	Evergreen; pendulous clusters, green or slate grey	H: 15–20 m W: 5 m Upright, graceful	Slow Cream, pink or red flowers from May to February; deeply furrowed, dark brown bark	Hardy; copes with heavy soil
Fagus sylvatica var. *purpurea* (copper beech) Central, Southern and Western Europe	Deciduous; crinkly edged, oval, glossy, coppery purple	H: 12–25 m W: 6 m Shapely, with dense, rounded crown	Slow Branchlets sit in flat sprays on elegant branches	Hardy, though best in cool, sheltered position
Fraxinus rotundifolia subsp. *oxycarpa* 'Raywood' (claret ash) Australian hybrid	Deciduous; in groups of three, green	H: 10–15 m W: 6 m Upright, symmetrical	Fast Holds rich, wine-coloured autumn leaves for some weeks	Hardy in most conditions if water available; best autumn colour in cool climate
Ginkgo biloba (maidenhair tree) China	Deciduous conifer; like giant maidenhair fern leaves	H: 10–15 m W: 7 m Upright when young, loose crowned when mature	Slow Buttery yellow autumn foliage	Prefers rich, deep soil

Ginkgo biloba.

TALL TREES				
TREE AND PLACE OF ORIGIN	**LEAVES**	**HEIGHT (H), WIDTH (W) AND FORM**	**GROWTH RATE AND SPECIAL CHARACTERISTICS**	**PARTICULAR REQUIREMENTS AND HARDINESS**
Liquidambar styraciflua (American sweet gum) Eastern United States of America, Guatamala, Mexico	Deciduous; maplelike	H: 6–18 m W: 5 m Upright, pyramidal	Moderate Provides dense summer shade; yellow, orange, red and purple autumn leaves; round, woody, spiny seed pods, annoying to bare feet	Very hardy and heat tolerant
Liriodendron tulipifera (tulip tree) Southern United States of America	Deciduous; symmetrical, four lobed, pale green	H: 15–35 m W: 6 m Upright, with conical crown	Fast Greenish gold tuliplike flowers, banded orange inside, in summer; golden autumn leaves	Prefers rich, deep mountain soil; wind-fast
Magnolia grandiflora United States of America	Evergreen; large, dark, shiny	H: 10–25 m W: 7 m Dome shaped	Moderate Large, lemon-scented, creamy white chalicelike flowers in summer	Hardy, though prefers rich, deep soil
Metasequoia glyptostroboides (dawn redwood) China	Deciduous conifer; short, fine, daintily fernlike on stiff branches	H: 12–15 m W: 5 m Elegant, pyramidal	Moderate Pale green leaves of spring darken, then turn apricot in autumn; sunset-coloured trunk	Well-drained soil
Pyrus ussuriensis (Manchurian pear) North-east Asia	Deciduous	H: 8–12 m W: 9 m Large, spreading	Moderate White blossom over whole tree in spring; good summer shade; burnished orange autumn leaves	Adapts to most well-composted soils; prefers open, sunny position; drought tender
Quercus robur (European oak) Europe, North Africa, western Asia	Deciduous; oblong, wavy lobed	H: 12–20 m W: 7 m Spreading, with dense crown and heavy branches	Moderate Acorn clusters; yellow, then brown autumn leaves	Hardy
Schinus molle (peppercorn) Western South America	Evergreen; fernlike	H: 12–20 m W: 7 m Spreading, with rounded, heavily branched crown	Fast Dainty yellow flowers in summer; pendulous clusters of rosy pink peppercorns; aromatic leaves	Generally hardy, though prefers hot, dry climate; wind-fast
Stenocarpus sinuatus (firewheel tree) New South Wales, Queensland	Evergreen; vary on tree from single to deep lobed, glossy	H: 8–30 m W: 4 m Upright, single trunked	Slow Wheels of scarlet flowers, late summer to autumn; may be slow to flower in cool areas	Prefers tropical climate; will reluctantly grow further south, though may only leaf and flower on sunny side

TALL TREES				
TREE AND PLACE OF ORIGIN	**LEAVES**	**HEIGHT (H), WIDTH (W) AND FORM**	**GROWTH RATE AND SPECIAL CHARACTERISTICS**	**PARTICULAR REQUIREMENTS AND HARDINESS**
Syzygium floribundum (weeping lilly pilly) New South Wales, Queensland	Evergreen; dainty, shiny green	H: 10–24 m W: 5 m Slightly pendulous	Fast in ideal conditions White berries; handsome, weeping foliage, particularly when new	Prefers warm, northern Australian climate
Tilia × europaea (linden or lime) Europe	Deciduous; large, heart shaped, finely toothed	H: 10–30 m W: 6 m Dense, shapely crown	Fast Fine, white-stalked flowers, with pale green bracts in summer; distinctive winged fruit	Hardy, though prefers cool mountain climate; drought tender
Ulmus parvifolia (Chinese elm) China, Japan, Korea	Deciduous to evergreen in warmer areas; small, toothed, glossy	H: 10 m W: 7 m Graceful, semi-pendulous, spreading, with loose crown	Moderate Elegant, mottled tan trunk	Hardy
Zelkova serrata Japan	Deciduous; heart shaped, narrow toothed	H: 12–20 m W: 7 m Compact crown, with outer branches semi-pendulous	Moderate Russet autumn leaves; smooth, grey bark	Easily grown in cool climate; prefers well-drained soils; drought tender

The maple *Acer negundo* 'Aureo-marginatum' has an upright, elegant form. It loses its leaves in winter.

Bauhinia.

MEDIUM TREES (HEIGHT 6–10 METRES)

TREE AND PLACE OF ORIGIN	LEAVES	HEIGHT (H), WIDTH (W) AND FORM	GROWTH RATE AND SPECIAL CHARACTERISTICS	PARTICULAR REQUIREMENTS AND HARDINESS
Acacia prominens (golden rain wattle) New South Wales, Queensland	Evergreen; small, pointed	H: 4–10 m W: 6 m Erect, with round crown	Fast Dense sprays of golden balls in late winter and spring	Prefers well-drained soil and protected, shady position
Acer buergeranum (trident maple) China, Japan	Deciduous; large, three lobed	H: 7 m W: 4 m Vase shaped	Fast Brilliant red autumn leaves	Prefers cool climate and alkaline soil
Acer griseum (paperbark maple) Central China	Deciduous; three lobed	H: 8–12 m W: 4–5 m Rather upright, though spreading with age	Moderate Orange-red autumn leaves; trunk bark peels in tight curls, revealing new orange-coloured bark	Cool climate; alkaline to slightly acid soil
Albizia julibrissin 'Rosea' (pink silk tree) Iran to Japan	Deciduous; fernlike	H: 8–10 m W: 6 m Upright, with loose framework of branches	Very fast Clusters of fluffy pink flowers in summer	Well-drained soils; open position in sun or light shade
Allocasuarina torulosa (forest oak) New South Wales, Queensland	Evergreen; fine toothed, on threadlike stems	H: 8–12 m W: 5 m Pyramidal	Fast Fine, pendulous branches; foliage moves gracefully and has autumn copper lights; intriguing tan, corky trunk; small, oval cones	Hardy, though prefers warm climate and position
Amelanchier canadensis (shad bush) North America	Deciduous; oval, with woolly underside	H: 5–8 m W: 4 m Small, compact, upright	Fast Clusters of small, white flowers create lacy effect over bare-branched tree in spring; maroon or purple fruit; russet autumn leaves	Cool climate; acid soil; sheltered position
Arbutus × andrachnoides (strawberry tree) Asia Minor, Southern Europe	Evergreen; elliptical, leathery, dark green	H: 5–6 m W: 5 m Dense crown, often multi-trunked	Moderate Small sprays of dainty, white, urn-shaped flowers in autumn and early winter; orange fruit; trunks have reddish cinnamon bark, peeling to reveal colour variations	Hardy; wind-fast
Bauhinia carronii (Queensland bean) New South Wales, Queensland, South Australia	Evergreen; consist of two leaflets	H: 6–9 m W: 5 m Light, spreading	Moderate White pea flowers, edged in purple, in spring	Sub-tropical coastal or inland climate; open, sunny position Stands some soil moisture; frost tender

MEDIUM TREES				
TREE AND PLACE OF ORIGIN	**LEAVES**	**HEIGHT (H), WIDTH (W) AND FORM**	**GROWTH RATE AND SPECIAL CHARACTERISTICS**	**PARTICULAR REQUIREMENTS AND HARDINESS**
Betula pendula (silver birch) Europe, north-east Asia	Deciduous; triangular, fluttery	H: 6–10 m W: 5 m Upright	Fast Dappled white trunk and main branches; fine branchlets; yellow-gold autumn leaves	Sunny, sheltered position Prefers cool, deep soil; withstands some soil moisture
Ceratopetalum gummiferum (New South Wales Christmas bush) New South Wales	Deciduous; consist of three narrow leaflets	H: 6–12 m W: 3 m Upright, dainty	Moderate Tiny, white flowers and pinkish red bracts in late summer and early autumn	Well-drained, fertile soil
Cercis siliquastrum (Judas tree) Southern Europe, western Asia	Deciduous; broad, heart shaped	H: 5–9 m W: 5 m Loosely upright, with trunk dividing close to ground	Moderate Masses of light magenta pea flowers cover the whole tree in spring; buttery yellow autumn leaves	Open, sunny position Prefers warm climate; tolerates alkaline soil; drought and frost tender
Citrus limon (lemon tree) India	Evergreen; shiny green	H: 5–7 m W: 3 m Open-textured crown	Medium Fragrant, waxy, white flowers in late spring to early summer; pale yellow, oval, juicy fruit	Well drained soil; open, sunny position Frost tender
Davidia involucrata (dove tree) Western China	Deciduous; heart shaped, with white felted underside	H: 6–12 m W: 5 m Mop-topped and can grow quite wide	Moderate 'Doves' are large, white bracts surrounding insignificant flowers in spring	Hardier than often supposed, though prefers cool climate
Diospyros kaki (Chinese persimmon) China, Japan	Deciduous; large, round to oval	H: 3–10 m W: 3 m Upright	Slow Tints of gold and scarlet in autumn leaves; red-orange fruit from autumn on	Rich soil, kept moist during summer
Erythrina crista-galli (coral tree) Brazil	Deciduous; grouped in threes	H: 5–10 m W: 3 m Rather gaunt, with loose, leafy crown	Fast Dense clusters of large, brilliant red pea flowers from mid-summer to autumn; prickly stems and branches	Hardy, though prefers warm climate
Eucalyptus torquata (Coolgardie or coral gum) Western Australia	Evergreen; long, narrow, blue-green	H: 3–8 m W: 3 m Light crown, with single trunk	Fast Decorative horned and corrugated buds whose caps turn bronze before buds open; bunches of white, pink or red flowers hang over long period through summer; bird attracting	Hardy; vigorous; frost tender when young

Betula pendula.

Hymenosporum flavum.

MEDIUM TREES				
TREE AND PLACE OF ORIGIN	LEAVES	HEIGHT (H), WIDTH (W) AND FORM	GROWTH RATE AND SPECIAL CHARACTERISTICS	PARTICULAR REQUIREMENTS AND HARDINESS
Eucryphia glutinosa (leatherwood) Chile, China, Japan, Korea	Semi-deciduous; fernlike, green	H: 6 m W: 2 m Erect, light, with glossy trunk	Moderate Large, single, almond-scented, pure white flowers, spring to summer	Cool climate; rich, acid soil
Fraxinus excelsior 'Aurea' (golden ash) Europe	Deciduous; fernlike	H: 6–12 m W: 6 m Broad, mop-top crown	Fast Leaves rich golden yellow in early spring and autumn, yellow in summer; branchlets revealed in winter are yellow, with black buds	Hardy; withstands warm climate and infrequent watering
Hymenosporum flavum (native frangipani) New South Wales, Queensland, New Guinea	Evergreen; elliptical, dark green	H: 5–12 m W: 3 m Upright, often sparse, candelabra	Moderate Clusters of fragrant, yellow tubular flowers, late spring to early summer	Warm coastal climate, warm position Moderately hardy, though frost tender
Jacaranda mimosifolia Central and South America	Deciduous, mainly in late winter; fine, fernlike	H: 5–12 m W: 6 m Spreading, loose branched	Fast Clusters of blue flowers in spring; leaves turn golden with cold, are held through winter	Prefers well-drained soil and warm position; not wind tolerant; frost tender when young
Koelreuteria paniculata (golden rain tree) China, Japan, Korea	Deciduous; large, composed of many leaflets	H: 5–8 m W: 5 m Erect, sturdy, with round crown	Medium Sprays of golden flowers in summer; large, three-sided pods; golden autumn foliage	Hardy in most conditions; very tolerant of alkaline soil; withstands hot, dry climate once established
Leucadendron argenteum (silver tree) South Africa	Evergreen; narrow, silver, clustered along straight branches	H: 5–8 m W: 2 m Upright, symmetrical	Moderate Ornamental silver foliage	Intolerant of lime, alkalinity and bad drainage; frost tender, particularly when young
Malus floribunda (Japanese flowering crab) Japan	Deciduous; elliptical	H: 8m W: 4–5 m Spreading, with round crown	Moderate Red buds, then white to pale pink flowers in early spring; yellow or reddish crab apples and autumn leaves	Open, sunny position Adapts to most soils if compost added; drought tender
Malus ioensis 'Plena' (bechtel crab) United States of America	Deciduous; elliptical, notched, blue-green	H: 6 m W: 4 m Upright candelabra	Fast Clusters of pale pink, cupped blossom, often paler to white inside, in mid-spring, usually among leaves; fine, dappled autumn leaves	Generally hardy, but not for hot climates

Malus ioensis 'Plena'.

MEDIUM TREES				
TREE AND PLACE OF ORIGIN	**LEAVES**	**HEIGHT (H), WIDTH (W) AND FORM**	**GROWTH RATE AND SPECIAL CHARACTERISTICS**	**PARTICULAR REQUIREMENTS AND HARDINESS**
Melia azederach var. *australasica* (white cedar) New South Wales, Northern Territory, Queensland, Western Australia, New Guinea	Deciduous; ashlike	H: 6–12 m W: 6 m Dense crown, with rather pendulous branches	Fast Loose, upright clusters of dainty, pale mauve, fragrant flowers in spring; dull yellow berries; golden autumn leaves	Thrives in warm inland climate, though only tall in tropics; slightly frost tender when young
Morus nigra (black mulberry) Iran	Deciduous; heart shaped, mid-green	H: 8 m W: 6 m Loose limbed, with broad crown	Slow Dark red fruit; buttery autumn leaves; bird attracting	Hardy
Picea pungens var. *glauca* (blue spruce) Western North America	Evergreen conifer; stiff, prickly, bluish needles	H: 6–12 m W: 5 m Stiff, pyramidal	Slow Short branchlets standing out in all directions	Generally hardy, though prefers cool mountain climate
Pittosporum phillyreoides (weeping pittosporum) Mainland Australia	Evergreen; willowlike	H: 4–9 m W: 3 m Upright, with pendulous branches	Slow Masses of yellow bell flowers, winter to early summer; quaint, heart-shaped, orange-yellow seed capsules	Low rainfall, warm inland climate
Prunus cerasifera 'Nigra' (purple-leafed cherry plum) Western Asia	Deciduous; elliptical	H: 7 m W: 5 m Upright, but can spread	Medium Fine, single, palest pink blossom in early spring; rich, plum-coloured leaves follow	Hardy; withstands warm, dry climate
Prunus serrulata 'Shirotae' syn. 'Mount Fuji' Japan	Deciduous; elliptical	H: 5–7 m W: 3 m Vase shaped	Medium Semi-double and single, white blossoms in mid-spring; rich, variously coloured autumn leaves	Cool and temperate climates Tolerates some soil moisture
Quercus suber (cork oak) North Africa, Southern Europe	Evergreen; small, glossy	H: 6–12 m W: 5 m Light branched	Slow Rough, corky trunk; small acorns	Suits warm climate; tolerates wide range of soils; slightly frost tender
Sophora japonica (pagoda tree) China, Korea	Deciduous; fernlike	H: 6–15 m W: 8 m Upright, spreading, with round crown at maturity	Moderate Sprays of cream pea flowers in late summer	Warm or cool climate; moist, well-drained position Hardy

MEDIUM TREES				
TREE AND PLACE OF ORIGIN	LEAVES	HEIGHT (H), WIDTH (W) AND FORM	GROWTH RATE AND SPECIAL CHARACTERISTICS	PARTICULAR REQUIREMENTS AND HARDINESS
Sorbus hupehensis (mountain ash or rowan tree) Western China	Deciduous; fernlike	H: 6–10 m W: 5 m Upright, though spreading with age	Fast Clusters of white flowers in summer; white berries gradually turn pink and hang on through part of winter; bird attracting	Hardy, though best in sheltered position; tolerates poor soil
Virgilia divaricata (spring-flowering virgilia) South Africa	Evergreen; fernlike	H: 8 m W: 5 m Upright, loose textured	Very fast Profuse, fragrant, mauve pea flowers in spring; tree's useful life only 10–15 years and best as filler while garden establishes	Adaptable to most well-drained soils; drought and frost tender

SMALL TREES (HEIGHT TO 6 METRES)

TREE AND PLACE OF ORIGIN	LEAVES	HEIGHT (H), WIDTH (W) AND FORM	GROWTH RATE AND SPECIAL CHARACTERISTICS	PARTICULAR REQUIREMENTS AND HARDINESS
Acacia cardiophylla (Wyalong wattle) New South Wales	Evergreen; fine, fernlike, soft green	H: 3–4 m W: 3 m Spreading, bushy	Fast Prolific small, yellow flowers in spring; pendulous branches	Light soil Hardy
Acacia howittii (sticky wattle) Eastern Victoria	Evergreen; tiny, sticky	H: 2.5–6 m W: 4 m Dense, conical, with leaf-draped branches	Fast Tiny, pale yellow flower balls dotted through fine foliage in early spring	Adapts to most conditions, though prefers moist soil
Acacia iteaphylla (Gawler Range wattle) South Australia	Evergreen; willowlike, silver-grey	H: 2–3 m W: 3 m Dense, shrubby	Fast Abundant short sprays of flowers from winter to spring; drooping branches	Hardy
Acacia spectabilis (Mudgee wattle) New South Wales, Queensland	Evergreen; fine, fernlike, blue-green	H: 3–5 m W: 2 m Sparse, dainty	Fast Racemes of fluffy, rich yellow balls beyond leaves in late winter	Hardy
Acer palmatum (Japanese maple) Japan	Deciduous; small, fine stalked, handlike	H: 3–5 m W: 4 m Vase shaped, layered	Moderate Tiny, delicate, pink flowers in early spring; all varieties have beautiful spring and autumn foliage, but large range of leaf colours and shapes	Prefers cool mountain climate and sheltered position; sensitive to hot winds, and mid- and late afternoon sun

Magnolia denudata.

SMALL TREES				
TREE AND PLACE OF ORIGIN	LEAVES	HEIGHT (H), WIDTH (W) AND FORM	GROWTH RATE AND SPECIAL CHARACTERISTICS	PARTICULAR REQUIREMENTS AND HARDINESS
Azara microphylla (box-leaf azara) Chile	Evergreen; small, arranged in flat sprays, glossy	H: 3–6 m W: 2 m Upright, vase shaped	Moderate Vanilla-scented, white flowers in spring	Hardy, though prefers cool, mountain climate and good soil
Crataegus × *smithiana* (red Mexican hawthorn) Victoria	Semi-deciduous; round to oval, blunt ended, glossy	H: 5 m W: 4 m Vase shaped	Moderate Clusters of small, white blossom in summer; bunches of large, red berries; thornless branches	Hardy
Dais cotinifolia (pompon tree, South African daphne) South Africa	Deciduous in cold climate, almost evergreen in warmer climate; simple, oval	H: 3–5 m W: 3 m Narrow and upright when young; spreading, with rounded crown, when mature	Fast Small, dense, round clusters of pink to mauve flowers in early summer	Light, well-drained soil Prefers warm climate; tolerates dryness once established; frost tender
Eucalyptus forrestiana (fuchsia gum) Western Australia	Evergreen; thick, shiny green	H: 2.5–4 m W: 3 m Bushy	Fast Bright yellow flowers in late autumn or early winter; pendulous scarlet pods	Prefers warm climate; will grow on heavy or sandy soil; frost tender when young; withstands some coastal exposure
Eucalyptus steedmanii (Steedman gum) Western Australia	Evergreen; thick, leathery	H: 4–5 m W: 5 m Shapely, rounded, with slender branches and foliage to ground	Fast Long, drooping, four-winged buds; peaked caps produce yellow flowers that cover tree for several months in summer	Hardy, though prefers warm climate; dislikes poor drainage; withstands moderate coastal exposure
Laburnum × *watereri* (golden chain tree, Voss's laburnum) Southern Europe, south-west Asia	Deciduous; consist of three leaflets	H: 3–6 m W: 4 m Semi-weeping, with branches often sparse	Fast Racemes of golden pea flowers in spring; little autumn change in leaves; green trunk	Suitable for most soils with adequate drainage, though prefers alkaline soils; dislikes coastal exposure
Magnolia denudata Central China	Deciduous; large, oval	H: 5–10 m W: 3 m Upright	Moderate Fragrant, creamy white, tuliplike flowers emerge from grey, velvety buds borne on bare, twiggy stems in spring; burnished-gold autumn leaves, often with black edges	Acid soil Prefers warm, moist climate and sheltered position

SMALL TREES				
TREE AND PLACE OF ORIGIN	LEAVES	HEIGHT (H), WIDTH (W) AND FORM	GROWTH RATE AND SPECIAL CHARACTERISTICS	PARTICULAR REQUIREMENTS AND HARDINESS
Malus aldenhamensis (Aldenham purple crab) England	Deciduous; roundish	H: 5 m W: 3 m Loose, spreading	Fast Massed, semi-double, deep pink to cerise blossoms in early spring; purple-red crab apples in autumn; bronze-purple new leaves, purple-tinged mature leaves, and burnished autumn leaves	Generally hardy
Malus 'Gorgeous' New Zealand	Deciduous; small	H: 2–3 m W: 2 m Vase shaped	Moderate White blossom in mid-spring; red fruit; russet autumn leaves	Generally hardy in cool and temperate climates
Mespilus germanica (medlar) Europe, Turkey	Deciduous; oval	H: 5 m W: 3–4 m Spreading, with stiff branches	Fast Hawthornlike clusters of small, white or pink flowers in summer; large brown fruit, with distinctive, clawlike sepals; autumn leaves colour richly in red, burnt orange and rose-pink	Cool climate or sheltered position in warm climate; frost to ripen fruit
Michelia doltsopa (evergreen magnolia) Western China	Evergreen; large, dark, glossy	H: 3–15 m W: 4 m Upright, rather conical	Moderate Fragrant, white, magnolialike flowers in August	Cool mountain climate; moist soil; sheltered position
Prunus mume 'Alboplena' (double white Japanese apricot) Eastern Asia	Deciduous; small	H: 3–6 m W: 2–3 m Vase shaped	Fast Fragrant, semi-double flowers of ice-pink in mid-winter	Generally hardy
Tamarix parviflora (early tamarisk) South-eastern Europe	Deciduous; fine, cypresslike, follow spring flowers	H: 5 m W: 3–4 m Short trunk, with loose tracery of overlying branchlets, dense crown	Fast Racemes of tiny, pale pink flowers along last year's growth in early spring	Hardy, though prefers hot, dry climate; tolerates alkaline, saline, heavy or poorly drained soil and hot, dry sand; frost tender when young
Telopea speciosissima (New South Wales waratah) New South Wales	Evergreen; stiff, longish, oval, leathery, with serrated edges	H: 2–3 m W: 2 m Upright, shrubby	Moderate Crimson flowers, contained in broad, red, conelike structures, ringed with red bracts, in mid-spring	Low-phosphorus, well-drained soil, sand or gravel, with humus mulch; warm position

Rhododendrons offer a range of flower colours and shrubby forms of varying size. 'Christmas Cheer', flowering in early spring, lightens up a garden corner.

SHRUBS

For many people shrubs are the all-important plants of the garden. They are a touch less grand than trees, more approachable and easier to manage. People can get to know them close up.

Shrubs are usually multi-trunked plants. While the great majority of trees put their efforts into growing a single trunk, only a few shrubs, such as the rhododendron, do this, and even then their branches start well down the trunk. Shrubs are smaller than trees, too. They are unlikely to be more than 4 metres tall, and most of them are about 2 metres.

SHRUBS IN THE LANDSCAPE

In a garden design the importance of shrubs and their role depend on the trees around them. Shrubs, such as *Viburnum tinus*, camellias, *Garrya elliptica* and many wattles, are frequently used to form a middle storey, providing a combination of permanent leafiness and seasonal interest. Often in a planting shrubs are graded from the largest, such as hibiscus and oleanders (*Nerium oleander*), at the back, through medium types, such as abelias and Mexican orange blossom (*Choisya ternata*), to the smallest, such as correas, heaths (*Erica*) and lavenders (*Lavandula*), near the front.

While you may only have one or two medium trees in a suburban garden, you are likely to need a number of shrubs to add variety and character, but beware the 'one of everything' look that mars many gardens. Choose plants that complement your theme and make a conscious effort to link visually the shrubs you use. Repetition of leaf types or of shrubs here and there gives plantings greater impact. In spring Mexican orange blossom, recurring through a border of white and creamy flower tonings, or *Spiraea* 'Anthony Waterer', reappearing among pink and crimson flowers and leaves, is most effective.

The flowers and leaves of shrubs are perhaps more significant in planning gardens than their shape and form. Evergreen shrubs give a leafy background of various constant colours, while deciduous shrubs – best planted in front of evergreens if you have both – turn from the rich colours of autumn to a haze of bare winter branches.

Evergreen shrubs can screen fences effectively. In warm places oleanders with their prolific flowers in late summer, banksias, callistemons, *Feijoa sellowiana*, clipped now and then, guavas (*Psidium guajava*), glossy-leafed escallonias and shrubby pittosporums are excellent. For all but the hottest spots, *Viburnum tinus* and *Camellia sasanqua* are suitable; *C. japonica* needs somewhat less sun to give its best. Melaleucas, acacias, pittosporums and evergreen viburnums are reliable lower-storey plants in windbreak plantings of trees. Shrubs make a sculpturesque feature set in a lawn if they are grouped; one shrub looks too lonely.

Play with textures and explore your plant books and people's gardens to find shrubs for seasonal highlight. Remember that shrubs are seen at closer quarters than trees, so detail matters more. Be restrained with variegated leaves. Plum- or copper-coloured foliage is more restful, toning rather than contrasting with other leaves.

Some striking autumn foliage effects can be achieved using shrubs rather than trees. The smoke tree (*Cotinus coggyria*) has superb autumn colours, as do most spiraea species, *Ceratostigma willmottianum*, the flowering currant (*Ribes sanguineum*) and the snowball tree (*Viburnum opulus* 'Sterile'). When it comes to autumn berries, too, shrubs offer a range of fine plants. Low-growing *Cotoneaster horizontalis* has superb red berries as well as fine autumn foliage, while the low-growing evergreen cotoneasters, including *C. dammeri* and *C. microphyllus*, give a permanent green form and seasonal flowers and fruit. Then there is one of the best, the tall *C.* 'Cornubia', and the Nepal firethorn (*Pyracantha fortuneana*), with its glossy, red berries, and its orange-berried counterpart *P. angustifolia*. *Duranta repens* has pale blue flowers late in summer and carries its yellow berries well into winter. It thrives in the tropics or temperate areas.

TALL SHRUBS (HEIGHT OVER 2 METRES)

SHRUB AND PLACE OF ORIGIN	LEAVES	HEIGHT (H), WIDTH (W) AND FORM	SPECIAL CHARACTERISTICS	PARTICULAR REQUIREMENTS AND HARDINESS
Acacia boormanii (Snowy River wattle) New South Wales, Victoria	Evergreen; narrow, grey-green	H: 4 m W: 3 m Dense	Rod-shaped, bright yellow flowers in spring	Moisture Hardy, though prefers sunny position; frost resistant
Banksia ericifolia (heath banksia) New South Wales	Evergreen; narrow, bright green	H: 2.5–4 m W: 4 m Upright	Striking, candlelike, yellow-orange flowers in winter; bird attracting	Easy to grow in well-drained, sunny position
Banksia integrifolia (coastal banksia) New South Wales, Queensland, Victoria	Evergreen; silver underside	H: 3–5 m W: 4 m Upright	Small, candlelike, greenish yellow flowers over long period	Sunny position Drought and frost resistant
Buddleja davidii (butterfly bush) China	Evergreen; long, pointy, deep green on top, felted and grey on underside	H: 2.5–3 m W: 2 m Upright, dense	Spikes of long, dense, fragrant, lilaclike, white, pink, bluish mauve or magenta flowers in summer; butterfly attracting	Easy to grow; fast growing in sun
Caesalpinia gilliesii (bird of paradise tree) South America	Deciduous; fine, fernlike	H: 3 m W: 2 m Loose, spreading	Distinctive yellow flowers with long, protruding, red stamens in summer	Rich, well-drained soil; very warm, protected position in part sun Frost tender
Camellia sasanqua China, Japan	Evergreen; glossy deep green	H: 2–3 m W: 2 m Upright to gracefully arching	Single or semi-double, mainly white or pink flowers, late summer to early winter	Moist, rich, acid soil Tolerates sun
Crataegus crus-galli (cockspur thorn) North America	Deciduous; narrow, rounded	H: 5 m W: 3 m Rounded, dense	Five-petalled, pinkish white flowers in spring; large, deep red, glossy berries in autumn	Suits most soils; drought and frost resistant
Garrya elliptica (catkin bush) South-west United States of America	Evergreen; wavy edged, grey-green on underside	H: 2–4 m W: 1.5 m Upright, with many branches	Green tassels in winter	Very hardy in all but hottest position
Grevillea rosmarinifolia (rosemary grevillea) New South Wales, Victoria	Evergreen; narrow, pointed, prickly, dark green	H: 2 m W: 3 m Dense	Pink and red flowers over long period; good screen	Exceptionally hardy; suits most soils; drought and frost resistant

TALL SHRUBS				
SHRUB AND PLACE OF ORIGIN	LEAVES	HEIGHT (H), WIDTH (W) AND FORM	SPECIAL CHARACTERISTICS	PARTICULAR REQUIREMENTS AND HARDINESS
Leptospermum laevigatum (coast tea tree) New South Wales, Queensland, South Australia, Tasmania, Victoria	Evergreen; small, thick, oval, greyish green	H: 2–5 m W: 2–4 m Loose, spreading	Small, open, white flowers in spring and summer; trunk often twisted, gnarled; good for binding sandy soils and for large hedge or screen	Hardy, though prefers light, open soil in sunny position; drought and frost resistant
Leptospermum petersonii (lemon-scented tea tree) New South Wales, Queensland	Evergreen; narrow, light green, copper coloured when young	H: 3–4 m W: 4 m Spreading, graceful	Small, open, white flowers in spring and summer; lemon-scented leaves	Quick-growing in well-drained soil in sunny position
Murraya exotica (orange jessamine) Queensland, India, South-east Asia	Evergreen; small, glossy green	H: 2–3 m W: 2.5 m Erect, branching	Fragrant, white star flowers, like orange blossom, in summer	Prefers warm position and protection from frosts and drought
Nerium oleander (oleander) Mediterranean	Evergreen; long, narrow, grey-green	H: 4 m W: 3 m Upright, spreading	Clusters of free-flowering, single or double, open, white, creamy pink, salmon, pink or red flowers, late summer to autumn	Sunny position Very hardy; drought resistant
Persoonia pinifolia (pine-leaf geebung) New South Wales	Evergreen; narrow, pinelike	H: 2–3 m W: 2 m Loose, branching	Golden flowers in clusters in spring; decorative fruits	Hardy, though prefers light, sandy soil in sunny position
Philadelphus mexicanus (Mexican mock orange) Mexico	Evergreen; dainty, heart shaped, pale green	H: 2–3 m W: 2 m Erect, branching, graceful	Pendulous clusters of white cup flowers, with heavy orange fragrance, in spring	Does well in rich soil in sunny to partly shaded position
Syringa vulgaris (common lilac) Eastern Europe	Deciduous; heart shaped, deep green	H: 2.5–3 m W: 2 m Erect, branching	Large clusters of fragrant, mauve flowers in spring; also pink, red or purple single or double varieties	Prefers cool climate and rich soil, with lime added
Weigela florida China, Korea	Deciduous; long, light green	H: 2 m W: 2 m Arching branches	Masses of small, white, pink or crimson trumpet flowers in spring; some varieties have variegated leaves	Regular moisture Fast growing; prefers sunny, open position; frost resistant

Nerium oleander.

MEDIUM SHRUBS (HEIGHT 1–2 METRES)

SHRUB AND PLACE OF ORIGIN	LEAVES	HEIGHT (H), WIDTH (W) AND FORM	SPECIAL CHARACTERISTICS	PARTICULAR REQUIREMENTS AND HARDINESS
Abelia × grandiflora (glossy abelia)	Evergreen; oval, glossy green	H: 1.5 m W: 1.5 m Graceful, arching stems	White flowers in summer and autumn; after flowering, reddish sepals remain on bush	Extremely hardy, though prefers full sun; drought and frost resistant
Abutilon (Chinese lantern) South America	Evergreen	H: 1–2 m W: 1.5 m Soft	White, yellow, orange, pink or red bell flowers, spring to autumn; some hybrids have showy, variegated leaves	Prefers well-composted soil and open, sunny position, though will take part shade; frost tender
Acacia drummondii (Drummond's wattle) Western Australia	Evergreen; fernlike, dark green	H: 2 m W: 1.5 m Round, compact	Spikes of tiny, bright yellow flowers in spring	Hardy, though prefers well-drained soil; takes sun
Boronia megastigma (brown boronia) Western Australia	Evergreen; fine, needlelike	H: 1.5 m W: 50 cm–1 m Slender, graceful	Fragrant, brown bell flowers, with yellowish insides, in winter	Can be short lived if not in moist, sheltered position
Cassia artemisioides (silver cassia) Mainland Australia	Evergreen; fine, divided, silver	H: 2 m W:1.5 m Rounded	Masses of buttercup-yellow flowers for many months	Sandy soil; warm, open position
Chimonanthus praecox (wintersweet) China, Japan	Deciduous; rough textured, bright green	H: 1.5–3 m W: 2 m Loose, vase shaped	Fragrant, waxen, brownish yellow star flowers on bare branches in winter	Easily grown in protected, sunny position; prefers moist, rich soil
Choisya ternata (Mexican orange blossom) Mexico	Evergreen; glossy deep green	H: 1–2 m W: 2 m Neat, dense, round	Masses of white flowers, with fragrance of orange blossom, in spring	Open, sunny position Drought and frost resistant
Eriostemon myoporoides (long-leaf waxflower) New South Wales, Queensland, Victoria	Evergreen; small, pointy, narrow, dark green	H: 1–3 m W: 1.2 m Branching	White star flowers, opening from pink buds in spring; leaves aromatic when crushed	Hardy in sun or semi-shade
Gardenia jasminoides 'Florida' (double white gardenia) China, Japan	Evergreen; glossy green	H: 1 m W: 1 m Open, branching	Fragrant, waxy, rich white double flowers in summer; good hedge in warm climate	Needs sunny, protected position; drought and frost tender

MEDIUM SHRUBS				
SHRUB AND PLACE OF ORIGIN	**LEAVES**	**HEIGHT (H), WIDTH (W) AND FORM**	**SPECIAL CHARACTERISTICS**	**PARTICULAR REQUIREMENTS AND HARDINESS**
Hydrangea quercifolia (oakleaf hydrangea) United States of America	Semi-deciduous; handsome, toothed	H: 1–2 m W: 1 m Erect	Pyramidal clusters of white to blush-pink flowers in summer and autumn; autumn colour	Moisture Will grow in most soils in sun or dappled shade
Indigofera decora (Chinese indigo) China, Japan	Deciduous; fernlike, light green	H: 1 m W: 1 m Clumpy, suckering	Sprays of soft pink pea flowers, spring to autumn	Rich, well-drained soil; sunny position or dappled shade
Lavandula angustifolia (English lavender) Mediterranean	Evergreen; narrow, smooth edged, greyish green	H: 1 m W: 1 m Compact, with straight branches	Fragrant, purplish mauve flowers, on erect spikes, for long period in summer; varieties with white or pink flowers, and dwarf forms	Well-drained soil; sunny position Hardiest lavender for cold climates; dislikes humidity
Plectranthus ecklonii (blue spur-flower) South Africa	Evergreen; slightly hairy, dark green	H: 1–2 m W: 2 m Scrambling	Mauve-blue or deep blue flowers, on long, upright spikes, flowering freely in summer and autumn	Prefers semi shade; grows easily in a protected, frost-free position
Protea cynaroides (king protea, giant protea) South Africa	Evergreen; round, leathery	H: 1–1.5 m W: 1 m Round, with thick branches	Large, silvery pink cup flowers in summer, with surrounding colourful, crownlike, often bearded bracts; cultivars available in different colours	Well-drained soil; open, sunny position Cannot tolerate fertiliser
Raphiolepis × *delacourii* (pink Indian hawthorn)	Evergreen; elliptical, leathery, glossy deep green	H: 1–2.5 m W: 2 m Spreading	Clusters of open, deep pink flowers at end of branches in spring, which contrast well with leaves	Hardy, though prefers moist soil, to which compost added, in sunny to shaded position; frost and drought resistant
Thryptomene 'Paynei' South Australia	Evergreen; fine, narrow, numerous	H: 90 cm–1.2 m W: 1.5 m Slender, with loose branches	Masses of tiny, light pink flowers in autumn and winter and into spring	Easy to grow in well-drained medium soil in sunny position; drought and frost resistant

Protea cynaroides.

SMALL SHRUBS (HEIGHT TO 1 METRE)

SHRUB AND PLACE OF ORIGIN	LEAVES	HEIGHT (H), WIDTH (W) AND FORM	SPECIAL CHARACTERISTICS	PARTICULAR REQUIREMENTS AND HARDINESS
Azalea kurume Japan	Evergreen; small, dark	H: 30 cm–1 m W: 1 m Compact	Masses of small, white, salmon-pink, red, crimson or mauve flowers in spring	Moist, acid, well-drained soil, with plenty of compost; semi-shaded position
Bauera rubioides (river rose) New South Wales, Queensland, South Australia, Tasmania, Victoria	Evergreen; narrow, close to stem	H: 60 cm–1.5 m W: 1.5 m Scrambling, with wiry stems	Tiny, pink or white cup flowers in spring and summer	Prefers moist soil; frost resistant
Callistemon viminalis 'Captain Cook' (Captain Cook bottlebrush) New South Wales, Queensland	Evergreen; soft, deep green	H: 60 cm–1 m W: 50 cm Dwarf, weeping, clump forming	Deep red bottlebrush flowers in spring; good for containers and rockeries	Well-drained soil; sunny position
Calocephalus brownii (cushion bush) New South Wales, South Australia, Tasmania, Victoria, Western Australia	Evergreen; tiny, narrow, silvery	H: 60–90 cm W: 1 m Moundlike, densely branched	Yellow balls of flowers, on silver, wiry stems, in summer	Open, sunny position Very resistant to drought, frost and salt
Correa reflexa New South Wales, Queensland, South Australia, Tasmania, Victoria	Evergreen; small, rough	H: 70 cm W: 2 m Open, spreading	Long, tubular, red or green flowers in winter; many varieties available	Semi-shaded position Hardy in cool, moist soil
Erica × *darleyensis* (Darley heath)	Evergreen; small, needlelike	H: 60 cm W: 60 cm Compact	Tiny, white or rose-pink bell flowers in winter and early spring	Very hardy; takes sun or part shade; will grow in limy soil
Fuchsia species and hybrids South America	Evergreen; oval	H: 30 cm–2.5 m W: 30 cm–1.5 m	Graceful, pendulous flowers, with central tube or cup, summer to autumn; flowers of the species are small and dainty	Moist, rich soil; filtered sun
Heliotropium arborescens (cherry pie, heliotrope) Peru	Evergreen; rough textured, dull green	H: 60 cm–1 m W: 1 m Loose branched	Clusters of small, lilac or purple flowers, with sweet, spicy scent, spring to autumn	Moist, well-drained soil Frost tender
Hypocalymma angustifolium (white myrtle) Western Australia	Evergreen; very narrow, soft	H: 30–90 cm W: 90 cm Weeping, lacy branched	White to deep pink flowers, in pairs up the stem, in winter and spring	Well-drained soil; sunny position Drought and frost resistant

SMALL SHRUBS				
SHRUB AND PLACE OF ORIGIN	LEAVES	HEIGHT (H), WIDTH (W) AND FORM	SPECIAL CHARACTERISTICS	PARTICULAR REQUIREMENTS AND HARDINESS
Santolina chamaecyparissus (cotton lavender) Mediterranean	Evergreen; consist of tiny, crowded, silver leaflets	H: 30–60 cm W: 1 m Erect, compact	Dense, yellow button flowers, spring to summer; nothing like lavender in leaf or flower; mainly grown for foliage, which is aromatic when crushed; good among annuals or perennials	Hardy; drought and frost resistant
Spiraea 'Anthony Waterer'	Deciduous; narrow, light green, with some yellow	H: 60–90 cm W: 60 cm Multi-branched	Terminal clusters of rosy carmine flowers in summer; yellow-red autumn leaves	Very hardy in sunny position; suits many soils

The russet tones of mollis azaleas add autumn colouring to a spring garden.

PERENNIALS

Many people take for granted the contribution of trees and shrubs, and passions for annuals come and go, but perennials seem to be almost everyone's favourite. In Australia, along with the fervour for cottage gardens, there has been quite a revival of interest in perennial plants in recent years. But the interest has gone beyond a passing fashion. More exotic perennials are available in this country than ever before, and we are still gathering information about their special needs and ways to make them flourish. As well, Australian perennials, such as *Helichrysum* and *Pultenaea* species, are proving valuable in domestic gardens.

Year by year, perennials, such as penstemons, lupins, chrysanthemums and delphiniums, are with us in their seasons. They are termed 'herbaceous' because they have no wood, just soft leaves and stems, which usually wither and die annually to be replaced with new growth, while their root clumps grow wider and stronger over the years.

At some time in the past perennials were dug up or their seed collected from the wild. Yes, they are really a collection of wildflowers. Some are still as they grew wild; others have been further developed in cultivation to improve the range, colour and form. Perennials come to gardens from many parts of the world, so the response of different ones to Australian conditions varies. It is largely a matter of trial and error – and research into their origins and requirements – to find the ones that will flourish in your garden.

OPPOSITE PAGE Part of the art of making a perennial border is having some plants coming on as early-flowering perennials fade. Add plants that flower late in the season to fill spaces where growth has been cut back.

PERENNIAL BORDERS

In Europe, and particularly the British Isles, perennial borders have been extremely popular for over a century. Gertrude Jekyll (1843–1932), the great English gardener, perfected the art of border making with her exquisite colour work and thorough attention to scale and grading heights. The experience of seeing her borders has been described by horticulturist Graham Thomas as like 'walking through a static rainbow'.

Perennial borders present tremendous challenges to the gardener. The classic border is quite deep – about 6 metres – although considerable grandeur can be achieved with a border only 2 or 3 metres wide and this is certainly the size beginners should start with. The behaviour, colour, height and demeanour of each species must be thoroughly understood, and each must be placed according to its ways, with repetitions throughout the border, to form a perfect picture. Above all, a successful perennial border is an exercise in timing. It is usual to draw a plan of a border before it is planted to check the likely result, and to make adjustments to the border as it grows and develops.

Establishing and maintaining a perennial border is demanding work, so you should be quite sure you want to put in the time before you start one. The soil is deeply dug and prepared with the addition of large quantities of compost (see Chapter 4). Sometimes the bed is mounded a little for sharper drainage. In Australia perennials often wither, wilt and tip over prematurely in the harsh and changeable summer weather unless they are carefully chosen and tended. Plant growth in the perennial border is stimulated at regular intervals with liquid manure, and, as they mature, some perennials need a light staking. Scruffy plants need to be tidied up, which in turn encourages a second flush of flowers. Dead-heading summer-blooming perennials to extend their flowering time into autumn helps to hide the gaps left as plants that bloom early or briefly begin to fade.

Spring-flowering geums have vivid but delicate flowers on tall stems above shapely leaves.

WHERE HAVE ALL THE FLOWERS GONE?

Because the majority of perennials flourish in spring, summer and autumn in temperate climates, perennial borders can look rather abandoned in winter, with just a few cut, dried stalks above ground. This does not matter so much in Europe, where cold, harsh winters keep people mostly indoors, but in most parts of Australia winter weather does not consistently keep people from their gardens. To ensure some interest in the garden during the cold months and into early spring, plant a guard of low evergreen shrubs, such as *Daphne odora*, *Thryptomene* 'Paynei' and *Rosmarinus officinalis* 'Blue Lagoon'; perennial plants, including *Helleborus*, *Primula*, *Bergenia* and *Saxifraga* species; and bulbs, such as snowdrops (*Galanthus*), snowflakes (*Leucojum*), crocuses, *Ipheion*, grape hyacinths (*Muscari*) and hyacinths (*Hyacinthus*). Also look out for perennials that bloom in winter and early spring in your area. A support planting of low evergreen plants, such as lavenders, marguerite daisies (*Chrysanthemum frutescens*), rosemaries, pelargoniums, prostrate cotoneasters, echiums and old-fashioned azaleas, can hold the fort throughout the year. French lavender (*Lavandula dentata*), the cigar flower (*Cuphea ignea*) and heliotrope, or cherry pie (*Heliotropium arborescens*), flower throughout the year unless it is extremely cold.

MIXED GARDEN BORDERS

Perennials and shrubs can be combined in endless variations. For instance, plant euphorbias, potentillas and helianthemums with thryptomenes and French lavender. Billowing white *Gaura lindheimeri* is striking skirting evergreen shrubs in summer and autumn, and you can use perennial wallflowers (*Cheiranthus cheiri*) for winter and early spring effects. Many of the plants in a mixed border also contribute interesting foliage when they are not in flower.

These same evergreen plants can shield perennials from the worst of the wind and sun in summertime and act as supportive planting just in case the perennials don't perform all that well! It may take two or three years for perennial plants to reach their full glory.

TALL PERENNIALS (HEIGHT OVER 60 CENTIMETRES)

PERENNIAL AND PLACE OF ORIGIN	LEAVES	HEIGHT (H), WIDTH (W) AND FORM	FLOWERING TIME AND SPECIAL CHARACTERISTICS	PARTICULAR REQUIREMENTS AND HARDINESS
Dietes bicolor (butterfly iris) South Africa	Bold, straplike	H: 50–80 cm W: 60 cm Clump-forming rhizome	Summer Yellow, irislike flowers, with open petals, over long period	Happy in sun or shade; drought and frost resistant
Digitalis (foxglove) Europe, United Kingdom	Large, textured	H: 2 m W: 1 m Tall, upright spikes	Summer Cream, pink or mauve bell flowers, with mottled throats, on tall spikes	Light, well-drained soil; sunny position
Gaura lindheimeri North America	Small, lacy, mid-green	H: 1–1.5 m W: 1 m Bushy, with long, arching stems	Summer to autumn Pink buds open to white butterfly flowers up stems	Easy to grow in moist soil and full sun
Hemerocallis (daylily) Asia	Long, narrow, straplike	H: 1 m W: 1 m Clump forming	Summer to autumn Open, yellow, orange, bronze or red trumpet flowers, on long stems, only last one day, but more follow; dwarf varieties also	Very hardy in sun or part shade; does best in moist, rich soil
Romneya coulteri (Californian tree-poppy) United States of America	Silvery grey	H: 1–2 m W: 3–4 m Spreading	Summer to autumn Large, poppylike, white flowers, with yellow centres and petals like crêpe-paper	Suits most soils; loves sun
Salvia patens (perennial salvia) North America	Oval, greyish	H: 1 m W: 1 m Clump forming	Summer to autumn Tubular, deep blue flowers, with two lips, on long spikes, over long period	Prefers moist soil and open, sunny position
Sisyrinchium striatum (spring bell) South America	Broad, blue-grey, bladelike	H: 60 cm W: 1 m Clump forming	Spring to summer Clusters of tiny, cream star flowers up stems, over long period	Easy to grow in sun or part shade
Thalictrum aquilegiifolium (meadow rue) Europe	Delicate, like maidenhair fern, light green	H: 1.5 m W: 1.5 m Tall, clump forming	Summer Fluffy clusters of white or pale mauve flowers above leaves	Hardy in most soils in sun or dappled shade

Gaura lindheimeri.

MEDIUM PERENNIALS (HEIGHT ABOUT 30–60 CENTIMETRES)

PERENNIAL AND PLACE OF ORIGIN	LEAVES	HEIGHT (H), WIDTH (W) AND FORM	FLOWERING TIME AND SPECIAL CHARACTERISTICS	PARTICULAR REQUIREMENTS AND HARDINESS
Achillea ptarmica 'The Pearl' (yarrow, milfoil) Europe	Long, fronded, deep green	H: 60 cm W: 50 cm	Summer to autumn Flat clusters of tiny, white button flowers on long stems; flowers profusely over long period	Quick growing; sun loving
Anthemis tinctoria (chamomile) Europe	Finely dissected, greyish green	H: 40 cm W: 1 m Spreading	Spring Masses of yellow daisy flowers	Hardy in well-drained soil and full sun
Aquilegia (columbine, granny's bonnet) Europe, United Kingdom	Consist of wedge-shaped leaflets, bluish green	H: 45 cm W: 40 cm Graceful, upright, clump forming	Spring Species are nodding, five-petalled, white, rose-coloured or blue flowers, with spur from back; many varieties	Moist soil; filtered sun
Astilbe	Fernlike, glossy green with some copper	H: 45 cm W: 30 cm Clump forming	Spring to early summer Plumes of white, pink or red flowers on spikes	Hardy in shade or sun; prefers moist, rich soil
Helichrysum bracteatum 'Dargan Hill Monarch' (straw flower) Australian cultivar	Tough, greyish	H: 45 cm W: 1 m	Summer to autumn Large, long-lasting, daisy flower heads, with yellow bracts	Full sun; very well-drained soil
Helleborus orientalis (Lenten rose, winter rose) Western Asia	Divided, leathery, deep green	H: 40–60 cm W: 50 cm Clump forming	Winter Nodding but open-faced, creamy white, rosy or mauve flowers rise above leaves	Partial shade under trees Prefers moist, well-drained, mulched soil
Hosta species (plantain lily) Asia	Range of different greens, some variegated	H: 30–50 cm W: 50 cm Clump forming	Summer Small, sparse, funnel-shaped, white or mauve flowers on tall, slender stems; some varieties fragrant; grown for beauty of leaves	Moist, rich soil; shade Attracts snails
Oenothera missouriensis (evening primrose) Southern United States of America	Narrow, long, glossy	H: 40 cm W: 40 cm	Summer, mainly at night Open-petalled, bright yellow flowers	Grows in most soils, in sun or part shade; drought and frost resistant
Sedum spectabile (ice plant) Asia	Thick, succulent, light green	H: 40 cm W: 50 cm Clump forming	Summer to autumn Clusters of pink star flowers; attracts butterflies; good for rock gardens or perennial borders	Hardy; loves sun; drought and frost resistant

Erigeron karvinskianus.

SMALL PERENNIALS (HEIGHT TO ABOUT 30 CENTIMETRES)

PERENNIAL AND PLACE OF ORIGIN	LEAVES	HEIGHT (H), WIDTH (W) AND FORM	FLOWERING TIME AND SPECIAL CHARACTERISTICS	PARTICULAR REQUIREMENTS AND HARDINESS
Ajuga australis (austral bugle) New South Wales, Queensland, South Australia, Tasmania, Victoria	Long, oval, green, purplish underside	H: 10 cm W: 1 m Spreading	Spring to summer Purple flowers, on spikes 10 cm high, above leaves	Very hardy; adapts to most soils
Armeria maritima (sea pink, thrift) Europe	Thin, green	H: 20 cm W: 20 cm Clump forming	Spring to summer Masses of small, white or pink balls of flowers on stems; good for rockery or border	Well-drained soil Drought and frost resistant
Bergenia cordifolia (elephant's ear) Siberia	Large, oval, glossy green, with pink-tinged edges	H: 30 cm W: 30 cm Clump forming	Spring Massed panicles of pale pink flowers on reddish stems	Will grow in open sun or under trees; adaptable to most soils; drought and frost resistant
Dianthus (pink) Europe	Fine, thin, deep green to grey-green	H: 15 cm W: 40 cm Clump forming	Early summer Highly fragrant, white, pink, red or lilac flowers, many with different-coloured centres; good for rockeries or borders	Well-drained soil; full sun
Dimorphotheca (African daisy) South Africa	Small, on lank stems	H: 30 cm W: 50 cm Scrubby, spreading	Summer Spectacular, white, yellow, pink or purple daisy flowers	Well-drained; open, sunny position Drought resistant; cut back by frosts
Erigeron karvinskianus (baby's tears) North America	Fine	H: 20–40 cm W: 60 cm Clump forming	All year Dainty, white daisy flowers, with touches of pink	Full sun to shade Hardy under most conditions
Heuchera (coral bells) North America	Rounded, geraniumlike	H: 30 cm W: 40 cm Clump forming	Spring Small, pink or crimson bell flowers on spikes	Moist, well-drained soil; sun or partial shade
Iberis sempervirens (candytuft) Europe	Deep green	H: 30 cm W: 30 cm Rounded, clump forming	Spring Clusters of small, white flowers, massed over plant	Pruning back to shape Suits most soils; drought and frost resistant
Nepeta × *faassenii* (catmint) Arabian peninsula	Rounded, soft, pungent, grey-green	H: 30 cm W: 45 cm Spreading	Summer Small, mauve-blue flowers, with a lip, in whorls up spikes 14 cm high; good for edges in border	Grows well in well-drained soil and sunny position; cut back by frosts

ANNUALS: A SHORT BUT MERRY LIFE

Of all plants, annuals as a group are the most colourful. These plants are sown as seeds, grow, flourish, flower and fade in the space of less than a year – though soon after they have died tiny seed leaves may appear in the soil, for annuals often self-seed. It's high-pressure living, and annuals are programmed to do so much in so short a time that, to grow them well, their needs must be understood and attended to or their moment may pass.

FORMAL BEDDINGS AND DRIFTS

Traditionally annuals have been planted in separate garden beds, sometimes in gaudy patterns and often with little regard for the total landscape. This type of bedding practice has given them rather a bad name, yet today there are some quite beautiful annual plantings, with carefully chosen colours and subtle patterns, particularly in civic gardens. Annual beds can be quite striking within gardens, particularly in soft, spring colours; plant, for example, a single species such as a dainty viscaria. Annuals can be used around a formal pond, fountain or statue: lobelias in mixed blues look sensational by water.

Annuals – sometimes of just one kind – can be planted in drifts, rather in the way that bulbs grow if left alone. Start with two or three, widening to ten or so plants across and then diminishing the number again perhaps, so that they seem to disappear between two shrubs.

MIXED PLANTINGS

Annuals can be used in garden borders among perennials, bulbs and shrubs. Unless you are quite sure that you want your annual plants set in straight lines, giving an ordered, crisp effect, you should plant them as if their seed had been sprinkled over the ground in a casual way.

Blue and mauve salvias look rich but soft planted in a mixed border. (Keep to the blue and mixed pink tonings for an elegant and harmonious effect.) Surround them with patches of blue petunias. Don't use pink petunias as well or they'll take over the whole show, and any hint of white will drain away the colours of the others. If there's room you could plant the perennial speedwell (*Veronica spicata*), with its tiny spires of pink or blue, in a ratio of about three-quarters pink to one-quarter blue, and some of the pink or cameo-mix alyssum. Dainty annuals, such as midnight phlox or viscaria, can be sown directly among the other plants. Plant some clumps of rhizomatous *Liriope*, so that deep blue, candlelike flowers appear quite suddenly in late summer and autumn, and pale pink perennial asters, which flower about the same time – quite a surprise!

Sometimes annuals can be closely planted to lap around the lower reaches of green shrubs, making a pool of light in an otherwise dark corner: for instance, creamy yellow petunias round the skirts of pyramidal conifers. Think of lime-green Molucca balm (*Moluccella laevis*) and small, random patches of white alyssum in front of a hedge planting of *Viburnum tinus* or one of the conifer species such as *Juniperus sabina*.

SOFT EDGINGS

Annuals make charming soft edgings. Avoid stiff, straight lines when you use them this way. Imagine a lacy, scalloped edge of white primulas, for late winter and early spring, with behind them patches of bulbs – *Narcissus papyraceus* 'Paperwhite', grape hyacinths (*Muscari*) and old-world freesias – worked round permanent crowns of perennials, such as *Helleborus orientalis*. As summer progresses the hellebores' leaves go darker green and brown at the edges and are gradually replaced with shiny, light green ones. By this time their crowns will have broadened; the primulas will have long been composted; and the spent flowers of the bulbs will have been removed to prevent seeds forming, and the stems and leaves allowed to wither, nourishing the bulbs for next year's flowers.

POTS AND WINDOW-BOXES

An acceptable way of segregating annuals is to plant them in window-boxes, tubs and pots, where they have special privileges. The too-stripy petunias and the too-carmine zinnias immediately become less vulgar confined to a container. The possibilities are endless, but plan your combinations carefully.

Iceland poppies (*Papaver nudicaule*) and *Gypsophila elegans* make a lively spring and early summer combination.

ANNUALS

ANNUAL AND PLACE OF ORIGIN	HEIGHT (H), WIDTH (W) AND CHARACTERISTICS	PLANTING TIME (PT) FOR SEEDS AND FLOWERING TIME (FT)	PARTICULAR REQUIREMENTS AND HARDINESS
Actinotus helianthi (eastern Sydney flannel flower) New South Wales, Queensland	H: 50 cm W: 3 cm Star flowers, with soft, creamy white, raylike petals	PT: spring FT: late spring to summer	Grows best in gravel or sandstone with perfect drainage
Alyssum maritimum syn. *Lobularia maritima* (sweet Alice) Central Europe, Mediterranean	H: 15 cm W: 20 cm Carpeting plant with tiny heads of white, cream, mauve-pink or mauve flowers; good edging paths or between bricks or pavers	PT: all year FT: all year	Sun or part shade
Bellis perennis (English daisy) Europe	H: 15 cm W: 20 cm Dainty heads of pink, red or white flowers on short stems; can be grown in lawns	PT: winter to spring FT: spring to summer	Sun or part shade
Cleome spinosa (spider flower) Tropical America	H: 1–1.5 m W: 30 cm Clusters of spiderlike, white, pink or violet flowers, on long stalks; good for massed effect behind smaller plants	PT: spring FT: summer to autumn	Sun
Cosmos Mexico	H: 1–2 m W: 30 cm Simple, white, pink or mauve single flowers on tall stems; also shorter orange or yellow varieties	PT: spring to summer FT: spring to autumn	Well-drained soil; sun Easily grown
Delphinium (larkspur) Europe	H: 1–1.5 m W: 40 cm White, pink, blue or mauve flowers on tall spikes	PT: autumn FT: spring to summer	Rich, well-drained soil Full sun
Eschscholzia californica (Californian poppy) United States of America	H: 20–45 cm W: 30 cm Masses of poppylike, orange flowers above soft, grey leaves; cultivars in cream, yellow, pink or red	PT: spring to early summer FT: spring to late autumn	Easily grown in poor soil; sun loving
Helianthus (sunflower) Mexico, South America	H: 1–3 m W: 30 cm Single or double, deep gold flowers up to 15–20 cm wide	PT: spring to early summer FT: summer to autumn	Rich, well-drained soil; full sun; protection from strong winds

Cleome spinosa.

Myosotis and *Bellis perennis*.

ANNUALS			
ANNUAL AND PLACE OF ORIGIN	**HEIGHT (H), WIDTH (W) AND CHARACTERISTICS**	**PLANTING TIME (PT) FOR SEEDS AND FLOWERING TIME (FT)**	**PARTICULAR REQUIREMENTS AND HARDINESS**
Helichrysum (everlasting daisy, straw flower) New South Wales, South Australia, Tasmania, Victoria	H: 30–50 cm W: 25 cm Papery, white, yellow, pink or red flowers; dried flowers last months	PT: autumn to spring FT: early spring	Moisture during dry periods Suits sunny position
Lathyrus odoratus (sweet pea) Mediterranean	H: 3 m W: 20 cm Fragrant, white, cream, pink, blue, mauve or rich maroon pea flowers; climbs	PT: mid-summer to late autumn; early spring in cool climates FT: spring to autumn	Plenty of sun; rich, well-drained soil; trellis
Myosotis (forget-me-not) Europe	H: 8–20 cm W: 25 cm Tiny clusters of white, pink or sky-blue flowers, with yellow centres; pale green leaves; good for edges, borders or ground cover under trees	PT: all year FT: mainly spring	Easily grown, though prefers moist soil and partly shaded position
Nemesia strumosa South Africa	H: 20 cm W: 30 cm Clusters of small funnel flowers in bright and pastel colours	PT: autumn FT: spring	Rich, well-drained soil
Nigella damascena (love-in-a-mist) Mediterranean, western Asia	H: 30–40 cm W: 30 cm Misty masses of blue star flowers, with spurred petals, among veil of bracts and fine foliage; seed pods dry well	PT: autumn and early spring FT: spring	Easily grown in most soils; prefers full sun or part shade; seeds readily
Papaver nudicaule (Iceland poppy) Arctic region	H: 40–45 cm W: 30 cm Single-petalled, yellow, lemon, orange, salmon, pink, red or cerise cup flowers; good behind border plants	PT: autumn FT: mid-winter to mid-spring	Rich, well-drained soil; plenty of sun
Salpiglossis sinuata (velvet flower) Chile	H: 75 cm W: 30 cm Dark-veined trumpet flowers in stained-glass colours	PT: early spring FT: all summer	Rich, well-drained soil; protected, sunny position; light staking
Viola (pansy and viola) Europe	H: 15–20 cm W: 30 cm Flat-faced, yellow, blue, purple, russet, brown or velvety black flowers; new pastel varieties available; good for edges or low borders.	PT: autumn to early spring FT: spring to early summer	Rich, well-drained soil; sunny position, though protected from late afternoon heat

BULBS

The term 'bulb' refers to a plant that stores food underground. There are true bulbs, such as tulips, daffodils and liliums; corms, such as gladioli; rhizomes, such as anemones, irises, kangaroo paws and cannas; and tubers, such as dahlias, cyclamens and colchicums. A true bulb is onionlike. It has a flat basal plate that develops roots for feeding and for holding it firmly in the soil. The outer layers protect the bud, or embryo plant. Bulblets (new bulbs) form around the base. These can be separated from the parent plant when it is lifted, but they can take up to four years to develop flowers.

A corm has a structure, like a swollen stem at the base of the true stem, which contains a mass of stored food, protected by thin scales. Roots form at the base and the bud at the top. Pips (baby corms) at the sides develop in time, but a new corm for the following year forms on top of the old one, which shrivels and dies. A rhizome is a creeping horizontal stem, with often quite superficial roots. New plants are produced at the shooting end and from swollen parts of the stem. Separate plants are grown from pieces of stem with at least one potential shooting spot. A tuber is a swollen root on a stem, which shoots from 'eyes' (buds). Tubers should be lifted and divided at the end of the flowering season.

There is an endearing self-sufficiency about bulbs. Each is a masterpiece of packaging, complete with food storage and protection for the next year's precious plant in miniature. Moreover most are not difficult to grow, despite their striking beauty.

Bulbs come in all shapes, sizes and habits and in a host of colours. Many are bright and cheery looking, some are grand or majestic and others have a gentleness, with their soft pastel shades and modest habit. Often there is a camellialike lustre to the petals.

OPPOSITE PAGE Claude Monet, the French artist, thought of his garden at Giverny as an enormous painting to which strikingly colourful adjustments could be made. Deep pink contrasted with a blue of the same intensity, against a background of amber and gold, provides inspiration for any gardener.

BULB MAGIC AND ROMANCE

The magic of bulbs is in the way their beautiful flowers appear, develop and open or unfurl so quickly, once the bulbs sense that it is shooting and flowering time. Some, such as nerines, appear overnight from bare ground, the right combination of moisture and warmth triggering them into action.

The romance of bulbs is in their history. Many were gathered in the sixteenth and seventeenth centuries from parts of Asia and Central and Southern Europe and sold for great prices in Europe's commercial centres, particularly Holland.

Can you imagine red tulips growing wild over the steppes of Central Asia? Narcissi mostly originated in Egypt, Spain and Portugal, but one species is widespread through Asia. Dainty crocuses come largely from the shallow soils of Greece and the islands nearby. Irises in the wild have been found in North America, Europe and Asia, and there is a genus of the iris family found in Australia, called *Patersonia*. Many lilies, with their vibrant colours, grow in the southern parts of Africa, which have a Mediterranean climate. Others flourish in Asia, and Australia also has its native lilies.

BULB GROWING IN AUSTRALIA

Southern and eastern Australia have an ideal climate for bulbs, many of which come from places with similar climates. The hilly areas west of Brisbane and the tablelands around Cairns are also well suited to many bulbs, as is the south-western corner of Western Australia. Some bulbs, such as *Tulipa* and *Fritillaria* species, require a very cold winter in order to flourish and do best in southern and eastern mountain districts. Certainly we should be more aware of how bulbs can complement our garden pictures and discipline ourselves to plant them when we should. We should also be aware of the charming native bulbs, such as the ones listed in the following table, that can add to our range of choice and are well suited to different areas of Australia.

There are many ways of using bulbs in all seasons, and the same flowering types used differently can create vastly different effects. Remember, though, that you must put up with withering leaves after flowering is over, while next year's bulbs are being nurtured; tying long leaves into granny-knotted bundles or flattening them down among leafy plants will help.

FORMAL AND SINGLE-PLANTING BORDERS

Plant bulbs in clumps or patches, with annuals, perennials or both. Wallflowers (*Cheiranthus cheiri*) and forget-me-nots (*Myosotis*) are two plants that work well with bulbs. Think of pale daffodils (*Narcissus*) with cream wallflowers and blue forget-me-nots or pink tulips among blue forget-me-nots and pale and deep pink *Ranunculus* and, if the border is deeper than this, perennials and shrubs behind.

Daffodils are fine as a single planting in a long border linking trees, particularly the gentler types such as *Narcissus papyraceus* 'Paperwhite' and pheasant's eyes (*N. poeticus*).

CONTAINERS

Decorative plantings of bulbs can be made in both large and small containers – happy combinations to brighten late winter, spring, summer or autumn days. Sometimes it helps to soften the plantings with a trailing or edging plant, such as lobelia – if it's not too hot – or alyssum. Plant snowflakes (*Leucojum*) edged with crocuses for late winter; daffodils edged with white primulas, or grape hyacinths (*Muscari*) with old-fashioned freesias and frothy white primulas, for spring. Clivias are particularly striking when their apricot lily flowers appear in spring (and sometimes in autumn, too), but, grown in terracotta pots that set off their straplike evergreen leaves, they are handsome throughout the year. Christmas lilies (*Lilium longiflorum*) and the Asiatic lilies look good flowering above a terracotta pot, perhaps with its edges softened by dwarf agapanthus if it is large. Nerines – white or a mixture of pink and white or yellow and red – can look charming near the house in autumn. *Hyacinthus*, either in a single colour or a mixture, often flower in early winter if planted at the beginning of February.

DRIFTS AND UNDER TREES

Everyone knows how well daffodils work as drifts, if left to naturalise. The strong yellow ones don't mix well with anything but other *Narcissus* species or bold flowers in clear red, purple, blue, orange or gold, such as tulips and poppies (*Papaver*). Equally striking can be patches of *Gladiolus carneus* growing in profusion in grass – perhaps mixed with rich blue babianas.

ROCK AND WATER GARDENS

Small bulbs such as hoop petticoat daffodils (*Narcissus bulbocodium*), crocuses, rock cyclamens and rock tulips are grateful for safe pockets in rockeries because they can be easily lost or dug over in garden beds. But make sure that they are not allowed to dry out as they are preparing to flower.

Some of the arum lilies (*Zantedeschia*) and many of the iris species are happy on the edge of a pond or even in the water (see the section on Pond Plants, later in the chapter).

BULBS FOR ALL SEASONS

Somehow when we think of the beauty of daffodils in early spring – and most of us do – the mind dances on to freesias, to grape hyacinths, to bluebells (*Hyacinthoides*), to irises and to *Gladiolus* species; then to summer and the brilliantly coloured and delicate lilies – *Lilium auratum* and the Asiatics – crinums, galtonias, the amazing range of dahlias and the dearly loved agapanthus, now in maxi and mini forms.

Come autumn, there are *Lycoris*, the autumn crocus (*Colchicum autumnale*), the crocuslike *Zephyranthes candida*, the queen of the autumn bulbs, the nerine – and the little rock cyclamens *Cyclamen hederifolium*, which herald a delightful season of cyclamens extending into winter. Another autumn classic is the Japanese windflower (*Anemone japonica*). It needs plenty of space for its rhizomes to roam free.

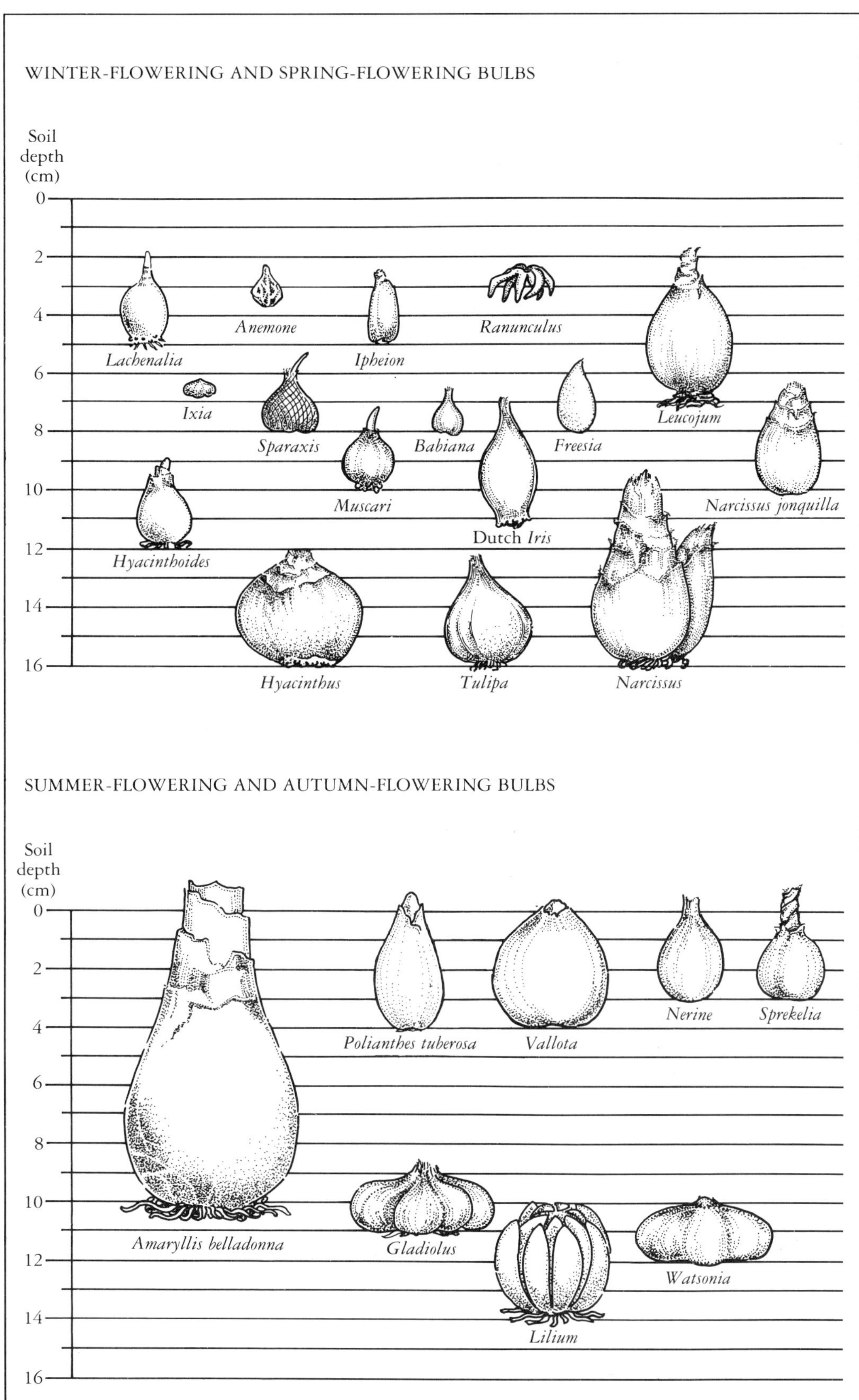

Plant winter-flowering and spring-flowering bulbs in autumn; summer-flowering and autumn-flowering bulbs in winter. Vary the planting depths shown, according to your soil type: bulbs should be planted a little more deeply in sandy soil than in heavy clay.

Fragrant old-fashioned freesias are planted with Spanish bluebells (*Hyacinthoides hispanica*) on a sunny bank.

Winter is more difficult, but cyclamens, *Iris unguicularis*, *I. germanica* and snowflakes are about, and perhaps apricot-coloured clivias running early or late. Suddenly crocuses and early jonquils (*Narcissus jonquilla*) appear, with hyacinths, daffodils, freesias and the soldierlike lachenalias following. Next it's the colour parade of sparaxis, anemones and ranunculi, with deep blue babianas; then bluebells and irises again.

COMMON GROUND

Although bulbs come from many different habitats they have certain characteristics and requirements in common.

- All bulbs have a growing season, and a dormant season during which they can be readily handled.
- When obtaining bulbs, choose the plumpest, healthiest ones: big flowers come from big bulbs.
- Bulbs prefer good-quality, well-drained soil with a generous supply of humus. Complete fertiliser must be worked in well in advance and not allowed to touch the bulb. Fertiliser high in phosphorus and potash is favoured.
- Most bulbs prefer slightly acid soil.
- Most bulbs should be planted at a soil depth twice their height – a little deeper if the soil is light and sandy. They should be planted two-bulbs'-width apart for a clumped, natural effect. Nerines and amaryllis prefer their necks just above the soil, and rhizomes are planted close to the surface.
- Bulbs need plenty of water while they are growing, but when their leaves die down after flowering they prefer dryness.
- Most bulbs are best lifted about every four years to be thinned out or divided and perhaps planted in a different place. Some, however, should be lifted each year after flowering, particularly tulips, hyacinths and gladioli. If you don't mind losing some occasionally or a deterioration in quality, you can leave daffodils and jonquils, grape hyacinths, colchicums, watsonias, freesias and bluebells to naturalise and form colonies.
- The best time to move bulbs is when their leaves are dying off after flowering. Make sure that you make a note of where you have replanted them before they disappear from view!

Anemone japonica.

BULBS, CORMS AND TUBERS

BULB AND PLACE OF ORIGIN	HEIGHT (H) AND WIDTH (W)	CHARACTERISTICS	PLANTING (PT) AND FLOWERING TIME (FT)	PARTICULAR REQUIREMENTS AND HARDINESS
Agapanthus 'Baby Blue' South Africa	H: 45–60 cm W: 40 cm	Evergreen; narrow, straplike leaves; small version of *A. praecox*; white form also available	PT: all year FT: spring to autumn (generously)	Generally hardy; thrives in sun or shade; multiplies readily
Agapanthus praecox subsp. *orientalis* (Nile lily) South Africa	H: 90–120 cm W: 75 cm	Evergreen; clump forming; large, round, blue or white flower heads borne on stiff stalks, above wide, long, straplike leaves	PT: all year FT: mainly summer	As for *A.* 'Baby Blue'
Allium giganteum (ornamental onion) Afghanistan, Iran and regions north	H: 120 cm W: 30–60 cm	Winter dormant; large, spherical flower heads of massed, lilac-purple florets on long stems, above narrow leaves	PT: late winter to spring FT: late spring to early summer	Well-drained soil; sunny position Withstands dry conditions
Alpinia coerulea (native ginger) New South Wales, Queensland	H: 2 m W: 1 m	Evergreen; white and red flowers in terminal clusters	PT: when available FT: spring or summer	Damp, humus-rich soil; protected, shady position
Alstroemeria (Peruvian lily) South America	H: 75 cm W: 40 cm	Summer dormant; bugle-shaped, cream to bright red-orange flowers	PT: autumn to early winter FT: late spring	Loose, open soil Grows in full sun or part shade
Amaryllis belladonna (belladonna lily) South Africa	H: 50–70 cm W: 75 cm	Large, perfumed, white or pink trumpet flowers on long stalks before leaves appear	PT: spring FT: autumn	Prefers open, dry, sun-baked position, though also grows in semi-shade
Anemone blanda South-eastern Europe, Turkey	H: 75 cm W: 10 cm	Winter dormant; daisylike, pale mauve flowers, shading to white near centre; finely divided leaves	PT: autumn FT: early spring	Dry, well-drained soil
Anemone japonica (Japanese windflower) Japan	H: 1 m W: 40 cm	Evergreen; simple, single or semi-double, white, rose-pink or deep pink cup flowers on long stems, above leaves	PT: all year FT: summer to autumn	Moist soil; sunny to shaded position
Anigozanthos manglesii (red and green kangaroo paw) Western Australia	H: 1 m W: 30 cm	Evergreen; pawlike, velvety, red and green flowers	PT: all year FT: spring to summer	Well-drained soil; sunny position

Anigozanthos.

BULBS, CORMS AND TUBERS				
BULB AND PLACE OF ORIGIN	HEIGHT (H) AND WIDTH (W)	CHARACTERISTICS	PLANTING (PT) AND FLOWERING TIME (FT)	PARTICULAR REQUIREMENTS AND HARDINESS
Babiana stricta (baboon flower) South Africa	H: 20–30 cm W: 7.5 cm	Evergreen; freesialike, blue or mauve flowers; sword-shaped leaves	PT: autumn FT: mid-spring	Well-drained soil; open, sunny position Hardy if well mulched in winter
Bulbine bulbosa (native leek) All Australian States except Western Australia	H: 50 cm W: 30 cm	Evergreen; small, yellow star flowers, among fans of narrow, pointed, grasslike leaves	PT: late summer FT: spring or summer	Light, well-drained, moist soil; protected position in semi-shade
Calostemma purpureum (garland lily) New South Wales interior, South Australia, Victoria	H: 40 cm W: 30 cm	Evergreen; clusters of wine-red to pink trumpet flowers, with yellow centres; straplike leaves	PT: all year FT: summer to early autumn	Open, sunny position
Canna (Indian shot) Caribbean	H: 1.5–2 m W: 70 cm	Evergreen; large-petalled, flaglike, yellow, orange, pink or red flowers; long, broad leaves	PT: winter FT: summer	Prefers moist, rich soils in sunny position
Chionodoxa (glory of the snow) Crete, Cypress, Turkey	H: 15–20 cm W: 5 cm	Summer dormant; white star flowers, tinged mauve; thin, stringy leaves	PT: autumn FT: spring	Cool, mountain climate, well-drained soil; sheltered position Drought tender
Clivia miniata (kaffir lily) South Africa	H: 40 cm W: 50 cm	Evergreen; clusters of apricot trumpet flowers; broad, straplike leaves	PT: autumn FT: spring and autumn	Well-drained soil; protected, shady position Frost tender
Colchicum autumnale (meadow saffron) Northern Europe	H: 10 cm W: 6 cm	Summer dormant; mottled rose-purple or white star flowers, followed by stringy leaves	PT: spring FT: autumn	Damp, humus-rich soil; open position
Crinum flaccidum New South Wales, South Australia	H: 1 m W: 10–40 cm	Evergreen; clusters of creamy white trumpet flowers, above tall, pointed leaves in rosettes	PT: all year FT: summer	Well-drained soil; open, sunny position Frost tender
Crinum moorei South Africa	H: 1–1.5 m W: 1 m	Evergreen; clusters of tubular, white or pink flowers; broad, glossy pale green leaves in rosettes	PT: autumn FT: summer	Moist, rich, well-drained soil; protected position
Crocus South-eastern Europe	H: 5–8 cm W: 2.5–5 cm	Summer dormant; large, yellow, pink, blue, mauve or violet cup flowers; fine, green, straplike leaves, with silver underside	PT: autumn FT: early spring	Mountain or cold-winter climate

Crinum moorei.

Cyclamen hederifolilum.

BULBS, CORMS AND TUBERS

BULB AND PLACE OF ORIGIN	HEIGHT (H) AND WIDTH (W)	CHARACTERISTICS	PLANTING (PT) AND FLOWERING TIME (FT)	PARTICULAR REQUIREMENTS AND HARDINESS
Cyclamen hederifolium (sour bread) Southern Europe	H: 10 cm W: 10–15 cm	Summer dormant; buds like folded umbrellas, opening to small, unusual, white, pink, red or mauve flowers; heart-shaped, blue-green, often mottled leaves	PT: autumn FT: autumn to winter	Humus-rich soil; filtered sun and some protection
Dahlia Mexico, South America	H: 1–2 m W: 60 cm	Winter dormant; generous daisy flowers in variety of shapes, sizes and colours	PT: spring FT: summer to autumn	Prefers humus-rich, well-drained soil in sunny position
Dahlia imperialis (tree dahlia) Mexico	H: 5–7 m W: 50 cm	Winter dormant; clusters of soft mauve flowers, hanging from bamboolike, arching branches	PT: spring to summer FT: autumn	Sunny, sheltered position
Dierama pulcherrimum (fairy fishing rod) South Africa	H: 1.5 m W: 45 cm	Evergreen; tiny, pink bell flowers on long, slender, nodding stems, above dainty, grasslike leaves	PT: autumn FT: late spring	Moist soil; sun or semi-shade Hardy
Freesia South Africa	H: 25 cm W: 15 cm	Summer dormant; medium to small, perfumed, cream to yellow trumpet flowers on slender stems	PT: autumn FT: early spring	Well-drained soil Easy to grow in full sun or light shade
Galanthus nivalis (English snowdrop) Central to Eastern Europe	H: 10 cm W: 15 cm	Summer dormant; dainty, white cup flowers, with curved, pendant outer petals	PT: autumn FT: early spring	Cool winter or cool, shady position in warm climate Naturalises if left undisturbed
Gladiolus × colvillei (sword lily) English hybrid	H: 50 cm W: 15 cm	Winter dormant; broad, open, white trumpet flowers, with cream markings, up stems; sword-shaped leaves	PT: autumn FT: spring	Easily grown in well-drained soil in full sun
Hippeastrum South America	H: 45 cm W: 30 cm	Winter dormant; broad, six-petalled, white, pink or red trumpet flowers, with thick, lustrous, velvety petals, on thick stems before leaves appear	PT: winter to spring FT: summer	Easily grown in humus-rich, well-drained soil in sunny position
Hyacinthoides hispanica (Spanish bluebell) Spain	H: 30–40 cm W: 30 cm	Winter dormant; clump forming; blue bell flowers arranged down stems	PT: autumn FT: spring	Easily grown in full sun or part shade
Ipheion uniflorum (star flower) North America	H: 15 cm W: 15 cm	Winter dormant; masses of small, blue star flowers, above grasslike leaves; good for borders	PT: all year FT: spring	Easily grown in most soils in sunny position

Muscari.

Bearded *Iris.*

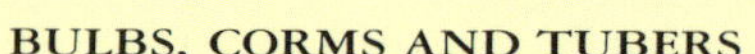

BULBS, CORMS AND TUBERS

BULB AND PLACE OF ORIGIN	HEIGHT (H) AND WIDTH (W)	CHARACTERISTICS	PLANTING (PT) AND FLOWERING TIME (FT)	PARTICULAR REQUIREMENTS AND HARDINESS
Iris, bearded	H: 1 m W: 40 cm	Evergreen; large, delicate flowers in many colours, with upright lateral petals in threes	PT: autumn FT: spring	Full sun, with rhizome partly above surface to bake in late summer sun
Iris kaempferi (water iris) Japan	H: 80 cm W: 30 cm	Evergreen; large flowers in many colours, with broad, flat petals; good pond-edging plant	PT: late autumn to early winter FT: late spring to early summer	Full sun Prefers moist to boggy soils
Ixia viridiflora (African corn lily, green ixia) Africa	H: 75 cm W: 15 cm	Winter dormant; clump forming; turquoise star flowers, with dark centres; narrow, straplike leaves	PT: autumn FT: early spring	Full sun; dry position Naturalises if left undisturbed
Lachenalia aloides (soldier boy) South Africa	H: 15 cm W: 20 cm	Winter dormant; dainty, yellow-green or yellow-red bell flowers, hanging almost vertically from straight, mottled stems; mottled leaves; good edging plant	PT: autumn FT: late winter to early spring	Well-drained soil; full sun Thrives in warm and coastal climates
Leucojum vernum (snowflake) Mediterranean	H: 30 cm W: 30 cm	Winter dormant; small, white cup flowers, with green spots on each petal	PT: autumn FT: late winter to spring	Well-drained soil Easily grown in full sun to semi-shade
Lilium (lily) Asia, Southern Europe	H: 1–1.5 m W: 25 cm	Winter dormant; clusters of stately trumpet flowers, often fragrant, at top of tall, leafy stems; many colours	PT: winter to spring FT: summer	Moist, humus-rich, well-drained soil; sun to part shade
Muscari (grape hyacinth) Europe	H: 15 cm W: 20 cm	Winter dormant; tiny blue or white bell flowers in terminal clusters up stems; good edging plant	PT: autumn FT: winter to early spring	Well-drained soil; full sun or semi-shade Easily grown in most soils
Narcissus (daffodil, jonquil) Europe, Mediterranean	H: 25–30 cm W: 20 cm	Winter dormant; white, gold, yellow or orange flowers, with central cup or trumpet surrounded by flat petals; clump forming	PT: autumn FT: late autumn to early spring	Prefers moist, well-drained soil; deeper planting needed in hot areas with sandy soil; naturalises
Nerine (spider lily) South Africa	H: 30–60 cm W: 30 cm	Winter dormant; dainty, upright clusters of small, white, gold, pink or red trumpet flowers, with protruding stamens	PT: spring to early summer FT: autumn	Well-drained soil Plant with neck above surface
Sparaxis (harlequin flower) South Africa	H: 15–30 cm W: 10 cm	Winter dormant; open, bright, colourful saucer flowers; good border plant	PT: autumn FT: spring	Full sun and some winter moisture Prefers good drainage

BULBS, CORMS AND TUBERS				
BULB AND PLACE OF ORIGIN	HEIGHT (H) AND WIDTH (W)	CHARACTERISTICS	PLANTING (PT) AND FLOWERING TIME (FT)	PARTICULAR REQUIREMENTS AND HARDINESS
Tulbaghia (wild garlic) South Africa	H: 30–40 cm W: 15 cm	Evergreen; clump forming; clusters of tubular, mauve flowers at top of stems; thin, straplike leaves	PT: autumn FT: spring to summer	Easily grown in sun or semi-shade
Tulipa (tulip) Central Asia, Mediterranean	H: 12–70 cm W: 15 cm	Winter dormant; upward-facing, bright or pastel-shaded cup flowers, with lustrous petals in various shapes and sizes	PT: autumn FT: spring	Cold winter (or put in crisper of fridge over autumn); rich, well-drained soil; protected position in full sun or semi-shade
Vallota speciosa (Scarborough lily) Africa	H: 30 cm W: 20–30 cm	Winter dormant; bold, flame red trumpet flowers, with gold stamens; good in outdoor pots	PT: winter FT: spring to early autumn	Well-drained soil; semi-shaded position Prefers dry soil
Zantedeschia aethiopica (arum lily) Eastern South Africa, tropical Africa	H: 1 m W: 50 cm	Evergreen; white cornucopia flowers, with yellow central rods; spear-shaped leaves	PT: all year FT: spring	Likes moisture, even permanent water to about 20 cm high
Zephyranthes candida (flower of the west wind) Central America, South America	H: 20 cm W: 20 cm	Winter dormant; white flowers, on thin stalks, start as cream trumpets and unfurl to stars	PT: spring to summer FT: late summer to autumn	Moisture in spring to early summer; well-drained soil; full sun or semi-shade Multiplies quickly if no competition

Sometimes one or two bulbs, such as this black tulip, can be planted to highlight a garden ornament – and you will remember where they are planted after they have disappeared from sight.

Large, repetitive plantings of various shapes and textures make a bold showing in an extensive rockery. Slow-growing dwarf conifers give accent to the clumps.

GROUND COVERS AND ROCK DWELLERS

Ground covers have a matlike quality or the ability to cascade down a wall or over rocks. Often people see ground covers as a solution when they run out of planting ideas; however, the use of ground covers is more of an art than a quick way out.

In planning gardens among the rocks and across the ground the selection of plants in terms of colour, harmony of shape and character is just as telling as in any other part of the garden. The objective is to create the feeling that the plants just happen to be growing there by nature, not design. A pleasing natural effect will be more likely to result from a simple combination of a few plants than from a wide collection of plants gathered together on the rocks, looking awkward. For instance, plant patches of autumn-flowering Japanese windflowers (*Anemone japonica*) or spring- and summer-flowering arctotis.

There are many interesting low-growing, ground-covering plants for sun, shade and exposed sites. The trick is to know the particular ones suited to your prevailing conditions so that they cover the ground quickly and well.

Ground-covering plants can be a foil for a garden statue, whereas taller plants may reduce its impact. In the same way, a uniform planting of ground covers around a simple pond will complement rather than compete. Sometimes a change of pace in the garden, with some flat patches filled with leafiness, is a good idea: patches of silvery grey snow-in-summer (*Cerastium tomentosum*) among lavenders, *Convolvulus mauritanicus* down a sunny bank between shrubby grevilleas or callistemons, and *Lamium* species coating the shadows between hydrangeas, for example.

Ground covers can be interspersed with evergreen bulbs, such as dwarf agapanthus and *Bulbine bulbosa*, or perennials, such as pulmonaria, with its dainty spotted leaves, and hellebores. Prostrate junipers make hardy and striking ground covers, and masses of Scottish heather (*Calluna vulgaris*) are effective on a more sheltered site.

GROUND COVERS (HEIGHT OVER 25 CENTIMETRES)

GROUND COVER AND PLACE OF ORIGIN	HEIGHT (H), WIDTH (W) AND FORM	SPECIAL CHARACTERISTICS	PARTICULAR REQUIREMENTS AND HARDINESS
Anthemis cupaniana (chamomile) Europe	H: 50 cm W: 50 cm Tufty	Bright yellow daisy flowers, in summer, rise above blue-green, fernlike foliage in rounded clump	Sunny position Adapts to most soils; drought tender; easily layered
Anthemis montana (chamomile) Asia, Europe	H: 25 cm W: 30 cm Tufty	White daisy flowers, with yellow centres cover broad bush in summer; silver-grey, fernlike leaves	Sunny position Adapts to most soils; drought tender; layers itself
Calluna vulgaris (Scotch heather) Great Britain	H: 45 cm W: 50 cm Tufty	Tiny, hanging, mauve bell flowers, summer to autumn; rather upright, small bush, with fine blue-grey or green leaves	Acid soil Prefers cool, moist climate; drought tender
Convolvulus cneorum Southern Europe	H: 45 cm W: 50 cm Shrubby	Open, white bell flowers, tinged with pink, spring to summer; silver leaves	Light to medium soil; sharp drainage; open, sunny position
Cotoneaster dammeri China	H: 30 cm W: 1 m Low, shrubby	Small, white flowers in summer; shiny scarlet berries; small, oval, glossy leaves on spreading stems	Adapts to most soils and positions; layers itself
Cymbopogon exaltatus (scented grass) Mainland Australia	H: 1 m W: 35 cm Low, clump-forming grass	Lemon-scented leaves	Hardy
Dampiera linearis (common dampiera) Western Australia	H: 45 cm W: 1 m Tufty	Bright blue flowers in spring and summer; leaves vary in shape; long stems	Prefers sandy soil and full sun; strongly suckering
Fuchsia procumbens (trailing fuchsia) New Zealand	H: 1.5 m W: 50 cm Trailing, climbing	Dainty, orange, green and purple flowers in summer; long, wiry stems, with semi-evergreen, tiny, round leaves; can spill over rocks	Rich, moist soil; protected position in semi-shade Drought tender; layers easily
Gardenia florida 'Radicans' China	H: 1 m W: 1 m Shrubby, dwarf	Fragrant, roselike, white flowers, all year in tropics, in summer in cool climate; glossy green leaves	Light to medium, well-drained soil; protected, warm position Drought and frost tender
Gazania (treasure flower) South Africa	H: 30 cm W: 50 cm Tufty, matting	Cream, yellow, gold, pinky bronze or rust-coloured daisy flowers, sometimes with dark-ringed centre, open with sun in warm months; long, narrow, green leaves, usually with silver underside	Adapts to any well-drained soil in open, sunny position; frost tender; easily layered
Goodenia, including *G. albiflora* Flinders Ranges in South Australia	H: 40 cm W: 40 cm Shrubby, erect	Large, fan-shaped, white flowers in summer; small, narrow leaves, with serrated edges	Hardy, though prefers well-drained soil in sunny position; suckering

Scaevola aemula.

GROUND COVERS

GROUND COVER AND PLACE OF ORIGIN	HEIGHT (H), WIDTH (W) AND FORM	SPECIAL CHARACTERISTICS	PARTICULAR REQUIREMENTS AND HARDINESS
Helichrysum petiolare South Africa	H: 1.2 m W: 1 m Loose, sprawling	Effectively covers ground with stems and velvety, grey leaves; 'Limelight' has lime-gold leaves	Hardy
Hypericum calycinum (rose of Sharon) South-eastern Europe, western Asia	H: 30 cm W: 1 m Creeping	Buttercuplike, yellow flowers, with prominent stamens, in summer; firm evergreen leaves	Quite hardy if protected from frosts and drought; needs watching as it can sucker profusely
Juniperus horizontalis (creeping juniper) Eastern North America	H: 1 m W: 3 m Shrubby	Jagged, blue-green foliage	Some protection from heat Best in cool to warm climate; layers itself
Kennedia prostrata (running postman) All Australian States	H: 1.5–2 m W: 1 m Flat mat	Bright scarlet pea flowers cover plant, spring to summer; hairy, three-lobed leaves	Warm inland climate
Lantana montevidensis (creeping lantana) South America	H: 50 cm W: 30 cm Spilling	Mauve-pink flowers most of year; good for rocky banks	Sun or semi-shade Spreads rapidly in sub-tropical climate by suckering stems
Myoporum parvifolium South Australia, Flinders Island in Tasmania, Victoria, Western Australia	H: 50 cm W: 1 m Prostrate, trailing	White star flowers for long period in spring and summer; small, mid-green leaves	Well-drained soil; sunny position
Pelargonium peltatum (ivy geranium) South Africa	H: 25 cm W: 2 m Loose, trailing unless supported	Clusters of white, pink, red or mauve flowers, summer to autumn; ivylike, succulent, green leaves	Light, well-drained soil; open, sunny position Hardy
Plectranthus ciliatus Africa	H: 45 cm W: 2 m Loose, spreading	Misty, upright spikes of white or mauve flowers in autumn; leaves with burgundy underside	Shade Easily layered
Pultenaea pedunculata New South Wales, South Australia, Tasmania, Victoria	H: 30 cm W: 1.5 m Loose, scrambling	Profuse, yellow pea flowers in spring and summer; narrow, dark green leaves; branches form mat	Light to medium, well-drained soil; open, sunny position Resistant to salt spray
Scaevola aemula (fairy fan flower) Australia	H: 50 cm W: 1 m Matting	Mauve-blue, fan-shaped flowers	Well-drained soil; full sun Layers itself
Stipa elegantissima Mainland Australia	H: 40 cm W: 30 cm Erect grass	Plumes of wispy, pink flowers, spring to summer; narrow, rough, silvery leaves	Light, well-drained soil; open, sunny position

LOW GROUND COVERS (HEIGHT TO 25 CENTIMETRES)

GROUND COVER AND PLACE OF ORIGIN	HEIGHT (H), WIDTH (W) AND FORM	SPECIAL CHARACTERISTICS	PARTICULAR REQUIREMENTS AND HARDINESS
Ajuga reptans (bugle flower) United Kingdom	H: 25 cm W: 1 m Matting	Purplish blue flowers, crowded on spikes, in spring and summer, above leafy, dark green rosettes	Adapts to most soils, if moist, and most positions; drought and frost tender; layers itself
Brachyscome multifida New South Wales, south-eastern Queensland, Victoria	H: 10 cm W: 40 cm Tufty	Small, daisylike, mauve flowers for long period over spring and summer; finely divided leaves	Well-drained soil; sunny position Drought and frost resistant
Campanula poscharskyana (Siberian bell flower) Europe	H: 25 cm W: 35 cm Matting	Pale blue bell flowers in spring; rosettes of round, pale green leaves	Spreads readily in moist soil and shady position; drought tender; layers itself
Cerastium tomentosum (snow-in-summer) Europe	H: 7.5 cm W: 30 cm Loose, scrambling	Dainty, white flowers, on slender stems, in summer; small, silver leaves	Sun-loving, though prefers mid-afternoon shade; drought tender; layers itself
Convolvulus mauritanicus North Africa	H: 3 cm W: 2 m Loose, scrambling	Open, china-blue bell flowers from late spring to autumn; small, grey-green leaves; can scramble over walls and appear taller	Light to medium, well-drained soils; open, sunny position
Heterocentron elegans (creeping lasiandra) South America	H: 4 cm W: 1 m Matting	Small, purple flowers in spring and summer; dainty, oblong leaves on reddish stems	Moist, rich, well-drained soil; protected, sunny position Layers itself
Mazus pumilio New South Wales, Queensland, South Australia, Tasmania, Victoria	H: 25 cm W: 50 cm Matting	Tubular, lilac flowers, on short stems, in summer; smooth, spreading stems, with leafy rosettes of bright green	Light to heavy soils, open, sunny position Drought tender; layers itself
Mentha requienii (Corsican mint) Mediterranean	H: 3 cm W: 30 cm Matting	Tiny, pale green leaves, sweetly pungent when crushed	Moist soil; protection from strong sun Layers itself
Pratia pedunculata New South Wales, Queensland, South Australia, Tasmania, Victoria	H: 3 cm W: 4 cm Matting	Tiny, white or blue star flowers in summer; dainty, fernlike leaves form over ground	Moist soil; open, sunny position Layers itself readily
Scleranthus biflorus Australia, New Zealand	H: 15 cm W: 75 cm Matting in tight, mossy cushions	Tiny, pale green flowers in spring	Ample moisture; full sun Layers itself

LOW GROUND COVERS			
GROUND COVER AND PLACE OF ORIGIN	HEIGHT (H), WIDTH (W) AND FORM	SPECIAL CHARACTERISTICS	PARTICULAR REQUIREMENTS AND HARDINESS
Soleirolia soleirolii (baby's tears, helxine) Italy	H: 1 cm W: 1 m Matting, mosslike	Tiny, green leaves form over paving and earth	Spreads quickly, by layering, in moist soil and shade
Thymus doerfleri (woolly thyme) Europe	H: 3 cm W: 45 cm Prostrate, matting	Lilac-pink flowers in summer; tiny, hairy, greenish grey leaves cover stems	Adapts to most soils, if well drained, and most positions; layers itself readily
Thymus serpyllum (Westmoreland thyme, wild thyme) Europe	H: 20 cm W: 25 cm Matting	White, pink or red flowers in summer; tiny, scented leaves; small, woody, creeping stems	Well-drained soil; open, sunny position Layers itself readily
Viola hederacea (native violet) Eastern Australia, Malaysia	H: 5 cm W: 15 cm Matting	Small, purple and white or white flowers most of year; rounded, green-leaves coat ground	Moist soil; full sun or part shade Layers itself

Ground covers on a large scale create a garden that is spectacular in itself yet takes the eye to the view beyond.

CLIMBING PLANTS

Some plants are really happier growing on walls and fences, rather than occupying garden beds. These are mainly plants that creep, climb or twine, but there are also some that just like to lean on things: shrublike plants with long, rather weak stems that are in need of support. As well, some shrubs lend themselves to being trained against a wall.

All of these climbers are important decorative garden ingredients and most of them have useful qualities (though some have pushy ways that need to be understood). In particular, they provide vertical interest in gardens, contributing flowers in season, leafiness and sometimes fine autumn colour. In small gardens and courtyards and narrow side pathways, they can decorate walls and fences, with an economy of ground space.

Climbers cover unsightly outhouses and walls and drape themselves over screens. Being quick growers mostly, they soon reach a useful height and provide decoration for some years before many a shrub or tree would have grown to that height. And, if a tree is actually part of the long-term master plan, a climber can be retired when the tree eventually arrives at the required height.

CREEPY CREEPERS

For all the creepers' good points, their name still sends some people into fits of horror, although, as you will see from the following descriptions, they are not always to blame for the troubles they cause.

- Many creepers are extremely vigorous, and on warm days after rain or a good watering you can almost see them growing, so they need close supervision. Those with ropelike stems, such as ivy, can eventually kill a tree, the tree's branches becoming strangled by the entwining stems. The weight of enthusiastic creepers can eventually topple a fence, and their twining stems often prise palings apart.
- Some creepers have young shoots that get themselves into small places, such as the air spaces in cast-iron decoration on verandahs, and the sheer strength of their growing and expanding stems eventually breaks the delicate lacework. We've all seen this with the irresistible wisteria, which should be kept well trimmed, with its framework tied to the cast iron, not growing through it.
- Some creepers establish a firm foothold wherever their stems touch ground. In this way the parent plant can have a family extending far from its roots. Members of the jasmine group, such as the recumbent, shrublike *Jasminum mesnyi*, do this. Worst of all is the much-loved spring-flowering *J. polyanthum*.
- Most floppy, shrubby climbers in need of support, such as *Jasminum polyanthum* and the bluebell creeper (*Sollya heterophylla*), wave their stems around for a while and, if support cannot be found, do a back flip, landing back on themselves. When a few thwarted stems do this, a hideous tangle results.

We are the ones who should be held responsible when creepers get out of hand because we have failed firstly to select a suitable one for the job in hand, and secondly to maintain and control the plant, with a proper regard for its individual habits and requirements. You can make climbers sociable by understanding their characters and needs.

OPPOSITE PAGE Wisteria, such as the white *Wisteria venusta*, is most people's favourite climber. Remember, though, that it is like a climbing tree.

Leaners

Leaners put out long, lax stems that need support to advance their position in life. In the wild, they achieve it by pressing themselves against tree trunks, but in the garden we usually prefer them to lean against walls and fences. A good example is the blue-flowered *Plumbago auriculata*. Climbing roses are leaning plants, too, although most of them use their thorns as barbs to hook into tree trunks, fences or walls.

In gardens leaning plants often need to be tied to screens, walls and fences every now and then, particularly if they are leaning outwards in search of light. Cutting away obstructing branches from surrounding plants gives them more light. Attach leaners with wall plugs that have eye screws or hooks and ties, or tie them to fence rails. Strengthen your plants by shortening the leafy shoots every now and then. A good overall clip after flowering time will encourage the next season's growth of flowers.

Self-clingers

Amazing self-clingers are self-sufficient when it comes to climbing. Virginia creeper (*Parthenocissus quinquefolia*) clings by discs on its tendrils. Boston ivy (*P. tricuspidata*) can cling to brick surfaces with its tendrils. The climbing hydrangea (*Hydrangea petiolaris*), ivy (*Hedera helix*) and climbing fig (*Ficus pumila*) have little hairy 'feet' – really aerial roots that come from their stems. Because of their larger aerial roots, tropical plants, such as the monstera, have the capacity to mount tree trunks, thus increasing their opportunities for space and light.

Self-clinging plants can get a firm foothold on all but the most slippery of surfaces. Watch them carefully and anticipate their progress or they will leave their footprints on paintwork when you remove them from forbidden areas.

Tendril climbers

Tendril climbers to begin with wave weak tendrils around in the air seeking nearby objects suitable for climbing on. Once successful, these tendrils speedily become tenacious, springlike coils. Passionfruit (*Passiflora*), grape vines (*Vitis*), *Pandorea pandorana* and *P. jasminoides* 'Princess Di' advance themselves in this way. Clematis uses the same principle, but has no

BELOW *Clematis montana* 'Rubens' is a light creeper that adorns any support with grace.

OPPOSITE PAGE Bougainvillea adds drama and a touch of the tropics to a conservatory.

tendrils so uses leaf stems instead – as does the spring jasmine (in addition to winding around and growing on practically everything).

Many climbers of this type, such as honeysuckles (*Lonicera*), banksia roses (*Rosa banksiae*), *Jasminum polyanthum* and *J. mesnyi*, have a mass of old, dead stems under their newer growth because they partly smother themselves with their fresh growth. Check for this from time to time and cut away the dead stems, taking care not to cut the main, living stems of the plant, and flatten the newer growth back against the wall or screen. Shorten waving new shoots straight after flowering, as well as pruning spent flowering stems, to keep your plant more compact.

Don't despair if your efforts to control these climbers are not completely successful: their business is vigour and coverage. Just keep an eye on what they're up to, and make sure that they don't go off limits.

Twiners

Twiners hurl their entire body into the business of winding around supports. Their stems wave about to find supports; once successful, around and around they twine, growing firmly into place. Then long new stems reach out for the next support. If none is found these exploratory stems flop back on top of the existing plant mass. Honeysuckles and the rather unfairly named beautiful Australian snake vine (*Hibbertia scandens*) are examples of this type.

Most twiners develop firm, ropy stems on their branches eventually. They can be used well on pergolas. As they twine around a post, cut back any waving side shoots to ensure dense growth and plenty of flowers. Once they have reached the top, fan out two or three long stems over the pergola. Frequent clipping back of the new, wandering shoots ensures a firm, permanent framework and makes discipline much easier – so don't weaken on the job.

Wisteria, that special twiner

The monarch of all climbing plants is *Wisteria sinensis*. Come October, or early November in cooler parts, it is indescribably lovely, with its festoons of blue-mauve pea flowers. Such is its beauty that even the most fervent creeper-haters are often moved to admire it in someone else's garden.

Wisteria is no usual creeper – it is a climbing tree with the capacity to form a large trunk and big, woody branches. It is capable of spreading its stems to a height of over 30 metres eventually. Take heed that you provide the room it needs for some degree of fulfilment, although you need not let it have its head completely.

If you give your wisteria a good pruning when it shoots after flowering and, through summer, cut its new, wavy stems right back to within two shoots of a more established stem, your climbing tree will be kept well in hand and do nothing but delight you.

Wall plants

Wall plants are not climbers in the strict sense. They are pliant, loose-stemmed shrubs that grow successfully in garden beds also. Wall plants are planted quite close to a fence or wall and their branches trained to display themselves in an informal espalier. Outward-growing shoots are shortened back and the best side branches are selected for display. The branches can be pinned to a masonry wall with plugs, large eye screws and ties.

Wall plants are far more easily controlled than most climbers, but they don't grow as fast. You can develop a tracery of wall plants flowering at various times of the year, or you can go for impact, planting several of the same type of shrub. Shrubs that lend themselves to this treatment are some of the grevilleas, callistemons such as *Callistemon viminalis* 'Hannah Ray', *Abelia* × *grandiflora*, *Garrya elliptica*, *Escallonia macrantha*, *Ceanothus* and sasanqua camellias. But there is no limit to the range of likely shrubs, so try something to suit your tastes.

Wall dwellers

The tiny inmates of cracks and crevices must have a mention because they add such sweetness to wall pictures. Don't pull them out in a drive for sterile tidiness; just cut them back if they get a bit unruly.

Among the dwellers are baby's tears (*Erigeron karvinskianus*), alyssum, lobelia and small *Campanula* species. Valerian, or kiss-me-quick (*Centranthus*), looks pretty through spring and summer but needs a firm hand now and then. Watch for its new seedlings and pull them out as you see them. You can also curb its spirit by constantly clipping it to the stem base. You might find a fern or two appearing in a wall. Let them be, but stop any ascendancy to power.

Do remember that plants growing close to walls often miss out on rain and that the soil there may be underworked. Since the walls are important display areas in gardens, treat climbers, wall plants and wall dwellers well by regularly watering and feeding them, and they will repay you a thousandfold.

Blue-mauve Chinese wisteria (*Wisteria sinensis*) relentlessly clambers along and through a fence.

ROBUST CLIMBERS

CLIMBER AND PLACE OF ORIGIN	LEAVES	HEIGHT AND SPECIAL CHARACTERISTICS	PARTICULAR REQUIREMENTS AND HARDINESS
Akebia quinata (five-leafed akebia, chocolate vine) China, Japan, Korea	Evergreen; consist of five-stalked, elliptical leaflets	3–5 m Dainty sprays of dusky pink, mauve and grey flowers in spring	Hardy under all conditions
Bougainvillea South America	Deciduous; small, green, on woody stems clad in barbed prickles	3–6 m Large, papery-looking bracts form the 'flowers', with small, black-red, creamy-mouthed true flowers at base of bracts, summer to autumn	Rich, well-drained soil; protected, sunny position Frost tender
Campsis grandiflora (Chinese trumpet creeper) China, Japan	Deciduous; large, fernlike, consisting of leaflets; on heavy, woody growth	5 m Sprays of orange-red trumpet flowers in summer and early autumn	Light to medium, well-drained soil Drought tender
Ficus pumila (climbing fig) China, Japan	Evergreen; small, oval to round, on fine, clinging stems, and becoming rather gross as plant matures	4 m Insignificant flowers	Hardy, though drought tender; likes light to medium soils in sun or semi-shade
Jasminum azoricum (summer jasmine) Madeira	Evergreen; dark, fernlike	4 m White star flowers, with lemony fragrance, for long period over summer and autumn	Hardy, though prefers moist, rich, well-drained soil; drought and frost tender
Jasminum mesnyi (primrose jasmine) China	Evergreen; elliptical, on loose, shrubby, scrambling stems	4 m Semi-double, citrus-yellow flowers, on arching green stems, in late winter	Hardy; adapts to most soils and positions
Lonicera japonica var. *repens* (Japanese honeysuckle) China, Japan	Evergreen; on scrambling, twisting stems	6 m Clustered heads of sweetly perfumed, creamy white and pink tubular flowers in summer	Hardy in sunny position
Mandevilla laxa (Chilean jasmine) Argentina, Chile	Deciduous, though evergreen in warm climates; heart shaped, green, on vigorously twining stems	3 m Clusters of fragrant, pure white trumpet flowers in summer	Rich, well-drained soil; warm, protected position
Pandorea jasminoides (bower of beauty) New South Wales, Queensland	Evergreen; large, consisting of dark, glossy leaflets	4–5 m Large, white or pink, red-throated flowers, usually in small clusters, in autumn	Best in sheltered, warm position

ROBUST CLIMBERS			
CLIMBER AND PLACE OF ORIGIN	**LEAVES**	**HEIGHT AND SPECIAL CHARACTERISTICS**	**PARTICULAR REQUIREMENTS AND HARDINESS**
Pandorea pandorana (wonga vine) New South Wales, Queensland, Tasmania, Victoria	Evergreen; divided, glossy	6 m Copious tubular, cream or brown flowers, smaller than those of *P. jasminoides*, with maroon or brown blotches, in spring	Tolerates cold, particularly if in rich soil; tolerates shade
Parthenocissus quinquefolia (Virginia creeper) Eastern United States of America	Deciduous; handlike, on tendrils that self-cling by means of tiny discs	9 m Brilliant blue-black berries in autumn; red autumn leaves	Adapts to most soils; drought tender
Parthenocissus tricuspidata 'Lowii' (Boston ivy, Japanese ivy, small-leaf Virginia creeper) China, Japan	Deciduous; small, eventually growing larger, variably shaped, with some divided, on self-clinging tendrils	15 m Red autumn leaves	Adapts to most soils; drought tender
Passiflora caerulea (blue passionflower) Brazil	Evergreen; handlike	3 m Slightly fragrant, whitish blue flowers, with blue, white and magenta centres, summer to autumn; showy, orange ornamental fruits	Light, rich, well-drained soil
Passiflora manicata (scarlet passionflower) Columbia, Ecuador, Peru	Evergreen; three pointed, almost divided	3 m Bright scarlet flowers, with central blue fringe, summer to autumn	Warm, frost-free climate; sunny, protected position
Solandra grandiflora (chalice vine) West Indies	Evergreen; large, elliptical, on thick stems	10 m Fragrant, cream flowers, like large goblets, winter to spring	Sub-tropical coastal climate Prefers dryness in early summer
Solandra maxima (cup of gold) Mexico	Evergreen; on long, arching branches	3 m Large, yellow trumpet flowers, with irregular, purple stripes on outside and fruit salad perfume, in summer	Warm-temperate and sub-tropical climates; rich, well-drained soil; full sun
Solanum jasminoides (potato vine) Brazil	Evergreen; small, divided, on twining stems	5 m White flowers, like those of potato, for most of year	Adapts to most soils
Tecoma × smithii Peru	Evergreen; ashlike, on stiff-stemmed, shrubby plant	5 m Clusters of bright yellow bell flowers, with orange tubes, spring to autumn	Tolerates most soils; best in sunny, protected position; frost tender

ROBUST CLIMBERS			
CLIMBER AND PLACE OF ORIGIN	LEAVES	HEIGHT AND SPECIAL CHARACTERISTICS	PARTICULAR REQUIREMENTS AND HARDINESS
Tecomaria capensis (Cape honeysuckle) South Africa	Evergreen; ashlike, on long, stiff, leaning stems	5 m Narrow, tubular, burnt-orange flowers, particularly late summer to autumn	Tolerates most soils in sun or shade; frost tender
Thunbergia grandiflora (blue trumpet vine) Northern India	Evergreen; large, heart shaped, on slender, weak stems	3 m Clusters of large, pale blue flowers, 7.5 cm wide, in early spring	Well-drained soil; sunny, protected position Frost tender
Vitis coignetiae (crimson glory vine) Northern Japan	Deciduous; grapevinelike	5 m Insignificant flowers; ruby-red autumn leaves	Adapts to most soils in part or full sun
Wisteria floribunda 'Macrobotrys' (long Japanese wisteria) Japan, northern China	Deciduous; ashlike, consist of leaflets, on strong, woody stems	10 m Long, fragrant, purple pea flowers in early spring; white and pink varieties; buttery yellow autumn leaves; gnarled trunk	Adapts to most soils; prefers sunny, protected position
Wisteria sinensis (Chinese wisteria) China	Deciduous; similar to *W.f.* 'Macrobotrys' but fewer leaves	10–30 m Clusters of fragrant, blue-mauve flowers on bare branches in spring; buttery yellow autumn leaves; white double form, 'Alba'	Hardy; vigorous grower under all conditions once established

The blue trumpet vine (*Thunbergia grandiflora*) makes an attractive choice for a warm or tropical garden.

Clematis aristata.

LIGHT CLIMBERS

CLIMBER AND PLACE OF ORIGIN	LEAVES	HEIGHT AND SPECIAL CHARACTERISTICS	PARTICULAR REQUIREMENTS AND HARDINESS
Allemanda cathartica (golden allemanda) Northern South America	Evergreen; long, leathery	3 m Large, open, bright yellow trumpet flowers in summer	Sub-tropical and tropical climates
Ampelopsis brevipedunculata (porcelain grape) Eastern Asia	Deciduous; large, heart shaped	3 m Insignificant, greenish flowers in summer; blue to turquoise berries	Hardy, but best in cool climate
Billardiera scandens (common appleberry) New South Wales, Queensland, South Australia, Tasmania, Victoria	Evergreen; waxy edged	4 m Pale yellow bell flowers in spring; bronze berries	Light to medium soil; open, sunny position
Clematis aristata (Australian clematis, old man's beard) All Australian States except Western Australia	Evergreen; consist of three leaflets, on twining stems	2 m Clusters of dainty, single, creamy white flowers in spring; white, fluffy seed pods	Filtered sun or part shade
Clematis armandii China	Evergreen; tapering, glossy	5 m Clusters of simple, white flowers, becoming pink tinged, in spring	Moist, rich soil; open, sunny position, but with roots kept shaded
Clematis × *jackmanii*	Deciduous	3 m Large flowers in summer; hybrids in many colours	As for *C. armandii*
Clematis napaulensis Nepal	Summer deciduous; divided	4 m Dainty, green bell flowers, among leaves, in winter	Sunny position, but with cool, moist root run
Cobaea scandens (cup-and-saucer plant) Central America, South America	Evergreen; alternating on stem, mid-green	7.5 m Cup-and-saucer, lime-green or green-turning-purple flowers, spring to summer; fast climber	Warm position
Gelsemium sempervirens (Carolina jasmine) Southern United States of America	Evergreen; small, shiny, on lightly twining stems	4 m Masses of small, yellow bell flowers, late winter to early spring	Hardy, though prefers well-drained soil in sun or shade
Hardenbergia violacea (purple coral pea) All Australian States except Western Australia	Evergreen; narrow, oval, dark green	3 m Profuse, small, purple pea flowers in spring; 'Rosea' has pale pink flowers, 'Alba' white	Endures hot, dry conditions

LIGHT CLIMBERS			
CLIMBER AND PLACE OF ORIGIN	LEAVES	HEIGHT AND SPECIAL CHARACTERISTICS	PARTICULAR REQUIREMENTS AND HARDINESS
Hibbertia scandens (snake vine) New South Wales, Queensland	Evergreen; shiny deep green, on strongly twining, brown stems	2 m Large, single yellow flowers, mainly spring to summer, but almost all year with good sun	Loose-grained, well-drained soil; warm position
Hoya carnosa (common waxplant) Southern China	Evergreen; waxlike	2 m Waxy, white star flowers, with pink centres, summer to autumn	Best in gravelly, well-drained soil in sheltered position; frost tender
Hydrangea petiolaris (climbing hydrangea) Asia	Deciduous; green	2 m Flat clusters of tiny, white florets in summer	Moist, rich, well-drained soil Drought and frost tender
Lapageria rosea (Chilean bell flower) Argentina, Chile	Evergreen; leathery, on slender, twining stems	1.5 m Long, firm, waxen, soft cerise bell flowers, summer to autumn; also white form	Cool climate; rich, well-drained soil
Mandevilla splendens Tropical America	Evergreen; heart shaped, on twining, woody stems	3 m Clusters of rose-pink trumpet flowers, summer to autumn	Moist, rich, well-drained soil; warm position in part shade Drought and frost tender
Manettia bicolor (cigar vine) Brazil	Evergreen; simple, dainty, on twining stems	1.5–2 m Small, tubular, red flowers, with yellow tips, most of year	Adapts to most soils given well-drained soil and warm, sheltered position; frost and drought tender
Petrea volubilis (purple wreath) Central America, Mexico, West Indies	Evergreen; simple, on rather shrubby plant	4 m Sprays of dainty violet flowers, with showy, blue-mauve, starlike outer petals, in summer	Tropical climate or warm position Drought and frost tender
Pyrostegia venusta (orange trumpet creeper) Brazil	Evergreen; divided	2–3 m Tubular, scarlet-orange flowers cover plant most of year	Warm climate Drought and frost tender
Senecio macroglossus (Cape ivy) Africa	Evergreen; small, triangular, deep green, on succulent stems	3 m Daisylike, yellow flowers in winter	Light to medium, well-drained soil Frost tender
Sollya heterophylla (bluebell creeper) Western Australia	Evergreen; small	3 m Tiny clusters of rich blue flowers in summer	Hardy in sun and light shade; can become a weed if uncontrolled
Stephanotis floribunda (Madagascar jasmine) Madagascar	Evergreen; long, shining green	3 m Clusters of fragrant, white star flowers, spring to summer	Prefers well-drained soil, to which compost added, and warm, sheltered position; drought and frost tender
Trachelospermum jasminoides (Chinese star jasmine) Southern China	Evergreen; shapely, shiny	7 m Fragrant, white star flowers in summer	Suits most soils, in sunny or shady position; drought tender

GRASSES, BAMBOOS AND SIMILAR PLANTS

Birds feel safe to drink here, protected by clumps of fountain grass (*Pennisetum alopecuroides*) and Australian shrubs.

Some people won't even pause to read this section, for grasses and bamboos can seem deadly dull or nuisances. (Even the domestic lawn has this same quality at times.) Nevertheless, grassy plants have some merit, particularly in modern gardens concerned with elegance and simplicity rather than variety and nostalgia.

Much of the importance of grasses and bamboos in garden design stems from their gently vertical lines and the wonderful sense of movement that big, grassy plantings give to a garden. The foliage of grasses and bamboos wafts about or rustles, depending on the leaf structure and the wind. Grasses and bamboos give a sense that there is water about, even if there isn't; a feeling of closeness to nature.

GRASSES

Grasses are quite important as part of a native garden, completing a bushland picture, and in sparse, stylised gardens, with pebbles or rocks and perhaps a modern sculpture. Small grasses, such as the blue-grey, tufty *Festuca glauca*, look great snuggled into a sunken tree stump or close by a sleeper or stone step. These grasses can also just be planted in patches here and there among low-growing plants or at the edge of a water dish or small pond.

The green *Restio tetraphyllus* has a lustrous glow about it. It fits best by a pond, where it combines happily with the green of waterlily (*Nymphaea*) pads. *Pennisetum alopecuroides* is a much livelier grass than either it or *Festuca glauca*: its fine, fawn and silvery green foliage moves in the wind, and its small pampas-like seed heads add extra interest through summer and autumn. Such a grass can be used well near water or to suggest water and a little fantasy. It can also be used here and there along the edge of a border or in the curves of a sweeping garden – such a use is described as punctuating.

Sword grass (*Gahnia radula*) offers a distinctive, grassy shape in a native garden or at the foot of a large outcrop of rocks. With its rushy, plumed flowers and seed heads it is well over a metre in height – a strong presence but never overpowering.

Native grasses and a mulch of twigs create a natural-looking environment.

BAMBOO: ALMOST A TREE

From time to time the sight of tall bamboos, moving, rustling and adorned in great style with green or black, shiny stems, is enough for you to throw to the winds all the warnings people have given you. But, although these giant grasses may look like slender-trunked, leafy trees, they are not. They are every bit a huge grass that will spread and invade, with hordes of shoots. Planted as screening plants, they have gummed up many a fence line, causing rifts between neighbours.

If you want tall bamboos, plant them in metal containers in the soil, and watch for the first shooting arm that appears outside limits. Alternatively, plant them in strong containers and use them decoratively in courtyards and on terraces. Large-growing bamboos crave water, and the condition of many fine plants deteriorates with the rigours of a pot, so water them well and frequently.

There are some interesting dwarf types of bamboo, which you may come across in aquatic or more general nurseries. Some of the dwarf bamboos are variegated green and white, others green and gold. All need a good water supply to avoid a withered look, and all should be planted in metal containers and sunk in the ground or watched carefully in gardens.

PLANTS SIMILAR TO BAMBOO

Some 'bamboos' qualify in common name only and are somewhat different from true bamboos in their growing habits. Nevertheless, treated as bamboos rather than the shrubs they are, their value in garden composition can be appreciated.

Sacred or heavenly bamboo (*Nandina domestica*) is a versatile native of Japan and China. It reaches a height of 1–2 metres and grows in all but the most extreme heat and shade, though its leaf colour will vary according to its growing conditions. Its stems are jointed and bamboo-like, but its leaves usually present as a flimsy umbrella head of dainty leaves on fine radial stems. The heads shoot here and there from the stems and at the top. Nandina has clusters of fine white flowers that may or may not become scarlet berries.

In the garden nandina has a slightly suckering habit; unwanted growths can be divided off with a spade and rooted pieces used elsewhere. It is good for difficult spots and as a flimsy evergreen that makes elegant, leafy silhouettes if you run out of ideas. As a hardy pot subject it is also exemplary, and will produce autumn-coloured leaves if its roots become constricted. Just keep it watered and enjoy it.

The dwarf form, *Nandina domestica* 'Nana', grows to only half a metre in height. It has leaves that curl at the edges and are a permanent, pale green and russet.

Chinese indigo (*Indigofera decora*) is a shrub that reaches no more than half a metre in height and has dainty leaves, quite like *Nandina domestica*, only smaller and a pale green. Unlike nandina it is deciduous, but, as if to make up for its bare branches, it produces sprays of pale pink, pea flowers for many months during summer. Chinese indigo suckers but is easily deterred. A native of China and Japan, it will thrive in harsh sun or semi-shade and on humid courtyards. It's good to have a ready source of pieces for other spots in the garden and for friends.

PALMS, CYCADS AND FERNS

Of all green plants, palms, cycads and ferns provide the most lush, intricate and delicate green foliage. They are known to have been in existence for millions of years. They can be used together quite comfortably – somehow they seem to have an affinity – and certainly some of them live in the same natural environment, whether tropical rainforest, arid regions or warm temperate areas.

It is satisfying to add an extra dimension to suitable spots in a native garden by including native palms, cycads and ferns. All three plant types can contribute to theme plantings: in a south-eastern or north-eastern aspect as a middle and lower storey planting near a large spreading tree, such as an Indian bean tree (*Catalpa bignonioides*) or walnut tree (*Juglans nigra*); as an interlude; as a band of palms or ferns or both, running across the width of the back garden, through which you walk on the way to a swimming pool or tennis court; or as an appealing backdrop to a formal or informal pool. Palms can be used with brightly coloured plants, such as tecomas, *Solanum rantonnetii*, hibiscus and ginger lilies (*Hedychium densiflorum*) for a tropical effect. Ferns can be planted in a shady but well-watered area along the side of a house, though tree ferns need at least 3 metres' width to spread their fronds.

Ferns and palms were widely planted during the Victorian era, so the Australian tree fern *Dicksonia antarctica* is an appropriate planting in a nostalgic garden.

SPECIAL NEEDS

Most palms and cycads favour well-drained soil rich in humus, leaf mould, well-rotted cow manure and compost. Some handle exposure to the sun and wind; others need shelter. They like a ready supply of water but must not become over-wet. It's best to let the soil dry out a little before watering again. Much of the water should be received from overhead.

Shelter and moisture are of the utmost importance to ferns. If needed, water can be supplied by a simple overhead spray system that contributes to the humidity of the garden area or fernery. Ferns like a moist, rich soil, full of compost or leaf mould, and an occasional dose of weak liquid manure; they do not require good drainage. They are content with filtered sunlight.

PALMS

It was the gardeners of the Victorian era who first recognised the grace and decorative potential of palms and our appreciation has been conditioned by theirs. Palms certainly have an urbanity and sophistication about them that is foreign to ferns.

There is such a variety of palms that you should have no trouble finding ones that appeal to you. Of course, the sorts of palm that are for you depend on your climatic conditions and soil as well as on their good looks. They are expensive to buy, so put time into selecting them. You also need some idea of the final height and size of species that you fancy.

Above all you need to have a vision of the effect you wish to create. You may want to plant your palms near a swimming pool or sun deck, or to use them in combination with ferns to create a rainforest atmosphere in a sheltered corner of the garden or in a high-ceilinged conservatory area. Be careful not to plant palms with thorny stems near swimming pools or other places where children could be endangered. The palms listed are ones suitable for a range of Australian conditions.

CYCADS

Although both palms and cycads have a trunk or trunks topped with an array of feathery leaves, cycads are not lesser-known palms but a distinct and unrelated group of plants. There are fourteen species in Australia.

Cycad leaves, which may be broad or narrow, are not soft like most palm fronds. They are usually stiff, with pointed ends, and some have thorny edges and can be tricky to handle. Some trunks are hidden underground, others are branched or clustered. Cycads have no flowers; instead they bear cones – male cones on one plant, female on the other. Some cones are quite beautiful.

Collectively, cycads are not as choosy as palms, and in warm temperate zones, without severe frosts or snow, most should grow successfully. The sago palm (*Cycas revoluta*), the Australian nut palm (*C. media*) and the Byfield fern (*Bowenia serrulata*) are three interesting cycads to plant. Remember their sharp-edged nature when you are handling them and choosing their site.

The sago palm is the most popular cycad. It has stiff, palmlike fronds of glossy green and grows to a height of 2–3.5 metres, preferring poor soils in protected spots. It is drought and frost resistant and very hardy.

Palms planted among shrubs create the mood of a tropical garden.

Shade-loving ferns and ground covers combine with well-set rocks to make a restful spot under sheltering trees.

The Australian nut palm has lovely long, leafy fronds of dark green, although the young ones have a rusty-coloured, hairy look. The plant grows slowly to a height of 3–5 metres. It prefers protected sunny spots and a light to medium, well-drained soil.

The lovely Byfield fern is often mistaken for a true fern. Its long-lasting fronds have been traditionally used in flower arrangements. A native of the central Queensland coastal region, it is suitable for warm, frost-free gardens as an understorey plant. It grows to about 1 metre and has a subterranean base, up to ten handsome, branched fronds and, in time, globular cones.

FERNS

Unlike palms and cycads, ferns need the overhead shelter of neighbouring trees for protection from hot winds and the sun's rays. They in their individual ways are evocative of the cool, shady, damp places in which they naturally occur. This is why they look so strange when arranged in a straight line.

If you have room and a sheltered spot, a ferny place can add a restful atmosphere to your garden. Australia's giant tree ferns can set the stage. Try to have at least three tree ferns in a group. *Dicksonia antarctica* is quite hardy if its trunk is dug well into the ground. It doesn't require the water one might suppose in order to flourish, once it is established. If you are concerned about dryness, try *Cyathea australis*, the rough tree fern. By nature it grows more on hills and in forests than in damp, ferny gullies.

Under these tall ferns, smaller ferns can mingle. The holly fern (*Cyrtomium falcatum*) has leathery leaves, and is extremely hardy, providing a good contrast to lacy ferns. The bird's nest fern (*Asplenium nidus*) is not too hard to grow in temperate districts, and a mixture of young and mature plants is appealing. Over rocks and ground surfaces the hare's foot fern (*Davallia pyxidata*) may get a foothold, carpeting the ground with its adventurous, furry feet. In damp, sheltered outdoor spots, the maidenhair fern (*Adiantum aethiopicum*) may feel at home and reward you with spray after spray of its dainty leaves.

PALMS

PALM AND PLACE OF ORIGIN	HEIGHT (H) AND WIDTH (W)	CHARACTERISTICS	PARTICULAR REQUIREMENTS AND HARDINESS
Archontophoenix alexandrae (Alexandra palm) Queensland	H: 15–30 m W: 5 m	Long, graceful fronds on smooth, upright trunk; cream to shell-pink flowers in autumn; round, red fruit in winter	Plentiful moisture or a moist, warm, protected position Will succeed in temperate as well as tropical climate if requirements met; frost tender
Butia capitata (jelly palm) Argentina, Brazil, Uruguay	H: 2–6 m W: 3 m	Densely packed, curving, blue-green leaves; edible, orange-yellow fruit	Hardy, though prefers moist, rich soil; grows in tropical and temperate climates in full sun or shade; slightly frost tender
Caryota mitis (clustering fishtail palm) India, Indonesia, Philippines	H: 5 m W: 3 m	Numerous clumped stems; each curving leaf has fishtail of wedge-shaped leaflets at end; pale cream flowers; orange to red fruits; good for outdoor pots while young	Protected, partly shaded position Grows successfully in temperate as well as tropical climates if requirements met; drought and frost tender
Chamaedorea elegans (parlour palm) Guatemala, Mexico	H: 3 m W: 1 m	Short-fronded, shortish leaves; yellow flowers; black fruit; good for indoor or outdoor pots	Hardy in tropical and temperate climates in sheltered position, though dislikes direct sunlight
Chamaerops humilis (dwarf fan palm) Mediterranean fringes of Southern Europe, North Africa	H: 5 m W: 3 m	Clustering, with one to several trunks; fan-shaped, rich green leaves; yellow flowers; brown fruit; beware of spines at base of leaf stems; good for pots, particularly outdoors	Hardy in most climates; tolerates shade, sun, coastal conditions, altitudes to 1000 metres and light snow
Howea forsteriana (kentia palm) Lord Howe Island	H: 3–20 m W: 5 m	Slender, ringed trunk; elegant form and large, arching leaves, with long leaflets; good for outdoor pots or indoor pots, with spells in warm, sheltered position outside	Hardy, though does best in temperate or sub-tropical climate in sheltered position; drought and frost tender
Livistona australis (Australian fan palm or cabbage tree palm) New South Wales, Queensland, Victoria	H: 7–20 m W: 2 m	Dense head of fan-shaped leaves, on a ringed, dark trunk; sprays of yellow flowers in early spring; reddish brown or black fruit	Prefers moist, warm coastal climate
Rhapis excelsa (lady palm) Southern China	H: 1.5 m W: 75 cm	Densely clumping, with slender trunks; segmented, fan-shaped leaves down the trunk; creamy flowers in short spikes; good in indoor or outdoor pots	Moist, rich soil; warm, shady position Grows in temperate or tropical climate; frost tender
Washingtonia filifera (cotton palm) Mexico, south-western United States of America	H: 10–20 m W: 3 m	Huge, fan-shaped leaves, fringed with cottonlike threads; creamy flowers; waxy, white fruit; spiny thorns on leaf stems near trunk; good in outdoor pots if well watered	Hardy; handles climatic extremes outstandingly, though prefers well-drained soil and open, sunny position

POND PLANTS

There is something intriguing and other worldly about a pond, its inhabitants and its surroundings. And the waterlily in its floating glory is surely a favourite of most people.

Nymphaea 'St Louis Gold' invites us to enter the realm of water gardens.

WATERLILIES

Waterlilies (*Nymphaea*) can be abundantly generous in sunny situations, yet in other places quite grudging, meting out a few buds during their flowering season, which peaks in midsummer. Waxlike but delicate flowers of white, yellow, pink or red are the ones most often seen. With the cooler months the leaves of waterlilies rot, and the plants disappear to the pond's depths for winter.

The warmer the water, the happier waterlilies are, and during summer they should be in sun for about three-quarters of the day. To do well they need to be in water at least 40 centimetres deep. Like most water plants, waterlilies are heavy feeders, and within their pond they like to be in rich soil. A dressing of decayed cow manure in some rich soil in spring encourages flowering in the following season. It should be dampened then squeezed to a firm, not wet, consistency and put into the lily container or by the roots in the pond. Some people add a layer of washed sand to prevent the water discolouring, others prefer their ponds a little murky!

If your pond is quite sunny, you may like to try some of the sub-tropical species, which grow on stems above their leaves. They come in vibrant blues, purples, reds, pinks, yellows and creams. Some people in temperate regions nurse their sub-tropical waterlilies through the winter months by keeping them in tubs or fibreglass pond shells in igloos or hothouses from March to November. Night-flowering tropical waterlilies are an interesting group. Usually their flowers open from 7 p.m. to 10 a.m. They are suited to sub-tropical as well as tropical parts. All the tropical and sub-tropical waterlilies listed in the table are fragrant to varying degrees.

Even if you don't have a pond, you can still keep waterlilies. Use a sound wooden half-barrel or a very large ceramic container and choose a perfect spot where they can enjoy the sun while you enjoy them.

OTHER DECORATIVE WATER PLANTS

Water poppies (*Hydrocleys nymphoides*) are pretty, lemon-cupped flowers, with dark stamens, on stems about 6 centimetres long. Their leaves are quite small ovals of glossy green, which rest on the pond's surface all the year.

Water clover (*Marsilea quadrifolia*) have dainty, four-leafed-clover leaves in brown and green tonings, which float on the surface, held by threadlike stems. In winter they retire, to reappear on the surface when spring comes.

Pale green water lettuces (*Pistia stratiotes*) – and sometimes their families of baby lettuces – sit happily on the water through the summer months. Unfortunately they are annuals and disintegrate during winter, so you'll probably need to replenish your supplies in the following spring.

The little floating fern *Azolla caroliniana* is a delight and a curse. It forms lichen-green patches over the water and provides a surface cover for the fish beneath, but multiplies rapidly and can cover an entire pond in no time. If you include it, you'll need to remove a lot of its offspring quite often. If reflections on the water are important to you, this plant should be avoided.

From late December through to March, smooth spikes of mid-blue flowers on tall stems appear on the glossy, evergreen, heart-shaped leaves of peacock hyacinths (*Pontederia cordata*). They should have 10–15 centimetres of water over the crown. When they become too broad they should be divided.

Many irises appreciate continually moist soils, and some thrive at the margins of ponds year after year. The Louisiana hybrids are a beautiful group of irises happy to dwell in water. *Iris kaempferi* will stand in water through the spring and summer, but its roots may rot if it's not kept dry during the winter. Its beautiful wide, flattish flowers may be white, cream, yellow, blue, mauve, purple or rose. *I. laevigata* is comfortable in shallow water or boggy soil but can tolerate drought. It has rich blue flowers with golden markings; its leaves do not have the distinctive midrib of *I. kaempferi*. *I. pseudacorus* grows in boggy ground or shallow water. Its flowers, shaped like *fleurs-de-lys*, are in a range of rich and soft yellows.

Arum lilies (*Zantedeschia aethiopica*) seem to grow more happily in about 14 centimetres of water than they do on land. They die down during summer and send up fresh new leaves in late winter.

WATERLILIES FOR YOUR POND

TEMPERATE CLIMATE	TROPICAL OR SUB-TROPICAL CLIMATE: DAY FLOWERING
***Nymphaea* 'Attraction'** Has semi-double, garnet-red to pink flowers, with white highlights and upright stamens; dark green leaves.	***Nymphaea* 'Afterglow'** Has variable peachy yellow, orange and pink flowers; green leaves, with hint of pink.
***Nymphaea* 'Gladstoniana'** Has semi-double, pure white star flowers, full of golden stamens; mid-green leaves.	***Nymphaea* 'Director George T. Moore'** Has rich purple flowers, with golden centre; leaves flecked with purple. Free flowering.
***Nymphaea marliacea* 'Carnea'** Has semi-double, soft pink star flowers, with golden stamens; dark green leaves.	***Nymphaea* 'Evelyn Randig'** Has magnificent, deep pink to magenta flowers; dark green leaves, mottled with pink.
***Nymphaea marliacea* 'Chromatella'** Has semi-double, yellow cup flowers, with deep gold stamens; olive-green leaves, mottled maroon and bronze.	***Nymphaea gigantea*** Has large white or powder blue flowers, with masses of incurved, golden stamens; green leaves, with purplish underside. Native to tropical Australia and requires tropical conditions.
***Nymphaea pygmaea* 'Helvola'** One of the smallest of cultivars; has semi-double, dainty, yellow star flowers; olive-green leaves, with purplish brown mottling.	***Nymphaea* 'Panama Pacific'** Has fragrant, deep blue flowers that become reddish purple with maturity; mid-green leaves.
SUB-TROPICAL CLIMATE, WARM POSITION OR HOTHOUSE	***Nymphaea* 'Yellow Dazzler'** Has large, plentiful, darkish yellow flowers; medium-sized, mahogany leaves.
***Nymphaea* 'A. Seibert'** Has deep rose-pink star flowers; green leaves.	TROPICAL AND SUB-TROPICAL CLIMATES NIGHT FLOWERING
***Nymphaea* 'Mrs George H. Pring'** Has pure white star flowers, with yellow stamens; large, mid-green leaves, with splashes of reddish brown and purplish underside.	***Nymphaea* 'Maroon Beauty'** Has burgundy flowers; coppery red leaves.
Nymphaea stellata Has pale blue flowers; leaves with purplish underside.	***Nymphaea* 'Red Flare'** Has flame-red flowers; mahogany leaves.
***Nymphaea* 'St Louis Gold'** Has large, yellow star flowers, with deep gold stamens; green leaves, spotted brown when young.	***Nymphaea* 'Trudy Slocum'** Has large, well-formed, white flowers on tall stems; green leaves.

Irises and waterlilies are the essence of water gardens.

Beside a pool, the bluish green foliage of a prostrate conifer contrasts with the yellow and green of a variegated grass.

MARGINAL PLANTS

While the irises and arum lilies discussed above can grow at the water's edge, they are happier in water up to about 25 centimetres deep, with the exception of *Iris kaempferi*. The following attractive bog plants can grace the water's edge but won't want to go right in.

Astilbes are long-flowering summer perennials with feathery heads of white, pale pink, mauve or crimson and attractive, peonylike leaves. Some are short and some are medium to tall growers. *Bulbinella hookeri*, with its yellow, starry flowers, is an Australian bog flower. Fairy fishing rods (*Dierama pulcherrimum*) have a sensational flowering season, during which they put forth chains of pale pink bells on elegant, slender stems. *Geum rivale* is suitable for the water's edge. The daylily (*Hemerocallis*) is a wonderful poolside plant, with its repeated flowerings. It comes in many lovely forms and colours. *Hosta* provides handsomely veined leaves and tall, dainty flower stems. Impatiens is quite comfortable in bog conditions, though its growth is more stunted there than in well-drained areas. *Physostegia virginiana*, with mauve, pink or white flowers in late summer, is a striking marginal plant. The lily *Schizostylis coccinea*, looking like a small gladiolus in red, pink or white, makes a special poolside contribution even as late as autumn.

SUBMERGED PLANTS

Submerged plants are critical to the health of the pond, though they are usually inconspicuous. They provide shelter for fish, and food to a lesser extent. Also they return oxygen to the water through the process of photosynthesis. It is important to have a number of oxygenating plants when establishing a garden pond. A pond should have a lot of submerged plants, so don't haul them out as an act of servicing the pond. If you are sure the pool is congested, just snip off a few pieces every now and then.

Crassula recurva is a creeping plant that grows submerged or at the pond's edge. *Egeria densa* has seaweedlike, ropy stems, covered in leaflets, and small, white, three-petalled, nectar-filled flowers are borne above water. *Elodea* species are excellent oxygenators, forming dense masses that release oxygen bubbles throughout the day. The water milfoil (*Myriophyllum*) is an attractive, lacy-leafed plant that provides a haven for fish eggs. Eel grass (*Vallisneria spiralis*), with its ribbonlike leaves, is easy to grow.

4/ MANAGING A GARDEN

The principle is always the same: you cannot expect your soil and your plants to go on giving you of their best if you are not prepared to give something back in return . . . This is as true of gardens as of human relationships.

VITA SACKVILLE-WEST

The pleasure of walking in your garden, sitting there with a quiet drink or enjoying it with your friends is not won all that easily. It's not so good being in gardens overtaken by weeds, with plants affected by fungal diseases and marred or devoured by marauding garden pests – snails, caterpillars, aphids and other nuisances. The neglect can carry through to dejected-looking trees and shrubs whose branches have become tangled or been broken off in a storm and left hanging like a half-mast cry for help. And certainly you won't be able to relax in a garden where the plants are drooping from thirst or stunted from lack of food.

A garden, like a household, has to be well run. Some aspects of gardening, such as knowing what is beautiful or the logical positioning of a path, can come to people fairly naturally. But some specialist knowledge is required to identify garden diseases, pests and weeds and to deal with them effectively. Even the basics about soil and its contents and how to supply plants with sufficient nourishment need to be learnt.

Bear in mind that much of the responsibility for how things are done lies with garden owners. By being in touch with what's going on in your garden, you can do a power of preventive work. Get into the habit of wandering about your garden. You'll catch the first leaf curled over by a leaf roller and the first muddled nest made by a webbing caterpillar. By stamping out a few big snails as you admire the garden after a shower, you'll prevent the birth of many new ones.

The pleasures of a garden cannot be enjoyed unless the plants are well provided for.

DOWN TO EARTH

As gardeners, we should be constantly concerned about managing our soil well. It is really on trust from nature. We get so much from the soil, we should give something back. And it is quite rewarding to see the soil we have helped to make, as well as the fruits and flowers of our efforts.

Soil is the upper layer of the earth, in which plants get a foothold, live and grow. The nature of a soil helps to determine the sorts of plants that will grow in it and the way they will grow. The good news is that, unlike weather, soil can be altered by various means to suit your needs. To understand your particular soil and how best to care for it, it is important that you learn something about soil in general.

The soil of a particular plot represents a stage in geological history. Over the ages various types of rock have crumbled and weathered, gradually mingling with decaying vegetable and animal matter. This mixture, 3–20 centimetres deep, together with air and water, is soil or, more specifically, topsoil. Below the topsoil lies the subsoil, a rather more basic soil, which lacks organic matter, bacteria, moisture and air.

Fine flowers come from good soil that meets their needs. Lupins (*Lupinus*), delphiniums and oriental poppies (*Papaver orientale*) revel in rich, deep soil.

Rivers and glaciers transport soil to new sites, adding variety to their composition. In areas that have been affected by volcanoes there is usually a clear demarcation between the soil of volcanic origin and the original soil.

What is in the soil? – crumbled rock, elements essential to plant life, living organisms, humus, water and air.

ROCK CRUMBLINGS

Rock crumblings can be very fine clay particles, slightly less fine silt, or coarser particles, known as sand, gravel and stones. The crumblings contain compounds of the elements that are crucial to healthy plant growth, although the mineral content of soil varies with the nature of the parent rock.

ESSENTIAL SOIL ELEMENTS

There are six elements that are especially valuable and a number of trace elements only necessary in very small amounts.

Nitrogen

The natural source of nitrogen is humus, made from the decomposition of vegetable matter, which occurs constantly in the soil. Nitrogen is important for strong, healthy leaf and stem development in grass, trees, shrubs and leafy vegetables and for the deep, rich shades of green that gardeners always admire.

Potassium

While there is usually enough potassium in heavy soils, sandy soils may need a supplement to produce healthy plants. There is potassium in burnt wood, vegetable ash and burnt seaweed, and it may be bought commercially as potash. Root tips, shoots and growing tips are made sturdy by this element, so it is a valuable nutrient for root vegetables. It is also essential for sap production and flowering. Together with phosphorus, potassium protects plants against disease.

Phosphorus

Phosphorus is deficient in some Australian soils, particularly limy soils, such as those of the Mallee in Victoria and South Australia. Bone meal and animal manures, especially horse and poultry manure, provide natural phosphorus. Phosphorus is needed for healthy root growth and so is very important for root crops, such as carrots, parsnips and turnips. It encourages flowering, the ripening of fruits and vegetables, such as tomatoes and beans, and the development of seeds, as well as helping plants to resist disease.

Calcium

In all but the most acid soils there is usually enough calcium. It is necessary for sturdy plant growth and assists in the development of healthy root and growing tips. It also makes soil more workable, by binding fine particles together.

Magnesium

Magnesium levels in soil are often low. However, liberal use of animal manures will improve the situation. Magnesium encourages the greening of leaves, as well as being generally nutritious for plants.

Sulphur

Sulphur deficiencies are quite unusual. This element, like magnesium and nitrogen, assists in the important process of making foliage green.

Trace elements

Trace elements are quite important, but only needed in such minute quantities that there are usually sufficient in the soil. They include boron, manganese, molybdenum, sodium, zinc, copper, iron, cobalt, chlorine and iodine. Iron contributes to the greenness of plants; a deficiency is recognised by the yellowing of leaves, particularly the top growth, although the veins may remain green. Iron deficiency is remedied by a dose of iron chelates or sulphate of iron. Other deficiencies are usually counteracted by an application of a complete fertiliser.

SOIL LIFE

Soil cannot be regarded as something static. It is alive with micro-organisms, minute creatures that are constantly assisting in the breakdown of animal and vegetable waste to form humus. Their action, and that of water, helps as well in the breakdown of rocks into the elements from which are formed the easily absorbed compounds needed by plants. Micro-organisms, which are mainly bacteria and fungi, form huge colonies in fertile soil, but are present wherever there is decaying organic matter.

Insects, too, live in the soil in their thousands, and their pulverising and aerating behaviour is most beneficial. Earthworms are generally considered the master gardeners of the soil. Their movements open up the soil and so improve its quality.

HUMUS

The end product of the decay of dead plants and creatures and animal manures is humus. This rich, brown, crumbly, sweet-smelling stuff is also our reward for composting. Whatever the nature of soil, humus will always improve the texture and add nutrients, especially nitrogen, but it needs to be constantly added to keep up the standard.

Soil rich in humus is warmer in winter and cooler in summer. It has less tendency to form a crust or to erode. It holds water well and is readily workable and crumbly, allowing roots to grow readily and nutrients to be taken up easily.

WATER

Water provides the means by which chemicals travel in the soil. By taking water through their roots plants receive the benefits of the soil's nutrients. Oxygen and hydrogen, which are so important for plant growth, are taken in from water in the soil – water that is there naturally and water from the hose of the attentive gardener.

AIR

Soil needs air to enable the normal passage of water. Air supplies plants with carbon, hydrogen and oxygen. The oxygen in air is essential to the creatures of the soil and also to plant roots. Without it soil becomes lifeless – you may already have discovered that tired, tight-knit soil becomes much easier to work when exposed to the air.

SOIL STRUCTURE

Soils are categorised as sand, sandy loam, loam, clay loam and clay. Soils vary from loose, large-grained, quick-draining sand through degrees of looseness or lumpiness to stiff, hard-to-drain, fine-particled clay. Within your garden the soil may vary from, say, sandy loam in one area to a large patch of solid clay in another. As well, you may have a few rocky outcrops breaking the surface, or the soil itself may be quite stony.

The way your soil is suggests what you can do and what you can grow. Even rocky outcrops can be incorporated into a garden plan. You may want to either modify your soil to make it more amenable to a variety of plants or learn about the sorts of plants that you can grow in the existing soil, by reading garden books, asking local nurseries for advice and talking to neighbours or other people who have to contend with the same type of soil.

Sand

Sand is easy to dig and work over, but, because it doesn't hold moisture, it dries out quickly and requires constant watering in dry weather. As water drains through the loose grains of sand, it washes out the minerals and the humus from which plants get their nourishment.

Sandy loam

Sandy loam is largely sand with enough silt and humus to hold it together. This soil holds moisture long enough for plants to take it in and retains nutrients, so plants do well. Sandy loam is a pleasure to dig because it is not too heavy.

Loamy soil

Loamy soil has equal parts of sand and clay. It retains moisture to the extent that it does not need to be watered quite so regularly as sand, but it still offers good drainage to plants. It makes a satisfactory garden soil.

Clay loam

Clay loam is a heavier soil, with some of the characteristics of clay, but it still gives plants reasonable drainage and access to nutriments.

Organic matter in soil improves its texture, making it easier to work with. As well, it adds valuable plant nutrients and attracts earthworms.

Clay

Clay is very hard to work, tending to dry out into a hard mass when it is not watered – something that often happens in Australia's long, hot summers. When this occurs, the soil has to be chipped rather than dug. In wintertime, when the clay is wet, surface puddles form. The water eventually drains through the fine, close-knit particles, but the whole ground then becomes a sticky mess that clings to your boots and spade so you seem to get nowhere.

CHANGING THE SOIL'S TEXTURE

You can take up the challenge and work towards altering the less satisfactory aspects of your soil. Sand and clay can be modified to make them more like sandy loam and clay loam. Eventually you can achieve an even loam, rich in humus and all that both gardeners and plants could ever wish for. This will not happen overnight, but, surprisingly enough, some results occur quite quickly.

Improving sandy soil

If your soil is too sandy, you must build as much organic material into it as possible to help bind the loose grains so that water and nutrients will be retained. Add organic material directly to the soil. The scope is great: kitchen scraps, garden prunings, old woollen or felt carpet, newspapers, feathers and household dust will all gradually break down into basic soil nutriments. The garden, however, can sometimes look a bit messy as a result, so you may prefer to make a compost heap (see below) with these materials – the brown humus that is produced can then be added to your garden.

Improving clay soil

The objective is to open up the close-knit, fine clay particles, enabling water to pass through. However, the solution is not as easy as just digging humus into the clay. If you have ever done that you will remember how you can almost see the organic matter becoming part of the clay. Instead, the time-honoured method is to add a substance called gypsum first. This amazing substance has the ability to open up the clay particles, so that the soil becomes receptive to humus. Sand can also be added and dug through, along with leaves, straw, bits of woollen carpet or anything else organic. But here's a Cinderella-style note of caution: after about six weeks the effect of gypsum wears off. If humus has not been added to the soil in that time, the loosened soil particles will tighten up again, becoming stiff clay once more.

INCREASING YOUR TOPSOIL

If you are unlucky enough to have only a thin layer of topsoil you should try to increase it, using compost to build up workable soil to a depth sufficient for planting. The subsoil below would need a lot of attention to bring it up to scratch, and it should not, as a rule, be disturbed in the course of gardening.

If you need to bring in soil as a supplement, it should be as close as possible in type to the indigenous soil. Only buy from a reputable firm because there is some risk of importing weed seed and extra creatures that you do not want with the soil.

SOIL ACIDITY AND ALKALINITY

It is important for you to understand the implications of having an acid or an alkaline soil, for some plants are quite sensitive to one or the other although there are many that are not so choosy. The level of acidity and alkalinity (pH) is assessed by measuring the concentration of hydrogen ions in solution in the soil. The higher the concentration, the more acid the soil is.

Most plants thrive in a neutral or slightly acid soil. The ideal level is about 6.5 pH. Those that can take more calcium, such as roses, carnations, delphiniums and some irises, are comfortable to about 7.5 pH. On the other side of the scale are acid-loving plants, such as the heath family, azaleas, camellias and rhododendrons, which can live successfully in soil down to a pH of four. Hydrangeas take a wide range of soils, but those that are not cream or white by nature will vary in colour with soil pH, from pink in alkaline soil to blue in acid soil. When planting by new buildings or freshly paved paths, be careful to remove visible lime, mortar or plaster left in the earth because it will make the soil nearby more alkaline.

Soil-testing kits are available from garden centres. They provide a simple method of testing a sample or two of your soil, using a colour chart as a guide to pH levels. The pH of your soil can be modified. Acid soils can be made more neutral by adding lime, while the addition of organic matter will make soils more acid. Adding composted oak leaves is a particularly effective method of increasing the acidity of your soil.

CARING FOR THE SOIL

The care and structural improvement of soil largely involve the application of nitrogen, converted into the nitrate form that plants are able to use. Nitrates only have a short life, so need to be applied often. We do this by adding compost, organic and inorganic fertilisers (see Feeding Plants, later in the chapter) and mulch. Nature does it by adding humus. Leguminous plants are also important in the nitrogen cycle. They are members of the pea family and include various peas, lupins, lucerne and beans. Nodules attached to the roots of such plants contain bacteria that convert nitrogen straight into nitrates in the soil ready for use.

Neutral

0 Acid soil — 4 5 6 7 8 9 10 — Alkaline soil 14

On the pH scale, 7 represents a neutral soil.

Camellias do well in acid soil. They fail to thrive in an alkaline soil.

MULCH

Mulch can look attractive. Cut straw helps the soil to retain moisture, suppresses weeds and will in time decompose, adding goodness to the soil.

Mulching is a technique for covering garden surfaces with protective material, both organic and inorganic. Mulching has four important functions:

1 it helps to retain moisture in the soil
2 it protects the soil from extremes of heat and cold
3 it stifles weed growth
4 it improves soil texture and goodness, if it is organic.

A mulch may be made up of straw, old leaves, compost, manure, sawdust, pine bark, mushroom compost, wood chips or even gravel.

Applying mulch

- For most mulch to be effective it must be 10–12 centimetres deep. However, mushroom compost, which is sold commercially and is a rich and valuable mixture of stable manure, straw and mushroom debris, should not be laid more than 5 centimetres deep and must be kept away from trunks and stems: it can be quite alkaline, and there have been reports of damage to acid-loving plants.
- Care must be taken, when using any organic mulch, not to put it too heavily around the stems or trunks of plants, which can be damaged by the heat generated as the materials decompose.
- If pine bark, sawdust or other unrotted organic material is used around a plant, the breaking-down process may cause a sudden nitrogen deficiency, which you can recognise by a yellowing of the plant's leaves. In fact it is advisable to mix blood and bone through the mulch in anticipation of this problem. Add two handfuls per square metre of ground.
- The ground should always be well soaked before a mulch is laid, for the mulch can prevent water from entering the soil.

COMPOST: AN ESSENTIAL OF GOOD GARDENING

BELOW A double bin allows you to build up a new store of compost while you are using your first lot on the garden.

ABOVE Bought plastic bins are an alternative to constructed wooden or brick compost bins.

The essential components of the compost process are:

- organic matter
- nitrogen
- air
- water.

Suitable organic materials include:

- food scraps (but not meat and bread, which attract rats)
- straw
- leaves
- small prunings
- woody stems and branches less than 5 centimetres thick
- small amounts of woollen carpet, underfelt, newspapers, feathers, household dust and wood ash.

Do not use:

- woody or prickly stems or branches (chop these up finely in a mulcher)
- plants that have been affected by pests or diseases
- plants that have been sprayed with pesticides or herbicides
- hardy perennial weeds, such as oxalis and couch grass
- ash from coke, coal or briquettes.

Containers and heaps

Compost can be made in a heap or a bin. A heap takes less effort but is not as orderly and easy to control as a bin. Develop a heap in a (preferably sunny) corner of the garden, where it is not an eyesore. Make it no more than 50 centimetres high and wide so that it does not become unwieldy. Leave it open to the air, without a covering.

The following containers make suitable bins:

- a commercial, ready-made plastic bin, usually about 1 metre high; some have air holes in the sides, some are solid and some have detachable sides
- a square, wire-netting cage, constructed around four posts, to a height of about 1 metre – one side should be removable so that the compost can be turned
- bales of straw stacked to a height of two bales (about 1 metre) to form a back and two sides; the straw can be used as organic layers in a new bin once it has begun to decompose
- a square or rectangular structure made from posts and boards to a height of about 1.5 metres, with removable boards at the front to provide access during and at the end of compost making
- a brick-sided structure to a height of about 1.5 metres, with air vents and a front of removable wooden slats
- a tumble bin, usually a forty-four-gallon drum suspended on a frame and turned with a handle.

Making the compost

Compost can become a very personal thing, and many gardeners swear by their own method. The important factor is to adhere to the basic principles of compost making.

1. Alternate 8-centimetre layers of organic matter of different textures with a good sprinkling of blood and bone or ammonium sulphate: the nitrogenous fertilisers speed up the breaking-down process. Traditionally, lime was added to compost to counteract the acidity of the other ingredients, but it is now rarely put in, especially if the compost is to be used around acid-loving plants.
2. Moisten the completed compost thoroughly.
3. Cover the compost with a plastic sheet or lid to increase the heat and encourage decomposition.
4. Leave the compost to rot for eight weeks, meanwhile starting a second compost heap or bin.
5. Fork the rotted compost onto garden beds or incorporate it into the soil as the beds are dug or trenched.

Compost bins need not be ugly. Here a fine pumpkin has sprung up in the side not in use.

PLANTING

When your soil is well dug, prepared with a good supply of organic matter worked through and rested for six weeks, you are ready to plant. As well as organic matter, such as compost or blood and bone, you can dig in a complete fertiliser when you prepare the soil. You can also use a slow-release fertiliser, which will give your plants nourishment over the next few months; because slow-release fertiliser is gentle with roots, it can be sprinkled into the hole at planting time, according to directions.

If you are planting seeds, it is important that you work the soil to a fine tilth, which means that the soil is dug and redug and undecomposed objects, such as bottletops, wire and silverfoil, are removed to make an even mixture. You can work either close to the ground with a hand fork or at the end of a hoe or a long-handled fork.

SOWING SEED

Seeds are either sown directly in the garden, or temporarily in perforated seed trays and then transferred to the garden.

Direct sowing

1 Moisten soil, worked to a fine tilth, before sowing.
2 Mix fine seeds with sand to ensure they are spread evenly as you sow; do not cover them with much soil. Press larger seeds into the soil.
3 Cover the seeds lightly with soil and moisten them. The seeds should be covered to a depth of about twice their size.
4 Water the seeds and seedlings regularly: moisture is critical to germination and subsequent growth. Watering should be gentle and even. Remember to water in the morning, to help prevent fungal infection.
5 Avoid overcrowding of the seedlings. Use tweezers to thin them out if necessary.
6 Apply weak liquid manure or liquid seaweed every two or three weeks to encourage growth.

INDIRECT SOWING

Before sowing, some seeds, such as those of wattles, need to have their hard coats softened. Soak them in boiling water overnight.

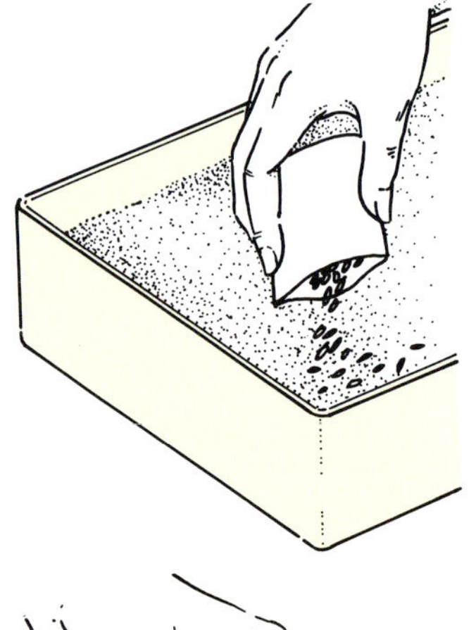

Sow seeds evenly in a seed-sowing mix that drains uniformly.

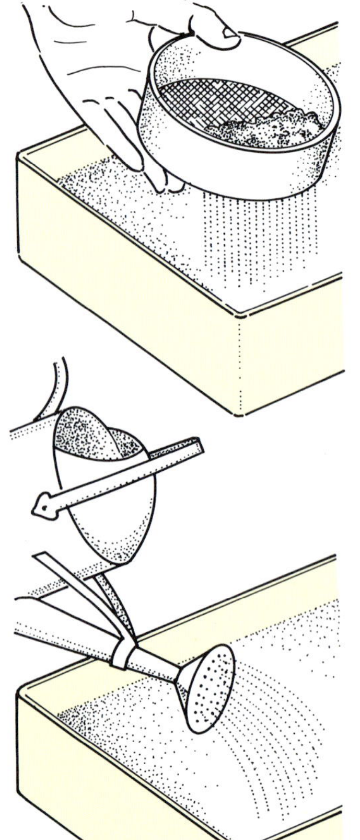

Cover the seeds with finely sieved soil.

Use a watering can that gives a fine spray to water in the seeds. Add a label to the tray, showing the date of sowing and the name of the seeds.

Indirect sowing

1 Put a commercial seed-raising mix in a seed tray and moisten it.
2 Press round the edges of the tray, so that the soil is lightly compressed, and level the top.
3 Scatter seeds finely over the mix, then press them in with a matchbox.
4 Cover the seeds lightly with sifted soil and water them gently.
5 Keep the tray in a light position, but not where the full sun will burn the plants and perhaps dry them out.
6 Transfer tray-grown seedlings to the garden as soon as their first two leaves have developed.

Planting out and transplanting

Deciduous plants are best bought, with their roots bare and packed in a water-retentive mulch, in winter, when they are dormant. The bare roots enable you to arrange them comfortably and well spread out in a hole dug plenty big enough to take them. Evergreen plants are usually bought in containers and are best planted in autumn or spring in the following manner.

1 Dig a hole that is twice as wide and a little deeper than the plant's container.
2 Soak the plant before planting it. Pot-bound or dry plants in particular should be thoroughly soaked and their roots freed a little by teasing them out with your fingers, but otherwise roots should not need to be handled.
3 Find the point at which the plant has been covered by earth in its pot or tube, and place the plant in the hole to that level – it must be planted neither too deeply nor too shallowly, though it's best to err on the shallow side. Mulch will help protect the plant if it is too far out of the ground.
4 Gently spade in soil around the plant in the hole. Make sure the soil is packed closely, leaving no air pockets around the roots, by tamping the soil down firmly at the surface.
5 Water the plant in well – a generous bucketful will give it a good start.
6 Keep the plant moist for several weeks after it has been transplanted from its container.

The same principles apply for transplanting as for planting out deciduous and evergreen plants. You can take a chance moving plants at other times, but there is a risk factor, though it varies with the nature of the plants.

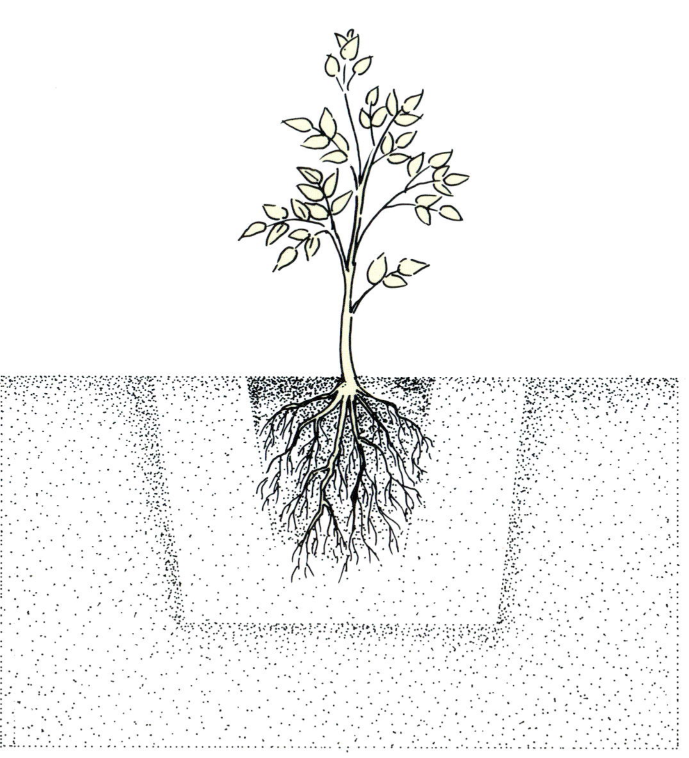

LEFT If the roots of a container-grown native or other plant form a tight mass, loosen them a little, ready for growing, before you plant as shown.

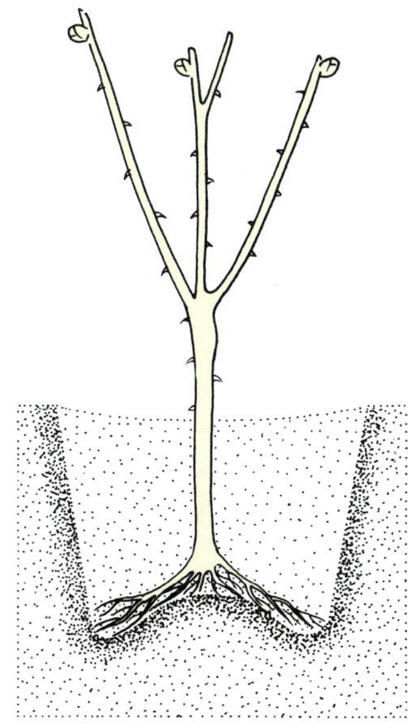

RIGHT To plant a rose bought bare rooted, spread the roots over a small mound of soil at the base of a prepared hole. Add soil until the hole is half filled, water it and leave it to drain. Then fill the hole in completely and water the rose well.

STAKING PLANTS

Staking is generally not necessary for young plants, unless they are growing in an exceptionally windy area. Young trees are best left unsupported to develop self-reliant, strong root systems. Larger transplanted trees, however, may need staking to anchor them while they establish strong roots in their new site. Three stakes set in a triangle are excellent for holding trees firmly and straight.

Wooden stakes are preferable; steel star-droppers are stronger for big plants, but take care because metal heats up and can burn plants. Before planting, hammer the stake firmly into the soil, not too close to the plant, to avoid damaging the roots. Ties used for staking must not cut into the bark, so use flexible materials, such as organic garden twine for small plants and Velcro or adjustable nylon straps for larger plants. Ties should be checked and adjusted or replaced if needed as the trees grow. Tie the material around the stake and the plant in a figure of eight to safeguard against bark damage and to allow for a small amount of movement.

Standard roses and other standard plants require staking at the time of planting: place the stake in the hole, close to the trunk, and tie it firmly to the trunk. Perennial plants that grow tall may need staking so that they are contained within a certain space and shown to their greatest advantage. The stakes used should be light and unobtrusive – green-painted metal or green bamboo sticks, perhaps, or little broken branches, so they don't detract from the overall picture.

BELOW If a rose, such as a climber, needs staking, the stake should be inserted before the rose is planted. Attach the rose to it, using flexible ties.

RIGHT A newly planted advanced tree may need to be staked for the first few years, particularly if the site is windy. Two or three stakes are required to secure the tree.

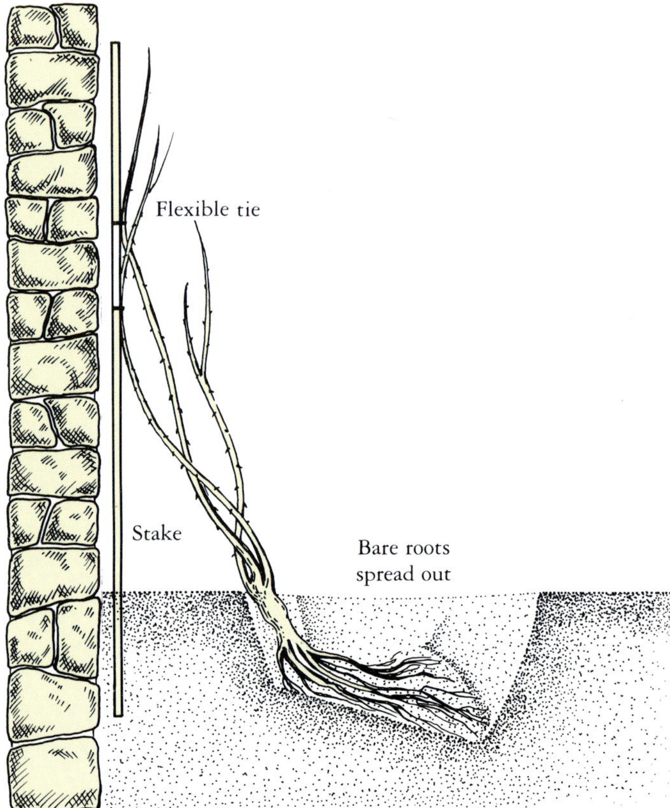

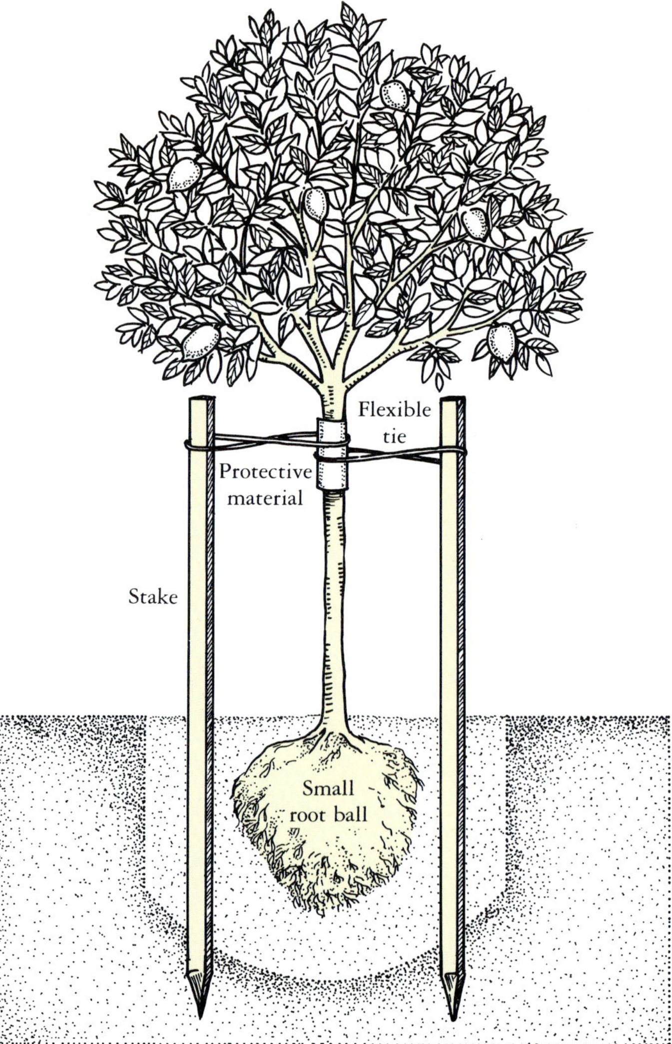

PROPAGATION: SOMETHING FOR NOTHING

There is something irresistible to many gardeners about creating new plants. Propagation of many species is not difficult, and, apart from the pleasure of passing plants on to friends or school fêtes, there's another important outcome: a number of healthy plants are produced from one plant or a few seeds, enabling you to produce lovely, massed garden effects quite economically.

It is important to find out which mode of propagation is appropriate for a particular plant: it may be by seed, bulblet, running root or piece of rhizome. Brambles, such as raspberries, and some shrubs arch their stems over, forming new roots where they touch the soil. These layered branches can be detached from the main plant and planted out as new plants.

Over the centuries gardeners have added other ways of propagating plants: slips and cuttings, root division, layering and the more complex methods of budding and grafting. Some people seem to sense instinctively the way to go about propagating various types of plants, but anyone can learn by trial and error and common sense. The enthusiasm that flows from a small triumph in the propagating field is amazing.

PROPAGATING SEED

Many types of seeds can be gathered successfully when pods or seed cases have ripened, turning yellow. Wattles (*Acacia*), for instance, have long, thin seed pods like peas, which should be collected when they turn from green to brown, and before they split open. Poppies (*Papaver*) have masses of seeds in their round pods and will release them easily when the pods die. Collect seeds in carefully labelled envelopes.

CUTTINGS FOR THE TAKING

Just which piece of the plant and how it should be taken are matters of inside information and experience. Some stems take best if they are hardened, woody pieces; others if they are soft, sappy tips of shoots. A 'heel', or little piece of parent bark attached to a newer stem, can help; many grevilleas and lavenders strike best with a heel. Sometimes it just seems to be the luck of the draw.

Cuttings are best taken in the early morning and kept moist in wet newspaper or a plastic bag, so that they don't dry out, until they can be planted. They are

The heads of oriental poppies (*Papaver orientale*) are a ready source of seeds for the following season. Gather the seeds in a paper bag when the heads are straw coloured.

usually started in pots, in a mixture of two or three parts of sharp sand to one part of peat moss. However, cuttings of some plants, such as marguerite daisies (*Chrysanthemum frutescens*), pelargoniums, begonias and fuchsias, can be placed straight into your garden where you want them to grow and will respond well.

Sometimes we are too busy to do our bits and pieces justice when we acquire them. It's a good idea to have a large pot or tub, preferably in an easterly aspect, in which to pop cuttings to keep them alive until you are able to deal with them.

WHEN TO TAKE CUTTINGS
Softwood cuttings (for example, impatiens, coleus, plectranthus and marguerites) At any time during the plant's growing season.
Semi-hardwood cuttings (for example, azaleas, camellias, daphne, abelia and marguerites) Throughout summer and autumn.
Hardwood cuttings (for example, hydrangeas, wisteria, grape vines and roses) During winter, when the plant is dormant.

Taking a softwood or semi-hardwood cutting

1 Look for a healthy stem – the topmost shoot or a strong side shoot.
2 Cut the tip off just below a node or pair of nodes (the junction of stem and leaf); the cutting should be about 10 centimetres in length.
3 Remove the side leaves on the cutting, leaving just four or five small ones near the top.
4 Place the cutting in damp propagating mix in a small pot, making a suitable hole for it with an old pencil beforehand to avoid damaging the end, and press it in firmly to avoid air pockets. Commercial propagating mixes are available, containing coarse river sand and peat moss or vermiculite.
5 Water the pot regularly, keeping it in indirect sunlight. A clear plastic bag or dome can be put over the top to increase the humidity and warmth to encourage growth. You may like to write the name of the plant and the date of planting on a plastic tag, using a waterproof pen. Store the tag down the side of the pot.
6 After the cutting has struck, remove the plastic covering. (Cuttings can take up to six or eight weeks to strike.) Continue to care for the cutting as you would a young plant, encouraging strong and healthy growth.
7 When the cutting has put out strong roots that are appearing through the bottom of the pot, gently tip the pot over, shake some of the propagating mix off the roots and plant the cutting either in the garden or in a larger container.

Taking a hardwood cutting

1 From the dormant plant, take a cutting about 15–20 centimetres in length, with three buds on it.
2 Put the cutting either into the ground directly or into pots, as for softwood cuttings.
3 Transplant to a permanent site several months later, when the cutting has rooted.

To take a softwood cutting from, for example, French lavender, cut a 7–10-centimetre length from the top of a stem, making the cut just below a pair of nodes. Remove the flower head and all but a few leaves. After several weeks in a propagating mix, the cutting will develop roots.

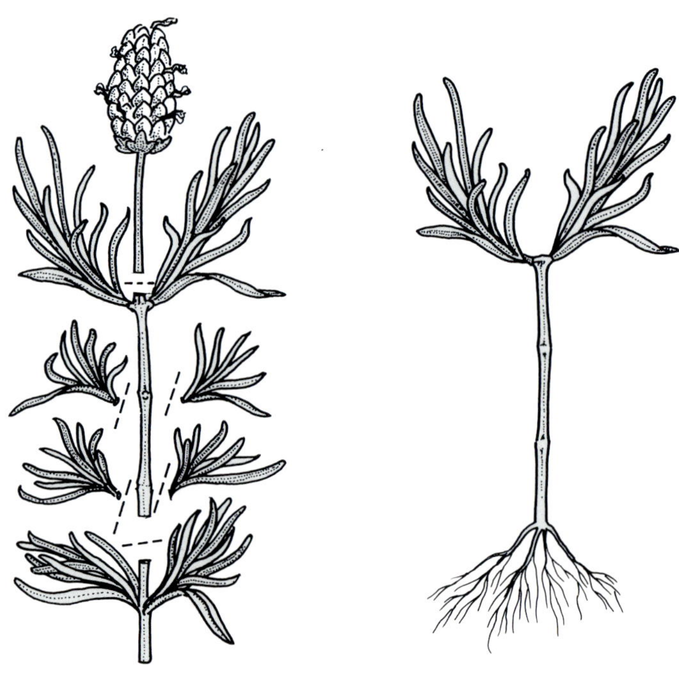

ROOT DIVISION

To divide a plant, lift it during the dormant season with a garden fork and remove as much soil as possible.

Many perennials, ground covers and shrubs can be divided or split up and new plants grown from the divisions. This can be done from autumn through to early spring.

1. With a spade, dig a circle round the plant, then lift the whole mass out.
2. Pull or cut the crowded clumps into smaller sections. They will usually divide quite readily.
3. Throw away any dead or diseased parts. The middle portion is also often discarded because it is old and tired. Younger, healthier shoots are at the edge; use these to start your new plants.
4. Plant the healthy divisions in well-prepared soil.
5. Water the new plants well to settle them in.
6. After the flowering season, cut the new plants' stems right down to 15 centimetres to encourage new spring growth. Divide the new clumps as before when they become too large.

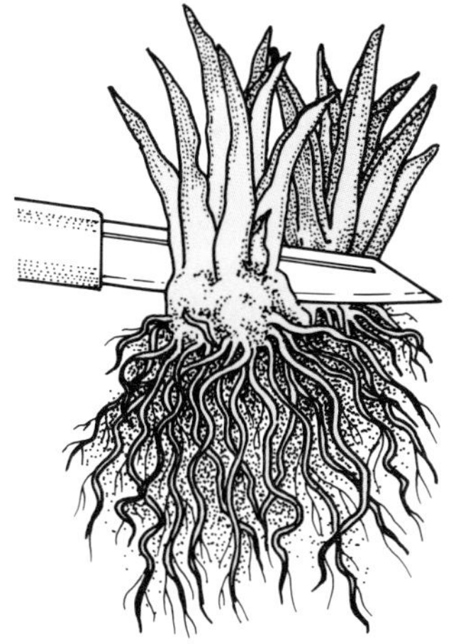

Cut through the plant's crown with a sharp knife.

Plant each piece containing roots separately.

LAYERING

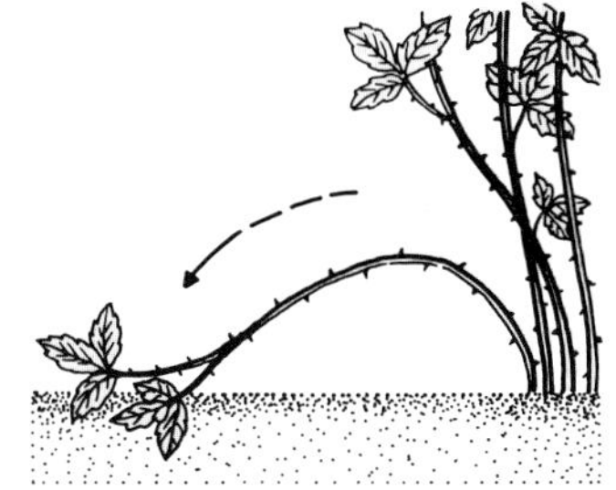

Bramble bushes and many other plants, such as rhododendrons, azaleas and magnolias, can be layered. Select a flexible stem on the parent plant to work with.

Using a technique called layering, you can capitalise on the tendency of many plants to root readily when their branches or stems come in contact with soil. Strawberries, rhododendrons, azaleas and climbers with creeping stems are good plants to try.

1. Bend a flexible branch down until it touches the soil.
2. Take off any leaves that will be under the ground, and scrape away a couple of centimetres of outer bark from the same area to encourage root growth.
3. Pin the bare area of branch under the ground; it will send out roots as a consequence.
4. Once new shoots have formed, cut the new plant from the parent stem. Lift it out carefully and resite it in your garden, or pot it up for later use or to give to friends.

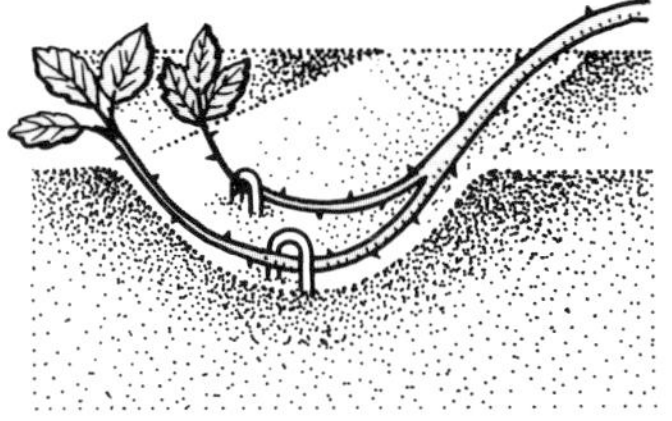

Dig a trench about 10 centimetres deep, and bend the stem down until it nestles at the bottom. Pin the tip down with a hooked wire or flat stone. Backfill the trench with soil and keep it moist.

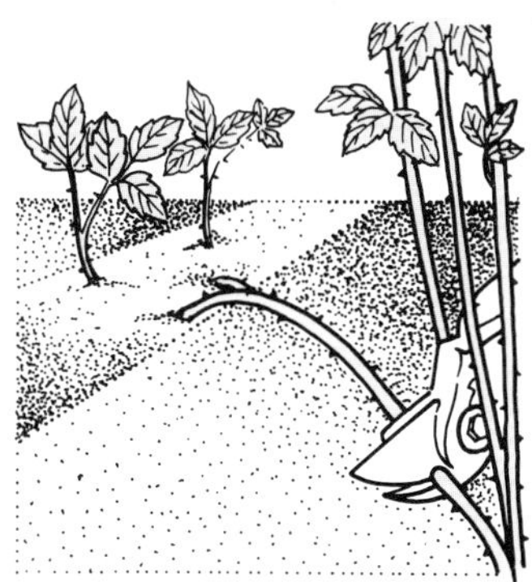

After a time, when the stem has grown roots, it can be severed from the parent plant and grown separately.

LAWNS IN THE LANDSCAPE

For some people, to own a fine lawn, maintained to perfection, is little short of ultimate happiness. To many it's an obsession. Others reluctantly mow and edge their way through alternate Sunday mornings! And some cunning people pay others to do the mowing or manage to own gardens so small that to plant a lawn just wouldn't make sense.

However, people who substitute hard surfaces miss out on the pleasure of living with a lawn – of sitting, walking, playing cricket or kicking a football with the kids on a broad expanse of grass. They miss out, too, on the pleasure of soft green spaces that provide a carpeted link between garden beds and of vantage points from which to admire the more intricate parts of the garden. We'd soon notice the loss if our public parks and gardens had no mown, grassy areas. So, for those who do want to live with lawns, here are some hints on acquiring and maintaining them, with a look at suitable types of grass and alternative forms of carpeted spaces.

SITE PREPARATION

You can acquire a lawn by sowing seed or laying turf, a ready-grown grass whose roots are matted 5 centimetres deep in earth and which is sold by the metre roll. There are sound arguments for and against the use of each – it's really a matter of what suits your purposes and matches your cash flow. Turf is instant, so best

Some people want their lawn to be an unbroken expanse of green, so daisies (*Bellis perennis*) are rooted out persistently. Others love the sense of a meadow that daisies bring.

where dogs and lively children might trample on seed. Both sown grass and turf require soil preparation.

1 Lay agricultural pipes if drainage is inadequate: good drainage is essential for good lawns.
2 Clear the area of rubbish, old grass and weeds. Physically remove the weeds or poison them, and then two or three weeks afterwards scrape the soil and remove the debris. Don't rotary hoe live weeds: you'll never find all the bits and pieces, and many will probably propagate and appear through the new lawn later. Remove all builders' rubble, sticks, glass, large clods and stones.
3 Loosen, as well as clear, the soil to a depth of 8 centimetres. Rake the surface of the soil smooth, following the contours that you want for your grassy area and evening out any hollows and lumps that you don't want. The top 2 centimetres of soil should be especially fine; you may need to bring in some top-quality loam for this.
4 Rake in a commercial lawn starter – a fertiliser used to accelerate growth.

SOWING GRASS SEED

A lawn can be planted at any time throughout the year, but spring or autumn are regarded as the best times for an efficient response.

1 Spread the seeds 30 grams (a handful) to a square metre of soil – cast half in one direction, the remainder in the other, to distribute them evenly, starting at the furthermost point of your area. And remember to cast enough to feed the birds.
2 Firm the soil down with a roller, or just walk all over the area gently, in flat-soled shoes.
3 Keep the seeds damp from sowing time until they shoot.
4 Continue to water the lawn well until it becomes established and looks quite green. Thorough watering encourages the roots to grow deep and strong.
5 Mow when the grass is 8–10 centimetres tall. Don't shave it closely – a short back and sides is *not* recommended in Australian climates. Frequent high cuts stimulate root growth and keep lawns fresh and green. Always leave the grass higher than 4 centimetres.

CHOOSING A GRASS

If you are buying turf, you may be offered a choice of lawn mixtures. A mixture of Kentucky blue and couch makes an attractive, strong lawn; finer mixtures are also available.

You have a wider choice of grass varieties if you are sowing your lawn. You can also use buffalo or kikuyu grass runners instead of seed, but you will have to find your own – they are not available commercially. Runners are usually planted in October.

***Agrostis tenuis* (bent)** Makes good-quality lawn that copes with drought, quickly recovering with watering, and is shade tolerant.

***Cynodon dactylon* (couch)** Drought resistant and suited to high temperatures, but sensitive to cold and frost and may look brown in winter. Although a sown lawn, it spreads by creeping stems.

***Festuca rubra* (fescue)** Makes good-quality lawn that copes with dry times, quickly recovering with watering, and also shade tolerant.

***Lolium perenne* (perennial rye)** Quick-germinating, fast-growing, hard-wearing grass that needs mowing often. Remains green throughout winter but does not tolerate heat and dryness.

***Pennisetum clandestinum* (kikuyu)** Aggressive, strong-growing stem spreader that needs frequent mowing and checking; drought and heat tolerant, though a little frost sensitive.

***Poa pratensis* (Kentucky blue)** Attractive, blue-green grass, drought and winter tolerant and able to grow in poorer soils; but slow to establish and better mixed with faster-growing types.

***Stenotaphrum secundatum* (buffalo)** Coarse, mat-forming grass, with creeping stems; forms a dense, springy lawn, inclined to brown off in cold weather. Plant runners about 14 centimetres apart.

The pleasant neutrality of green lawn is a foil for the more intense colours of flowering plants.

PLANT ALTERNATIVES TO LAWN

If your kind of gardening doesn't meet the requirements of a lawn, look at some plant alternatives before resorting to paving, particularly if the area involved is not too big.

Chamaemelum nobile **(chamomile)** An appealing, lime-green plant, with fernlike leaves, that thrives in sunny, well-drained areas; forms a thick carpet that releases a delicious fragrance when crushed underfoot. The species to use for a lawn is a sterile version, *C. n.* 'Treneague', that does not produce flower heads or require mowing.

Dichondra repens Small, heart-shaped leaves carpet the ground. Plants remain green through all seasons, need no mowing, take full sun or partial shade and do not require good drainage. Generally purchased as seed.

Lippia nodiflora A hardy ground cover, with mid-green leaves and tiny flowers that are dull white to pale pink. Likes sandy, well-drained soils, but generally obliging in most soils; withstands heat, cold and drought.

Mentha requienii **(Corsican mint)** Grows in a flat mat and has tiny, pungent leaves. To grow well needs cool, damp position.

Thymus **(thyme)** Edible herb that doubles as lawn. Has fine leaves and matting habit and is a tough ground cover, useful for planting in paving pockets also. Fresh fragrance rises as it is crushed underfoot. Needs a sunny aspect and well-drained soil. There are several carpeting types, including Westmoreland thyme (*T. serpyllum*).

Chamomile (*Chamaemelum nobile*) is an alternative to grass. Its fragrance rises as it is walked on, but it is not suitable for heavy traffic.

LAYING TURF

Be ready to lay your rolls of turf when they are delivered, for they dry out easily. It's best not to keep turf rolls even overnight, especially in summer.

1 Unroll the rolls and lay them in lines, using secateurs or a strong knife to cut the turf to fit the shape of the garden beds and paths.
2 Press all the cut edges well down, with the back of a metal rake.
3 Water the turf until it is soaking wet.
4 Do not walk on the turf for a day and a half, and keep it quite damp while it is settling in and establishing roots in the base earth.
5 Water the turf thoroughly and regularly for a few months afterwards.

MAINTAINING A LAWN

It is customary to mow a lawn every second week, but in spring it may need cutting weekly, while sometimes in winter every three weeks is sufficient. Never mow closely in very hot weather – the short grass can burn easily, and the roots can be damaged.

Once established, a lawn should not be over-watered. If there's not much rain about, the lawn should have a good soaking once a week to encourage healthy, deep roots able to withstand dry, hot weather.

A lawn should be fertilised four times a year for best results. Water the grass thoroughly, then fertilise it with a food high in nitrogen and water it thoroughly once more.

For a near-perfect lawn you need to keep it uniformly grass by removing the weeds that appear from time to time. A small-pronged tool called a flat-weeder can be very helpful.

The edges of a lawn should be trimmed after each cut or every second cut. A brush-cutter is an efficient implement for cutting grass around rocks, although grass that is difficult to get at can be hand trimmed with a swivel-bladed clipper that rotates at various angles, if the area is small.

COMBATING WEEDS

Weeds are plants that have invasive growing habits outweighing their practical and decorative value. Much depends on environmental conditions: a plant may be a weed in some areas, a prized possession in others. There are two major groups of weeds: annuals and perennials.

ANNUAL WEEDS

Annual weeds, such as wild grasses and milk weed (*Euphorbia helioscopia*), germinate, flourish as plants, seed and die within the space of a year in the same way as flowering annuals. Grasses that are weeds may include the overflow from a lawn nearby and perhaps some of the native grasses that once covered the site. Milk weed, willow herb (*Epilobium*), which has quite a pretty pink flower, and flick weed grow all too readily and, if left, spread seeds galore through the garden. You will also get the odd blow-in annual weed, which is usually brought by the wind but may come as seed in some incomplete compost or from someone's sock.

All annual weeds can be pulled out readily if their ranks are small or they are young. Many can be dug in as green manure, but don't do this with mature plants bearing ripe seeds or you may be inadvertently sowing your next crop of weeds. Gently remove mature plants if you can to prevent the seeds dispersing, and catch next year's weed crop earlier.

Once you get the weed numbers down, regular maintenance should be quite easy. Learn to attack weeds as you see them, even on a trip to the letter box. It can take some keen gardeners all of an hour to collect the mail! Hide somewhere handy a small container, such as a 20-centimetre flowerpot or bucket, that you fill on such sorties.

PERENNIAL WEEDS

Perhaps the main difference between coping with annual and perennial weeds is that, as well as hiding a container, you will need to have at least a trowel or hand fork hidden in the bushes to combat the perennials. Perennial weeds, like perennial garden plants, go on living for years, their root crowns growing ever larger and their flowers seeding annually. Formidable foes indeed if they are let be. Examples – and some of you will shudder at their names – are dock weed (*Rumex crispus*), thistles (*Cirsium* species), paspalum and the pink-flowered *Oxalis corymbosa* and yellow-flowered *O. pes-caprae*. Some of these perennials, such as the grass paspalum and wild buttercups (*Ranunculus*), are actually rhizomes, which spread by root and seed. Some, such as onion weed (*Nothoscordum inodorum*), are bulbs, which, as well as spreading seed from their often pretty flower heads, grow tiny bulblets that fall off to create many new bulbs.

Unless perennial weeds are quite young, their roots will be tough enough to resist your pulling, or a few leaves or leaflets will break off, leaving the plant still growing. So dig them out properly or you may as well not weed at all.

Oxalis pes-caprae invades both garden beds and lawns, multiplying by tiny bulbs.

Winter grass (*Poa annua*) is a weed that should be dug out before it takes over a newly established lawn.

A prepared bed should be weeded just prior to planting.

GETTING RID OF WEEDS

The motto with all weeds is catch them young and be tough. They should be extracted from the soil as quickly, efficiently and harmlessly as possible. In most cases this means physical removal. It is best to weed after rain or a deep watering: weeds are easier to remove and there is less disturbance to shallow-rooted plants, such as annuals and vegetables, than if the ground is dry.

Weeds with big tap roots can be removed by cutting through the roots as far down as possible under the soil, with an old knife. If your weeds have grown well-clad seed heads, stop their spread by clipping off the heads into a bin, and get to the root of the matter as soon as you can.

For larger areas mow or slash, then scalp or dig off the soil surface, perhaps using a bobcat. Smaller areas do by hand and spade. Perennial weeds should not be rotary hoed or you will inadvertently spread fertile root pieces through the ground. Unless your compost bin is very efficient, do not compost perennial weeds; put them in the garbage bin.

Many people think weeds and poison in the same instant. However, spreading toxic substances through our precious earth, which produces the food we eat, is not too clever and, where weeds such as onion weed and oxalis are concerned, not particularly effective. The odds may seem overwhelming, but, taken patch by patch, your weeds can be conquered. Don't be discouraged by their bullying numbers. Each week set yourself an area to clear, and get out there as often as possible with your hand fork or long-handled fork and bin or barrow. Don't be too ambitious, though: you may only be able to weed effectively a small patch each time. Listen to your favourite music or the football as you work to make the time pass pleasantly.

Weeds in rock crevices and paving joints are hard to get at, but many weeds become disheartened if their heads are continually chopped off, even though you can't get at their roots. If they really get you down, use a systemic poison to eliminate them, preferably applying it carefully with a brush; never handle poison on windy days. Glyphosate-based herbicides, which kill plants if they touch any green part, are acceptable weedkillers.

Mulching the garden, after it has been weeded, with either organic materials, such as seaweed, newspaper, pea straw or pine bark, or inorganic ones, such as scoria or pebbles, will keep further weeds at bay, as well as conserve soil moisture.

CONTROLLING PESTS: NATURE'S WAY AND COMMON SENSE

On the principle that there's no such thing as a free lunch, many garden pests have to face the consequences of their actions in gardens. Damage caused by various bugs and creatures can be quite disheartening, and pests must be challenged. However, it is all too easy to use poison to wipe out colonies of small creatures that, to be fair, are only going about their natural tasks.

Using poisons is environmentally unfriendly. It is unwise to pump poison over our surroundings; the side effects are sometimes more severe than the problem itself. Bees, for example, which are so important in the plant pollination process, can die from toxic sprays, such as carbaryl, that are directed at pests. As well, if you wipe out a colony of trouble, you are likely to be wiping out the food supplies of creatures that actually do some good in gardens.

The contributions of those we might call goodies and baddies are woven into a fine and interdependent system. Nature left alone offers some solutions to our problems – almost certainly more than we are aware of. A ladybird beetle eats fifty to sixty aphids a day, its wingless larvae a further twenty-five per head. Ladybirds also eat woolly scale for a change of diet. Praying mantis feed on aphids and other insects. Small wasps and flies feed on caterpillars, some beetles and scale, or the eggs of other creatures. Spiders hunt harmful creatures or catch them in their webs. Birds catch small prey in the air or from the branches of trees and shrubs. It is not hard to allow birds a few of our precious earthworms, on their way through.

Another of nature's controls is the change of seasons. Creatures that thrive in the summer can be devastated by the autumn chill and disappear from sight and mind till the warmer weather; for most, the life cycle is short. Sometimes a summer downpour and cooler temperatures will reduce thrips, which thrive in hot, dry heat, while aphids, which favour damp heat, frequently also diminish in number under these conditions.

Allium deter aphids, which feed on roses and other plants.

Overhead watering reduces pests and keeps them on the move; many hate getting wet. Unfortunately, the increasing use of sprinkler and drip systems creates conditions favouring pests. Some pests, such as aphids, thrips and passionvine hoppers, rest happily on the top growth of plants while the sprinklers water beneath them.

COMMON PESTS AND HOW TO CURB THEM

There are ways of curbing the influence of some common garden pests, taking up the challenge of using non-toxic ways. Only when some additional form of control seems absolutely necessary are toxic sprays given here or in the table that follows, and then only those considered no more than mildly toxic for garden goodies and people.

Aphids

Aphids suck the sap of new green shoots and buds, from spring to autumn. Roses are a favourite: you will see the tiny insects clustered around the stems of new shoots and buds. It's best to remove aphids by hand or with a tissue soaked in a solution of household detergent. A bucket of soapy water or a water jet from a hose will also disperse them. Low-toxic sprays, such as garlic or pyrethrum, sprayed regularly, will control them adequately if physical methods become too arduous.

Beetles

Harlequin beetles, soldier beetles, Christmas beetles and various other beetles can be removed with a tissue and squashed.

Caterpillars

Just one or two caterpillars can do quite a lot of damage on shrubs and other plants. By walking around your garden and inspecting the plants, you are likely to catch them early. Check the backs as well as the fronts of leaves. There are many sorts of caterpillars: furry ones; green or fawn smooth-skinned ones; ones that, particularly on native plants, look like twigs; ones that crawl in an easily spotted looping style; and leaf rollers and webbing caterpillars (see below). Try to remove caterpillars physically – in your fingers or on a damp tissue – then squash them. Use pyrethrum spray for bad infestations.

Leaf rollers

Look out for rolled leaf tips on citrus, camellias, gardenias and other ornamentals. Unroll an affected leaf with one hand and hold a tissue in the other, below the leaf. If you are quick with the tissue, you will probably catch a tiny, fast-moving caterpillar that would otherwise feed on your precious new shoots.

Mealy bugs

Looking like tiny cottonwool blobs, mealy bugs are found mainly on indoor plants, although they also feed on daphnes and perennials. Sponge them with soapy water or methylated spirits, or use pyrethrum spray.

TOP Young stems on roses and many other plants provide juicy food for sap-sucking insects, such as aphids. The body colour of aphids ranges from yellow to green and darker colours.

BOTTOM If bugs, such as this crusader bug, are not in plague proportions in your garden, remove them by hand rather than with pesticides.

Passionvine hoppers

Passionvine hoppers appear from late September to April, in temperatures above 20 degrees Centigrade. These triangular-shaped flies, 7–8 millimetres in length, suck foliage, soon giving leaves a grey-bronze appearance. You'll see passionvine hoppers on fern fronds and the stems of passionfruit, azaleas and other shrubs. They are agile creatures that duck away if you try to squash them – so are the nymphs (their young), which can be identified by their fluffy, white tails. Use hose jets and pyrethrum spray to get rid of passionvine hoppers.

Pear and cherry slugs

The tiny, black, sluglike grubs known as pear and cherry slugs appear on the leaves of flourishing plum, pear and cherry trees, both fruiting and ornamental, in late spring and summer. They also affect hawthorns, medlars and a few other ornamental shrubs.

One suggestion for the eradication of pear and cherry slugs on trees is to dust the leaves with lime in early summer.

Red spider mites

Tiny red spider mites occur in huge numbers with warm, dry weather. Foliage misting or a spray of a strong, soapy solution, particularly to the undersides of leaves where they gather, disturbs them. Alternatively, you can use sulphur dust.

Scale

The presence of scale is often indicated by a procession of ants along the trunk or stems of plants. The ants are there because they feed on scale secretions. They do not eat the scale – it is up to us to cope with them. As well, you may see a black, sooty mould on leaves and stems, which is a fungus that grows on the honeydew produced by the scale. You will spot the scale themselves – which are black, white, red or brown and have a protective shell – on leaves (particularly the undersides) and stems.

If there are not too many scale, remove them with a cloth soaked in a solution of household detergent. A bucket of soapy water can be tipped over small infected plants. In severe cases, white oil can be sprayed over infected areas, smothering the scale.

Snails and slugs

Snails and slugs work to destroy garden plants mostly at night or after rain. If you make a nightly circuit of the garden, with a torch or the garden lights on, you can catch these prolific garden pests in the act and remove them for squashing underfoot. Also, an effective snail bait is obtainable. Use it around young seedlings and precious plants, otherwise you will have to keep watch all night, but be careful when cats and dogs are about because the bait can kill them. Put the pellets in a narrow-necked container sunk in the ground or placed on its side so that only snails and slugs can get at them. Another way to deal with snails and slugs is to offer them a saucer or two of beer, sinking the saucer in the ground.

TOP Check plants regularly for leaf-eating caterpillars, such as the painted apple moth caterpillar. The damage they cause can be quite dramatic.

BOTTOM Thrips are tiny, sap-sucking creatures that cause leaf destruction to a wide range of plants from callistemons to roses.

Thrips

Thrips are minute flies that look like 2-millimetre-long pieces of hair. They are found on rose blooms, carnations, gladioli, onion foliage and some ornamental shrubs. Repeated hosings can help combat them. Thrips thrive in the heat and are largely controlled by the weather if you can stay your hand from spraying.

Webbing caterpillars

You will notice the round, matted webs of webbing caterpillars among the foliage of tea trees and other native shrubs and occasionally on exotic shrubs. Probably the best way of dealing with them is to prune out the matted foliage and webs so that new growth can begin. Watch susceptible plants carefully to catch new attacks early.

Whiteflies

Tiny, elusive whiteflies suck the sap of healthy leaves in summer, leaving them yellow and mottled. Overhead watering from a hose or watering system disturbs them, making them less likely to lay their eggs on your plants. Use pyrethrum spray weekly, or even three or four times a week, on infected areas. Pyrethrum is as successful as more toxic sprays, but does little harm to the tiny wasp that lives on the eggs of whiteflies.

NON-TOXIC AND LOW-TOXIC PESTICIDES AND FUNGICIDES

Always follow the instructions provided when using commercial pesticides and fungicides.

Bordeaux powder General fungicide used for powdery mildew, rot in stone fruit, curly leaf and diseases in bark; considered only mildly toxic at normal spray strength, and vegetables can be used within a few days of treatment but should be washed.

Garlic Natural product, non-toxic to humans, that deters many damaging insects on contact, but needs to be sprayed regularly to be effective.

Lime sulphur Used for control of scale insects and fungal diseases, such as powdery mildew, but is not compatible with many other pesticides; can burn leaves if used when plant is actively growing and, although non-toxic, can irritate skin.

Proprietary fungicides Used for many foliage diseases, such as powdery mildew, black spot and rust, but can irritate skin and respiratory tract.

Pyrethrum Natural product, extracted from the pyrethrum flower, that is non-toxic to humans (though not to be freely inhaled), but toxic to fish, so cover ponds during spraying and for a couple of hours afterwards.

White oil Petroleum-based product that smothers scale insects.

Spitfire caterpillars are found mainly on gum trees. They look more harmful than they are.

DEALING WITH DISEASES

Watchfulness and anticipation are major weapons in overcoming plant diseases. Some plants are more susceptible to fungi and viruses than others, and problems are likely to occur when plants are grown in unsuitable soils or aspects. Some may die, others will show their resentment by contracting disease. For instance, a 'Lorraine Lee' rose will most likely get mildew if planted against a wall where there's no free passage of air. Callistemons, on the other hand, will grow healthily in a wide range of soils and sites. Knowing the special needs of plants and choosing plants not prone to disease in your locality are further weapons.

COMMON DISEASES AND WHAT TO DO

The table on the preceding page and the following discussion of common diseases suggest ways of combating plant ailments.

Black spot

You may notice black spots, with surrounding yellow patches, on your rose leaves late in the flowering season, mid-summer to autumn. Infected leaves can be pulled off, although they will dry and fall of themselves. Gather them up and dispose of them in the rubbish bin or burn them because they harbour the spores of next year's brood. However, a little black spot late in the season is preferable to the use of a systemic fungicide, such as a triforine-based rose spray.

Black spot flourishes in humid conditions; roses are seldom troubled by it in dry climates. If a certain rose is continually plagued by this fungal disease in your garden year after year, you may prefer to remove the plant and use a less disease-prone type, such as 'Sarah van Fleet' or 'Iceberg'.

Collar rot

Collar rot is a fungal disease that commonly affects the trunk bark of citrus, at ground level. The bark flakes and the wood rots, resulting in the tree losing vigour as nutritional processes are disrupted.

To treat, the diseased area should be scraped away and the clean wood beneath painted with a paste made from Bordeaux powder. When planting citrus, make sure the graft union is well above the surface of the soil. Other precautionary measures are to keep the trunk surface free from mulch and to encourage air circulation under the tree canopy. Poor drainage increases susceptibility. Remember, too, that citrus require good drainage.

Curly leaf

The leaves of peaches and nectarines (*Prunus persica*) can become blistered and curled due to the curly leaf fungus. A Bordeaux spray at precisely the time that flower buds are showing colour should control this.

Damping off

Damping off is a fungal disease that can cause tiny seedlings to fall over and die. Thin seedlings out early to avoid overcrowding and, to reduce favourable conditions for the disease, avoid watering them late in the day. Spray affected seedlings with a fungicide.

Damping off in lawns can be avoided by using a fertiliser high in phosphorus, rather than nitrogen, and by not over-watering.

In humid weather, fungal diseases, such as black spot, can be prevalent.

The foliage of peaches and nectarines (*Pumila persica*) often blisters and curls due to curly leaf fungus. The leaves eventually fall off.

Grey powdery mildew occurs on leaves in humid weather.

Mildew

Powdery mildew – an ashlike film – blotches the leaves and sometimes the buds of roses and crêpe myrtles (*Lagerstroemia indica*) in particular, if drainage is not efficient enough for the plant or there is insufficient sun. Treat this fungal disease with sulphur dust or a Bordeaux mixture.

Downy mildew, which shows as tufted spots of grey under a leaf or near leaf nodes, needs stronger treatment. A Bordeaux mixture may control it, but proprietary fungicides are more powerful.

Petal blight

Often azaleas, particularly frilly hybrid types, will be about to unfold their fat, coloured buds when instead they shrivel and rot, though they remain sadly clinging to the plants. Petal blight is the work of a fungus and should be treated with a contact fungicide, sprayed weekly while buds are showing colour and applied also during the flowering season, after rain. As well, the surrounding ground should be sprayed to kill spore-carrying toadstools, which are part of the cycle of petal blight. Remove all diseased petals and put them in the rubbish bin.

Rust

The orange-gold spots of rust form on the foliage of pelargoniums, fuchsias, English daisies (*Bellis perennis*), calendulas and snapdragons (*Antirrhinum*). Where feasible, infected leaves should be pulled off and burnt; alternatively, spray with a fungicide. In cases of extreme infection, the entire plant should be pulled up and burnt, as well. A pelargonium pruned back to healthy shoots near the ground in late autumn is far less likely to contract rust than one thought to be too beautiful to touch and left unpruned through winter.

WATERING IS CARING

Watering can be a relaxing exercise in the garden and provides a good time to observe what your plants are doing. All plants need water. It's shameful to let a plant wilt or die.

Many of the plants around us are from other countries and are accustomed to a more generous water supply than are Australian natives. However, while plants from the more arid areas of Australia have the capacity to survive lengthy periods without rain, not all Australian plants have such an inbuilt survival device.

Plants, like animals, have a high water content. They take water up from the soil through their roots. Some is used to keep the plant cells functioning properly, and insufficient water will cause wilting. Some is lost through evaporation from the leaves – a form of temperature control called transpiration. And some is used by the leaves to manufacture sugar sap to help in the development of shoots and leaves and the formation of flowers, fruits, seeds, wood and bark.

Plants particularly need water during their growing season. In spring, it is important for them to have a steady water supply to encourage flowering and fruiting. In summer, watering well will reduce the plants' stress. Water thoroughly; it is a waste of time to give plants a light sprinkle, because this causes shallow roots to develop, which become over-dependent on surface water. Watering is best done in the morning before the heat of the day. Water when the top few centimetres of your soil are dry, and soak the ground thoroughly enough to last a few days. You can check the water's penetration of the soil by digging with a trowel to a depth of 10 centimetres or so.

Any plants that have been transplanted or newly planted need immediate watering and the soil must not be allowed to dry out until the roots are established. Young seedlings need frequent waterings as do seeds, which need to be kept constantly moist until germination.

Try to understand the individual water requirements of the plants in your garden. Keep a weather-eye on the amount of water they are receiving naturally to establish how much you should be supplementing it, bearing in mind not to over-water. This applies whether you have an automatic sprinkler or a manual system or water by hand.

SYSTEMS OF WATERING

There are various methods of watering gardens. A watering can allows you to control closely the flow of water to pot plants and delicate plants, and to measure and apply liquid manure accurately. Hoses of suitable lengths can be fitted with a range of appliances; there are hand-held sprays, including finely misting ones, and fan-shaped spikes and sprinklers that give a 360-degree coverage – some with devices for restricting the spray to part of the full circle.

Hoses allow you a fairly exacting control over the amount of water your plants in different areas receive. Because you are actively involved in the watering programme, you are in your garden more and better able to notice the early stages of insect invasion, and any changes in the condition of your plants due to soil deficiencies or disease. Of course, the operating of hoses is time consuming. Care must be taken not to drag a hose across the corners of garden beds: pegs or carefully placed rocks can be used to protect them. Then there is the problem of storage. A neat way to store a hose when it is not in use is a hose arm, screwed to a house wall or set on a garden post. In either case it should be completely or partially concealed, while remaining accessible. Hose reels placed about a garden are not attractive and sometimes jump around, displaying a mind of their own.

There is a range of systems consisting of poly-tubing or PVC pipes, usually laid in the soil, and fittings or heads set at intervals. The fittings may provide a drip, trickle or spray. A spray system can have micro-fittings for a fine spray, macro-fittings for a stronger spray or two separate systems to meet the needs of individual plants and garden spaces. Sometimes inverted mister or sprinkler systems are installed in ferneries, shadehouses, igloos and glasshouses.

Poly-tubing systems can be easily installed by garden owners or landscapers. They may be operated by a simple time switch started manually but turned off automatically after the requisite period. Alternatively, they can be fitted with a battery-operated computer, programmed to start and finish at set times: daily, every few days or weekly. These systems are best suited to small or average-sized suburban gardens and require a reasonably good water pressure to function efficiently. A fully automatic system of a more complex nature, with a system of solenoid valves and operated by computer, allows the sequential watering of a large garden. It can be installed by an irrigation specialist or a handyperson.

POP-UP SPRINKLERS FOR A LAWN

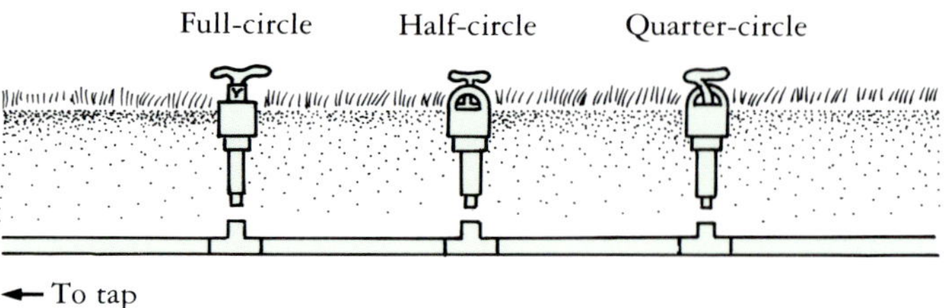

DRIP SYSTEM

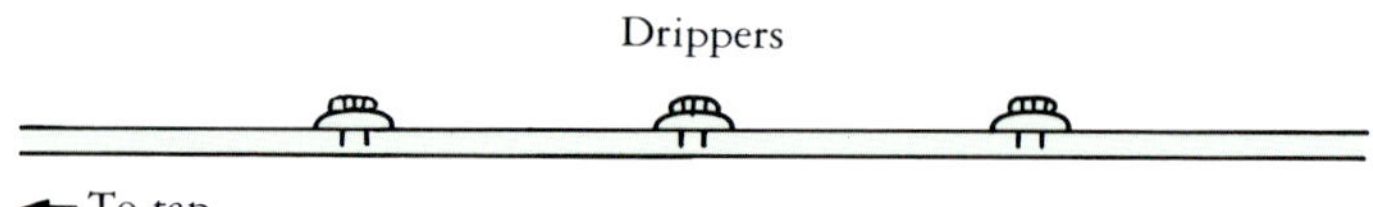

SPRINKLER SYSTEM FOR GARDEN OR LAWN

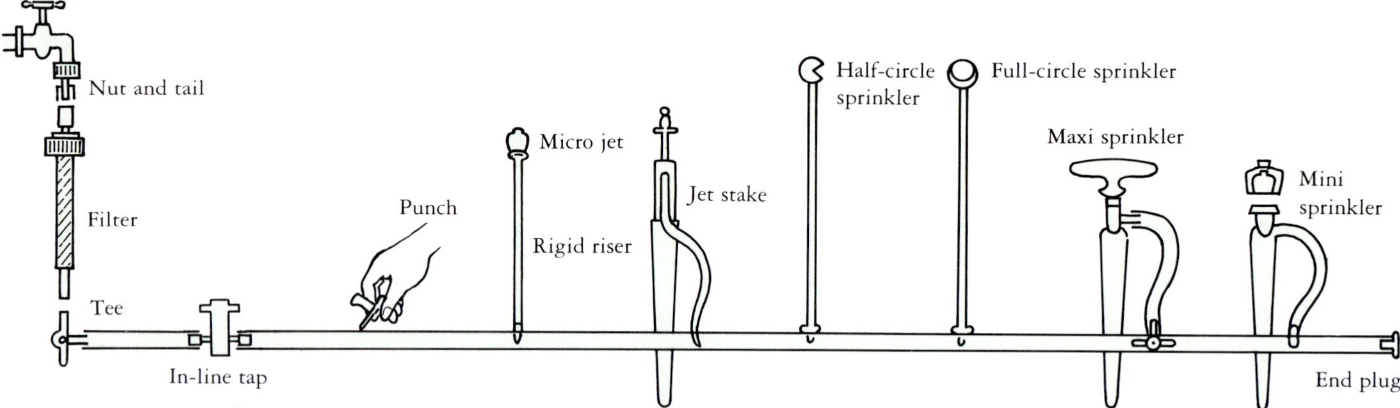

ABOVE These are the types of equipment needed for simple watering systems in different parts of the garden.

LEFT For flourishing plants and lawn regular watering is needed in dry weather.

REGULAR AND SPECIAL CARE

Pruning and fertilising are tasks that need to be carried out in gardens at specific times. Just how relevant they are depends on the nature of each garden. However, for most gardens it certainly helps to have a working knowledge of both pruning and fertilising to call on from time to time, and for some gardens a proper understanding is essential.

PRUNING

Some gardeners are most respectful of the science and art of pruning and inclined not to do it, or to get an expert in. Others, with little knowledge and even less artistic appreciation, are ears back and into it. We should aim for the middle way of mastering the fundamentals of pruning and becoming competent and comfortable with the job. Most of it is common sense.

Pruning is important for the well-being of many plants. The removal of any diseased wood allows them to channel their resources into healthy growth. The seasonal pruning of many plants stimulates and encourages new, vigorous growth and improved flowering and fruiting. Sometimes plants are pruned to improve their shape and contribution to a garden picture, and sometimes they need to be pruned because they have spread beyond their allotted space.

Even the loveliest gardens can grow unruly. Gardens need careful weeding and judicious pruning to ensure their beauty in the following season.

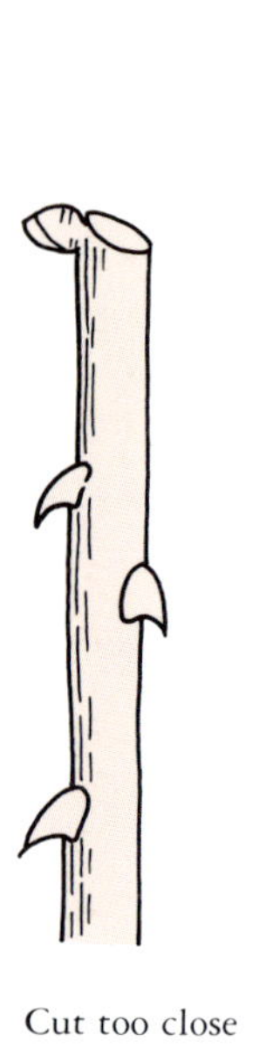

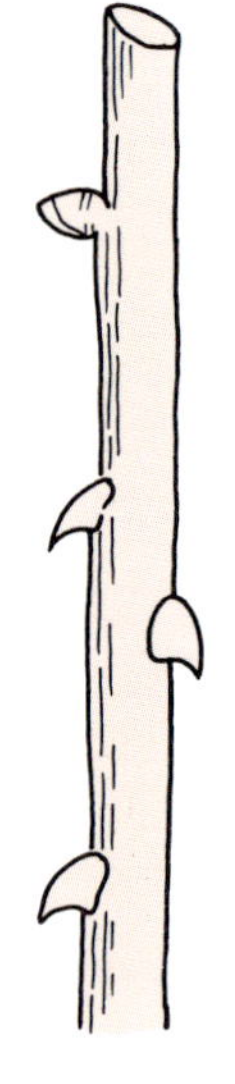

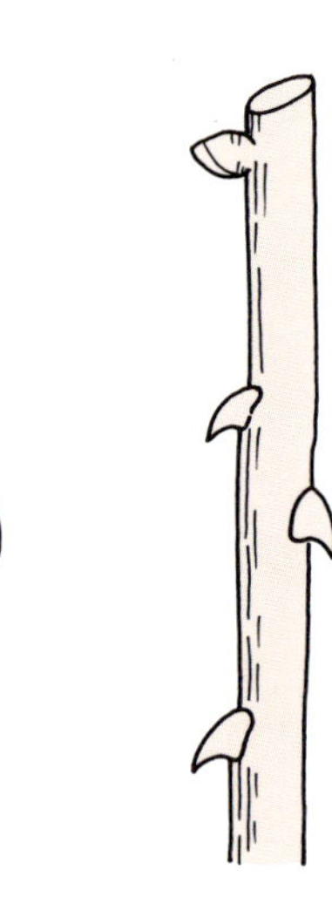

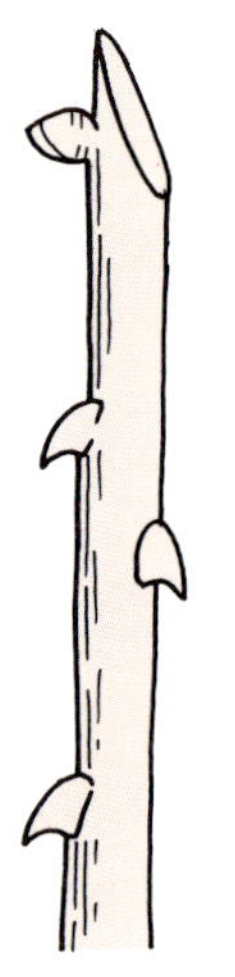

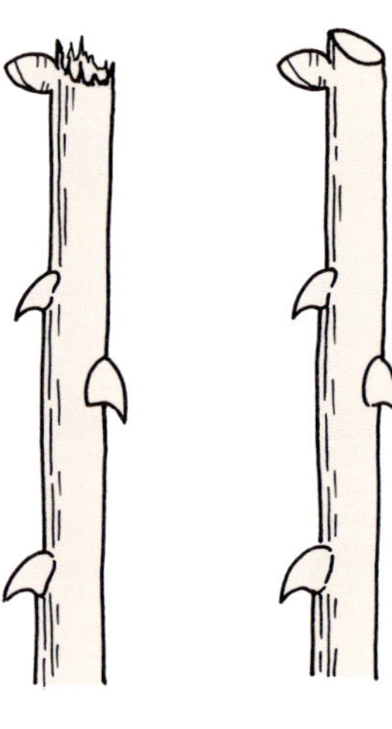

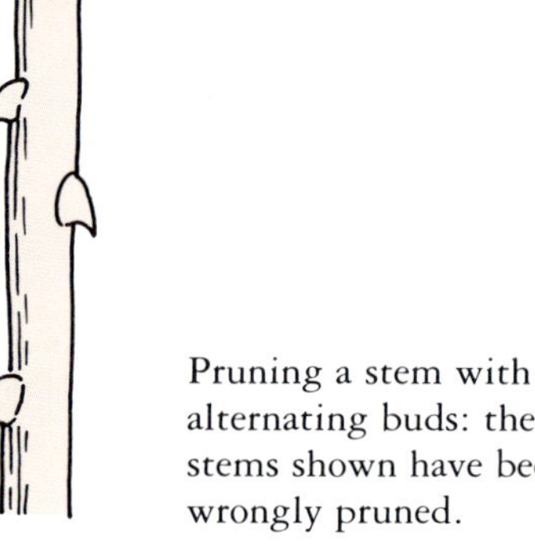

Pruning a stem with alternating buds: the first five stems shown have been wrongly pruned.

Principles of pruning

With the exception of the elimination of an entire branch or stem because it is in the way, not needed, dead or diseased, pruning always requires a cut made at a point just above a shoot or the place where a shoot might reasonably appear. You'll notice some shoots grow in pairs along a stem or branch. In this case the cut is made straight across, above a pair of healthy shoots or potential shoots. If shoots alternate along a stem, the cut is made diagonally and just above an outward-facing node from which a shoot is almost certain to appear. This encourages growth to occur outwards.

An entire branch that has to be removed should be taken off so that no bark of the trunk is harmed, and just sufficient of the limb bark – about 4 centimetres of a big branch – is left to enable healing and the formation of scar tissue over the wound. Scaled down, the same principle applies to any cut made on a branch or side stem. To leave a lot of stem above the outward-facing node will only risk disease, and to intrude into the trunk or main stem is deleterious to the whole plant.

Shrubs and some trees need seasonal pruning. Corrective pruning, the removal of diseased limbs and overgrown branches and general cleaning out can be done whenever the need arises, but never do a rushed pruning job. As well, small in-between pruning tasks beckon the sensitive gardener all year round. Whatever the time of year, it is best to prune when the sun is shining because this encourages quick healing. As well it makes for a more enjoyable time in the garden.

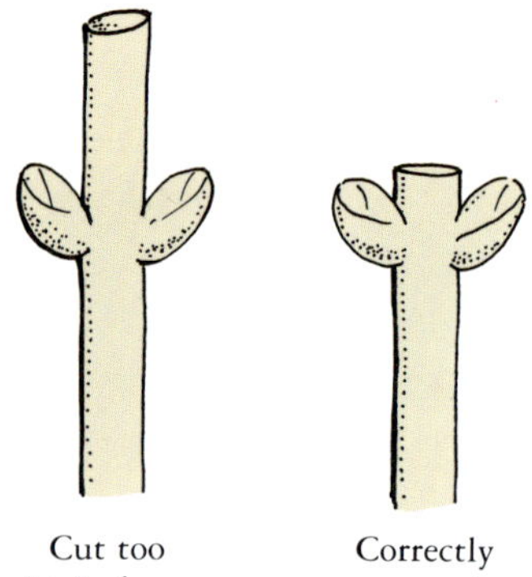

The correct way to prune a stem with bilateral buds is shown on the right.

Seasonal pruning

Roses are usually pruned in the last week of June and the first week of July. Of course you do not need to be precise, but adhering to this rule is a useful discipline. Prune roses to keep the shape of the plants and to allow good air circulation in the centre. Remove all dead or diseased wood, and cut all remaining canes back by at least one-third. Select a strong, outward-facing bud, and cut at a slant just above it. Climbing roses can be pruned after they flower, taking off plenty of newly flowered wood so that new canes will develop.

The first pruning of a deciduous fruit tree should be when it is newly planted. Cut the year's stems back hard to within 25 centimetres of where the tree branches. Try to keep your fruit tree branching low to the ground so that the trunk is only 30–45 centimetres high. In later years keep the branches at an angle of 45 degrees so that the tree's centre is open to the air and sun. Old, neglected deciduous fruit trees, such as apples (*Malus pumila*) and pears (*Pyrus communis*), need to have one-third of their branches cut hard back every three years. Side shoots should be shortened back to the last three or four buds and long growths lightly shortened. Grape vines (*Vitis*) should be pruned hard; cut back most of the previous year's growth to leave short spurs consisting of two or three buds. Kiwi fruit (*Actinidia chinensis*) should be cut back in early winter, well before the sap starts to run; cut back the fruiting wood to a few buds. Citrus trees can be pruned, if they look neglected, in early spring once the danger of frost is over. Evergreen fruit trees, such as feijoas (*Feijoa sellowiana*) and loquats (*Eriobotrya japonica*), need little pruning in their lifetime apart from an occasional shaping.

Spring-flowering deciduous shrubs, such as *Viburnum* × *burkwoodii*, spiraeas and philadelphus, flower on wood formed in the previous year, so prune them after flowering to give buds for the following spring a chance. Clean out all the old canes. Summer-flowering shrubs and small trees, such as hydrangeas, hibiscus and crêpe myrtles, flower on wood produced in the same growing season, so prune them in late winter to encourage new buds and growth, but make sure it is after the risk of frosts is over. It is not necessary to prune evergreen shrubs annually. If they become leggy or too large for their allotted space, they can be shortened back to a point above a node. The best time for this is after flowering.

Maintenance pruning

Most plants in the garden need corrective pruning to remove dead, damaged or diseased wood, branches that are crossing and any suckering growth.

Many plants should be 'picture pruned' to reveal their colourful and decorative bark and their beautiful natural form. For example, branches of a Japanese maple (*Acer palmatum*) can be selectively pruned to reveal its elegant structure and contribute to the overall garden picture. Limbing out – the removal of a tree's lower branches – reveals the trunk and raises the canopy.

Australian plants require considerable maintenance pruning. In gardens they tend to grow quickly, often becoming long and lank, whereas in natural stands they are kept in check by neighbouring plants. Cut them back after flowering – whatever the season – and whenever they start to straggle. By pruning and encouraging more vigorous, purposeful growth, you will ensure that your Australian plants live longer in your garden.

Many plants need pruning to encourage new growth. An overgrown plant that has been flowering poorly or fruiting badly will be revitalised. Pinching back – the removal of a terminal bud or a growth point by hand – produces bushiness, prevents lank growth and improves the growth of herbs, annuals and perennials. Fuchsias respond well if pinched back regularly in spring.

Fruit trees, shade trees and ornamental shrubs, in particular, often need thinning out. This means opening them up to the air and light.

Root-pruning is used to prepare plants, especially larger ones, for transplanting. A season before transplanting, dig a circle around the plant, just beyond the main roots, leaving them intact. This encourages new roots to grow more compactly, making it easier for the plant to be moved.

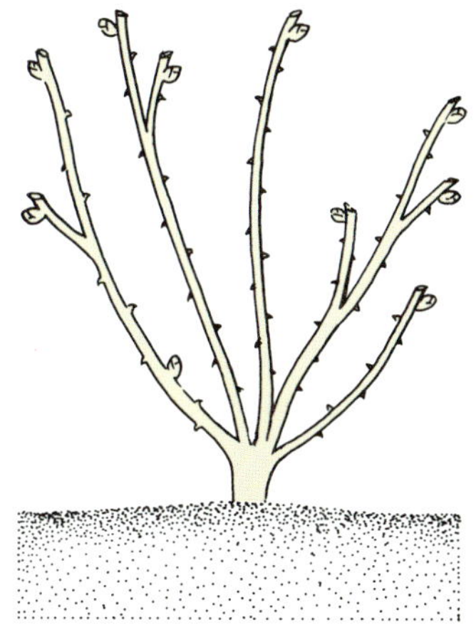

To prune a rose, remove dead or diseased branches and ones that cross each other, so that air can circulate in the middle of the bush. When shaping a rose bush, always prune the stems to an outward-facing bud.

FEEDING PLANTS

Nutrients are needed to sustain healthy plants; without them deficiencies result. Feeding also encourages plants to perform well, to produce bigger, more luxuriant flowers for longer periods and larger, healthier leaves. Bigger, brighter fruit and vegetables are another result. When plants are uprooted or planted in non-indigenous areas their diet may need to be supplemented. The signs of nutrient deficiencies and their remedies are given in the accompanying table.

PLANT DEFICIENCIES

NUTRIENT INVOLVED	PLANT SIGNALS	SUPPLEMENTS
Nitrogen (N)	Leaf yellowing, stunted growth, weak stems	Humus or compost, horse or sheep manure, blood and bone, sulphate of ammonia
Phosphorus (P)	Purplish leaves, stunted growth, poor yield of fruit and seeds	Poultry or horse manure
Potassium (K)	Scorching or mottling at leaf edges, browning of growing tips, poorly coloured flowers and fruits	Wood ash or potassium sulphate
Calcium (Ca)	Distortion of young leaves, ragged leaf edges, stunted root system	Gypsum or lime (lime will alter the pH of soil, increasing alkalinity)
Magnesium (Mg)	Leaf yellowing (of older leaves first), premature leaf fall	Epsom salts (magnesium sulphate): 1 tablespoon in water per square metre
Iron (Fe)	Leaf yellowing, though veins often remain green	Sulphate of iron or iron chelates

Just like people, plants have a wide variety of needs and tastes, and as gardeners we have to know how often we should feed plants for the best results and what with. Plant food, usually called fertiliser, comes in two ways – as organic (or natural) fertiliser and as inorganic (synthetic or chemical) food.

Organic fertilisers

Organic fertilisers include compost, seaweed, well-rotted cow, horse or sheep manure, bought blood and bone, and leaf mould. They are gentle and slow to release their nutrients and therefore do not burn the plants. They improve the soil texture as they decompose. Compost, because of its mildness and promotion of general well-being in all plants, can be applied throughout the year. Fowl manure in particular, but any animal manure, can be too strong unless it is well rotted.

Inorganic fertilisers

Inorganic fertilisers come in various forms: as liquids, water-soluble powders and granules. Some are quick releasing and, particularly the water-soluble ones, are soon absorbed by the plant. Other inorganic fertilisers are slow releasing, enabling the chemical nutrients to be taken up and used by growing plants over a period. Inorganic fertilisers do not improve the soil structure and soon leach out of soils, particularly sandy soils, so their effect is for a limited period.

Each major chemical item is listed on the packet. The type of inorganic fertiliser you buy should be appropriate for the needs of your particular plants. Commercial inorganic fertilisers are available as complete fertilisers, predominantly containing nitrogen (N), phosphorus (P) and potassium (K), or as specific fertilisers for plants, such as roses, camellias and citrus, that have particular likes and dislikes. The proportions of nitrogen, phosphorus and potassium are always stated on the packet of commercial complete fertilisers. Using a balanced commercial fertiliser is safer than applying these three nutrients individually. Remember always to follow package directions and never to overdo chemical fertilisers.

Always apply chemical fertilisers to damp soil. Water the soil again, when work is complete, to partially dissolve the fertiliser and reduce its strength.

WHAT AND WHEN TO FEED

Annuals These can be planted in a soil that has had a complete fertiliser, containing a high potassium content, dug into it about six weeks beforehand; or they can be given a very light dressing of such a fertiliser, well watered in, at planting time. Apply liquid manure from a watering can every three or four weeks as the annuals grow.

Australian native plants These do not need a rich diet, and if you plant them with a little slow-release fertiliser for a good start that's almost enough. Just a sprinkling of blood and bone in spring provides a supply of the nutrients they would have received in the wild, so encouraging healthy growth. Do not use other fertilisers or you could kill them.

Bulbs At planting time feed bulbs with a prepared food or a dressing of bone meal or blood and bone – just sprinkle it over moistened soil, then water it in. Feed the bulbs again as their leaves die down, when they are making bulb growth for the next year's flowers.

Citrus It is usual to feed citrus twice yearly with a complete fertiliser, giving a large dose in early spring and a summer supplement in late January or early February.

Deciduous flowering shrubs In early spring a complete fertiliser high in phosphorus will encourage next season's flowers. Evergreen shrubs such as daphnes, azaleas, pieris, kalmia, camellias and rhododendrons need a complete fertiliser high in potash, as well as organic fertilisers and compost; a special preparation is commercially available.

Fruit trees In early spring, and again after flowering, fruit trees should be given a complete fertiliser.

Herbs These easy-to-grow plants don't need fertiliser, just an application of compost every now and then. Too much fertiliser means less-fragrant leaves.

Perennials Different perennials have different requirements, but, if you are unable to research these and cater for them, add compost and blood and bone when the bed is prepared. Add a slow-release fertiliser at the time of planting. Each spring add a dressing of cow manure and blood and bone, and keep a good layer of compost round them throughout the year.

Roses Given a good winter feed, roses will reward you with plenty of blooms. After pruning in June or July, add horse, sheep or cow manure, blood and bone or a commercial rose food. You can add manure and compost whenever a flush of blooms finishes; however, the most important supplementary feeding time is at the end of January, following a light pruning. Give a commercial rose food or an organic fertiliser at this time. Roses are big feeders – but keep fertilisers and compost away from their trunks to avoid heat damage.

Trees Young trees, in particular, will benefit from a dressing of fertiliser high in nitrogen and a mulch of compost and cow manure. It is important not to ignore mature trees, though, and, if it is feasible, a mulch of compost will be appreciated where there would otherwise be only bare earth over the roots. Unfortunately, sometimes obsessional gardeners and strong winds tidy away the fallen leaves that trees offer as their own natural compost.

Vegetables The ground can be prepared with a complete fertiliser or manure before planting time, or these constituents can be gently watered in at planting time should you be running late. Use liquid fertilisers after you have transplanted seedlings and as leafy vegetables develop. As they are growing, side dress rooting and fruiting vegetables with a fertiliser high in phosphorus, and leafy crops with a nitrogenous fertiliser.

A DAY IN THE GARDEN

A garden needs regular, overall care, which can be given as often as you want to, or once a fortnight if you need to programme it into a busy schedule. There are lawns to be mown, beds to be weeded, paths to be swept, intrusive plants and branches to be taken back to within acceptable limits and plants to be watered.

Good tools are important for pleasurable and efficient gardening – no old, rusty blades and splintered handles! Make sure each implement is well designed for comfort and balance. You'll need sharp secateurs for pruning; a hand fork and a long-handled fork for weeding; a stout spade for digging (preferably with the longest handle available to save bending your back); long-handled secateurs and a pruning saw for the larger pruning jobs; a cane rake and straw broom for sweeping; a mower, if you have a lawn; a barrow; bins; and any pet tool that you like to use – even an old dessertspoon may suit your needs.

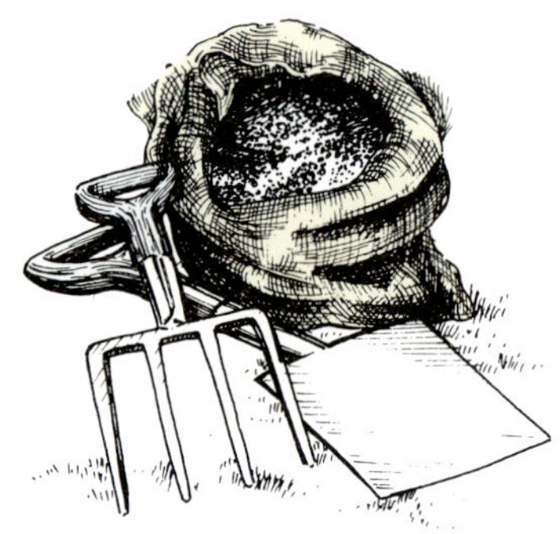

There's much to be said for a day in the garden – for the luxury of time to wander round inspecting and time to set about doing the tasks. Even if you've thought you won't like the hours of chores that have to be done, you may be surprised to find yourself enjoying the day.

A day's work indoors, cleaning and beautifying, can be pleasing, but after a week's wear and tear the house will be in need of touching up again. Out of doors you continue to reap the rewards of your efforts. Watch the seedlings and bulbs you once planted come into flower. See the tree you pruned and styled to lean across water combine with the long, green fronds of the ferns you shifted, to become the perfect setting for your pond. Investments indeed. Of course there's the day-to-day maintenance along the way, but, if you know what you are doing, this is varied, interesting and directed towards the ultimate goal of a lovely garden.

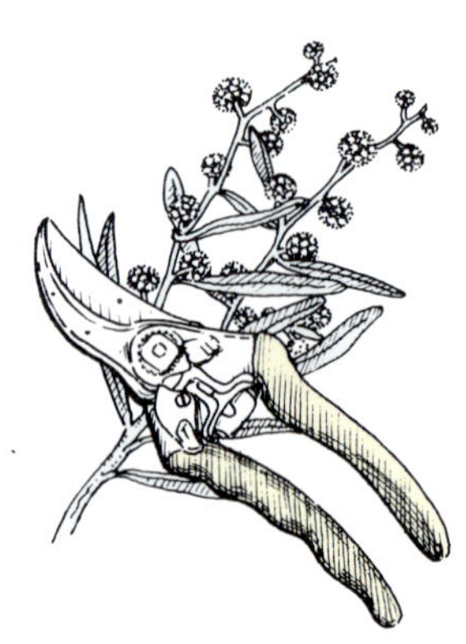

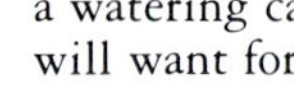

Gloves, forks, secateurs, fertiliser, a wheelbarrow, a watering can and things to plant – these are what you will want for a happy day in the garden.

5/ Garden Features

The area of garden features holds more traps and dangers than any other aspect of garden making. The reason for this is that often a garden is perfectly all right or even lovelier without embellishment.

To the basic layout or bones of your garden you will probably want to add various features, according to your needs and inclinations. Understanding how to select and site these additions is critical to their success. Garden additions fall into three categories – functional, ornamental and recreational – but at all times their aesthetic qualities must be considered.

Fences, walls, screens and pergolas, for example, fulfil the important outdoor functions of creating privacy, keeping out stray animals (and perhaps stray people) and giving shelter from sun and wind; they also offer decorative opportunities. Walls and fences, with their accompanying gates, are the outer clothing of our gardens, a way of wrapping up our houses and gardens – and of presenting our properties to the outside world. Screens and pergolas may be built primarily for protection from the weather, but it is important that their materials and style suit their surroundings. Some strongly built stone walls and pergolas with stone pillars are integral parts of the garden's bones, but these are exceptions. Most modern walls and pergolas are constructed of lighter materials, such as timber, and essentially qualify as garden features.

Sometimes a garden picture can be made more special using a decorative piece, such as a fountain, a little pond, a small statue or a modern sculpture in metal, concrete or even fibreglass. Some ornamental features, such as a pretty birdbath, a well-chosen garden light or a garden seat set in a shrubby alcove, achieve a very equitable balance of function and aesthetics.

Good judgement, common sense and restraint: these are the constants in deciding on the style, number, proportion, size and placing of garden additions.

Water enhances any garden. Here, bridged by a bluestone slab, it links a terrace to a lawn covered in fallen jacaranda flowers.

MAIL
6

DRESSING UP THE BOUNDARIES

Most people favour a boundary structure for the reasons already mentioned, and because it is conventional to have them. However, in many suburban neighbourhoods, structures along the front boundaries of properties are discouraged, giving the street a very open, free appearance and directing attention beyond, into the garden. Side walls and fences and garages then take on the responsibility for security.

If you live in such a suburb, you have the challenge of creating an interesting fenceless garden to suit your house. You will also need to watch for intrusive litter and perhaps build some safeguards against the curious or playful dogs that will visit. Try rocky outcrops under shrubs, and grow hardy plants and even a prickly plant or two – most dogs soon learn to leave them alone. You may like the notion of no front boundary structure, even if there is not a neighbourhood precedent; if so, your decision will result in quite a saving because walls and fences are not cheap.

CHOOSING A FENCE OR WALL

There are several important points to be considered when you are choosing a fence or wall: height, material, style and shape. It is important to check local council regulations before building a fence or wall. There may be a policy about height and materials, and it is usually necessary to obtain a permit to construct a masonry wall.

Height

How high your fence or wall is depends on how you feel about security and privacy and whether you feel that you want a high backdrop to the garden within. You may prefer the friendly feeling that a low fence generates and the idea of sharing your garden with passers-by. If your neighbours' houses and gardens are attractive you have the opportunity to share those pleasant surroundings more closely, while at the same time they can enjoy your garden. Remember, too, that if your front garden is small a high fence may seem claustrophobic and out of proportion; in contrast, a low fence, a tiny garden and perhaps a large pot or two will look pleasing from the street.

The larger environment may also guide your choice of fence height. On looking around your street, you may notice there is a general standard for height and, for that matter, other aspects of wall or fence construction, such as style. By conforming, you contribute to the unity and harmony of the streetscape.

OPPOSITE PAGE The low picket gate and soft plantings of this gateway offer an invitation to enter the garden beyond.

RIGHT A brush fence is not just a garden backdrop, but a handsome feature in itself.

Materials

The material you choose will in fact determine whether you have a wall or a fence. Walls are built of masonry – stone, rock, concrete blocks or brick with a concrete footing. Fences are built of timber or metal or some plant derivative, such as brush, tea tree or cane. They are supported by timber or metal uprights, sometimes set in concrete, with timber or metal bracing.

There is a permanency about masonry structures that only the most sturdy timber fences can remotely approach. Height for height they will probably be much more expensive than timber structures; the materials are costly and the labour intensive. But once built, their maintenance is minimal in comparison with that of a timber fence, which requires regular sanding and painting.

A pleasing unity is achieved when the type of bricks used in the house construction is repeated in the boundary walls. Sometimes cement mouldings are superimposed on a brick wall to create a wall in the Italianate or Georgian style. Sometimes brick walls are rendered and bagged. They may also be painted to match the external paintwork of the house. But remember that once something is painted, it will require regular upkeep.

Fences can be constructed from metal materials, such as galvanised chain mesh, barley-sugar-twist wire, cast iron or aluminium pickets. These have the lasting qualities of most metals. Sometimes some of the original iron lacework, metal pickets and stone pillars of Victorian fences and gates remain. They can be professionally repaired and replicated. Aluminium copies are also available, which have the advantage of being much lighter and cheaper and not so prone to rust.

Timber is a favoured material because timber fences, on the whole, do not cost as much as masonry walls, and timber is a versatile material that lends itself to a range of decorative schemes. Careful choice of timber and correct treatment of end grains and exposed surfaces can considerably lengthen the life of a fence. Posts and the plinth that runs along the base of a fence are best made of a rot-resistant timber, such as jarrah, red gum or treated pine. Other parts of the fence that do not touch the soil can be made of a less durable hardwood timber given a coat of timber preservative or paint to help it last.

Fences of brush are tremendously versatile: they have the capacity to look comfortable with both quite formal gardens and houses and more rustic concepts. It is usual for them to have metal posts set in concrete, with a timber or concrete footing. The brush is kept together with lacings of wire. Wooden gate posts should be set at the gateway if a timber gate is to be used. Brush gates are extremely heavy and quite difficult for children, the infirm and elderly people to manage. To finish off the fence, it is usual to have a timber capping or a rolled-brush thatch wired to the top of the fence. This also preserves the brush. Brush fences are usually erected by expert contractors – construction is not as easy as it looks, though simple brush screens are within the scope of a handyperson. Brush can be brought in small panels from landscape suppliers.

A brush fence extended around the perimeter of a property is expensive but creates a wonderful garden backdrop, and views from side windows are immediately enhanced by the dressiness of such a fence. If your property is small and you can work in with your neighbours, such a project is worth considering. You do not need to coax your plants into quickly covering the fence; instead just a few plants are needed to grace it here and there.

Tea-tree fences are appealing and rustic. A timber frame of posts, plinth and rails is built, to which uniform tea-tree saplings are individually nailed. The result is not a long-lasting fence, due to natural defects and irregularities in the saplings; however, if the framework is sound, it can be maintained by regular patching up.

Side fences usually define the boundary line between adjacent properties. They give privacy and keep domestic animals in or out. They are most likely to be of palings – the traditional boundary fencing – though they can be of brush, iron, aluminium or any other material that neighbours agree upon. If you have a choice of whether the timber posts and rails of a paling fence are on your side or not, think carefully. Rails are handy for climbing on and tying plants against, but you may prefer the sleek look of the other side.

Wooden trellis is a versatile material. The use of *treillage* in the conservatories, arbours and ornate screens of European gardens pre-dates Queen Victoria.

ABOVE A front fence need not form a straight line. This fence allows part of the garden to be shared with the street.

LEFT A span of brick wall can be recessed to create a raised bed filled with hardy flowering plants.

One of its most valuable modern uses is as an upward extension of paling fences along the sides or at the back of properties to block out unattractive views and to achieve privacy. Climbing plants can romp to the top and over and through; more disciplined plants can be tied and trained to a greater height. A timber capping gives trellis a dressier appearance.

Many free-standing Australian houses have internal garden gates set in fences that stretch from a house wall to a side fence. These fences and gates provide security and keep inquisitive animals out and resident children and animals in. They can be made of the front fence material for continuity or from simple vertical boards. Sometimes arched timber overhead, draped in a few strands of a climbing plant, can add charm.

Style

The style of the fence or wall you choose must be in keeping with your house and the mood of your garden. So be careful, for your favourite fence style introduced into a setting that does not suit it just will not look right. This does not mean that you are limited to one type of fence; but, after seeking out fences that might work, you should choose the one that best blends with and complements your property.

For example, if you have a Victorian house you might consider a cast-iron or aluminium fence with a bluestone base, in the traditional manner, a small corrugated iron and timber fence or a picket fence. You will have the fun of choosing post tops – metal caps, acorns, balls, pineapples or just a simply notched post top. But in your enthusiasm make sure that the result is not overdone or funny. Edwardian houses traditionally had timber, red-brick or fine corrugated iron and timber fences. Just as there is a link between house and fence styles, so there should be a link between their degree of grandeur. This applies to any property. The simpler the house, the less ornate the

OPPOSITE PAGE A fine pink kurrajong tree (*Brachychiton populneo-acerifolius*) has been saved by incorporating it in the pleasing design of a modern trellis fence.

RIGHT A local craftsperson made this wrought-iron gate to suit the surrounding garden.

fence should be. Fence ornamentation should never be used to compensate for the plainness of a house.

There are some simple modern fences where the most outstanding feature is the pleasing proportions of the timber, laid in an open-board style vertically or horizontally. Sometimes these have a simple timber capping. Post-and-rail fences have a rural feel and look best in outlying suburbs.

Shape

Fences and walls do not have to be built straight along the boundary. Often a front boundary looks much more exciting with a cut-off corner, creating a small street garden, and perhaps a centrally placed gate or a recessed gateway; or if it takes a right-angled turn to run parallel to the drive, with a gateway half-way down. A small garden on the street side gives a generosity and warmth to a boundary wall or fence and has a softening effect on a high wall, which can be augmented by a creeper on the house side gently falling in a leafy, flowering mass over the top.

Internal fences can be used to section off or divide spaces within a garden to support climbing plants, to screen off utility spaces or to separate a vegetable garden or orchard from other garden areas.

GATES

Gates complete the privacy that a wall or fence provides, allow access and offer an opportunity for decoration. It is important that they work well with the house, just as walls and fences should. They must also fit in with the parent wall or fence, and be of good proportion in relation to the surroundings. They should open logically, offering direct access to the house.

The gates of a property are the climax of the boundary. This does not mean that they should be grand – a display of opulence may be totally out of keeping with the atmosphere of the house and garden – but they should give people some idea of what to expect within. Are they too grim, haughty or uninteresting? Or is their degree of stateliness and dignity utterly appropriate, so that justice has been done to the house and garden beyond?

Even the positioning of a gate along a fence is a project in itself. If there is a view to be framed or a vista noticed, a gateway can offer the means. Above all, although a gate should provide the degree of privacy desired, it must welcome your visitors.

LIVING SCREENS AND WALKS

It is not necessary to have a brick, stone or solid timber fence to give an air of permanency to a garden. The alternative is a planting of trees or shrubs to form a hedge or living screen. The plants do not even need to be set in line but can be arranged in a rather solid group or clumps.

As well, plants can be trained to formally decorate pathways and drives and to form fancy screens more suited to the interior of a garden than the boundary. Nature can be coaxed and coached to perform a variety of roles as garden structures and decorative devices.

HEDGES

Hedges can define areas within a garden, as well as the boundaries, and some of the best are quite fine. They vary greatly in shape, size and type from edgings of low-clipped English box (*Buxus sempervirens*) to superbly cut, towering cypress hedges.

Abelia × *grandiflora* makes a lovely low hedge that looks good kept 1.5–2.5 metres high. With its permanent, green-to-bronze, glossy foliage, white summer flowers, red flower bracts in autumn and robust health, it has earned a spot in many suburban gardens. Mexican orange blossom (*Choisya ternata*) is another reliable, shrubby hedging plant. Sasanqua camellias provide a glossy green hedge on a larger, firmer scale, growing about 3 metres tall eventually. Hedges of sasanqua camellias need not be too hard-clipped – just a periodic shaping and shortening back is required.

A successful hedging plant of recent origin is *Pittosporum tenuifolium* 'James Stirling', which combines quick growth with beauty. These plants can be rough-clipped and their heads trimmed off every so often to keep them at the height required, but left alone they can grow 4–5 metres tall.

Some wonderful effects – a tracery of bare stems in winter, then a great burst of flowers and leaves – can be had by planting massed deciduous shrubs of the same kind, such as weigela, spiraea or mollis azaleas, perhaps even with colours mixed and matched. Flowering quince (*Chaenomeles japonica*) works well planted this way also and can be a fine sight through late winter.

Hedge roses sound and are romantic. Rugosa roses, with their bushy growth, interesting foliage, flowers and autumn colour and hips, make good hedges. The evergreen rose 'Lorraine Lee' has made a classic hedge for many a front garden and, with its willingness to flower in a sunny spot through much of the year, it is still regarded by many as a remarkable plant. Even the primrose-coloured evergreen *Rosa banksiae* 'Lutea' can be clipped and shaped to form a firm hedge though its flowers are borne only in the spring.

WALKS

A walk is created by a symmetrical planting of uniform trees on either side of a path. The trees are trained and trimmed through the years to form an overhead fretwork or arcade. A classic walk consists of laburnums, commonly known as golden chain trees. *Laburnum* × *watereri* can be seen to perfection at the great Bodnant Garden, in northern Wales: the light branches have been tied to a metal framework, and in spring panicles of golden pea flowers hang from them like spun gold. Wisteria also lends itself to this type of treatment, and in some warm European gardens orange trees are formed into a walk.

While the beauty of these concepts is undeniable, the challenge for Australians is to create new concepts, using other plants including some indigenous to Australia. For instance, a wattle walk could be tried, making sure that sufficient space is left between the branches for sunlight to filter through and keep the plants healthy: *Acacia spectabilis* and *A. mearnsii* could be suitable candidates.

PLEACHED SCREENS AND ALLEYS

The technique of pleaching encourages trees to form a living screen, or dense 'suspended hedge', usually revealing bare trunks beneath. Trees of the same type are planted in line at uniform intervals and usually shortened back regularly to avoid branches interfering with each other and to direct growth according to the design. A pleached alley is a walk with pleached trees on either side.

In Europe the most commonly used trees for pleaching are linden trees (*Tilia* species) and hornbeams (*Carpinus* species). But there must be many trees that would lend themselves to this treatment. Be on the lookout for other suitable plants if the concept appeals to you. *Prunus cerasifera* 'Nigra', with its rich plum-coloured foliage and dainty, palest pink blossoms, is one suggestion, or you might experiment with native frangipani (*Hymenosporum flavum*) in a sunny spot.

OPPOSITE PAGE Evergreen banksia roses (*Rosa banksiae* 'Lutea') form a hedge.

RIGHT Lilac (*Syringa vulgaris*) hedges provide living walls.

AVENUES

Avenues are tree-lined approaches, usually formed by one or more rows of trees planted on either side of a drive or a broad path. Lombardy poplars (*Populus nigra* 'Italica') on either side of a broad concrete-slab path leading to the lake of Bolobek, at Macedon, Victoria, are a fine example of an avenue, made even lovelier by the side plantings of pheasant's eye narcissus (*Narcissus poeticus*).

PLACES TO SIT

Sitting areas are important in gardens. They offer spaces for leisure and places from which to appreciate individual characteristics of the garden surroundings. Although a terrace or patio is often built as part of the house or added on later, paving can be set in a pleasant spot anywhere in the garden. The types of paving materials available and how to use them are discussed in Chapter 2.

Timber decking can also be used. Timber decks are really raised sitting areas. They can be incorporated into garden and house design in several ways, usually as an adjunct to the house or pool, but sometimes as a separate feature incorporated into the garden to bridge depressions and cover swampy places.

The need for an adjoining deck should only arise if the floor level of the house is well above ground level or the land slopes away sharply beyond the house wall, making a paved terrace a complex operation; or if the house is built on sandy soil, making a firm base difficult to achieve. An adjoining deck can be a broad balcony commanding a fine view of ocean or valley and hill. It is best if the deck is part of the essential house structure, though it can be a later addition. Purists believe that decks should only be used with timber houses.

It is important to understand the different influences that a deck and a terrace have on a garden. From a deck you look down over the garden, and you may feel somewhat apart from it. A terrace at ground level or a few steps up is more likely to feel part of the garden and so might you, as you sit there. Always consider how the deck or paving you have in mind will look from the garden and how it will blend with your house.

SEATING

As long as there have been gardens, those who cared about them have loved to sit in them. For this, timber benches, stools, turfed couches, elaborate seats carved from stone, and comfortable rocks have been used.

There is something entirely suitable about a bench made from stone or chunky natural timber, surrounded by garden. Benches are visually appealing, but they are not the most comfortable of seats. However, they can be used as a place on which to perch for a few minutes and leave tools and equipment, glasses and mugs. Be careful if you choose a classical bench of moulded concrete. Some are rather elaborate and only suitable for traditional formal gardens.

OPPOSITE PAGE A simple timber seat looks right in an informal garden.

OUTDOOR FURNITURE

When it comes to sitting at length, reading or chatting, you need seats with backs. The traditional slatted park seat is usually light (unless you get an original cast-iron-framed one), not too dear and very comfortable. But make sure it suits your garden.

There is a host of outdoor furniture to choose from. You should be quite sure of the look you are after when you choose pieces. Some are bright, cheery and obvious and look best near recreational areas, such as a pool or tennis court, rather than in places where the natural colours of the garden and seasonal changes are of most importance. In these latter spots furniture that is more low key and merges discreetly with the backdrop of your house or garden may be more appropriate.

Be careful if you choose teak or western red cedar chairs. Some of them are extremely heavy and ornate – far too gross to be beautiful in many gardens. If you choose a solid-looking table, you might consider fold-away directors' chairs to complete your table setting. Always check that the furniture you choose can be safely left outdoors.

RIGHT Light folding chairs that can be moved from sunny to shady spots and stored away are ideal for a courtyard.

GARDEN ORNAMENT

Many beautiful garden effects are dearly won: entirely happy combinations of colour, texture and seasonal transition, or the first flowers of a rare magnolia after fifteen years of waiting. Perhaps this is why many people let their hair down when it comes to garden ornaments; the quick transformation ornamentation achieves in a garden is very enticing. Make sure that you hasten slowly, paying due attention to the size and proportions of your garden spaces and to individuality, appropriateness and restraint. You will enjoy the result of careful forethought and wise selection, without a lingering concern that perhaps your statue does not suit your garden's style, your pots are too large or your metal sculpture is in the wrong place.

STATUES

Classical statues have a place in traditional gardens, whether these are large or small, formal courtyards or merely an alcove in a side garden, seen from a window.

Various moulded-concrete statues are available commercially, but should be chosen with great care because they are with you for a long time after you have acquired them. The same applies to original pieces, whose quality varies. A good reproduction of a famous original may be preferable to a lesser original work. When you are considering a statue (or any sculpture), the most important criterion is that you like it. It must be affordable, also. Look closely at a statue to see if there is anything unappealing about it – crudely executed eyes, an awkward nose, unconvincing hands or, in a reproduction, a distracting mould line. Take time to find one that really endears itself to you because of its grace, strength, humility or other qualities. There are many more ways to fill a garden space than with an indifferent statue.

Remember that a white statue makes a harsh contrast in a garden, in comparison with the sandstone or terracotta colour of many cast pieces. Some statues have an instant ancient quality created by an antique finish; however, in time untreated concrete pieces in shady places will acquire an appearance of antiquity for lichens and mosses will grow on them. Smear statues with yoghurt, if you can bear it, for a quicker result.

Not all moulded concrete statues are of classical inspiration. Many are of children, animals or birds, particularly ducks. They are appealing in the gardens of contemporary houses.

With statues of all kinds there is safety in lack of numbers. Be moderate – even when you have installed them to amuse the grandchildren! Statues are at their best when partially obscured, hidden in shrubberies along walks so that visitors come upon them quite suddenly, or placed in gloomy spots under trees. They are also ideal used as part of the vista at the end of a path. In all these instances their influence is strong but does not dominate.

LEFT A little statue is in keeping with a small, formal pond.

OPPOSITE PAGE A fine statue requires simple plantings that complement rather than compete.

OTHER SCULPTURES

There is an endless range of lovely objects that you can use to add interest to your garden. Try to be aware of the decorative possibilities of anything you see.

Sundials

As with all ornamentation, different styles of sundial are appropriate for different styles of garden. Sundials do not have to stand formally in the centre of a garden: they can be set on a stone low to the ground; on a tree stump; on a pedestal of stone or moulded concrete, perhaps in a garden bed; or at the end of a low stone or brick wall. To be functional they must be in full sun.

ABOVE A garden can become an outdoor gallery for original sculpture.

TOP A pair of terracotta ducks and a sundial form an appropriate grouping for a country garden.

ABOVE Pieces of slate stacked on top of each other make a casual low stand for a decorative sundial.

A carved stone piece is sensitively sited to be discovered by a visitor wandering through the garden.

Metal sculptures

Metal sculptures are ideally suited to gardens, given a little thought about where they should go. You can commission a piece not too expensively or find something ready-made. You may like to incorporate a stair rail, a gate or a decorative piece for a garden alcove. The concept of metal sculpture can be extended to arches and arbours for a fresh, individual note. Sculptured pieces can also be in the form of attractive metal curves placed on top of a boundary wall, over which roses can clamber. Natural finishes are always gentle in a garden, but metal can also be painted Chinese red or chrome yellow – whatever seems right for a rather dashing garden.

Pots as sculptures

You may have a pretty pot, urn or chimney pot that you can use as a sculptural piece. Some pots have necks too narrow for planting and are better as sculptures. A bold group of three or four compatible objects is more effective than a number of smaller, indifferent ones. Just one large pot at the edge of a garden bed skirting a path makes a decorative accent that asks the passer-by to take more notice of the garden. A large pot or urn by an extensive hedge relieves the monotony of a uniform planting.

Flotsam and jetsam

Hefty old red-gum branches, weathered driftwood, such as barnacle-coated planks and bleached tea tree, ancient, rusty chains and other treasures make decorative pieces for relaxed rural, native and cottage gardens. Hang the chain from a shed wall or over a tree branch. The boughs or plank can be near a rocky outcrop, by some pots or against a wall. Make sure, however, that you don't have too much happening all at once.

Rocks and stones

Sculptured by nature, rocks can be arranged to form a lovely composition. Be careful, when you handle rocks, not to knock off any moss. Dig them, mossy side up, into the ground until they look comfortable. If you have natural rocky outcrops on your land you may be able to take the earth away from around selected groups to reveal more or add more rocks to improve the composition.

Attractive sculptural effects can be created using river-washed rock, with nearby a few small river pebbles and a suitable plant, such as Corsican mint (*Mentha requienii*), if there is filtered shade, or the native silver cushion bush (*Calocephalus brownii*) for the sun.

A GARDEN WITH A CENTRAL ORNAMENT

A detailed, formal plan lends itself to a central decorative feature, such as a fountain, birdbath or sundial.

PERGOLAS

Pergolas originated centuries ago as simple structures on which to spread vines so that the sun could reach as many of the leafy stems, shoots and grapes as possible. The first pergolas were probably made of rough-hewn saplings, set upright in the ground at regular intervals in pairs linked by rafters and cross beams. No doubt the overhead timbers were tied to the upright poles, and the whole would have looked quite pretty, though this was not the primary aim.

Constructing a rustic pergola is quite within the capabilities of amateur carpenters.

In this hot garden, beauty and function combine. A flourishing grape vine draped over a broad pergola provides necessary protection from the sun.

USES

The basic design of pergolas has not changed, though today the uses have expanded and constructional materials and methods vary according to purpose and chosen style.

Supports for fruiting vines

The original function of pergolas still holds. A pergola to support fruiting vines can be erected as a free-standing structure somewhere in a garden. It makes an appealing and useful entranceway to an orchard or vegetable garden. Kiwi fruit (*Actinidia chinensis*), black and banana passionfruits (*Passiflora edulis* and *P. mollissima*) and grapes (*Vitis*) are suitable climbers for the pergola.

Screens

Pergolas, with their climbers, provide a windbreak or partially screen off an area of the garden. They can also mark a boundary between two spaces.

Shade

A pergola with a climbing plant over its sheltering rafters and beams provides summer shade. The climber should preferably be deciduous or sparsely evergreen to let winter sunlight into the sitting area beneath. Often the area below is paved, providing a firm surface for tables and chairs.

Decorative covered ways

A free-standing pergola in a garden is usually set over a path to form a covered way. Being a structure of some substance, it provides vertical and overhead strength in a garden. Its visual impact from within and without is considerable, so careful maintenance is required.

Display

Pergolas can also be structures for the grand display of one or more spectacular or particularly beautiful climbing plants. Plant, for example, a clematis, such as *Clematis montana* 'Rubens', with an evergreen honeysuckle (*Lonicera*); climbing 'Lorraine Lee' (an evergreen rose that is suitable for an airy pergola only); summer jasmine (*Jasminum azoricum*) and Carolina jasmine (*Gelsemium sempervirens*); the ornamental grape *Vitis coignetiae*; or *Wisteria sinensis*, or *W. floribunda* 'Macrobotrys', perhaps intermingled with a 'Black Boy' rose.

Extensions to houses

Pergolas that are extensions of houses need to follow the architectural lines of the buildings so that they appear part of them.

Over driveways

A pergola makes an attractive entrance to a driveway, particularly when it straddles double gates that have been set in a metre or two from the street and it extends in from the fenceline. The structure can support an evergreen or deciduous climbing plant.

STYLES AND MATERIALS

Where you are using a pergola as part of your garden layout it can reflect the character of your house or follow a more rustic style, particularly if it is well-removed from the building.

Pergolas built of rough-hewn logs or log uprights with rough-sawn timber cross-members have a rustic feel. Pillars half stone and half log, and uprights made entirely of stone, rendered brick or concrete, offer pleasing alternatives.

ARCHES, ARBOURS AND GAZEBOS

Arches, arbours and gazebos are probably descended from the pergola; they have in common a need to be used as part of an overall garden plan or strategy, not as exclusive decorations or features in their own right. When you are planning to introduce one of these dominant pieces of garden architecture, be careful to examine your motives, and think about the visual and spatial implications carefully before you proceed.

ARCHES

Usually an arch is made of strong wire or steel and forms a curved overhead structure across a path. Timber versions of an arch may be peaked rather than curved or just have two simple beams across, like a narrow pergola section. An arch is made especially lovely by being partially covered with climbing plants, particularly roses. The climbers should be well maintained, not left to wave aimlessly in the air, and regular cutting and feeding will result in increased floweriness. Attention should be given to the clearing out of dried leaves and stems on the underside of the arch.

The worst thing that can happen to an arch is for it to be used as a free-standing decoration. An arch is a narrow structure and will look exposed and contrived if set this way. It must be used functionally to mark a gateway or the entrance to a garden or, incorporated into hedges, fences or screens, to denote a division between two garden spaces.

An arch is best not used so that it cuts across the architectural lines of a house façade, unless the house itself is rather plain. The composition becomes too confusing to be attractive when an arch is placed in front of an elaborate Victorian or Edwardian house. It is better to train a climbing rose up a verandah post than to have a decorative arch and verandah competing at close quarters.

ARBOURS

An arbour is a small, open structure, rather like the cross-section of a pergola, with seats – a decorative shelter for sitting in out of doors. Probably the first arbours were vine clad, but the decorative possibilities would soon have been translated into roses. Arbours are usually made of trellis or wrought iron; some can be quite elaborate pieces. An arbour is sometimes used to embrace a classical urn of flowers or a fountain, rather than a seat.

An arbour may be a small oblong or semi-circular structure, set against a wall or fence, or a free-standing one, usually of wrought iron and possibly domed, set over a spot where two pathways cross. People can meet here and sit.

As a rule a free-standing arbour should have at least a space three times its height all the way around, give or take a few softening plants. An arbour nestled in a corner site can have planting to the back and sides but should have a clearance in front of at least three times its height.

A wall arbour both pleases the eye and offers a place to rest.

GAZEBOS OR SUMMERHOUSES

In Europe the idea of viewing the garden from a small home away from home has been prevalent among the well-to-do for centuries. People wander in the garden until they eventually arrive at a gazebo to rest and view the garden in comfort. Traditionally, gazebos were free-standing structures, usually octagonal or hexagonal, though sometimes oblong, with views all round or from the parts not walled in.

In recent times there has been a revival of building gazebos or summerhouses. In itself this is commendable, but it is important to put time into siting a gazebo and deciding if there is, in fact, sufficient space to include it without committing the misdemeanour of overcrowding. Fitting one into a shrubbery so that only half of the hexagon or octagon is revealed, while the other is hidden by plants, produces an economy of space; the rear portion can be filled in, possibly with vertical pine lining-board.

Ready-made gazebos are usually more economical than gazebos built for specific sites. Some styles are quite elaborate, with roofs of copper, slate or shingles. Off-the-hook gazebos come in all shapes and sizes and various materials, including treated pine and western red cedar, and usually have galvanised-iron or shingled roofs. Floors can be concrete, paving or tiling or just have gravel or pine bark on the earth. A few stepping stones leading to the threshold provide a welcome. Roses are the classic plant adornment: a pillar rose, such as 'Buff Beauty' or *Rosa devoniensis*, sparse of stem and flowery, makes an excellent gazebo rose, and a few branches spreading across the roof should not matter too much.

OPPOSITE PAGE Much can be learnt from the historic gardens of Australia. The fine gazebo of Buda, at Castlemaine, Victoria, is fitting for a nineteenth-century house and extensive garden.

TOP A neo-classical structure is appropriate in a rather grand garden.

BOTTOM A summerhouse turns a corner of a garden into a quiet retreat.

FERNERIES AND GLASSHOUSES

Ferneries and glasshouses exist more for the growing of plants than for visual gratification. But, if thoughtfully chosen or built, they can be quite an ornament to your garden.

Growing in ferneries and glasshouses plants that it might be impossible to establish outside can become a fascinating occupation. Some people who are not able to cope with the size of a conventional garden can relate to these small spaces where things seem very personal, easily controlled and safe.

FERNERIES

Ferneries are protected homes for ferns and other shade-dwelling plants, perhaps when there is no suitable spot in the garden. Among the plants, other than fern species, that thrive in ferneries are primulas, impatiens, saxifrages, heucherellas, begonias and some orchids.

Ferneries, sometimes also called shadehouses, are usually made of slatted wood, trellis or a timber frame covered with shadecloth to create an effect of filtered sunlight. They are usually fitted with shelves and a work bench so that plants can be displayed and potting and pruning attended to. A sprinkler system – preferably a misting type directed from the roof – is ideal for the plants housed in ferneries.

The buildings themselves can be made quite pretty, with pitched roofs and finials to suit a traditional setting or with external plantings, stepping stones and even a simple porch for more rustic surroundings. Sterilised pine bark makes a suitable floor for rustic ferneries.

Ferneries can be a place for walking through, with benches and shelves kept to the sides, or a very personal place with not much space for other people. Ferneries can also be designed as a natural garden, with rocks and a pool providing a setting in which the plants will thrive – a garden picture to be maintained and developed.

GLASSHOUSES

Glasshouses provide opportunities for plants that love sun and protection to thrive. These glazed structures are available commercially in many shapes and sizes, some of them traditional, and are extremely attractive in gardens.

Glasshouses, like ferneries, have shelves and benches, and again an automatic watering system is well worthwhile. Artificial heating can be installed, which accelerates the growth rate of plants and enables a wider range of heat-loving plants to be grown. Because maximum sun and light are captured through the glass and a humid atmosphere develops in the presence of so many enclosed plants, glasshouses create an ideal environment for the propagation and growth of plants. When summer comes, the windows or some panes can be whitewashed or covered with shadecloth to protect particular plants.

In a glasshouse all manner of seeds can be germinated and later planted out, and many hardwood and softwood cuttings, including daphne, begonias, bougainvilleas, lilies, frangipanis and gardenias can be struck. In cooler climates a glasshouse protects heat-loving plants during winter.

OPPOSITE PAGE Tree ferns and fernery seem to have grown together over the years.

ABOVE Lush palms and ferns in a courtyard beyond a glass-walled sitting-room create the impression of living in a spacious fernery.

WATER IN GARDENS

Water has always been closely allied with gardens. Its ornamental qualities were clearly understood long ago, the beauty of natural lakes, streams and waterfalls suggesting its potential for garden design. As a formal decorative element water dates back at least to the ancient gardens of Islam, yet today people find water in a landscape just as appealing.

There are a number of ways of presenting water in gardens, from large ornamental lakes to the simplest birdbath or low dish of water on a terrace; and from stepped cascades, waterfalls and towering fountains to a water spout. Some form of decorative water is available to everyone. Water has its own vitality and can look as close to perfection in a dish, with a single flower or leaf floating on it, as jetting and plummeting from a costly fountainhead.

Some gardens have natural water passing through; where they don't, owners sometimes create running water of their own. But water does not need to be tinkling or splashing. It is a matter of preference. There is something tranquil about a still pond whose contribution is reflection. It draws our attention to patches of the prevailing sky and to the surroundings mirrored in its surface.

STYLE AND SITE

If you have a yen for water in your garden, you will need to consider exactly where you want it, what form is suitable for your house and garden and whether you have sufficient space. If, for example, you want something lovely outside a certain window and your ground slopes away from your house you might think of a formal pond – a perfect circle edged in brick, with some lavenders nearby – or a birdbath with a planting of hardy grevilleas and banksias to one side. Alternatively, if your house is on level ground, you could make an informal pond, nestling it into the ground a little, with an exciting natural setting of Australian native plants.

Whatever you do with water in your garden, it should fall clearly into either the formal or the informal category. If you fail to acknowledge the difference, resulting in a confusion of styles, your water feature will not be entirely successful, and as you gather understanding your disappointment will grow.

The distinction is clear. An informal design can only be set where there is some likelihood that the water could have got there of its own accord. An artificial waterway should run down a hill or along a depression, and an informal pond should settle in a depression or hollow. Free shapes and natural materials should keep company with the informal. In nature there are few hard edges and straight lines. These and geometric shapes – circles, triangles and rectangles – are the property of formality.

FOUNTAINS

By definition fountains are splashy things and people and the nearby ground are invariably subject to wind-borne spray. Bearing this in mind, if you do not have to have your fountain right in the middle of a lawn or terrace, you could have it in a fernery or a courtyard with frothy plants close up, delighting in the spray.

Traditional free-standing fountains

Traditional free-standing fountains, the stylish prima donnas of the garden, are all about show. Today there are plenty of cast concrete or terracotta fountains in the form of statues or shafts ornate with classical symbols, fruit and flowers. As well, there are elegant metal reproduction Victorian fountains; some original pieces also appear for sale periodically.

Traditional free-standing fountains are usually set in a round pond, which should be wide enough to accept most of the spray. Some fountains come with their own small bowls, although they, too, can be set in a wide pond. Free-standing fountains need a space around them of at least twice their height – more if they are heavy and very grand.

A tiny, homemade pond is tucked under a Japanese flowering cherry (*Prunus serrulata*) and a cut-leaf Japanese maple (*Acer palmatum* 'Dissectum').

Contemporary free-standing fountains

Contemporary fountains may be extremely formal – metal sculptures set in a pond – or a series of cascades and receptive cups, the water eventually forming a pool at ground level. Alternatively they may be made from a superb rock or two: a veritable sculpture set in a formal pool.

Wall fountains

Wall fountains are quite magical. They were used as drinking fountains long ago, and in Italy and Spain you still come across them tucked into an old wall in a narrow street. If there is no room for a large fountain in your garden and you are after something traditional and formal, a wall fountain may be perfect.

You can buy some excellent concrete reproductions, or build your own wall fountain. If you do build one, you can give it a larger trough, rising from the ground, with a sitting edge. To complete the picture add a climbing rose to the wall – 'Madame Alfred Carrière' perhaps – mingling with an informally espaliered sasanqua camellia, for evergreen strength and a bonus of autumn flowers, and the soft mauve or rich purple of musk-perfumed heliotrope. In gardens the aim should be to achieve the romantic without mentioning it much, but these wall fountains are the stuff of romance.

A wall fountain need not be traditional; the concept can be interpreted in many interesting ways. For instance, add to a blank wall a series of ceramic dishes, shaped to collect and disperse the water as it courses down to a trough.

CASCADES AND WATERFALLS

Because water has to run somewhere, a cascade or waterfall will need a pond of some sort or a natural-looking watercourse to collect it when it ceases to tumble. Cascades can be formal, evenly stepped falls of water, such as those used near contemporary buildings, the whole unashamedly unnatural.

Waterfalls in the strict sense occur when the course of a river or creek is interrupted by a cliff or steep hill. Look at some real waterfalls to understand the principles to apply, if you want to achieve a natural-looking, scaled-down waterfall in your own garden. See the way the rocks seem to hang on a slope and how a branch remains dramatically suspended within the composition. The waterfall tumbling in your garden need only be four rocks high, with some shrubs behind, but the same principles of natural beauty should still apply.

ABOVE A traditional free-standing fountain usually needs a spacious setting if it is not to look overpowering.

OPPOSITE PAGE Stepping stones across a pond make an ornamental walkway. Pastel-coloured flowers harmonise with the soft greens of shrubs and water plants.

PONDS

Ponds can be formal or informal and can be lined in a number of ways. You need to choose the style and materials best suited to your house and garden and your pocket.

Formal ponds

Formal ponds have a regular, geometric shape – rectangular, square or circular. They can look extremely decorative and make suitable central features for terraces and courtyards. Large circular ponds can be grand, small ones delightful. Rectangular ponds have a special elegance and serenity. A fountain or a simple statue makes an appropriate centrepiece for a formal pond. Surround a formal pond with a square-cut paving material, such as bricks, slates, tiles or concrete blocks, in keeping with its shape; or set it as a bold centrepiece, perhaps edged with cut stone, in a square, rectangle or circle of lawn, choosing a shape to suit.

Plantings around this type of pond, if any, usually have a formal note. A ring of low roses or lavenders, clumps of iris, planted opposite each other across the water, or potted plants in a definite arrangement complement a formal pond. Rectangular ponds look most effective with just a patch or two of iris or set in a lawn with no surrounding plantings, only waterlilies and other water plants within the pond itself.

If running water is needed, it can be provided by a central fountain or a wall fountain playing into a narrow rectangle or semi-circle of water. A false side can be built on a formal pool to create a wall fountain if there is a strong planting of evergreens behind it. Water can enter the pond in some other stylised manner but never from a 'natural' waterfall.

Informal ponds

An informal pond is a celebration of everything that is not geometric or restrained. Since it must look as if the water came there naturally, it should be set at the

bottom of a slope, nestled in a ledge on the way down or tucked into a little hollow on level ground.

It is quite normal for a landscaped informal pond to have a front, even quite a broad one, made perhaps from slate or pebbles and facing the approach from which the pond is usually viewed. Such a pond can be surrounded by a curve of well-set rock on three sides and by rock plants – low growers that overhang the water, with taller shrubs and bushes behind. The approach might consist of flat slate pieces set in the lawn.

The materials suitable for an informal pond are natural rock and slate. Sometimes a sleeper can be set flat, just above the waterline, to form the back of the pond. As a rule, square-cut material near a natural pond does not work. The exception is where square-cut paving, particularly brick, runs up to the pond edge at the approach only.

Australian native plants make appropriate plantings for an informal pond. Try bird-attracting wattles, callistemons, banksias, correas and grasses. Or you may prefer exotic plants surrounding your pond: Chinese lantern bush (*Abutilon*) could form the backdrop, with sheltering oak-leafed hydrangeas (*Hydrangea quercifolia*), sasanqua camellias and *Raphiolepis* × *delacourii* for solid evergreens low to the ground and in the middle storey. And what about a rose with arching branches, such as 'Buff Beauty' or 'Cornelia' or beautiful 'Maigold', to droop a little over the water. There could be iris at the sides near the front or *Dietes bicolor* and some *Bergenia cordifolia* and forget-me-nots (*Myosotis*). This planting is not native, but it and the pond, with its well-set, mossy rocks, are entirely informal.

An informal pond can have a small waterfall or cascade – but not too high a one unless you have a genuine hill behind the pond. Artificial hills or mounds are uncomfortable things, best avoided.

Pond construction

Fibreglass shells can be bought ready-made in a wonderful range of shapes and sizes. A fibreglass shell must be set very firmly on sand, with sand tucked under its rim. Rock or another edging can be set here and there round the margin, with plants growing in between. Slate can be set over the exposed fibreglass ledge at the pond's approach or plants encouraged to grow over it. A mortar bed can be used to secure the rocks and slate, but the mortar should not be visible.

A shallow bush pond can be made by lining a hollow with concrete. It should be reinforced; for a small, curved pond, two or three folds of chicken wire can be used. It is then rendered, using a commercial waterproofing compound in the render. The render should extend up to and over the undersides of any rocks used to edge the pond; however, the rough edges of these ponds are quite interesting in their poured state, with plants and forest-floor litter softening the edges.

Large ponds can be built with brick sides and a reinforced concrete base, using steel reinforcing wire, the whole rendered. This type of pond can be made to suit a particular site, and, when it is extra large, can be made even stronger with double brick and additional reinforcing.

Sometimes, as an added precaution, rendered ponds are painted with a black waterproofing paint, following the instructions on the container. This helps to make the water look natural, and the paint forms an extra waterproof membrane while not harming the life within the pond.

WATER TECHNOLOGY

Fountains usually have electric pumps, to recirculate water, and a filter. The pump must be concealed in a box, perhaps under a paving slab or rock. Alternatively, a submergible pump, like the filter, can be put in the water, disguised by a plant or stone. Power leads also need to be safely concealed. Waterfalls also require pumps, but hiding the mechanism is not as difficult with an informal pond and rock surrounds as with a fountain set in a formal pond in a paved area.

Power must be brought to the fountain or pond site by underground conduit. If required, lighting can be installed at the same time. The pump and lights can be operated from a switch in the house.

With fountains, in particular, it is necessary to keep an eye on the water level, since they lose quite a lot of water as spray and splashes. Pump filters need checking and cleaning every two weeks to keep the pump functioning well.

Some people like to have a pump and filter in their still pond, though it does not really need one. However, it is advisable to flush out any pond a little every two to four weeks to keep it from stagnating. If possible a pond should be fitted with an overflow pipe, leading into the stormwater system, to assist with flushing and floodwater.

Water snails, fish and water plants provide an ecological cycle that includes the filtering or cleaning of their pond; this works effectively so long as the balance is maintained. In the process, the fish eat the larvae of mosquitoes, which float on the surface; the snails keep the algae in control; the water plants provide oxygen, shelter and a little food for the fish; and the algae supply micro-organisms helpful to the plants.

Granite slabs and crushed granite form a shore on which to linger and enjoy the water.

LEFT A spill of white roses and a crooked tree trunk soften the effect of a formal birdbath.

BIRDBATHS AND WATER DISHES

The standard commercial birdbath can be quite attractive, though some are more distinguished looking than others. They should be chosen carefully to suit your house and garden – nothing too ornate or classical for a rustic garden.

If you can find a large rock with a depression in it, or you are able to hollow one out, it will make a more interesting birdbath than the set pieces. A low dish – perhaps a handmade ceramic one – also makes a simple birdbath, particularly for gardens where cats do not come. Such a dish looks pretty near an overhanging shrub, tucked beside a path or placed at the edge of a paved sitting area.

Whether formal or informal, all the birdbaths and water dishes illustrated have two things in common: they have been chosen and positioned with care to give focus and individuality to their gardens; and they have been enhanced by soft, simple plantings.

BARBECUES

Several issues must be addressed in planning a barbecue area: the location of the outdoor cooking area; the type of barbecue; and the design of the setting, if the barbecue is to be built in.

LOCATION

Certain points need to be taken into account when you are planning the site for a barbecue area (though, of course, if you are planning to have a movable barbecue, some of the following points will not be of such importance or relevance):

- nearness to the kitchen or service pantry
- closeness to the outdoor eating area – though some owners prefer food to be cooked quite a distance from where people will be eating
- attractiveness of the surroundings
- space for people to circulate – family and friends often like to gather round while the food is being cooked
- privacy from and for neighbours
- aesthetic considerations – a barbecue is not always an attractive item and is best sited where it is not too obvious in the garden
- aspect – it is not advisable to place a barbecue in the line of a windfunnel or in full sun.

TYPE AND SETTING

You have the option of several barbecue styles. Consider each one carefully; the one you choose should suit your house, garden and way of life.

Portable barbecues

Portable barbecues range from fold-away wood-burning models to charcoal-burning ovens. Some have their own benches built around the cooking grid. Portable-gas models are available and enable food to be cooked much more quickly than on a conventional fire.

Fixed wood-burning barbecues

Some people prefer to make their own wood fire in a fixed fireplace according to their pet notions about the perfect barbecue. The barbecue can be set low to the ground, serving well as an auxiliary fireplace. However, a great deal of bending is required during cooking, and it is possibly better to set the barbecue at bench height for convenience.

Some enthusiasts have a semi-portable design, consisting of bluestone pitchers and a strong iron grid. The bluestones can be rough-built to any level, with the grid inserted somewhere between them. Although the barbecue is liable to be set up for long periods on one site, it can be dismantled and reassembled elsewhere at short notice or stored somewhere as required.

When a wood-burning barbecue is built in, grids and hotplates can be custom designed. One good idea is to set an old ploughshare into an oblong grid of strong, fine mesh wire, cutting a hole for it with tin snips. This provides a well-drained hotplate as well as space for direct open-fire cooking.

In designing the surrounds for a more conventional built-in wood-burning barbecue, care should be taken to make them simple and functional. An alcove for wood storage may be required and perhaps a place for a few utensils, oil, sauces and seasonings. A bench for ingredients and for serving from, on one or both sides, is handy. A working drawing should be done before construction is begun.

Bulky surrounds detract from the appearance of a built-in barbecue, and it is aesthetically preferable not to raise any part of the barbecue beyond bench height to accommodate shelves, chimney and so on. The intrusion of a barbecue chimney to conduct smoke away is hardly justified by the amount of interference from downwind smoke that occurs. At all costs you must aim not to build an ugly outdoor kitchen in your back garden.

Surrounds are usually of bluestone, rock, brick, slate or tiling. If building in rock, it is important to use only dense rock close to heat. The air-vesicles of

A bluestone barbecue nestles in a sloping expanse of lawn.

honeycomb rock can expand with extreme heat, causing an explosion.

Bluestone walling can look quite hefty and should only be constructed by experts; fine rockwork is attractive but requires intensive skilled labour. Brick, being a neat, rectangular unit, is more straightforward. Slate and tiles are usually veneered over brickwork and require skilled labour.

Electric and mains-gas barbecues

Electric and mains-gas units are set in a permanent site, and electricians and plumbers are needed to link them to the domestic supply. Installation is expensive, but once completed the barbecue is permanently 'stored', and the owners have the satisfaction of a permanent set-up and can plan other amenities around it. There are many hotplate styles and sizes from which to choose.

While some electric and mains-gas models are completely free-standing or sold with a framework, many are table models that need to be set into masonry surrounds, and the discussion relating to fixed wood-burning barbecues applies to them. Where a unit has a hood or canopy, sometimes housing a rotisserie, the intrusion above bench height cannot be avoided, but there is no need to surround it with masonry. The appearance is best softened by the forgiving branches of a nearby shrub. Unless you really want a striking modern feature, strong colours, such as vermilion, red and yellow, should be avoided in favour of more neutral colours: black, olive green, royal blue or burgundy.

CHILDREN'S PLAY AREAS

Many types of commercial play equipment for children are available, some brightly painted, others in bush colours. They often incorporate a number of items, including swings, ladders, climbing frames, monkey bars and tunnels, some complex, others less challenging; so it is a matter of deciding what is likely to suit your children's needs, your garden space and your pocket. Some children are thoroughly absorbed for hours at a time and use the equipment for many years. Others are not so attracted.

A children's playground should have some protection from the sun to enable lengthy playing periods out of doors. Children should be encouraged to wear hats and sun-screening cream. Especially when they are young, their sandpit should be shaded from sun, perhaps by a portable screen.

Firmly set log offcuts are fun for children to climb over in dry weather.

In any playing area safety factors must be the first consideration. Young children need to be watched while they are playing. Older children value privacy and prefer their play area to be out of the line of vision from the house. The amount of supervision is something parents, who know themselves and their children best, must sort out. Portable sandpits and wading pools are handy for little ones and can be set up to suit the occasion.

A fixed sandpit is easily made by digging out a suitable space and lining it with heavy-duty black polythene in which drainage holes have been made. It is then filled with clean sand, ready for action. This design has no hard edges or splintery wood. Sandpits need a cover to keep out cats and drifting garden litter.

It is not a good idea to put too much money into play areas, because children's interests change quickly. Given creative opportunities, children's imaginations will provide the details of games, challenges and adventures to be had. Children need a few loose materials because they may soon tire of fixed equipment over which they have little mastery. Logs and offcuts of tree trunks, small planks and old sheets of Masonite, carpet and linoleum hold a great deal of excitement for young children. Given a few fruit boxes, old saucepans, baking dishes and other ex-domestic paraphernalia, children will be absorbed for a long time. A small tent left pitched for a while will give rise to extra fantasies and can be quickly taken down when the novelty wears off. And even an old metal-framed school desk complete with seat soon becomes part of a game.

Children like to climb trees and practically everything else. For their own and the garden's protection, they should be told which trees are zoned for climbing. It is advisable to put a thick mulch of soft pine bark underneath the climbing trees, in case of accidents. At some stage children will probably want and get – given a suitable tree and obliging parents – their own custom-built treehouse. There is something special about a house in a tree; it appeals to children's desire for a place of their own.

Down on the ground, children can have a scarecrow, made from crossed sticks set in the ground. From time to time little ones will enjoy the fun of outfitting it in all manner of attire. It is also a good idea to have a couple of seats so children – and parents – can take a break. A few old tree stumps still *in situ* can be smoothed off at different levels or log cross-sections set in the ground at different heights to provide stools and stable climbing equipment.

As your children get older and you become less concerned about watching them, a screen of brush or trellis can be erected to give them a sense of privacy and you an opportunity to look at a climbing plant or two for a change.

TRAMPOLINES

Trampolines are large objects to have in a garden but can be a useful source of exercise and entertainment for all members of the family. Sometimes they can be unobtrusively hidden around corners. Alternatively, they can be worked into the contours of the garden, either sunk flush with a level surface or set into sloping ground. If the sight of a trampoline in the garden is unattractive, a brush screen, trellis or hedge planting can do much to hide it.

6/ GARDENS WITHIN GARDENS

Rose gardens, herb gardens, vegetable plots: there are many plantings that form a garden within the larger garden. A garden that contains one or more special areas within it, like any successful garden, will have cohesiveness – a harmony of style and spirit.

Some gardens flow from one part to the next: from a concentration of roses, perhaps, to fewer roses and then none as other plants create a new garden picture. Others are much more clearly divided into sections: a planting of roses may be formally hedged with *Pittosporum tenuifolium* 'James Stirling', clipped to 1.5 metres in height, or with low lavenders. In one garden plantings of vegetables may merge with plantings of herbs and perennials in a long border, while in another vegetables and herbs may be a separate planting behind a hedge of rosemary or a picket fence.

Some gardens within gardens, such as vegetable gardens and picking gardens, contribute to the practical running of a home; others, such as children's gardens or specialised gardens of cacti or orchids, are closely related to the needs or interests of individuals. Many, such as shade gardens or sunken gardens, contribute to the depth and richness of the whole and are closely linked to the aesthetics of garden design.

The development of a lovely garden within a garden may capture your enthusiasm, but it will also demand hard work. If you declare that there is to be a shade garden, it means that you have taken up the challenge of shade gardening, and half-hearted groups of sun-deprived plants and invasive fishbone ferns must become a thing of the past. If part of your garden is in sun most of the year, you must direct your efforts to creating an attractive, sun-hardy garden, with no more misunderstood, frizzled-up plants.

Time has enabled this giant hawthorn tree (*Crataegus*) to form a natural archway to a garden within a garden.

ROSES EN MASSE

The rose in its many forms and with its wide variety of blooms has been loved by countless people through the ages. Today it is as much cherished and used in gardens as ever. There are roses to suit all preferences: modern cultivars, older roses, bred more than fifty years ago, and species roses, which originally occurred naturally.

Modern roses have been bred from older forms to produce plants with good-quality cutting flowers. They have been hybridised for longer stems, firm form, clear colours and long lastingness. These hybrids need special care to preserve their fine quality.

Modern roses, though individually lovely, look too proud in a mixed planting; they do not blend. It's best to choose from the various tones within a particular colour group or to plan a pleasing contrasting-colour strategy, rather than to plant roses of different colours randomly. For instance, plant apricot-toned roses, such as 'Iced Ginger', 'Apricot Nectar' and 'Just Joey', or a mixture of pink and crimson roses, such as 'First Love' (pink), 'Queen Elizabeth' (pink), 'Mr Lincoln' (crimson) and 'Papa Meilland' (crimson).

Old roses usually belong to one of the great rose families, which include gallicas, damasks, albas, centifolias, bourbons, moss roses and rugosas. They are hardier than modern hybrids and less disease prone. As well, they require less formal pruning than modern roses. Old roses, including species roses, have many forms and rich or delicate colours. Perhaps it's because of their soft and often unruly form that they can be mixed in a planting and look as if they belong.

OPPOSITE PAGE Often by selecting roses of similar tonings or just one modern rose, such as the floribunda 'Mic Mac', a lovelier effect can be achieved than by growing roses of assorted colours.

PLANNING A ROSE GARDEN

Probably the best way to start a rose garden is to list your favourite roses, noting the colour, form and size of their flowers and the size, shape and style of the bush. You will need to know when they flower – whether in spring, summer, autumn or throughout the warmer seasons. Are they splashy and dramatic or a touch reticent? Observe the varying textures of their leaves and degree of evergreenness. Some leaves are large and shiny, some small, some rough textured and others fernlike. There are quite a few evergreen or almost evergreen roses, though most are deciduous. Some, like so many other shrubs, develop autumn colour in their leaves before they fall. And some roses have no thorns or only a few, while many are prickly.

Once your list of favourite roses is ready you can start to think of interesting ways to weave them into your rose garden design. You may find you need to add some extras or eliminate one or two – or just make the whole area bigger to fit them all in.

Of course you may not have the space for a complete rose garden, in which case you can limit your selection to a few varieties, planted among other shrubs, or make a special rose space, with a sundial or urn as the focus – separate, but still part of the larger garden picture. Perhaps you just have a spot for a climbing rose.

Roses can be trained in interesting ways to further beautify your garden. They can be grown on chains looped between tall, ladderlike posts up which they first clamber. Bush roses with long canes are shown to effect with many of their canes fastened to the ground with metal pegs or tied to the strong branches of a tree. Some roses can be trained up pillars, poles or tripods by gradually winding them round and round. Leave enough room for expansion, though, as the stems fill out. The roses 'Buff Beauty' and 'New Dawn' are suitable for this.

As you consider the places in your larger garden where you could have a rose garden, keep in mind the requirements and characteristics of roses. They need at least four to five hours of sun each day to flower at their best. The spreading varieties of old roses also require space or they become hemmed in and perform meanly. If bare rose branches for some months worry you, make sure plants nearby perform well over winter. Camellias provide a good backdrop for deciduous roses. 'Iceberg', 'Sea Foam', 'Mermaid', 'Lorraine Lee' and *Rosa banksiae* 'Lutea' are roses that keep most of their foliage during winter.

When planning and planting, use the knowledge gained from your research on the mature size of each rose type. Place smaller roses near the edge of the bed and around ponds or garden ornaments. Well-behaved medium roses should come next and some of the smaller spreading types. Tall bush roses and those large, shrubby roses that want to climb are for the back, as are the big ramblers and climbers.

UNDERPLANTINGS FOR ROSES

UNDERPLANTINGS FOR ROSES
***Alyssum maritimum* (sweet Alice)** Clump forming, with mauve, white or pink flowers.
***Aquilegia* (columbine, granny's bonnet)** Single or double flowers from white to pink to blue and purple; for sun or dappled shade.
Aster × frikartii Mauve-blue flowers and dark green foliage.
***Dianthus* (pink)** Sweetly scented flowers on grey mounds of leaves.
***Lavandula* (lavender)** Avoid *L. dentata* 'Allardi' because it grows too big.
***Santolina* (cotton lavender)** Silver-grey foliage with yellow flower heads.
***Stachys lanata* (lamb's ears)** Grey-white, furry leaves.
***Thymus* (thyme)** Ground cover with fragrant leaves.

Pathways are quite important for defining planting areas and the mood of a rose garden. Because most roses are thorny, there must be clear places to walk through. For showing off climbing roses, and because it's good to have places in which to sit, arbours are often used. Alternatively, an arched way can be created, using a timber structure with some lattice-work on horizontal braces, or a wrought-iron arch. Soon a rose will be clambering over it. A sundial in a small, open clearing, an urn, a pond or a formal fountain can be part of the decoration of your rose garden and may even form the central focus.

The appearance of a rose garden is usually improved by other simple plantings: for instance, an underplanting of dwarf lavenders or other low-growing evergreen shrubs. They provide softness and some interest beneath the bare branches of wintry roses; hellebores and winter-flowering bulbs are particularly suitable. Dainty, low-growing, evergreen edging plants add a finished look to rose beds, but remember edging plants are for

Roses tumble in an extravagant display over ladders linked by scallops of chains.

edges – not for romps through the entire bed. Companion plantings of garlic, onions and shallots (*Allium* species) help to keep aphids and other pests at bay.

PLANTING AND LIVING WITH ROSES

Roses perform best in a fertile soil including plenty of organic matter. Dig the soil well to two-spades' depth and add compost and well-rotted manures. Let it rest for a few weeks. Don't use sites in which roses have previously died. At the time of planting add a teaspoon of slow-release fertiliser to the hole.

June is rose-planting time; order roses in advance if you can. Plants should be bare rooted, with smooth young bark and thick stems. Wrinkles and withering suggest that the plant has dried out. Leaf buds should be swelling, not burst, and some buds should face outwards. Keep the plant moist until planted. Dig a hole to about a spade's depth and twice as wide, with a mound at the bottom over which spread the plant's roots. The diagram on page 145 shows how to plant the rose. Leave any rough stems on until the plant is well shot, then tidy the rose up a month later: prune each stem to a suitable outside shoot and remove dieback and stubby growth. Your rose should now be ready for a long and happy life.

Roses can be transplanted in winter when bare stemmed if the roots aren't too deep and old. Potted roses can be carefully planted out at any time if their roots are firmly set in the soil.

Pruning

How to prune roses is explained and illustrated on pages 164 and 165. Modern roses, in addition to being pruned in late June or early July, should be given a light pruning in late January or after summer flowering to stimulate autumn flowers. Rambling roses are usually pruned in November after flowering to make way for the strong young growth that will bear the next year's flowers. Old-fashioned roses get by very well left alone for two or three years, apart from the removing of obvious dead wood. The aim of pruning old-fashioned roses is to select out old, unproductive stems. The long stems are not shortened but left to fly free. Avoid the pruned modern hybrid look.

Always appraise the rose before you start pruning, looking it over for healthy shoots, and for any old, gnarled canes that need removing. Sometimes with pruning you must compromise to make sure that you have something of the plant left in the end. Ideally the remaining stems should be at least as thick as a pencil.

Keep a lookout for suckers on rose plants. Roses are grafted on briar roses quite often, and if suckers are not removed at the point where they leave the main stem below the graft they will grow vigorously, taking over the food supply of the rose, which eventually withers.

Feeding and watering

What and when to feed roses is explained on page 167. Roses like water and good drainage, but they are best off with a good soak twice weekly through the summer months – preferably of the surrounding ground, not their leaves. They should be watered in the early morning because dampness during the night encourages disease.

A FORMAL ROSE GARDEN

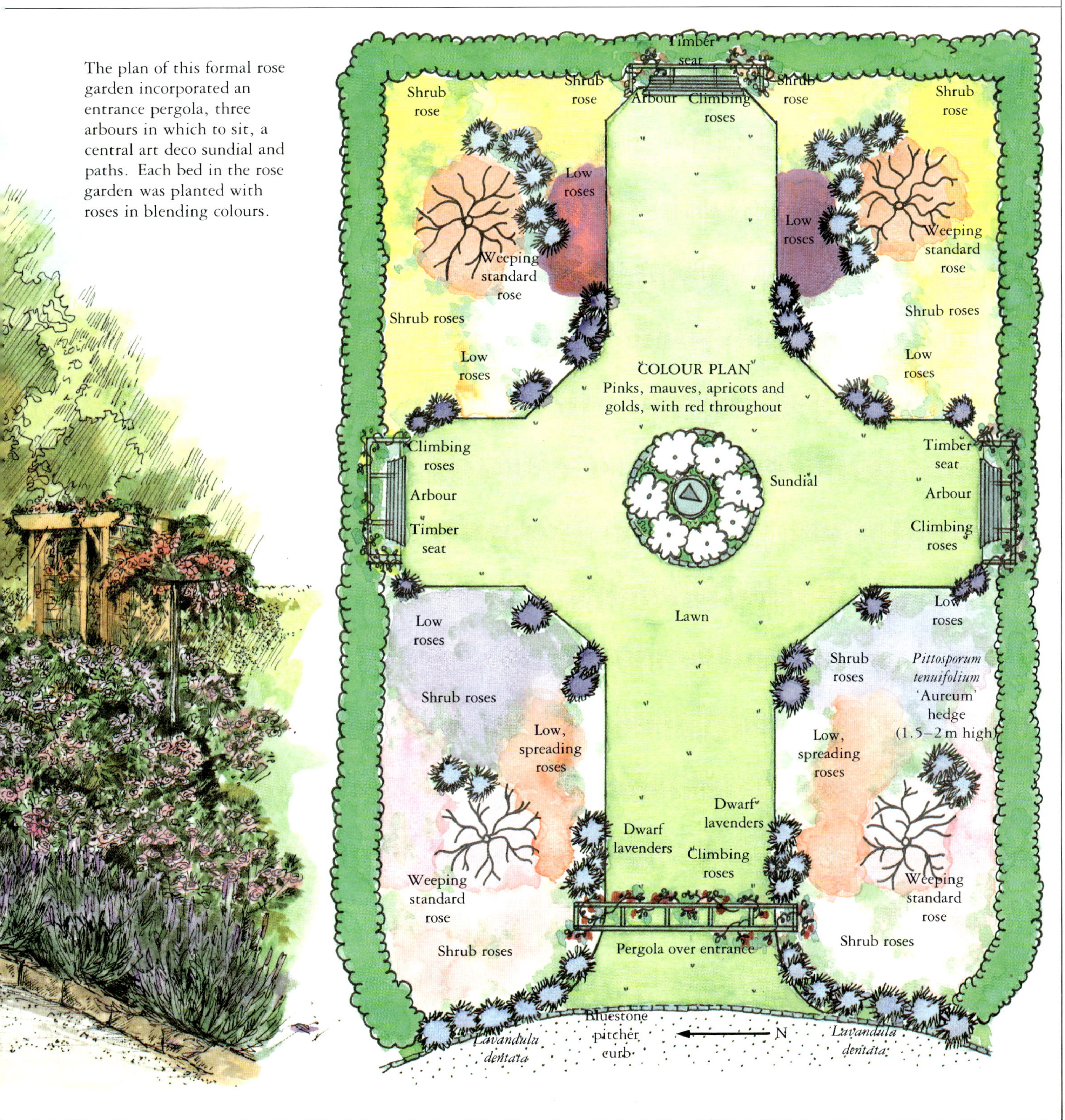

The plan of this formal rose garden incorporated an entrance pergola, three arbours in which to sit, a central art deco sundial and paths. Each bed in the rose garden was planted with roses in blending colours.

A SELECTION OF ROSES

NAME AND YEAR INTRODUCED	FORM AND HEIGHT	BLOOMS	LEAVES, STEMS AND HIPS
SPECIES ROSES AND HYBRIDS			
Rosa banksiae 'Lutea' 1824	Large climber Over 2 m	Small, double, primrose-coloured in dense clusters, in spring and autumn	Evergreen Sparse thorns
R. bracteata 'Mermaid' 1918	Large climber Over 2 m	Large, flat, fragrant, single, yellow, in spring, summer and autumn	Semi-evergreen Very thorny
R. micrugosa 1905	Large shrub 1.5–2 m	Delicate, single, fragrant, ice-pink, in spring	Deciduous, rough-textured leaves turning russet in autumn Fine thorns Fat, orange-red hips
R. moyesii 'Geranium' 1938	Medium shrub 1.5–2 m	Medium, single, tomato red, with rich gold stamens, in spring	Deciduous; russet leaves in autumn Bundles of long, pendulous, bright scarlet hips
GALLICAS AND HYBRIDS			
R. 'Cardinal de Richelieu' 1840	Medium shrub 1–1.5 m	Large, double, fragrant, rich crimson-purple, in spring	Deciduous Sparse thorns
R. 'Duchesse de Montebello' 1829	Medium shrub 1–1.5 m	Medium, double, fragrant, soft pink, in spring	Deciduous Thorns
R. gallica 'Versicolor' (Rosa Mundi) Before 1580	Medium shrub 1–1.5 m	Large, semi-double, pink, white and red striped, recurrent	Deciduous Thorns
ALBAS			
R. 'Great Maiden's Blush' Before 15th century	Large, upright shrub 1.5–2 m	Medium, double, fragrant, soft pink, with centre quartering and button eye, in spring	Deciduous, dull blue-green leaves Thorns
R. 'Madame Plantier' 1835	Large semi-climber 1.5–2 m	Medium, double, fragrant, creamy white, with centre quartering, in spring	Deciduous Almost thornless
CENTIFOLIAS			
R. 'Chapeau de Napoléon' 1826	Medium shrub 1–1.5 m	Large, double, fragrant, mid-pink, with button eye, in spring; mossy, crested buds	Deciduous Thorns
R. 'Fantin-Latour' Unknown origin	Medium shrub 1.5–2 m	Large, double, pale to deep pink, in spring	Deciduous Sparse thorns

A SELECTION OF ROSES			
NAME AND YEAR INTRODUCED	**FORM AND HEIGHT**	**BLOOMS**	**LEAVES, STEMS AND HIPS**
BOURBONS			
R. 'Madame Pierre Oger' 1878	Medium shrub 1–1.5 m	Medium, double, fragrant, lilac-pink, recurrent	Deciduous Thorns
RUGOSAS AND HYBRIDS			
R. 'Blanc Double de Coubert' 1892	Large shrub Over 2 m	Medium, semi-double, fragrant, pure white, recurrent	Deciduous, rough-textured leaves Thorns
R. 'Pink Grootendorst' 1923	Large shrub 1.5–2 m	Small, single, dianthuslike, clustered, clear pink, recurrent	Deciduous, rough-textured leaves Thorns
R. 'Sarah Van Fleet' 1926	Large shrub 2 m	Large, semi-double, fragrant, clear pink, recurrent	Deciduous, rough-textured leaves Thorns
R. 'Scabrosa' 1939	Medium shrub 1.5 m	Large, single, fragrant, almost magenta, recurrent	Deciduous, rough-textured leaves, turning russet in autumn Thorns Bright tomato-coloured hips
HYBRID MUSKS			
R. 'Buff Beauty' 1939	Medium semi-climber Over 2 m	Medium, double, clustered, fragrant, buff-apricot, recurrent	Deciduous Thorns
R. 'Cornelia' 1925	Medium semi-climber Over 2 m	Small, double, clustered, fragrant, apricot-pink, recurrent	Deciduous Thorns
MODERN SHRUB ROSES			
R. 'Dainty Bess' 1925	Medium shrub 1.5 m	Medium, single, dusky pink, recurrent	Deciduous Thorns
R. 'Iceberg' 1958	Large shrub 1.5–2 m	Medium, semi-double, fragrant, white, recurrent	Deciduous Sparse thorns
R. 'Lorraine Lee' 1924	Large shrub Over 1.5 m	Large, double, fragrant, salmon-pink, recurrent	Evergreen Thorns
R. 'Peace' syn. *R.* 'Madame A. Meilland' 1945	Large shrub 1.5–2 m	Large, double, fragrant, cream and sunset shades, recurrent	Deciduous Thorns
R. 'Ophelia' 1912	Medium shrub 1.5 m	Medium, double, fragrant, flesh-pink, deepening in centre, recurrent	Deciduous Thorns
SHRUB-CLIMBERS, CLIMBERS AND RAMBLERS			
R. 'Albertine' 1921	Large rambler Over 5 m	Large, semi-double, coppery pink, in spring	Deciduous Thorns
R. 'Black Boy' 1919	Large climber Over 5 m.	Medium, double, fragrant, rich blackish crimson, recurrent	Deciduous Thorns

A SELECTION OF ROSES			
NAME AND YEAR INTRODUCED	FORM AND HEIGHT	BLOOMS	LEAVES, STEMS AND HIPS
SHRUB-CLIMBERS, CLIMBERS AND RAMBLERS			
R. 'Clair Matin' 1960	Shrub climber 1.5–4 m	Medium, semi-double, slightly fragrant, salmon, in spring	Deciduous Thorns
R. 'Frühlingsmorgen' 1942	Large semi-climber Over 1.5 m	Large, single, fragrant, pale pink, with yellow centre and stamens, in spring and intermittently in summer and autumn	Deciduous, with some autumn tonings Thorns
R. 'Lavender Lassie' 1959	Shrub climber 3 m	Large, double, clustered, fragrant, lavender-pink, recurrent	Deciduous Thorns
R. 'Madame Grégoire Staechelin' 1927	Large climber Over 5 m	Large, double, fragrant, pale pink to mid-pink, in spring	Deciduous Thorns Handsome, orange hips
R. 'Maigold' 1953	Large semi-climber Over 4 m	Large, semi-double, fragrant, coppery apricot, in spring and intermittently in summer and autumn	Deciduous Thorns
R. 'Nancy Hayward' 1937	Large climber Over 5 m	Large, single, dull crimson, with golden stamens, in spring and intermittently through year	Deciduous Thorns
R. 'New Dawn' 1930	Large climber Over 5 m	Medium, double, fragrant, silvery pink, recurrent	Deciduous Thorns
SMALL SHRUB ROSES			
R. 'Cécile Brunner' 1881	Medium shrub 1.5 m	Small, double, fragrant, loosely clustered, pale pink, recurrent	Deciduous Some thorns
R. 'The Fairy' 1941	Small shrub Up to 1.75 m	Small, double, clustered, clear pink, in spring	Deciduous Some thorns
R. 'Green Ice' 1971	Small shrub Less than 1 m	Small, double, clustered, green, white and pinkish, recurrent	Deciduous Thorny

A jug of 'Iceberg' roses and a few blooms of *Rosa* 'Scabrosa' is almost too lovely to take inside. The posy is just two stems of *Rosa* 'Pink Grootendorst'.

SHADY PLACES

Shady gardens present a challenge, particularly if you have inherited them rather than specifically created them. There are several types: gardens under deciduous trees; gardens under evergreen trees; south-facing gardens; ferny places in gardens; and ferneries and bush-houses. You need to stand in your shady places and try to get to know their characteristics. What you can do with them depends on your answers to a number of questions.

- What do you see when you look up? Overhead structures greatly influence the environment beneath, reducing the direct light and the amount of water received. Notice the extent of eave structures, pergolas and other intrusions before you make planting decisions. There may be some light-reducing branches of trees that can be removed.

It is spring along this gold and silver pathway. The garden faces east and is sheltered from the afternoon sun.

- What is the water supply to the area like? Is the ground permanently damp? If so, you will need to grow helxine, mosses, ferns and other moisture-loving plants. Or is the ground sheltered by overhanging eaves, getting no natural water? If so, is it controlled so that the spot is watered mechanically even when the other, more open areas are not? If not, you may need to hand-water the areas under the eaves regularly. The gold dust plant (*Aucuba japonica* 'Variegata'), the ginger lily (*Hedychium*), the Japanese sacred bamboo (*Nandina domestica*) and periwinkles (*Vinca minor*) can withstand dry shade.
- Does air move around the plants? Or is it still and airless in your shady spot? Protective walls or fences, tree trunks and the overhead canopies of large trees can all prevent air flowing freely in the area they are shading. Again, judicious pruning may be the answer.
- Do the sun's direct rays reach the spot at any time of the day or at some time during the year? If sunlight is able to filter through, the shady place can have a much wider variety of plants than if it is in dense shade. However, *Fatsia japonica*, mahonias, nandinas, *Pseudopanax* species, *Mackaya bella* and *Symphoricarpos* species will tolerate considerable shade.
- What is the soil like? If the shade is created by a tree the soil's nutrients may be depleted and there may also be a number of roots running through the ground. To revitalise tired soil turn it over thoroughly, soak it, dig in organic matter, including blood and bone, and then rest it six weeks. Remove any dead roots from previous plants as you work the soil.
- How wide and long is your shady place? Area will determine to a large extent the size and number of plants you can grow. A tree fern, for example, can span 3 metres and looks out of place in a confined spot. If there is a path running through the area, it, too, will influence the plantings you have on either side.

TRIAL AND ERROR

It is no good pretending that shady places are easy. Sun, in varying degrees, is important to most plants. The more that dappled sunlight gets into your shady places and the more you learn about the plants you want to grow the more likely you will be to succeed. After a year or so if a plant does not seem to be thriving, you may need to move it, come winter, to somewhere less difficult.

Trees that like shade are much fewer than those that give it, and one tree under another is not usually visually pleasing. The Japanese maple (*Acer palmatum*), with a good supply of water and organic mulch, is a suitable under-tree, being dainty, low branched and small in all but mountainous districts. It can be used effectively as a link with a larger tree; however, a single Japanese maple looks quite awkward if not taken seriously as part of a composition. Camellias, particularly the japonica group, can brighten up a dull spot, given good water, mulch and food. They are not disease prone and in every way are handsome plants.

Instead of a mixture of plants, a mass of the one plant, such as a ground cover, can look striking, particularly under a large tree. Cut ground covers back to the lower shoots in winter or early spring to avoid lankness. Ferns, more than any other plants, are ideal for a shady area. They do not require much sun at all, although some light is needed. But they do need moisture: if your shady spot has reasonable drainage and a reasonable water supply from rain, hose or sprinkler, ferns will thrive. Choose them carefully, though: some need more warmth and protection than others. And plan your planting with care, remembering you are making a picture. Near the front you may need a few low, mossy rocks in which the smaller plants can nestle.

Structural solutions

Sometimes a shady garden can be greatly improved with the addition of a large urn or pot, a garden seat, a low stone bench or even a statue set among ground-covering ivy (*Hedera*) or rose of Sharon (*Hypericum calycinum*). It is most important to site the feature well, paying proper attention to adjacent plants, tree trunks and buildings. Somehow a low bench along a quite narrow side area makes it feel wider. On such a bench you can put a low pot plant in flower, something perhaps that has grown in a sunnier spot and will not be affected for a while by the shade.

OPPOSITE PAGE A garden picture does not happen accidentally. This shady garden is the result of careful planning and planting and a profound belief that simple things in the end are the loveliest.

PLANTS FOR SHADY PLACES

SHRUBS (HEIGHT 1–2 METRES)

***Artemisia arborescens* (wormwood)** Evergreen whose branches of deeply cut, silver leaves fill awkward spots; can stand periods without moisture.

***Aucuba japonica* 'Variegata' (gold dust plant)** Evergreen, large-leafed, green-stemmed shrub that creates patches of gold in the dullest areas and needs little direct sunlight – do not decide that you do not like it before you have thought what else you could use instead.

Cestrum elegans Evergreen, with narrow, rich coral-pink bells growing on arching branches, mid-winter to spring.

Cestrum nocturnum Evergreen that is as tough as old boots, even in a dry, shady corner; has fine, yellow flowers, spring to autumn.

Eupatorium megalophyllum Evergreen that is like a huge ageratum; needs protected position.

Fatsia japonica Evergreen whose stylish, big, fan-shaped leaves fill a corner; formal clusters of tiny, lime-green berries turn black.

Fuchsia magellanica Evergreen, dainty, old-world fuchsia able to survive in more sheltered spots than modern hybrids can; likes moisture.

Hydrangea macrophylla Deciduous, with white, pink, blue, mauve or purple flower heads, summer to autumn; needs dappled sunlight and moisture.

***Impatiens oliveri* (perennial balsam)** Evergreen, with pale lilac flowers in all seasons; fleshy stems. Grows easily in well-drained soil if given plenty of water, and is a useful bushy gap-filler, growing 1–2 m tall.

Jacobinia carnea Evergreen, with long plumes of carmine flowers, summer to autumn; plum-coloured leaves; softwood stalks. Cut it back by one-third after flowering and remove tatty old stalks.

***Kalmia latifolia* (mountain laurel)** Evergreen, with charming, white or pale pink flowers, like handmade lanterns, in late spring; glossy dark green leaves. It will either like the spot you give it or not – don't push it too far into shade, and transplant to more sunlight if it does not thrive after two years.

Mackaya bella Evergreen, with mauve bell flowers in spring; light copper-coloured leaves. A distinguished member of the shade dwellers.

SHRUBS (HEIGHT 1–2 METRES)

Mahonia Evergreen, striking, broad-leafed, prickly, palmlike plant whose unusual structure must be understood and used sensitively in picture making.

***Nandina domestica* (Japanese sacred bamboo)** Evergreen, at home in sun or shade. Will grow nearly 2 metres tall.

***Pieris* (andromeda, lily of the valley tree)** Evergreen, with dainty flowers like lilies of the valley in spring. Likes cool root run, acid soil and filtered sun. Grows about 1.5 metres tall.

***Plectranthus ecklonii* (blue spur-flower)** Evergreen, with a mass of arresting, dainty, purple-blue flower spikes; undemanding, soft-stemmed, quick-growing shrub that is lovely in autumn. Cut back by one-third after flowering, to keep compact. Grows readily from cuttings.

CLIMBING PLANTS

***Akebia quinata* (chocolate vine)** Evergreen, with dainty sprays of pink, mauve and grey flowers in spring. Charming in shade or sun.

***Gelsemium sempervirens* (Carolina jasmine)** Evergreen, with yellow bell flowers in late winter.

***Hedera helix* 'Glacier'** Evergreen, greenish-grey-and-white variegated ivy that brings some light into a dull corner. Invasive, so should be given firm limits.

***Solanum jasminoides* (potato creeper)** Evergreen that always tries to reach sunny spots, but gives white flowers on the way in all seasons.

PERENNIALS AND BULBS FOR MIDDLE BORDER

***Agapanthus* (Nile lily)** Evergreen bulb whose white- or blue-flowered dwarf varieties flower quite well in summer in rich soil. Has good, straplike leaves.

***Anemone japonica* (Japanese windflower)** Evergreen, with white, ice-pink or rose-pink cup flowers, late summer to autumn. Prefers moist, rich, light soil and partial shade, but grows in sun if kept moist.

***Aquilegia* (columbine, granny's bonnet)** Perennial, with nodding, pastel flowers, spring to summer; rosettes of blue-green leaves.

***Bergenia cordifolia* (elephant's ears)** Perennial; blossomlike, pink flowers in winter; broad, shiny leaves.

***Clivia miniata* (kaffir lily)** Evergreen bulb, with apricot lily flowers, autumn to spring; straplike leaves.

PLANTS FOR SHADY PLACES

PERENNIALS AND BULBS FOR MIDDLE BORDER

Begonia Perennial that is most rewarding in suitable conditions. Some species need more sunlight than others.

Crinum moorei Evergreen bulb, with white, pink or pale mauve lily flowers in summer; tall, pale green leaves.

***Epimedium* (dog-tooth violet)** Perennial grown mainly for fresh green young leaves, becoming deep glossy green. Low and spreading plant.

***Geranium robertianum* (herb Robert)** Perennial that can be a menace in gardens, seeding insidiously, yet in a poor, shady place provides a handy, evergreen leaf. Its nondescript pink flowers are best removed before seeding time.

***Heliotropium arborescens* (cherry pie, heliotrope)** Perennial, with dense heads of purple-lavender flowers and fragrance of musk. Shrubby plant for dappled shade or sun.

***Helleborus* (Lenten rose, winter rose)** Perennial, with delicate white or pastel flowers in winter; handsome, leathery leaves.

***Hemerocallis* (daylily)** Evergreen bulb, with yellow, apricot, copper, pink or red through to purple flowers, summer to autumn. Left undisturbed in moist soil, it will flourish. Will take part shade.

Hosta Winter-dormant plant, with dainty, white or mauve flowers; wonderfully textured leaf, often variegated. Impassions snails.

***Hyacinthoides* (bluebell)** Summer-dormant bulb that should be planted informally in woodland and left to establish colonies.

***Leucojum* (snowflake)** Summer-dormant bulb, with dainty, white cup flowers, spotted green, late winter to early spring.

***Lunaria* (honesty)** Not a perennial but a self-seeding annual, with white, magenta or purple flowers in summer; seed pods, dried out and peeled, make good floral decoration.

Primula Perennial that likes rich, well-drained to moist soil in filtered sun to shade and flowers autumn to spring. Remember *P. obconica*, in wonderful pastel shades, but use gloves to handle it.

***Salvia uliginosa* (bog sage)** Perrenial that likes sun but tolerates medium shade. Cut back after it flowers, summer to autumn.

GROUND COVERS

***Hypericum calycinum* (rose of Sharon)** Evergreen, with yellow flowers, containing many stamens, in summer; leathery leaves. Able to tussle with tree roots. May take time to establish, then must be watched.

***Lamium* (aluminium plant)** Evergreen, the variegated species of which makes a dappled mat once established. The mauve or yellow flowers are insignificant.

Plectranthus argentatus Evergreen, with attractive, feltlike, silver leaves. A native of Queensland and very frost tender.

Plectranthus ciliatus Evergreen, with pale mauve flowers in autumn; greenish purple leaves. Roots where it touches and spreads easily.

Plectranthus oertendahlii Evergreen, with silver-veined, bronze leaves. Spreads for about 22 centimetres.

***Vinca* (periwinkle)** Evergreen, with white or blue flowers in spring. There are small-leafed types, such as *V. minor*, and large-leafed ones.

EDGING PLANTS

***Erigeron karvinskianus* (baby's tears)** Perennial that flowers most seasons. It likes some protection but will not thrive without some sunlight.

***Fragaria* (wild strawberry)** Perennial; has dainty leaves, yellow flowers in spring and pushy ways, but, kept controlled, makes a pretty edging.

Impatiens Annual and perennial, succulent-stemmed plant, with flowers ranging from pastel to vibrant colours, summer to autumn. Prefers moist, fertile soil. One of the best plants for shady spots.

***Myosotis* (forget-me-not)** Annual that always finds a spot in which to grow. Flowers in spring mainly.

Pratia pedunculata Evergreen, with tiny, blue or white star flowers, spring to summer. The dainty, fernlike foliage will delight you, edging a path or pond.

***Saxifraga* (mossy saxifrage)** Perennial that favours semi-shade and makes a fine edging, with its firm, round rosettes of leaves and sprays of flowers, on dainty stems, in spring.

Tiarella Semi-evergreen plant for cool, rich soil, which throws up wonderful heads of heucheralike, pale green flowers in spring.

Viola Evergreen that needs sun to produce many flowers, but foliage flourishes in shady spots.

A PLACE IN THE SUN

You will know how important sunlight is to plant life if you have ever watched, over some years, the changes a maturing tree has made to a temperate garden with a sunny aspect. The plants underneath, once compact and healthy, become weaker and more straggling and the flowers smaller and paler as the shade extends.

If you have a sunny garden plot, make the most of it and don't drive all the sun away by growing a big tree, unless you need it to shade your house or an outdoor living space. Take up the challenge of creating a sun-loving garden within a garden.

PLANNING

Consider the space your garden in the sun will occupy before you begin. Perhaps it is a deep, oblong border, along the boundary, or an open, central area, or a sun-trap created by a house or garden wall? If the space is large, you may need to plan some judicious shade. A backdrop or hedge of *Feijoa sellowiana*, guava (*Psidium guajava*) or silvery wormwood (*Artemisia arborescens*) may provide sufficient shade and protection. If more is required, consider a light deciduous tree that offers a tracery of shadows when the harsh summer sun is in the western sky. A shady spot also allows you to introduce a seat from which to view the splendour of your sun-filled garden.

An open garden lends itself to a sundial, as a central focal point, or a formal square or round pond, perhaps with a fountain to provide cooling splashiness. Deep or dull colours are best for paving areas and paths in such a garden: cream or white is too harsh and dazzling. Materials such as sawn bluestone, dull slates or earth-toned bricks make suitable surfaces.

OPPOSITE PAGE Some plants need hot sun to thrive and look their best. Many have brightly coloured flowers and quite a few have silver foliage.

CHOOSING PLANTS

In choosing plants for your sunny places, it is important to know how much sun each requires and how each will look and behave when there is less sun during winter. Some plants are born and bred only for sunny positions and even thrive in sun-baked soil, growing mean and lank or rotting and withering if they are given anything less. You will need to establish whether your district suffers from frosts and the frost tolerance of the plants you choose. Remember that the origins of your plant species will give you clues about their heat tolerance and watering needs.

It is reassuring to know that if you look after plants that do not need full sun they will, in fact, often perform better in a sunny place than in a shady spot where they are neglected. A well-watered plant, such as a *Camellia japonica*, its roots kept cool with a 7–10-centimetre mulch and growing in soil of good texture, will survive and flourish in the sun, where a neglected one will get yellow, sunburnt leaves and appear stressed. On the other hand, some annual and perennial plants that thrive in moderate heat pack up when the sun hits them full force – although, once again, their tolerance will be greater if they are well fed and watered.

RIGHT Good drainage and a spot in the sun are all that these two neat cactuses need.

PLANTS THAT CRAVE SUN

***Centaurea cineraria* (dusty miller)** Perennial, with thistlelike, purple-blue flower heads in summer; silver leaves.	***Iberis sempervirens* (perennial candytuft)** Perennial, with small, snowy white flowers, winter to spring.
***Centranthus ruber* (kiss-me-quick, valerian)** Perennial, with white, pink or red flowers, spring to autumn.	***Iris unguicularis* (winter iris)** Bulb, with pale blue-mauve flowers among slender-bladed leaves in winter.
***Dianthus* (pink)** Perennial often grown as an annual, with perfumed, single or double, white, cream, pink, mauve or purple flowers, often with serrated edges, spring to summer.	***Ixia viridiflora* (African corn lily)** Winter-dormant, hardy bulb, with dainty, turquoise star flowers in spring.
***Echinops* (globe thistle)** Perennial, with white or blue thistlelike flowers, summer to autumn; grey or green leaves.	***Lavatera cachemiriana* (tree mallow)** Perennial, with abundant, hibiscuslike, pink flowers in late spring; shrubby bush.
***Euphorbia wulfenii* (wulfen spurge)** Perennial, with yellow-centred, lime-green flowers in spring.	***Limonium* (statice)** Perennial, with clusters of tiny, everlasting, white, yellow, pink, blue or mauve flowers, summer to autumn.
Gaura lindheimeri Perennial, with pinkish white butterfly flowers, on long stems, summer to autumn.	***Nepeta* × *faassenii* (catmint)** Perennial, with spikes of dainty, blue flowers, summer to autumn; pungent leaves.
***Gazania* hybrids (treasure flowers)** Perennial, with cream, yellow, orange, pink, red or rust-coloured daisy flowers, spring to autumn.	***Oenothera odorata* (evening primrose)** Bright yellow flowers at dusk in summer.
***Helenium autumnale* (sneezeweed)** Perennial, with yellow daisy flowers, which have conical centres, in summer.	***Rudbeckia* (cone flower)** Perennial, with yellow daisy flowers, which have conical centres, in autumn.
***Helianthus annuus* (sunflower)** Annual, with large, yellow daisy flowers in summer.	***Salvia leucantha* (Mexican mint bush)** Perennial, with velvety textured, violet or white flowers in autumn; sagelike, grey leaves.
	Salvia patens Perennial, with intense, pure blue flowers in summer.

In your sunny garden within a garden you might like to have annuals, perennials and shrubs from different warm countries to give you a wide range of plants and a flow of seasonal pictures. You might plan the area around the colours of plants born and bred for the sun: a garden of mainly silver-foliaged plants, many of which come from the Mediterranean region, the Canary Islands and South Africa. On the other hand, you might prefer to use plants that you know come from the warm regions of Australia and will suit your conditions year round. The list provided here will give you ideas for annual and perennial plants, but consult also the information and planting list in the section on A Garden Hot and Dry in Chapter 7.

The proven methods of conserving moisture are particularly important when it comes to growing plants in open, sunny spots and suntraps. Organic mulch, in conjunction with periodical watering, cannot be overstressed; it keeps roots cool, it protects the ground from moisture loss through evaporation, and, as it breaks down, improving the soil's texture, it increases the soil's water retention. Of course not all plants require the same quantity of water. For instance, while *Grevillea endlicherana* or the African native plant diosma (*Coleonema pulchrum*) can die from over-watering or a poorly drained site, hibiscus and bougainvillea species like their heat with plenty of water.

HERB GARDENS

A herb is usually defined as a plant with fragrant leaves containing volatile oils or one with roots, flowers or stems useful to humans. Herb gardens are inextricably linked with history. There are evocative and romantic aspects to these plants, and people over the centuries have loved to have herbs round them. As well, herbs have provided medicinal cures and comforts, food-enhancing flavours and cosmetic extracts.

If you only have room for a small garden but it faces north, east or west, you could not do much better than to make a herb garden. If you have more space, you could grow your herbs in their own garden within your larger one. By the time the lavenders, old roses, scented pelargoniums and lemon verbena (*Lippia citriodora*) for pot-pourri are planted with your herb collection, you will have a garden indeed.

LAYOUT

Some of the early herb gardens were made within monastery walls, where the plants' qualities were observed and tested. These gardens were orderly places and the strong-growing plants were segregated from the less pushy types. The idea of separate herb gardens evolved for such reasons of control and, so it seems, from the sheer joy of making beautiful and sometimes quite intricate patterns that were a delight to passers-by and those who viewed the gardens from upstairs windows.

Today, with a greater variety of plants, attractive small herb gardens can be made, perhaps containing neat paths and a small statue, birdbath or sundial.

Decorative herb gardens can be highly formal, like this one, or more informal and flowing, as the plan that follows shows.

A herb garden should be a nostalgic place. A seat can add to the pleasure of being in your herb garden.

The colours of herbs are largely foliage colours – emerald, blue, mid-green, olive, copper and silver. The flowers of herbs are purple, mauve, blue, white and yellow, with an occasional pale pink, carmine or red. Many of the flowers are small and restrained rather than showy. Therefore a great deal of the beauty of a herb garden comes from its low-key blending of foliage colours and the thoughtfulness of the layout. If you find yours is a little dull, add something bright, such as nasturtiums, Oriental poppies (*Papaver orientale*), a red rose or foxgloves (*Digitalis*) – even sunflowers (*Helianthus*) are permitted. And faithful borage (*Borago officinalis*) can always be relied on to thrust up its jewel-like blue flowers.

Your herb garden need not be too formal; the plants can be massed as in a cottage garden. Alternatively, you can plant a band of herbs around your vegetable patch: it can add charm and improve the appearance between seasons. A planting of English lavender (*Lavandula angustifolia*) or rosemary (*Rosmarinus officinalis*) makes a definite and pretty edging or hedging, neatening the edges and defining spaces, paths and borders.

HERBS TO PLANT FOR COLOUR

BLUE-MAUVE FLOWERS

Allium (chives, garlic, shallots)
Borago officinalis (borage)
Cichorium intybus (chicory)
Hyssopus officinalis
Linum perenne (flax)
Nepeta × *faassenii* (catmint)
Rosmarinus officinalis (rosemary)
Salvia officinalis (sage)
Thymus vulgaris (thyme)
Veronica spicata (speedwell)

PINK-RED FLOWERS

Centranthus ruber (kiss-me-quick, valerian)
Lavandula angustifolia 'Rosea' (pink English lavender)
Monarda didyma (bee balm, bergamot)
Salvia involucrata 'Bethellii' (Bethell sage)
Salvia rutilans (pineapple sage)
Saponaria ocymoides (soapwort)
Thymus serpyllum (creeping thyme)

YELLOW FLOWERS

Anthemis tinctoria (chamomile)
Oenothera missouriensis (evening primrose)
Phlomis fruticosa (Jerusalem sage)
Potentilla recta (cinquefoil)
Tanacetum vulgare (tansy)

CULTIVATION AND USE

Most herbs need a sunny position, with as much northern sun as possible, to give them the best chance to develop their properties of fragrance and volatile oils. Good drainage is important for all but a few herbs, although they should have no additional compost, animal manure or fertiliser because the leaves become too lush and yield less oil. Herbs are resistant to disease and tougher than many other garden plants. As well, they are easily propagated by slip, division or cutting, particularly in late winter and early spring. Marjoram (*Origanum majorana*), chives (*Allium schoenoprasum*) and the different mints (*Mentha*) can be divided then and sage (*Salvia officinalis*) and rosemary cuttings taken, although they tend to root readily at most times.

Some annual herbs, including parsley (*Petroselinum crispum*), dill (*Anethum graveolens*), coriander (*Coriandrum sativum*), anise (*Pimpinella anisum*) and chervil (*Anthriscus cerefolium*) are best sown direct. Basil (*Ocimum basilicum*), another annual, can be bought as seedlings in mid-spring. Snails love it, so be careful. Parsley and chervil are inclined to favour a shadier spot than many herbs.

Herbs should be cut for use when they are thriving; this also keeps them stimulated, shapely and producing good-quality growth. Mints and thymes (*Thymus*) become tough once they are seeding; cut them back to their bases immediately after flowering so that new leaves develop. Use your herb clippings for cooking, gifts, cuttings, fuel for aromatic barbecues or open fires and compost.

To dry herbs, pick them mid-morning, tie them in small bundles and hang them in airy spots. To store dried herbs, make sure first that they have thoroughly dried out, then strip the leaves from the stems or extract the seeds and store them out of the sun in airtight containers.

CREATING AN INTIMATE SPACE: A HERB GARDEN

The informal design of this herb garden allows many herbs to be grown in a small but special space.

COLOUR PLAN
Soft tonings and grey, green and golden foliage

KEY

1 *Prunus armeniaca* 'Moorpark' (Moorpark apricot), espaliered
2 *Psidium littorale* (cherry guava), clipped
3 *Pyrus communis* 'Beurre Bosc' (brown pear)
4 *Vaccinium corymbosum* (bush blueberry)
5 *Passiflora edulis* (black passionfruit)
6 *Heliotropium arborescens* (cherry pie, heliotrope)
7 *Prunus salicina* 'Satsuma' (satsuma plum)
8 *Ribes vulgaris* (redcurrant)
9 *Ribes grossularia* (gooseberry), on frame
10 *Allium ascalonicum* (shallot)
11 Space for extra planting, e.g. *Coriandrum sativum* (coriander), *Allium sativum* (garlic)
12 *Thymus* (thyme)
13 *Cheiranthus cheiri* (wallflower)
14 *Artemisia dracunculus* (French tarragon)
15 *Allium schoenoprasum* (chive)
16 *Anthriscus cerefolium* (chervil)
17 *Anethum graveolens* (dill)
18 *Ocimum basilicum* (basil)
19 *Salvia officinalis* (sage)
20 *Satureja montana* (winter savoury)
21 *Citrus limon* (lemon tree)
22 *Nepeta* × *faassenii* (catmint)
23 *Mentha spicata* (spearmint) in pot
24 *Punica granatum* 'Nana' (dwarf pomegranate)
25 *Laurus nobilis* (bay tree) in pot
26 *Rosmarinus officinalis* 'Blue Lagoon' (blue lagoon rosemary)
27 *Calendula officinalis* (pot marigold)
28 *Origanum vulgare* (oregano)
29 *Tanacetum vulgare* (tansy)
30 *Petroselinum crispum* (parsley)
31 Space for small, quick-growing vegetables, e.g. *Lactuca sativa* (lettuce), *Raphanus sativus* (radish), *Beta vulgaris* var. *cicla* (silverbeet)
32 *Santolina chamaecyparissus* (cotton lavender)
33 *Salvia officinalis* 'Variegata' (variegated sage)
34 *Salvia officinalis* 'Purpurascens' (purple sage)
35 *Borago officinalis* (borage)
36 *Tropaeolum majus* (nasturtium)
37 *Origanum marjorana* (marjoram)
38 *Lavandula dentata* (French lavender)
39 *Sanguisorba minor* (salad burnet)
40 *Lepidium sativum* (land cress)
41 *Lavandula angustifolia* (English lavender)
42 *Pelargonium* (scented geranium)
43 *Foeniculum vulgare* (fennel)
44 *Symphytum officinale* (comfrey)
45 *Monarda didyma* (bergamot)
46 *Lippia citriodora* (lemon verbena)
47 *Salvia rutilans* (pineapple sage)
48 *Digitalis purpurea* (foxglove)
49 *Armoracia rusticana* (horseradish)
50 *Angelica archangelica*
51 *Vitis vinifera* 'Isabella' (Isabella grape)
52 *Lonicera pericylmenum* 'Belgica' (honeysuckle, sweet woodbine)
53 *Pelargonium peltatum* (ivy geranium) in pots
54 *Feijoa sellowiana* hedge
55 *Rosa moyesii* 'Geranium'

VEGETABLE GARDENS

We have only to look at the gardens of a few serious vegetable gardeners to realise that these plots need by no means lack beauty, and, from a practical point of view, they cannot be surpassed. Vegetables have much to be said for them as garden occupants. They are interesting and varied in shape and form, with an intriguing range of colour; they reward us by growing quickly; they are good to eat and good for us. Vegetable gardens, as a rule, represent nature well controlled and garden components well and truly compartmentalised: rows of onions, cabbages, cauliflowers, peas, beans, beetroots, carrots, parsnips and leeks; rectangular plots of potatoes; patches of zucchini and pumpkins.

POTS AND POTAGERS

Vegetables are not too fussed about where we plant them. Given a fertile, well-drained soil in a sunny spot, many fine products, such as lettuces, will even grow in polystyrene boxes. Half-sized wooden barrels offer sharp drainage for tomatoes, zucchini and other vegetables. Potatoes are being grown with some distinction in car tyres, and a cut-down forty-four-gallon drum is a time-honoured vegetable pot. If you do not have a large space for vegetables, you can train peas and beans up walls, wires or trellis.

You may choose just to mix a few vegetables in with your general garden, and, provided you remember to keep an eye on them, there is no reason why you should not. In fact, if you feel the urge to turn your front garden over to vegetables, this is quite logical in an age of scarce resources. Your front garden, after all, may be your sunniest spot. You can make an appealing garden that will be the envy of passers-by.

If you do have room for a fully fledged vegetable garden you might like to design a simpler, smaller version of the potagers originating in France. Any vegetable garden, however, should not be too far from your kitchen and should be approached by a solid path to allow for wet-weather access. Your potager will soon become an absorbing hobby, and, once it is established, you might like to try some of the exciting new varieties of vegetables, such as rocket, radicchio, rainbow chard and golden capsicums, available through specialist sources.

MANAGING YOUR VEGETABLE GARDEN

The overriding principles of a well-run vegetable garden are regular watering and crop rotation, involving three or four types of crop. The theory behind crop rotation is that soil-borne pests and diseases do not build up year after year. Soil nutriments are also made available to the plants most needing them. You can, for example, rotate:

1 leguminous vegetables, such as peas (*Pisum sativum*) and beans (*Phaseolus*), and different types of onion (*Allium*)
2 *Brassica oleracea* varieties, such as cabbages, cauliflowers, kale and Brussels sprouts
3 root crops, such as carrots (*Daucus carota*), parsnips (*Pastinaca sativa*) and beetroots (*Beta*).

These three categories of vegetables require richly organic soil in decreasing order. Crop rotation, using three types of crop such as these, takes three years to fully implement. How to rotate the three crops is explained in the accompanying table.

Tomatoes (*Lycopersicon lycopersicum*) and potatoes (*Solanum tuberosum*) should be planted in a new area each year over a four-year period. Because they belong to the same family, they should never follow each other in less than four years.

As well as annuals you will probably want to allow space for permanent crops, such as asparagus and rhubarb (*Rheum rhaponticum*), and perhaps some berry fruits. Seed packets and seedling punnets give clear instructions about planting times and requirements, including spacing, which should be followed.

Part of the art of vegetable growing is to regulate your crops so that you do not have too many vegetables at once, and to grow them a little out of line with the peak commercial seasons so that when they are particularly expensive you can supply your own. This will take you some time to perfect.

For an average family, six tomato plants should give an adequate crop, with successive plantings every six weeks of six lettuces (*Lactuca sativa*), cauliflowers or cabbages to provide a continuous supply.

OPPOSITE PAGE A neatly kept vegetable garden can be easily incorporated in a larger garden.

CROP ROTATION
YEAR ONE
Set aside three plots in your vegetable garden. The first year dig the first plot over deeply and manure well. Add lime (one handful per square metre) six weeks before planting, to prevent diseases, such as club root, and to break down heavy soils. The prepared soil should be firm and flattish. Plant legumes and onion types.
YEAR TWO
Replace the legumes and onions in the first plot with brassicas. Legumes have nitrogen-fixing bacteria in their roots, which will have left the soil ready for the nitrogen-loving brassicas. All you will need to add is some complete fertiliser. Prepare the second plot as you did the first one originally, and plant it with legumes and onions.
YEAR THREE
Replace the brassicas in the first plot with root crops, making sure the soil is broken up finely and free of stones. Follow the legumes and onions in the second plot with brassicas. Both plots will need only the addition of a complete fertiliser. Prepare the third plot as you did the first two originally, and plant it with legumes and onions.
SUBSEQUENT YEARS
Continue to rotate crops in the three plots in the same order.

HEALTHY PLANTS

The healthier plants are – which is determined largely by good stock, watering, composting, fertilising and attention – the less prone they will be to pests and diseases, and, of course, the better they will be to eat.

Applications of liquid fertiliser are important to accelerate the growth of most vegetables from the early stages. A vegetable's life in your garden should be short but indulged.

When pests or diseases do attack, try to deal with them conservatively, using physical removal, natural soapy solutions and organic sprays. Sometimes it may be more expedient to remove a crop or what is left of it than to spray. Rest the soil for a season where a disease has caused problems. If you avoid poisonous sprays you have no need to worry about contamination of yourself and other living creatures. Try to ignore a munched-up leaf or two – there are a lot of leaves on a cabbage.

DESIGNING A VEGETABLE GARDEN

When you are designing your vegetable garden, a number of requirements must be met.

- Vegetables need a sunny position that is sheltered, particularly from drying winds, and is screened if a windfunnel exists. They also require well-drained, fertile soil.
- Plant vegetables in rows running north–south to attract the maximum sun. The width of the beds depends on the vegetables grown: cabbages and cauliflowers need a good 60 centimetres, onions 25 centimetres and carrots and parsnips 45 centimetres. Convenient access to all parts of the vegetable garden, via firm-surfaced paths, is essential. However, for easy access to plants and weeds without damaging the growing vegetables, no bed should be wide, except perhaps for patches where potatoes or pumpkins are grown. There must be sufficient room for wheeling a barrow between the beds and turning it near the compost bins. Paths also provide a permanent framework and are an important design element from an aesthetic as well as a practical point of view.
- Most vegetables must have a regular water supply as they develop. Carrots, lettuce, celery and tomatoes, in particular, deteriorate if the soil dries out. An automatic sprinkler system, providing regular watering, is helpful, but a nearby tap and hose are also handy so that the special needs of seeds or certain plants can be met without involving the whole garden. A tap is also useful for washing your hands and the harvested vegetables.
- Keeping up a regular supply of organic matter to vegetables is important, so have compost bins nearby. Leafy vegetable trimmings can be put straight into the compost before the cleaned vegetables are taken to the kitchen.
- Low hedges or edging plants define and neaten the perimeters of a vegetable garden; rosemary (*Rosmarinus officinalis*), English box (*Buxus sempervirens*) or lavenders (*Lavandula* species) make suitable hedges. A thick planting of lobelias or marigolds (*Tagetes*) looks striking edging beds, and the latter are well known for repelling soil-borne pests, such as nematodes.
- Fruit trees, and in particular lemon trees (*Citrus limon*), are handy near a vegetable garden. Certainly one can be planted as a screen if it is not likely to cast shadows over the vegetables during the day. Guava (*Psidium guajava*) and *Feijoa sellowiana* make protective and productive hedges. Espaliered fruit trees on walls or free-standing frameworks can also be incorporated, especially where space is limited.
- A low wall or a bench is important as a place to put tools, seed packets and cut vegetables and for you to rest on. You might carry the concept to the next phase: a table at kitchen-bench height near the compost bins where you can remove the unwanted leaves, roots and stems of your freshly picked vegetables.
- If space allows, decorative features, such as tubs of nasturtiums, chimney pots and old farm machinery or other rustic, cottagey bits and pieces, add to the pleasure of trips to the vegetable garden. And don't forget a scarecrow – scarecrows may delight us more than they frighten the birds, but they are nice to have around.

This country vegetable garden is surrounded by a rabbit-proof wall. It is divided by paths for easy access to the crops.

OPPOSITE PAGE Fine tomatoes (*Lycopersicon lycopersicum*) are one of the joys of having a vegetable garden.

GARDENS IN CONTAINERS

Gardens in outdoor pots, window-boxes and hanging baskets offer rich opportunities for combining flowers and marking the seasonal changes. The choice of plants, containers and positions is seemingly endless.

POTS AND SPOTS

The fact that pot plants can be moved from spot to spot provides tremendous flexibility. You can grow your plants in warm, sunny places until they flower, then take them round the corner to eastern or southern aspects, feeding them dilute liquid manure every three weeks.

There is a wide selection of terracotta pots and glazed ceramic pots, some in oriental styles, as well as pots of moulded concrete and reconstituted stone, in

BELOW Caring for a collection of potted plants can become an absorbing hobby.

OPPOSITE PAGE A pot overflowing with pretty plants adds a master touch to a garden space.

dressy formal and classical styles or less complicated shapes. Warmly coloured terracotta is a most desirable natural material, but it is porous and loses water more quickly than does a glazed pot. Use them by all means, but keep them well watered. Cement and reconstituted stone have the same porous qualities. Wood is a poor conductor of heat, so roots can be kept reasonably moist inside wooden containers.

Plants are best transferred from the plastic pots they come in to more flattering containers. You do not necessarily need to transfer them to expensive commercial pots, however: sometimes old paint tins and drums are ideal (at least until they rust) and can be painted a suitable colour. Try also a hollow log. Halved wooden barrels with drainage holes provide containers of varying sizes. Polystyrene boxes are useful for growing cuttings, lettuces or herbs, when a wide surface area is required; they have the advantage of being light as well – but keep them out of sight.

In choosing and siting pots it is important to consider proportion and scale just as you would for any other aspect of garden making. Try to visualise a pot near your house, matching it for style and shape. Sometimes a single large pot looks strange and contrived, whereas if you put a wide, low pot next to it, and perhaps a medium-sized one as well, the group immediately becomes integrated. Of course, this does not apply to large classical urns designed to be seen in the round as an architectural feature; they need to be arranged formally, never randomly.

A family of straight-sided pots – clay pipe cross-sections with no bottoms are fine if permanently sited – often work well with modern architecture. In contrast, there is something cottagey about a chimney pot at ground level, filled with plants or just used as a sculpture.

Sometimes handsome urns are best left empty. They should be sited carefully so that their beauty can be admired. This is the epitome of low maintenance. When you are despairing of a dingy corner or a boring side pathway think of an elegant pot as a decoration, but do not overdo the effect.

Pendulous fuchsias make a perfect planting for hanging baskets.

Place a big pot of herbs in a sunny spot near the kitchen (small pots are more demanding to manage). Window-boxes are delightful, too, outside kitchens – and for other rooms. However, they must not be allowed to spoil the fenestration; they are best placed on the sills of windows set half-way up a wall, although they can sometimes look attractive at the base of full-length windows. Window-boxes also give a froth of garden at upstairs windows.

PURPOSES

Growing plants in containers, and not in the garden, isolates them for special attention. There are some practical reasons for doing this:

- your garden may have little topsoil or sour, root-packed soil
- you may have some small and precious plants that you do not want to risk losing
- you can set limits for a rampant plant – ivy (*Hedera*) or violets (*Viola odorata*) are charming but safely contained as they tumble from pots
- you can hide once-a-year stars from sight when their moment is over and move them back to centre stage when they are at their peak again
- you can make pictures on wheels by moving groups of pots around, using a hand trolley to save your back
- if you have a small garden, you can make quite an impact with a few well-chosen, well-planted pots.

CARE

Potting mixes offer sharp drainage, which is critical to successful growing in pots. Badly drained pots retain water and eventually drown their plants. The mixes often have little or no true soil content, being largely made of dry, sterilised bark, sand and charcoal. Brands vary, so experiment until you find a good-quality one.

Hanging baskets are best set in a moulded fibre or wire frame lined with sphagnum moss. An inner lining of clear plastic, punctuated with drainage holes, improves water retention. Plastic containers held with chains are best used when the sides are to be covered with growth.

Plants in containers are exposed from top to toe to the extremes of conditions experienced in gardens. The sun bakes the sides and base of the container and quickly dries out the potting mix, and severe cold penetrates all over. Therefore plants should be checked for dryness and watered regularly. Plants, with the exception of native ones, should also be fed regularly, using liquid manure or a slow-release fertiliser rather than concentrated chemical fertilisers, which can be too powerful for captives.

Plants should not look too large or too small for their containers. Repot a plant in a container one size larger when roots appear through the drainage holes of the present one. Early spring is the best time for repotting.

New arrivals in pots, such as weeds, erigerons, forget-me-nots and privet seedlings, need to be checked or they can take over.

PLANTS FOR POTS

When combining plants in a pot do not get slapdash: your combinations must look good to the eye. However, unless you are planting a solitary conifer, standard box (*Buxus*) or similar plant, it is safe to say that you will find pots of any size or shape look better the fuller they are. Abundance, particularly in gardens, is a great concept.

Mix annuals and small perennials according to seasons. A lovely combination is trailing lobelias, convolvulus, pink African daisies (*Dimorphotheca*) and sweet Alice (*Alyssum*) in a large pot. Try velvety purple petunias with rich orange-gold marigolds (*Calendula* and *Tagetes*), or a mixture of pastels – the pink rose 'The Fairy' and sweet Alice or blue *Felicia amelloides* and mauve *Brachyscome multifida* daisy flowers.

Most bulbs enjoy the sharp drainage of a pot. They can be displayed at their height and then tucked out of sight as they decline. Precious, small and unusual bulbs are also safe in pots. Compost should be added each year if they remain in a pot.

Succulents also lend themselves to pot life, coping well with temporary drying out, and make interesting and different pot plants. Yuccas and palms, too, have a place in containers.

Food at your fingertips

Vegetables, such as *Capsicum annuum*, Chinese cabbage or pak choy (*Brassica chinensis* var. *chinensis*), Japanese senposai or mizuna (*B. japonica*), silverbeet (*Beta vulgaris* var. *cicla*), spinach (*Spinacea oleracea*) and tomatoes (*Lycopersicon lycopersicum*), can be successfully grown in pots. Most culinary herbs can also be grown, given suitable-sized pots, sunlight and good drainage, although angelica, because it grows tall, is best left in the ground. Remember that parsley (*Petroselinum crispum*) and chervil (*Anthriscus cerefolium*) take some shade. The mighty bay tree (*Laurus nobilis*) needs regular watering in a pot, but is well curbed if you keep clipping its leaves.

Other food-bearing plants for pots include blueberries (*Vaccinium*) and strawberries (*Fragaria*). The latter will drip down the sides of a tall pot in wonderful abandonment. Dwarf fruit trees – apples (*Malus*), pomegranates (*Punica granatum*) and nectarines and peaches (*Prunus persica*) – are at their best in pots. Guavas (*Psidium guajava*) and *Feijoa sellowiana*, too, can be contained in large pots. Citrus, particularly the small-fruited cumquat (*Fortunella*) and the 'Meyer' lemon, look extremely decorative in medium to large pots.

PLANTS FOR POTTING

PLANTS FOR SUNNY SPOTS

Alyssum maritimum (sweet Alice)
Brachyscome multifida (rock daisy)
Calendula officinalis (pot marigold)
Chrysanthemum frutescens (marguerite daisy)
Dianthus (carnation, pink)
Geranium (crane's bill)
Iberis sempervirens (candytuft)
Lantana
Lathyrus odorata (sweet pea)
Petunia
Torenia fournieri (wishbone flower)
Tropaeolum majus (nasturtium)
Verbena
Vinca (periwinkle)
Viola (pansy, violet)

PLANTS FOR SHADE OR FILTERED SUN

Azalea
Begonia
Camellia japonica
Camellia sasanqua
Campanula poscharskyana (Siberian bell flower)
Francoa sonchifolia (bridal wreath)
Impatiens
Lamium maculatum (aluminium plant)
Lobelia erinus (edging lobelia)
Nandina domestica (Japanese sacred bamboo)
Primula

Ferns are also suitable.

BULBS

Agapanthus 'Baby Blue' (dwarf Nile lily)
Clivia (kaffir lily)
Crocus
Freesia
Hyacinthoides (bluebell)
Hyacinthus (hyacinth)
Lilium (lily)
Muscari (grape hyacinth)
Narcissus (daffodil, jonquil)
Tulipa (tulip)
Zephyranthes (flower of the west wind)

SUCCULENTS AND UNUSUAL PLANTS

Crassula
Euphorbia
Kalanchoe
Portulacaria afra (jade plant)
Sedum (stonecrop)
Sempervivum
Zygocactus truncatus (Christmas cactus, crab cactus)

JUST FOR THE PICKING: CUTTING GARDENS

The idea of a picking garden originated with stately properties; the main gardens were large and rather formal and so the picking flowers were relegated to a place near the back of the house, where they tended to be planted in rows like a well-drilled squadron. This concept might be attractive to some who have the interest and space.

It must be a fine feeling to gather armfuls of, for instance, one type of yellow rose with which to fill large vases. Most of us, however, do not have the space to devote to a formal picking garden. In fact the concept seems a rather narrow interpretation of the cut flower, for almost every plant is capable of being used decoratively – whether for its flowers, leaves, stems, fruit, berries or bare branches. So, when you are planning a garden, try to fit in as many interesting plants as you can. Later you will enjoy the thrill of the hunt – of walking around the garden with basket and secateurs, finding all manner of treasures.

When you are short of flowers (or even when you are not) try to think laterally about what to use in vases. Look for the unusual, for plants that you might not consider at first glance: dried bracken, grasses or rushes; dead tree-fern fronds; the dry seed heads of parsley, love-in-a-mist or acanthus; lichen-covered branches; rose hips and cumquats on branches.

If you are doing large arrangements you will be glad of a foliage framework. Foliage adds a mellow touch to posies – sometimes you can make an entire posy of leaves. Some of the loveliest leaves are the silver-grey ones of *Eucalyptus*; the russet leaves on the arching boughs of *Melaleuca hypericifolia*; the pale green, maple-like foliage of *Grevillea glabrata*; the glossy green leaves of *Azara microphylla*, camellias and the mirror bush (*Coprosma*); and the speckled foliage of the gold dust plant (*Aucuba japonica* 'Variegata'). Some of the evergreen conifers have lacy foliage in tonings from grey-blue through green to burnished autumn colours.

Autumn gleanings – dried bracken fronds, the seed pods of love-in-a-mist (*Nigella damascena*), branches of green fig (*Ficus carica*), dull blue sloe fruit (*Prunus spinosa*), chrysanthemums, cornflowers (*Centaurea*), wheat ears, grapes, olives, nuts and a pumpkin – glow in an indoors arrangement.

COLOURFUL CUTTING PLANTS

SPRING SHRUBS

***Acacia* (wattle)** Yellow, lemon or gold flowers.

Camellia japonica White, cream, pink or red flowers.

***Chaenomeles japonica* (flowering quince)** White, pink or red flowers.

***Choisya ternata* (Mexican orange blossom)** White flowers.

SPRING ANNUALS, PERENNIALS AND BULBS

Anemone White, yellow, orange, pink or red flowers.

***Aquilegia* (columbine, granny's bonnet)** White, yellow, pink or mauve flowers, often in combination.

Arum White flowers.

***Dianthus* (carnation, pink)** White or pastel flowers.

Euphorbia Lime-green flowers.

Freesia Cream, yellow, red, blue or mauve flowers.

***Iberis sempervirens* (candytuft)** White flowers.

***Lathyrus odoratus* (sweet pea)** White, pink, red or mauve flowers.

***Myosotis* (forget-me-not)** Pink or blue flowers.

***Narcissus* (daffodil and jonquil)** White, cream, yellow, apricot or orange flowers.

***Nigella damascena* (love-in-a-mist)** Blue flowers.

***Papaver nudicaule* (Iceland poppy)** White, yellow, orange, pink or red flowers.

***Tulipa* (tulip)** Bold and pastel flowers.

***Viola odorata* (violet)** Mauve flowers.

SUMMER SHRUBS

***Abutilon* (Chinese lantern bush)** White, yellow, orange, pink or red flowers.

Hydrangea White, pink, blue or mauve flowers. Some fade to russet.

SUMMER ANNUALS, PERENNIALS AND BULBS

***Alstroemeria* (Peruvian lily)** Cream, yellow, orange, pink or red flowers.

***Antirrhinum* (snapdragon)** White, yellow, pink, red or mauve flowers.

***Campanula* (bell flower)** White, pink, blue or mauve flowers.

SUMMER ANNUALS, PERENNIALS AND BULBS

***Chrysanthemum maximum* (shasta daisy)** White flowers.

Cosmos White, yellow, orange, pink or magenta flowers.

***Delphinium* (larkspur)** White, blue or mauve flowers.

***Eryngium* (sea holly)** Blue-mauve flowers.

***Gerbera* (African daisy)** Pink or red flowers.

***Gladiolus* (sword lily)** White, cream, green, pink, red or mauve flowers.

***Gypsophila* (baby's breath)** White or pink flowers.

Iris Dark or pastel flowers.

***Lavandula* (lavender)** White, pink or mauve flowers.

***Lilium* (lily)** Bold or pastel flowers.

***Molucella laevis* (Molucca balm)** Pale green flowers.

***Rosa* (rose)** White or cream through to mauve flowers (also orange or red autumn hips).

AUTUMN SHRUBS AND TREES

***Berberis thunbergii* 'Atropurpurea'** Rich red-mauve leaves.

***Cornus florida* (dogwood)** Red leaves (also cream and pink bracts in spring).

Cotoneaster Red berries (also white spring flowers).

***Crataegus* (hawthorn)** Red berries (also white spring flowers).

***Euonymus alatus* (cork bush)** Purple berries (also red summer flowers).

Fuchsia White, pink, red, mauve or purple flowers.

***Malus* (crab apple)** Red or yellow crab apples (also white or pink spring blossom).

***Physalis alkekengi* (winter cherry)** Cherry-red berries.

***Quercus palustris* (scarlet oak)** Orange and scarlet foliage.

***Sorbus* (rowan)** Scarlet berries.

***Viburnum opulus* 'Sterile' (snowball tree)** Russet leaves (also white flowers in spring).

COLOURFUL CUTTING PLANTS	
AUTUMN ANNUALS, PERENNIALS AND BULBS	**WINTER SHRUBS**
***Aconitum* (monkshood)** Deep blue flowers.	***Hamamelis mollis* (witch hazel)** Yellow flowers.
***Amaryllis belladonna* (belladonna lily)** White or pink flowers.	***Jasminum mesnyi* (primrose jasmine)** Yellow flowers on arching stems.
***Aster* (Easter daisy, Michaelmas daisy)** White, pink or mauve flowers.	***Mahonia*** Yellow flowers (also evergreen leaves).
Chrysanthemum Flowers all colours but blue.	***Rhododendron*** White, yellow, pink, red or mauve flowers.
Dahlia Yellow, orange or red flowers.	***Viburnum tinus* (laurestinus)** White to pink flowers (also glossy evergreen leaves).
Rudbeckia Yellow or orange flowers.	**WINTER ANNUALS, PERENNIALS AND BULBS**
Salvia Pink or mauve flowers.	***Anthemis cupaniana*** White daisy flowers, with golden eye; lacy, silver leaves.
WINTER SHRUBS	***Bergenia cordifolia* (elephant's ear)** Pale pink flowers in clusters into spring.
Camellia japonica White, pink or red flowers.	***Cheiranthus cheiri* (wallflower)** Fragrant clusters of yellow, gold, brown, mauve or maroon flowers.
Ceratostigma willmottianum Russet leaves (also blue autumn flowers).	***Leucojum aestivum* (snowflake)** Small, white bell flowers, with green spots.
***Chimonanthus praecox* (wintersweet)** Yellow flowers on bare branches.	
***Garrya elliptica* (catkin bush)** Yellow-grey tassels.	

DRIED FLOWERS AND OTHER ARRANGEMENTS

Remember that many flowers and seed heads by being first hung and dried can have an extra life as decoration. They need to be hung from a rack in a warm, dry place. Flowers well suited to this way of handling are honesty (*Lunaria*), larkspurs (*Delphinium*), lavender, love-in-a-mist (*Nigella damascena*), sea holly (*Eryngium*) and paper daisies (*Helichrysum*).

Other flowers and foliage can be preserved by being placed in a mixture of two-parts glycerine to one-part water. Hydrangeas, freshly picked beech (*Fagus*) and *Garrya elliptica* lend themselves to this method.

When there seems to be nothing in the garden you can even make a posy from herbs. Add a few cottagey flowers and leaves as well if you want to: lavender leaves, cotton lavender (*Santolina chamaecyparissus*), nasturtiums (*Tropaeolum*), alpine strawberry (*Fragaria*) leaves, scented pelargoniums, feverfew (*Chrysanthemum parthenium*), rose hips, heartsease (*Viola tricolor*) and chives (*Allium schoenoprasum*) flowers among sprigs of thyme or bronze fennel (*Foeniculum vulgare* 'Nigra'). A posy made of such gatherings is called a tussie-mussie – a reminder of Elizabethan times.

GARDENS FOR CHILDREN

Starting a gardening habit early can have a lasting effect on how a person feels about plants. Of course, as with many childhood interests, enthusiasm often wanes. There is so much to fit in when you are very young. But the experience is there as a foundation for later.

Some children enjoy limited periods of helping their parents. While tasks often take twice as long, it is a valuable learning experience. Composting, in particular, often intrigues children. They see how, over time, kitchen scraps and leaves, weeds and clippings are magically changed. The task of spreading compost is simple to explain and execute.

Children should be taught quite young to use and look after tools, and any dangers, such as walking on a rake or running with secateurs, should be clearly explained. As well, they should be taught the rituals of care: gathering up tools and cleaning spades, forks and trowels at the end of any work, and periodically oiling secateurs and saw blades.

It is important that children working in the garden wear suitable clothes: shoes and jeans or tough-wearing clothes. A cotton hat provides protection in warm or cold weather, and skin should be protected against the sun's rays and the wind. Teach your children to wash their hands after gardening tasks are finished. It is advisable for them to have regular tetanus injections just as it is for any gardener.

If you can make a space for the children to have a garden of their own, it will mean something special to them. They can grow seeds and cuttings there and watch plants flower. They may learn how snails eat the best things first and how plants thrive when they are well watered and fed. Hang a bird-feeder on a nearby tree for extra appeal.

Share your garden with children when they are young and they will care about gardens when they are older.

Small fibre-glass ponds are easy to install, perhaps in the children's own garden. One with oxygenating plants, snails and fish will fascinate children and provide an important lesson in caring for creatures.

FOR CHILDREN

FLOWERS

Alyssum maritimum (sweet Alice)
Aster (Easter daisy, Michaelmas daisy)
Calendula officinalis (pot marigold)
Cosmos
Helianthus (sunflower)
Lunaria (honesty)
Nigella damascena (love-in-a-mist)
Papaver (poppy)
Tropaeolum majus (nasturtium)
Viola (pansy, violet)

VEGETABLES

Beta (beetroot)
Beta vulgaris var. *cicla* (silverbeet)
Lactuca (lettuce)
Lycopersicon lycopersicum (tomato)
Phaseolus (bean)
Raphanus sativus (radish)

HERBS

Allium schoenoprasum (chives)
Mentha (mint)
Origanum majorana (marjoram)
Petroselinum crispum (parsley)
Thymus (thyme)

To many children, the fun of pulling up carrots and beetroot and of discovering potatoes in the soil can be irresistible. Gathering tomatoes, looking for berries and picking fruit are all interesting and rewarding experiences. If children are taught about the pleasure of fresh herbs, they will run to collect them when they are needed for pot or salad.

From learning about the things that we eat from the garden, children can be helped to understand about the things that we don't – which should be everything else that grows in the garden. So many plants or parts of plants, and even some of the loveliest flowers, are extremely poisonous and eating them can produce reactions ranging from minor irritations to serious illness and death. Some leaves and stems produce an immediate allergic response in many people who touch them. Among the offenders are the rhus tree (*Rhus succedanea*), some grevilleas, agaves, primulas, particularly *Primula obconica*, and the ripe fruit of the Norfolk Island hibiscus or pyramid tree (*Lagunaria patersonia*). This does not mean that they should not be planted, but that they should be treated with respect.

Children's gardens do not have to be outdoors. They can have flowering plants in window-boxes and a miniature garden in a terrarium. Cress, bean sprouts and mung beans can be grown indoors, on damp cotton-wool in saucers. The progress of cuttings can be watched in a mini-propagator.

There are also many objects that children will enjoy making from garden materials: pot-pourri, lavender bags, acorn-and-matchstick people and seed-pod creatures, with eyes made from dried peas or split beans.

7/ GARDENS FOR TODAY

What is a garden? A piece of ground where nature is organised and controlled by human beings for their particular needs. A garden can be rocks and driftwood, and a cactus; no more. Or it can be a place of trees and flowers and fruits. Or both.

Through the centuries in China, Japan and most Western countries, master gardeners and designers developed gardens according to the demands of those who could afford them and the means at hand. While fine castles and monasteries had fine gardens to match, cottagers and peasants developed the art of growing from slip, root and cutting in tiny plots. Some of their plants – herbs with which to flavour cooking, for instance – may have filtered down from the grand estates on which the people worked. Other bits and pieces were probably found in the forest and wild places. And, from the beginning, different kinds of gardens evolved in different parts of the world as well as within countries.

These days the categorisation of gardens is quite arbitrary and most gardens, when it comes to style, are either a mixture or a mix-up. The main thing is to grow plants that you like in a setting that is comfortable for you, your house and its environment, carefully mixing and matching to make a lovely and practical garden. On that basis, you may find that you like a mixture of native and imported plants. You may choose a design with a heavy emphasis on style – perhaps a formal Italian garden full of masonry and controlled plants, all elegance and restraint. If you are a busy person, working long hours away from home, you will probably be after ways to create a lovely garden using a few shortcuts.

This chapter offers you a selection of garden styles and practical information to help you discover and achieve the garden that is for you.

An ancient fig tree inspired the development of this garden. Informal, curving flower beds and lawns suit many Australian houses.

AN AUSTRALIAN NATIVE GARDEN

Picture a garden with lots of foliage throughout the year: blue-greens and yellow-greens mingled; some leaves quite fine, others bold. There are flowers among the leaves, mostly in dainty, interesting shapes and bright colours. Fresh fragrances of leaves and flowers mingle, and birds chirp and call. The birds feed on insects near the ground or do acrobatics to reach into the flowers to find their favourite nectars. There are rocks, moss-covered, set well into the ground, with small plants growing in the cracks. Paths are of earth, gravel, brick paving or slate pieces, but nothing too ornate. Chances are you're in an Australian native garden.

Yet, in Australia regrettably there has been tremendous destruction of indigenous plants and fauna in the process of clearing the land. Ironically the bush has often been replaced with gardens of plants from other parts of the world, ones frequently far less suitable to Australian climates and requiring more care and water than most native plants. In some areas clearing of native flora is no longer permitted. In any case, if you have a bush block, why not enjoy this ready-planted garden? But a native garden is an option for any garden builder or renovator. Its informality has an affinity not only with the landscape but also with both modern Australian styles of architecture and the simple styles evolved in the past in response to the environment.

Native gardens take several forms. In their purest form they include only plants that grew in the area originally. To develop this kind of garden involves considerable research, but the Society for Growing Australian Plants and local groups can assist. Other native gardens include any plant indigenous to Australia. However, it is possible also to mix native plants with favourite exotic plants, such as roses, camellias and lavenders: the way in which they are blended largely determines their success. If such gardens are planned sensitively, with regard to the special attributes of each plant – colour, texture, size, form and seasonal behaviour – these gardens can be interesting to plan and exciting to have. The designs of all native gardens have in common an attempt to create a setting something akin to the natural sites from which the plants have come, and to position rocks, plants and other materials in groupings that could be found in the natural habitat.

OPPOSITE PAGE This natural-looking garden epitomises the Australian native-garden style. If an overseas plant is included, it is because it is the best one for the site and overall composition.

TOP The colours of some Australian plants are quite dazzling. The intense blue of *Dampiera linearis* is set off by the softer colouring of *Pityrodia dilatata*.
BOTTOM Red heath (*Epacris impressa*) and golden *Acacia leptospermoides* glow against the dull greens of other native plants.

PLANNING

Almost without noticing, you will find yourself emulating the look of the bush when you set out your native garden. It would be most unusual to achieve a formal native garden, for Australian trees and shrubs do not lend themselves to lines or avenues. Walk in the bush or climb a mountain for a refresher course if you need inspiration. Look at the way the rocks have weathered in groups and are well settled in the ground and how small rocks and gravel form from the crumblings under the parent rocks. Notice the sorts of plants and the way they grow – trees and shrubby bushes together, with lower bushes and ground-covering plants in the clearings.

Before you start, as always with good design, you must have some idea of the shape you want your garden to take and the facilities you wish to include. Try to incorporate any existing trees rather than remove them. With a little thought, sympathetic supplementary planting, native or ornamental, can be used to unite a rather different-looking existing ornamental tree with native plants: for instance, the flower colours and dainty leaves of *Westringia glabra* can reinforce an isolated *Spiraea thunbergii*.

Think about your land. Does it slope? Do you need a retaining wall? If so, rocks or railway sleepers will be appropriate materials to use. Some of the sleepers used in the retaining work can be arranged to form sitting places, or you might place a couple of sleeper seats in appealing spots. Paths have their own logic in a native garden. Instead of the paths dictating the plantings to either side, trees and bushes take precedence and the paths have to find their way around them.

An informal pond or a large dish filled with water and placed at the end of the terrace or close to a tree will add to the charm of your native garden and delight the birds. Often people with native gardens encourage a natural or ephemeral pond, like a tiny waterhole, in a hollow with a clay base. It will dry out with lack of rain, and some of the small surrounding plants may wither, but, come the rain, the little pool will fill again and small plants will flourish once more. Surface water can be conducted by means of an open cement drain lined with pebbles. The effect of a tiny, intermittently flowing creek bed is achieved. A necessary drain becomes an interesting feature, instead of being hidden underground with grid catchments here and there. A constructed pond should be sited at a low point of the garden where you might expect it to occur naturally.

THE PLANTS

Some people believe that any native plant can grow happily anywhere in Australia. That's hardly fair. Australia is huge, with a large range of conditions. Some native plants are adaptable, while others are quite choosy. Just what you can plant depends on your district and soil. Do some research on what grows well in the neighbourhood. Make a list of the plants that you'd like to try, then check them out in local nurseries. Note their flowering habits to help you plan your garden pictures. Plants from similar conditions overseas can also be considered. We feel that a plant shouldn't need to show its passport to be allowed in: if it looks good and fits in that's fine. African proteas, serissas and diosmas look entirely at home among our native plants. Even exotic plants from dissimilar climates can blend. Ceanothus, which originated in California, looks stunning planted close to a spring-flowering, scarlet bottlebrush, and picture blue and yellow Dutch irises beneath a wattle tree (*Acacia*).

Keep your plantings informal and remember how important it is to have something lovely to look at in one spot or another in the garden all through the year. Some grevilleas, such as *Grevillea* 'Poorinda Leane', flower twice a year. Plant some trees in a clump of three, four or five, with shrubs tucked around them, and another of the same kind planted a short distance away. A shrub might lean out from a tree stump or grow hard by a rock. Let ground covers romp over surfaces as they might naturally. Plant tufts of native grasses and Australian bulbs in sheltered rock pockets and large cracks here and there. Keep in mind the smaller native plants and lush ferns for the shady spots beneath taller plants. However, don't plant ferns before sheltering plants are sufficiently grown. Above all remember that, although it takes a lot of willpower, you will achieve a more natural effect by working with a limited number of plants rather than by adding 'one of everything'.

A GARDEN OF AUSTRALIAN PLANTS

This native garden has been designed to be seen from the long windows of the house.

KEY

1 *Pandorea jasminoides*
2 *Pandorea pandorana*
3 *Hardenbergia violacea*
4 *Melaleuca diosmifolia*
5 *Callistemon viminalis* 'Captain Cook'
6 *Hibbertia scandens*
7 *Billardiera ringens*
8 *Clematis aristata*
9 *Prostanthera lasianthos*
10 *Callistemon viminalis* 'Hannah Ray'
11 *Eriostemon myoporoides*
12 *Brachyscome multifida*
13 *Alyogyne huegelii*
14 *Anigozanthos flavidus*
15 *Westringia glabra*
16 *Eucalyptus woodwardii*
17 *Eucalyptus leucoxylon* var. *macrocarpa*
18 *Hymenosporum flavum*
19 *Grevillea* 'Poorinda Leane'
20 *Hibiscus tiliaceus*
21 *Dianella*
22 *Billardiera cymosa*
23 *Indigofera australis*
24 *Grevillea* 'Sandra Gordon'
25 *Cordyline australis*
26 *Scaevola aemula*
27 *Baeckea linifolia*
28 *Grevillea glabrata*
29 *Leptospermum petersonii*
30 *Correa baeuerlenii*
31 *Baeckea ramosissima*
32 *Prostanthera ovalifolia*
33 *Restio tetraphyllus*
34 *Correa reflexa*
35 *Scleranthus biflorus*
36 *Acacia mearnsii*
37 *Kunzea ambigua*
38 *Bauera rubioides*
39 *Acacia drummondii*
40 *Banksia ericifolia*
41 *Pratia pedunculata*
42 *Banksia marginata*
43 *Thryptomene* 'Paynei'
44 *Grevillea endlicherana*
45 *Astartea fascicularis*
46 *Eucalyptus nicholii*
47 *Viola hederacea*
48 *Dicksonia antarctica*
49 *Banksia spinulosa*
50 *Eucalyptus ficifolia*
51 *Acacia spectabilis*
52 *Acacia pravissima*

OPPOSITE PAGE This pathway is like a track through a well-stocked forest. There are bush birds everywhere, although the garden is close to the city.

LEFT Strong, simple structural elements and materials suit Australian native gardens.

PLANTING AND MAINTENANCE

Just because native plants have a reputation for hardiness doesn't mean that they like to be dumped in unprepared ground. In fact they appreciate well-dug ground, with as much well-rotted organic matter as possible turned into it, whether it is sandy or clay. After that add a sprinkling of blood and bone in early spring, although no other fertiliser should be necessary. Compost can be added at any time. Native plants, like most plants, are glad of a mulch – most have been used to a forest or scrubland floor in the wild. Leaf litter and small twigs or fine pine bark that will eventually break down are ideal. Even coarse gravel can be used as a mulch.

Native plants are best bought small. Young native plants are particularly vigorous, whereas the more advanced ones suffer from being handled and grow more slowly. It is unwise to interfere with the roots of native plants, so if the plants are pot-bound soak them in a bucket of water for an hour or two. Then, if they are planted in a hole dug to twice their depth and width, the backfilled soil will be soft enough for the roots to feel free to move out into the surrounding earth. About a teaspoonful of a specially formulated slow-release fertiliser can be sprinkled lightly in the hole and around the plant before the hole is filled in. Staking is not advised. The growing roots of young native plants should be encouraged to develop strongly, so that they bear the weight of their plant without aid.

Once native plants have taken off they can find transplanting quite disturbing. Those, such as eucalypts, that develop a long tap root (a strong single root) are particularly at risk. Young plants that have not been in the ground long can be lifted if necessary.

Even a native garden requires water and is not entirely maintenance free. However, many Australian plants are well adapted to a rigorous environment and have drought-tolerant growth habits and leathery leaves – ideal for a tough spot in the garden. Some native plants even deteriorate from too much watering and fertilising.

As native plants grow they need regular cutting back to keep them compact, not woody and straggly. Shorten any lank stems when you plant; then, after they have flowered, cut the plants back, removing spent heads. Always cut to healthy growth – above the nodes from which buds appear on stems. In summer check for new, lank growth and tip-prune this so that the plants make stronger, shorter shoots.

GARDEN BONUSES

Native gardens can provide some unexpected bonuses. If you like cottage-garden effects, try the low-growing *Brachyscome* species, with their daisy flowers of mauve or mid-pink, dainty straw flowers (*Helichrysum*), enchanting *Helipterum*, rose-pink rice flowers (*Pimelea linifolia*), *Eriostemon* species, white flannel flowers (*Actinotus helianthi*), native violets (*Viola hederacea*) and irislike *Patersonia occidentalis*. Remember kangaroo paws (*Anigozanthos*) for your back line in a border.

Native plants also provide endless cut-flower inspirations. Flowers, seeds, pods, foliage and branches can be used and many stems last well. Just a few flowering favourites are banksias, particularly *Banksia marginata*, Western Australian flowering gum (*Eucalyptus ficifolia*), kangaroo paws, waratahs (*Telopea*), the treasured brown boronia (*Boronia megastigma*) and *Thryptomene* and *Astartea* species. Foliage from a healthy *Grevillea glabrata* plant is lovely, too. *Melaleuca hypericifolia* offers graceful arched branches for arrangements. Use also the silvery grey eucalypts, particularly the spinning gum (*Eucalyptus perriniana*) and the elegant leaves and flowers of *E. caesia*.

When your native garden is finished, pause to sit on your rough-hewn sleeper seat. Whether your native garden is in a large city or on the edge of bush, it will have the feel of a special place, close to nature. Your garden has not been too hard to make and will be easy to care for – and don't worry, the birds will find you.

NATIVE ORCHIDS FOR THE ENTHUSIAST

Why not grow some native orchids? You don't have to live in the tropics to grow some of the orchids available, and the results will be thrilling. You can obtain native orchids at specialist nurseries or through orchid societies; people are not permitted to lift them from natural stands in the bush.

Good drainage is needed, and commercial orchid mixes probably provide the best growing medium. Watch out for snails.

***Dendrobium bigibbum* (Cooktown orchid)** Found naturally growing on rocks, this dainty pink orchid is the floral emblem of Queensland and is best grown by enthusiasts in northern Australia.

***Paphiopedilum* (slipper orchid)** Nodding buds on separate stems rise from among the leaves; flowers in tones of olive, bronze and gold appear in winter.

***Sarcochilus falcatus* (orange blossom orchid)** Given some frost protection, it will grow even in the cooler parts of southern Australia.

HARDY PLANTS FOR NATIVE GARDENS

TREES (HEIGHT 4–10 METRES)

Acacia howittii (sticky wattle)
Acacia podalyriifolia (Mount Morgan wattle)
Acacia pravissima (Ovens wattle)
Acacia spectabilis (Mudgee wattle)
Allocasuarina torulosa (forest oak)
Banksia integrifolia (coastal banksia)
Banksia marginata (silver banksia)
Brachychiton acerifolius (flame tree)
Ceratopetalum gummiferum (New South Wales Christmas bush)
Eucalyptus caesia (gungurru, silver bell gum)
Eucalyptus forrestiana (fuchsia gum)
Eucalyptus leucoxylon var. *macrocarpa* (yellow gum)
Eucalyptus perriniana (spinning gum)
Eucalyptus woodwardii (lemon-flowered gum)
Hymenosporum flavum (native frangipani)
Leptospermum petersonii (lemon-scented tea tree)
Melia azederach var. *australasica* (white cedar)
Telopea speciosissima (New South Wales waratah)

TALL SHRUBS (HEIGHT TO 5 METRES)

Acacia drummondii (Drummond's wattle)
Astartea fascicularis
Baeckea virgata (tall baeckea)
Banksia ericifolia (heath banksia)
Banksia spinulosa (hairpin banksia)
Bauera rubioides (river rose)
Boronia muelleri (forest boronia)
Callistemon viminalis (weeping bottlebrush)
Callistemon viminalis 'Hannah Ray'
Correa baeuerlenii (chef's cap correa)
Eriostemon myoporoides (wax plant)
Grevillea biternata
Grevillea endlicherana (spindly grevillea)
Grevillea glabrata
Grevillea 'Ivanhoe'

TALL SHRUBS (HEIGHT TO 5 METRES)

Grevillea 'Poorinda' hybrids
Hakea laurina (pincushion hakea)
Hakea salicifolia (willow hakea)
Indigofera australis (Australian indigo)
Kunzea ambigua (tick bush, white kunzea)
Melaleuca fulgens (scarlet honey myrtle)
Melaleuca hypericifolia (hillock bush)
Melaleuca incana (grey honey myrtle)
Melaleuca pulchella (claw flower)
Prostanthera melissifolia (native mint)
Thryptomene saxicola (rock thryptomene)
Westringia glabra (violet westringia)

SMALL SHRUBS (HEIGHT TO 1 METRE)

Boronia denticulata (mauve boronia)
Callistemon 'Captain Cook'
Correa decumbens
Correa pulchella
Crowea saligna
Epacris (native heath)
Westringia fruticosa (coast or native rosemary)

CLIMBERS

Billardiera scandens (common appleberry)
Clematis aristata (Australian clematis, old man's beard)
Hardenbergia violacea (false sarsaparilla, purple coral pea)
Hibbertia scandens (snake vine)
Pandorea jasminoides (bower of beauty)

GROUND COVERS

Ajuga australis (austral bugle)
Helichrysum baxteri (straw flower)
Helichrysum bracteatum (paper daisy)
Kennedia prostrata (running postman)
Myoporum parvifolium (boobialla)
Viola hederacea (native violet)

A GARDEN HOT AND DRY

In hot inland regions, it is tempting to believe that garden making is just not worthwhile. The excessive dry heat experienced by so much of inland Australia exhausts would-be gardeners as much as plants.

The available water has a direct bearing on the size and type of garden and plants possible. Many outback gardens have a yearly rainfall below 25 centimetres. In many instances water is in extremely short supply and every skerrick from the laundry and dishwashing must be recycled if there is to be a garden. Even when a supply is available from a bore, dam or river, it should not be squandered in low rainfall areas.

In the past, the possibilities for dry interior gardens have been limited, but today's greater understanding of plants, water conservation and good design can help to overcome the two major problems: high temperatures and low rainfall. Hardy, shade-giving trees, windbreaks and overhead structures, such as rustic wooden pergolas and arches, are fundamental to the success and enjoyment of gardens in the harsh sun, and should be incorporated in your initial design and work.

Thriving heat-tolerant plants, such as grevilleas and melaleucas, make paths seem cooler in hot, dry areas.

It can take many years for large trees to become established in dry conditions so they must be planted as soon as possible and all future needs for trees anticipated. Windbreaks and shade trees, uniform plantings and broad paths of cool gravel can be used to create a coherent structure for the subsidiary garden projects.

If you hanker for a few plants that need more water than the environment permits, plant them in the shelter of the house – in the aspect that best suits them. There it will be easy for you to hand-water them. This applies also to herbs that thrive in warm, rather dry conditions. It is possible to grow lawn in drier areas. One hundred per cent fescue (*Festuca*) or a fescue blend copes reasonably well with arid conditions.

Sleeper seats here and there in shady places suit the setting. Rock sculptures, natural outcrops and groupings of rock make strong focal points.

CHOOSING PLANTS

Shady relief can be provided by such trees as the coolibah (*Eucalyptus microtheca*), *E. lehmannii*, the silver bell gum or gungurru (*E. caesia*), the peppercorn (*Schinus molle*), the white cedar (*Melia azedarach*), the Judas tree (*Cercis siliquastrum*) and the desert kurrajong (*Brachychiton gregorii*). The athel tree (*Tamarix aphylla*), with its soft pink flowers, and the weeping pittosporum (*Pittosporum phillyreoides*) are smaller types.

A mixture of shrubby plants provides a screen against the wind's dust and an understorey for shade-giving trees. Among suitable shrubs 1 to 2 metres tall you could choose the silver wormwood (*Artemisia arborescens*), with its aromatic, deep-cut leaves, *Lavatera plebeia*, with its plentiful, hibiscuslike flowers, the lovely desert banksia, *Banksia ornata*, flower-of-the-Incas (*Cantua buxifolia*), with its rose-red or golden flowers, and *Olearia pimeleoides*, with its large, white daisy flowers. Of the taller shrubs, the Mount Morgan wattle (*Acacia podalyriifolia*), *Cassia tomentosa*, with its yellow flowers, the fuchsia gum (*Eucalyptus forrestiana*) and the coral gum (*E. torquata*) are just a few that provide an interesting shrubby screen.

Experiment with plants from other parts of the world with conditions similar to yours. Species of the rock rose (*Cistus*) from the Mediterranean area make low, attractive shrubs for a clump or low hedge. The mauve daisy bush *Felicia fruticosa*, gold and green *Euphorbia wulfenii*, the pretty native *Micromyrtus ciliata*, *Santolina chamaecyparissus*, with its silver, fernlike leaves and golden button heads, and the small blue daisy *Felicia amelloides* could make a cheery mixed border or garden plot that basks for weeks in the sun; edge it with the deep blue native *Dampiera rosmarinifolia* and the pink or white native *Myoporum parvifolium*. Succulent plants, with their ability to store water for later use, can be usefully worked into the garden. Friendly pigface (*Mesembryanthemum*), the annual Livingstone daisies (*Dorotheanthus bellidiformis*) and the annual portulacas are some of these. For a list of possible annual and perennial plants see the section on A Place in the Sun in Chapter 6.

Many culinary herbs from the Mediterranean are suited to hot, dry conditions. Bearded irises and lamb's ears (*Stachys lanata*) also revel in warm, dry soil.

TREES AND SHRUBS FOR HOT, DRY AREAS

TREES

***Acacia aneura* (mulga wattle)** Spiked, yellow flowers in spring.

***Acacia farnesiana* (perfume wattle)** Deep golden flowers in spring.

***Acacia pendula* (weeping myall)** Yellow flower balls in spring; pendulous form.

***Acacia rigens* (nealie)** Golden flower balls in spring; needlelike leaves.

***Acacia victoriae* (bramble wattle)** Pale yellow flower balls in spring.

***Allocasuarina cristata* (belah, black oak)** Branches upturned at ends.

***Allocasuarina luehmannii* (bull oak)** Upright tree.

***Brachychiton acerifolius* (flame tree)** Masses of red bell flowers when branches almost bare in summer.

***Brachychiton gregorii* (desert kurrajong)** Fragrant, pale yellow bell flowers, spring to summer; tapering trunk.

***Callistemon teretifolius* (Flinders Ranges bottlebrush)** Crimson brushes in spring.

***Callitris columellaris* (Murray pine, white cypress-pine)** Upright, compact tree.

***Cassia artemisioides* (silver cassia)** Yellow flowers in summer; silver leaves.

***Cercis siliquastrum* (Judas tree)** Light magenta flowers along branches in spring.

***Eucalyptus erythrocorys* (illyarie)** Yellow flowers, with red caps, autumn to summer.

***Eucalyptus microtheca* (coolibah)** White flowers, spring to summer; grey leaves.

***Eucalyptus nutans* (red-flowered moort, nodding gum)** Crimson flowers in spring. Suitable tree for hedging.

***Eucalyptus steedmanii* (Steedman gum)** Yellow flowers in spring; multi-trunked.

***Eucalyptus torquata* (Coolgardie gum, coral gum)** Masses of pink flowers, spring to summer.

***Eucalyptus woodwardii* (lemon-flowered gum)** Bright, showy yellow flowers in spring.

***Fraxinus oxycarpa* (desert ash)** Deciduous, leafy tree.

Hakea francisiana Red flowers in spring.

***Hibiscus tiliaceus* (coast cottonwood, native hibiscus)** Yellow flowers, with dark brown centres, all year in tropics.

***Melia azederach* var. *australasica* (white cedar)** Perfumed mauve flowers in spring.

***Olea europaea* (olive)** Olives, summer to autumn; grey-green leaves.

***Phoenix canariensis* (Canary Island date palm)** Long fronds; thick, chunky trunk.

***Pittosporum phillyreoides* (weeping pittosporum)** Cream flowers in spring, followed by bright orange seed capsules.

***Schinus molle* (peppercorn)** Pink peppercorns, in summer.

***Washingtonia filifera* (cotton palm)** Huge, fan-shaped leaves.

SHRUBS

Agave attenuata Nodding, pink to red flower spikes, spring to autumn; succulent, blue-green leaves.

***Aloe arborescens* (tree aloe)** Deep red flower spikes, spring to summer; rosettes of fleshy, spiked leaves.

***Alyogyne huegelii* (lilac hibiscus)** Clear violet-blue flowers, all year in tropics; greyish leaves.

***Atriplex nummularia* (old man saltbush)** Grey leaves. Hedging plant.

***Buddleja salviifolia* (winter buddleia)** Plumes of fragrant, mauve flowers in spring.

***Dodonaea* species (hop bush)** Winged, pink or red fruits.

***Duranta repens* (sky flower)** Sprays of dainty blue flowers, in spring, followed by yellow berries.

***Echium candicans* (pride of Madeira)** Plumes of rich blue flowers, spring to summer; rough grey leaves.

Eremophila alternifolia Tubular pink or red flowers, spring to autumn; narrow, aromatic leaves.

***Grevillea endlicherana* (spindly grevillea)** Fine, pinkish white flowers most of the year; fine silver-grey leaves.

TREES AND SHRUBS FOR HOT, DRY AREAS	
SHRUBS	**SHRUBS**
Lavandula dentata **(French lavender)** Velvety lavender flowers in summer; silver leaves.	***Phlomis fruticosa*** **(Jerusalem sage)** Yellow flowers in spring; grey-green leaves.
Melaleuca bracteata Small clusters of white flowers, spring to summer.	***Plumbago auriculata*** **(Cape plumbago)** Clusters of pale blue flowers, summer to autumn. Hedging or wall plant.
Myoporum debile **(sprawling myoporum)** Tubular lavender-blue flowers in spring, followed by pink berries.	***Punica granatum*** **(pomegranate)** Deciduous, with waxen, vermilion flowers in summer.
Nerium oleander **(oleander)** Branched clusters of white, apricot, pale pink, deep pink or crimson flowers in summer.	***Teucrium fruticans*** **(shrubby germander)** Blue-mauve flowers, spring to autumn; grey leaves.
Pelargonium **(geranium)** White or colourful flowers, summer to autumn.	

Wisteria is a very hardy plant. Grown on a pergola, it provides a cool canopy for the summer months.

CARE

There is no doubt that garden making and tending under these harsh circumstances is extremely frustrating and soul destroying. The growing of plants is always precarious. Within the certainties of heat and limited rain there can still be quite a large variation in conditions from season to season.

Heavy, thorough mulching with organic materials is absolutely essential to retain moisture in the soil (see Chapter 4). Organic matter dug into the soil will improve the texture and increase water retention. Commercial wetting agents help retain water over long periods, but are expensive for large areas.

Frequent light watering is a waste of time as well as water. Encourage roots of new young plants to penetrate deeply by watering them very well and deeply periodically: weekly perhaps at first, then every two or three weeks. Subsoil should be left as undisturbed as possible to help hold the moisture at a level where roots can get to it.

A TROPICAL GARDEN

Even within the areas of Australia broadly defined as tropical there are marked regional variations. Therefore if you live in tropical Australia you need to be aware of the characteristics of your local climate and to adapt your gardening practices accordingly.

Lawns, large shade trees and water should be considered as surroundings for entertainment areas because of their cooling effect during the extreme heat of December through to February and at all times. Native Queensland blue couch and other couch varieties are ideal for lawn because the winter temperatures are warm enough to keep them growing. Relaxing evenings out of doors, perhaps beside a pool, are a way of life in some tropical parts, so lighting that enhances the night garden and fragrant plantings should also be part of the design. Think carefully before planting warm-temperate plants that struggle in the excessive humidity when there are so many beautiful plants that will grow in tropical conditions.

Tropical gardens lend themselves to secluded sitting places and to shrinelike spots. Meeting one or two sculptures along a lush path can be an exciting interlude.

There are many ornamental trees and shrubs that provide the luxuriance of growth found in the tropics (see the accompanying table). You can also grow a wide variety of luscious fruits, such as bananas (*Musa sapientum*), mangoes (*Mangifera indica*), pawpaws (*Carica papaya*), avocados (*Persea americana*), guavas (*Psidium guajava*), pineapples (*Ananas comosus*), starfruit (*Averrhoa carambola*) and custard apples (*Annona*), not to mention macadamia nuts (*Macadamia integrifolia*) and coconuts (*Cocos*). Remember, too, the orchids that originate in the tropics; the Cooktown orchid (*Dendrobium bigibbum*), for example, flowers for many months and can be tied to the trunk or branch of a tree.

It is hard to imagine a more restful place than this tropical summerhouse near a pool.

PLANTS FOR THE TROPICS

TREES

***Archontophoenix alexandrae* (Alexandra palm)** Evergreen, with long, graceful fronds; for other suitable palms see the list in the Palms, Cycads and Ferns section of Chapter 3.

Bauhinia blakeana Small evergreen, with lovely white, pink or mauve 'butterfly' flowers.

***Brachychiton acerifolius* (flame tree)** Deciduous, large tree, with massed red flowers on leafless branches in summer.

***Cassia fistula* (golden shower, Indian laburnum)** Deciduous, spreading, weeping, medium-growing tree, with long, drooping sprays of spectacular yellow flowers.

***Delonix regia* (royal poinciana)** Deciduous, with spreading branches, fernlike leaves and fine red and gold flowers in early summer.

Jacaranda mimosifolia Deciduous, with ferny leaves and blue flowers in summer.

***Syzygium* (lilly pilly)** Evergreen, with often bronze-pink new foliage and always attractive berries.

***Xanthostemon chrysanthus* (golden penda)** Evergreen, magnificent, medium-growing tree, with glossy leaves and bunches of lime-yellow flowers.

SHRUBS

Calliandra Evergreen, with powder puffs of white, pink or red flowers.

Cassia corymbosa Evergreen, with sprays of rich yellow flowers.

***Clerodendrum ugandense* (blue butterfly bush)** Evergreen, with sprays of violet-blue 'butterfly' flowers.

SHRUBS

***Codiaeum variegatum* (croton)** Evergreen, with leaves variegated yellow, orange, pink or red.

***Euphorbia pulcherrima* (poinsettia)** Evergreen, with scarlet flowers in time to deck Christmas tables.

***Gardenia jasminoides* and *G.* 'Radicans'** Evergreen, with superbly fragrant, rich white flowers.

***Grevillea* 'Robyn Gordon' and *G.* 'Sandra Gordon'** Evergreens that, like other grevilleas, do exceedingly well.

***Hibiscus tiliaceus* (coast cottonwood, native hibiscus)** Evergreen, with yellow flowers that have rich brown centres. There are other tropical hibiscus.

Murraya exotica Evergreen, with fragrant flowers like orange blossom.

Mussaenda Evergreen, with colourful, creamy or pink bracts.

***Plumeria rubra* (frangipani)** Deciduous, with sweetly scented, waxy, pink or red flowers; *P. r. acutifolia* has white flowers.

CLIMBERS

Allemanda cathartica Evergreen, with large yellow flowers and glossy, dark green leaves.

Bougainvillea Evergreen, with brilliantly coloured bracts.

Petrea volubilis Evergreen, with masses of dainty violet flowers.

***Pyrostegia venusta* (orange trumpet vine)** Evergreen, with clusters of tubular, orange flowers. Formerly *Bignonia venusta*.

Solandra nitida Evergreen, with large, golden flowers.

LEARNING FROM THE TROPICS

In more temperate parts, even as far south as Melbourne, the summer is hot enough to produce tropical flowers of amazing vividness. Some people think they are vulgar and will not allow them in their garden. Others like to be surrounded by brightness. If you are one of these, it's an absorbing challenge to create a tropical-style garden, perhaps around an informal pond or a swimming pool.

To capture the mood of tropical gardens, you must start with an illusion of lushness – the feeling that everything is bursting with growth, birds, butterflies and do-gooding insects. Bright colours are vital to the effect, with no colour rules except that anything in the least pale or insipid is not allowed. There should certainly be no silver foliage, just rich, verdant shades. Palms, plants with palmlike leaves and ferns are part of creating a sense of the tropics. So are fruit trees and strong-growing perennial plants. Perennials with grasslike blades or broad, flat leaves provide a good middle storey. Then there will be low, sprawling plants spilling out from under the larger plants. Something still is missing – climbing, clambering plants that give a sense of urgency and movement as they struggle for a place in the sun. Lastly, add a few orchids, crowded into tall pots with curved sides. Powerful ingredients indeed.

Caring for your 'tropical mix'

The collection of plants suggested has a wide variety of tastes and thirsts. Make sure you learn the needs of any you choose, but a good general rule is to apply compost everywhere and provide blood and bone for all but the ferns. Watering is another matter. You will probably find that you have to hand-water as often as is needed to satisfy the wants of each plant. Misting sprays and warmth to create humidity are essential if you are planting tropical plants down south.

OPPOSITE PAGE Royal poinciana (*Delonix regia*), shown on the far left, and frangipani (*Plumeria rubra* var. *acutifolia*) are among the loveliest plants of the tropics.

RIGHT A small waterfall and shady plants at the edge of a swimming pool have a cooling effect on a tropical garden.

A GARDEN ON THE COAST

A garden by the sea is one of the greatest challenges for a garden maker, although the nature of the problem depends a great deal on the particular sea or ocean and the aspect and degree of exposure of the site. Plants are likely to experience salt-laden winds at all times of the year, with some seasonal variation. Salt can cause severe leaf burn or defoliation and many plants will develop slowly and show stunted growth, particularly on the seaward side. Sometimes sand abrasion adds to the damage done.

Sadly, a great deal of restraint and curbing of gardening ideas is often necessary. Some plants just cannot handle exposed sites or salt. However, there are some hardy warriors that will give you a strong front line against invading winds and weather. It is also worth experimenting with hardy but unproven plants.

A walk through the area that surrounds your garden may lead to some discoveries about which plants do well under harsh coastal conditions. As well, you can get guidance from local nurseries and you may like to check out the local indigenous stars at the nearest branch of the Society for Growing Australian Plants.

A balcony takes advantage of the views and the climate.

BARRIERS AGAINST THE WIND

If you are building on a block near the coast make sure only minimal disturbance to the existing vegetation occurs. Try to save existing trees and shrubs. Their roots bind the soil, while their branches provide shelter. Thoughtless removal can greatly increase wind erosion. Be sure that people working on the site understand your wishes.

To reduce the force of the wind, barriers must be formed by artificial screens, trees and shrubs or both. The efficiency of any windbreak is determined by its height and density.

- Artificial screens have the advantage of being erected quickly. Brush, tea-tree saplings, weatherboard, trellis, brick or stone are suitable. Screens are more effective if air can pass through openings in the structure, breaking the force of the wind.
- A community of plants, particularly those indigenous to the area and accustomed to growing together, make a strong wind barrier, given time to grow. Using three or four stakes per plant, support the trees or shrubs during the early stages of growth until the roots are set, but remove the stakes as soon as you feel the plants can stand firmly without them. Low plants and ground covers, such as gazanias, *Mesembryanthemum* species and *Convolvulus mauritanicus*, are also an important part of a living screen. They bind the soil and help protect the roots of the larger plants from sun and wind.

DESIGN

The direction of the prevailing wind and winds bearing salt need to be considered when you are siting your house and garden. Whether you nestle your house into a slope or sit it high on a hill may also depend on whether you put panoramic views or shelter and greater possibilities for a garden first. Sometimes a compromise is possible. Some rooms might lead outside to secluded and protected gardens, others to terraces overlooking the sea (and perhaps a swimming pool). Whatever your decision, outdoor sitting areas, as well as the house, should be oriented to make the most of the environment.

The African daisy (*Dimorphotheca*) is a tried and true plant for the seaside.

Outdoor living becomes even more attractive than usual in the sea air, and plenty of outdoor space should be allowed for casual entertaining of family and friends. Benches made of sleepers or slatted wood provide easy seating in such areas and on terraces surrounding swimming pools; they also act as low boundary walls, partially defining spaces. Make sure you have a range of sitting spots offering shade at various times of the day.

When you are creating a seaside garden, emulate the freedom of the sea shores and cliff tops. Have gently curving paths or a string of cleared spaces. Choose surfaces kind to bare feet and not slippery: sand, earth, bricks, concrete blocks or slate. Rocks are particularly appropriate in a coastal setting, well dug in to look like natural outcrops or used as garden edging.

Site taps and grids for washing sandy feet near house entrances or the swimming pool. The clothesline should also be close by for wet bathers – but well concealed.

HARDY, SALT-RESISTANT PLANTS: THE FRONT LINE

TREES

Acacia suaveolens
Agonis flexuosa (weeping myrtle)
Allocasuarina stricta (drooping sheoak)
Arbutus unedo (strawberry tree)
Banksia integrifolia (coast banksia)
Eucalyptus botryoides (southern mahogany)
Eucalyptus ficifolia (Western Australian flowering gum)
Callistemon viminalis (weeping bottlebrush)
Crataegus pubescens (Mexican hawthorn)
Cupressus macrocarpa (Monterey cypress)
Grevillea robusta (silky oak)
Koelreuteria paniculata (golden rain tree)
Lagunaria patersonia (Norfolk Island hibiscus)
Melaleuca
Melia azedarach var. *australasica* (white cedar)
Metrosideros excelsa (New Zealand Christmas tree)
Olea europaea (olive)
Phoenix canariensis (Canary Island palm)
Pittosporum tobira
Prunus × *blireiana*
Quercus ilex (holm oak)
Tamarix parviflora (early tamarisk)

SHRUBS

Abelia × *grandiflora*
Acacia saligna (golden wreath wattle)
Agave attenuata
Banksia ericifolia (heath banksia)
Brachysema lanceolatum (Swan River pea)
Buddleja salviifolia (winter buddleia)
Coleonema pulchrum (diosma)
Coprosma repens (mirror bush)
Correa reflexa
Echium candicans
Escallonia macrantha
Eucalyptus forrestiana (fuchsia gum)
Euonymus japonicus (Japanese spindle tree)
Hebe
Hibiscus

SHRUBS

Kunzea ambigua (tick bush, white kunzea)
Lavandula
Leonotis leonurus (lion's ears)
Leptospermum laevigatum (coast tea tree)
Leptospermum petersonii (lemon-scented tea tree)
Nerium oleander (oleander)
Phlomis fruticosa (Jerusalem sage)
Plumbago auriculata (Cape plumbago)
Raphiolepis × *delacourii* (Indian hawthorn)
Rosmarinus officinalis (rosemary)
Westringia fruticosa (coast or native rosemary)

PERENNIALS

Artemisia arborescens (wormwood)
Calocephalus brownii (cushion bush)
Canna indica (Indian shot)
Chrysanthemum frutescens (marguerite daisy)
Euryops pectinatus
Limonium sinuatum (sea lavender, statice)
Narcissus jonquilla (jonquil)
Nepeta (catmint)
Pelargonium
Santolina chamaecyparissus (cotton lavender)
Zephyranthes candida (flower of the west wind)

GROUND COVERS

Alyssum maritimum (sweet Alice)
Arctotis (aurora daisy)
Cerastium tomentosum (snow-in-summer)
Dimorphotheca (African daisy)
Juniperus horizontalis (creeping juniper)
Lantana montevidensis (creeping lantana)
Mesembryanthemum (pigface)
Myoporum acuminatum (boobialla)
Polygonum (knotweed)
Stachys lanata (lamb's ears)
Vinca (periwinkle)
Viola hederacea (native violet)

The New Zealand Christmas tree (*Metrosideros excelsa*) makes a hardy front-line plant for a coastal garden.

HARDY, SALT-RESISTANT PLANTS: THE SECOND LINE
TREES
Abutilon (Chinese lantern) *Aucuba japonica* 'Variegata' (gold dust plant) *Callistemon* (bottlebrush) *Crataegus oxyacantha* (hawthorn) *Dryandra* *Feijoa sellowiana* *Hakea salicifolia* (willow hakea) *Tristaniopsis conferta* 'Variegata' (Queensland brush box)
PERENNIALS
Babiana (baboon plant) *Cheiranthus cheiri* (wallflower) *Clivia miniata* (kaffir lily) *Convolvulus cneorum* *Crinum* (spider lily) *Gaura lindheimeri* *Hemerocallis* (daylily) *Indigofera australis* (Australian indigo) *Liriope muscari* (lily turf)
GROUND COVERS
Achillea (yarrow) *Ajuga reptans* (bugle plant) *Bergenia cordifolia* (elephant's ear) *Brachyscome multifida* (rock daisy) *Dianthus* (carnation, pink) *Fuchsia procumbens* *Gazania* (treasure flower) *Scleranthus biflorus*

Native gardens are suited to houses at the coast; draw heavily on the types of native plants that still survive in your district. Some plants, such as cushion bushes (*Calocephalus brownii*), coast rosemary (*Westringia fruticosa*) and the white-flowered *Correa alba*, adapt readily to most coastal conditions; see also the section in this chapter on A Native Garden.

You might like to give your sunny, sheltered spots the brilliance of the tropics (see the section in this chapter on A Tropical Garden) or follow the colourful planting suggestions for A Place in the Sun in Chapter 6 and those for A Garden Hot and Dry in this chapter; among the plants listed there are a number of silver-leafed ones that suggest another successful type of sunny coastal planting. Olive trees (*Olea*) and oleanders (*Nerium oleander*) could be used as tall background plants and possibly *Buddleja salviifolia*, native to Central and South Africa. Yellow-flowered Jerusalem sage (*Phlomis fruticosa*) can grow more than a metre tall. A mauve form also exists. Wormwood (*Artemisia arborescens*) forms a silvery, fernlike shrub about 1.5 metres high and 1.5 metres wide. The same size, pride of Madeira (*Echium candicans*), with its superb plumes of blue, starlike flowers and deep pinky red stamens, is excellent in a sunny corner or for a bold patch in a deep border. Along the edges of a border or for low plantings here and there among rocks, *Cerastium tomentosum* and gazanias present a strong front.

PLANTING AND CARE

Plants grow slowly in harsh conditions, so the smaller they are the less adjustment they have to make to their new environment. Tube-sized plants will be able to establish their tiny roots more readily than large plants, building a firm foundation for later buffeting.

All young trees and shrubs should be planted with tree guards to protect the growing shoots. Shadecloth supported by firm stakes can be used to guard seedlings and developing perennial plants and vegetables. A light foliage watering every two or three weeks, or after salt-laden winds have blown themselves out, will relieve the build-up of salt deposits that reduce the plants' growing efficiency.

Good soil management assumes a special importance under harsh coastal conditions. Organic matter worked into the soil helps to retain moisture and nutrients among the roots of plants. Animal manures and compost should be added twice a year. A mulch of twigs, eucalyptus litter or fine pine bark is a wise precaution, particularly until windbreaks are firmly established. Seaweed is one of the best mulches. Add it after the garden has been soaked.

An automatic sprinkler system, even just a simple one, is important where gardens are to be left to fend for themselves, sometimes for weeks on end. Just a good soak every one or two weeks, depending on the type of plants in the garden, can keep them going without pampering them. Provided they can receive water, lawns are a fairly inexpensive and refreshing ground cover near the house.

A COTTAGE GARDEN

The term cottage garden tends to be associated with small, English-style gardens. However, the concept of a mixed garden made up of this and that – purely decorative plants, herbs, fruits and vegetables all in together – is fairly general throughout Europe and Western societies. It is not difficult to make a cottage garden, but to keep it looking lovely takes time and effort.

The main structural components of a cottage garden are paths. They define the garden spaces and beds and may be straight or curved. An island bed, encircled by a path that leads to the front gate on one side and the front doorway on the other, is characteristic. Strong, intrusive structures, such as garages, carports and blank walls, should be given adjacent plantings or climbers, such as roses and summer jasmine (*Jasminum azoricum*), to soften and screen them. A low hedge, perhaps of Mexican orange blossom (*Choisya ternata*), clipped sasanqua camellias or plumbago, can be grown to screen a broad driveway.

You do not need to have a cottage to have a cottage garden, but such gardens are usually associated with modest houses rather than grand ones. Houses can be old or new, but they should not be elaborate or attention grabbing. It is the plants – their colour, their form and their composition – that should form the main decorative feature. Light picket fences are associated with cottage gardens; they let air and sunshine in and allow the garden to be viewed and admired by passers-by. Low stone walls, with their rugged natural appearance, also mark the boundary – and make a simple seat – without dominating.

PLANNING

First work out where your paths are to be and your major plants, including a tree or two, a few shrubs and large, shrubby roses such as 'Sarah van Fleet'. Cottage gardens do not have elaborate paving or masonry. Retaining walls and flights of steps are used only if the land fall is steep. Paths of gravel (crushed toppings rather than river pebbles) are suitable. Avoid modern pavers if you want a traditional garden. Work out a pretty pattern with old or mellow bricks, instead. Edge the paths with bricks or period terracotta edging tiles if the adjacent flower beds are higher. Alternatively, use edging plants – sweet Alice (*Alyssum*), pinks (*Dianthus*), ajuga and thyme for the sun, small campanulas, lobelia and *Lamium maculatum* for the shade.

Fountains and other elaborate garden ornaments are out of place in a cottage garden. If you want more than a birdbath or a low dish, have a simple pond. A completely circular pond, edged simply in brick flush with the lawn or one brick up, looks right.

Plain arches of wire or timber, with a climbing rose perhaps, can be used to good effect, but they look out of place as an exposed feature. They should mark a garden entrance, be at the side of the house or be part of an internal boundary that sets apart a special herb, vegetable or rose garden. If a pergola is to be incorporated into the garden design, it should be built on simple lines in rustic or dressed timber to suit the house. You could paint it one of the colours used in the house or coat it with clear wood preservative to protect the raw timber.

GETTING STARTED

If you are starting from scratch, some of the plants already in the garden may need to be transplanted elsewhere. For instance, a young Douglas fir or banksia in the lawn is quite inappropriate for a cottage garden. Even some of the lawn may need to be converted to beds. The next step after this is to mark in your paths, bed and border shapes and the sites for any seats, birdbaths or other features. Then prepare the soil (see Chapter 4).

OPPOSITE PAGE In the traditional cottage garden the path is hard to find, so abundant are the flowering plants.

LEFT A visit to a cottage garden brings a surge of anticipation. There will be precious – and often spare – plants tucked here and there.

OPPOSITE PAGE A cottage garden is never more at home than when accompanying an old or simple house.

Mark the position of the plants with upturned pots, using big pots to indicate the largest trees and shrubs. Plan a small, fine tree or two, such as a suitable crab apple (*Malus*) or a lemon tree (*Citrus limon*), and some shrubs, such as dogwoods (*Cornus*) or oleanders (*Nerium oleander*). Perfumed shrubs, such as lilacs (*Syringa*), mock orange (*Philadelphus coronarius*), wintersweet (*Chimonanthus praecox*) and the flowering quince (*Chaenomeles japonica*), are particularly appealing. Old-fashioned roses, such as 'La Reine Victoria', 'Madame Pierre Oger', 'Frühlingsgold', 'Fantin-Latour' and 'Stanwell Perpetual', are the essence of cottage gardens, as are climbing roses, clematis and jasmine. The plantings already sound beautiful, but there must still be room for all the bits and pieces that are integral to a cottage garden.

As you set out your plants, give thought to the mature height and shape of each. If you have a rather square or triangular bed in front of the house, for instance, build up its centre with tall plants, extending them to the centre back if no shrubs are included there, or place a tall, shrubby rose in the centre and build perennials and smaller plants round it to establish a focus.

Grading your garden from high to low will certainly achieve the right effect, but be careful not to become pedantic or your garden will be too perfect, taking on the air of a formal border and losing its cottagey atmosphere. Build in some lesser high points, away from the focal point or in a bed on the other side of the path, and plant to keep the garden pictures interesting.

With colour combinations, too, you must not strive for perfection. Do not attempt to closely grade your colours or, again, you will be in the league of magnificent formal borders. However, avoid having two garish colours together by following a simple planting rule such as 'only pinks, blues, creams, mauves and silvers' or 'no oranges allowed'. In this kind of garden, where flowers are the focus, part of the challenge will also be to work out pictures for different times of the year. The plant lists in Chapter 3 will help.

When you are working out the plants you want in your garden, you must, of course, take into account aspect and local influences, such as a brick wall or the movement of shadows cast by a tree. Don't forget the warm pockets and shady spots that will be created as you plant. These allow sun-loving plants to appear in positions where you would not normally plant them and for some shelter-loving plants to take their place in quite a sunny bed. The bonus of the unexpected is one of the joys of gardening, particularly in cottage gardens.

PLANTING OUT A COTTAGE PLOT

Here is a planting scheme for a large cottage garden bed with an open, sunny aspect.

Tall perennials

Vertical lines are very important. Even in winter the clear green spikes of Dutch irises can provide strength, perhaps in front of bare-stemmed shrubs. Then in spring the irises flower, as do other tall perennials: lupins (*Lupinus*), hollyhocks (*Althaea rosea*), delphiniums, foxgloves (*Digitalis purpurea*) and Queen Anne's lace (*Ammi majus*). Azure-blue bog sage (*Salvia uliginosa*) is a summer bloomer, but, as its flowers and stems are fine, it can go in front of stronger flower heads, such as those of the hollyhocks and sunflowers (*Helianthus*). Yellow evening primroses (*Oenothera missouriensis*) – just one or two – might form a clump at one side of the bed, and monkshoods (*Aconitum*), *Gaura* and penstemons could be in front of these. Thus you have a strong vertical statement in the centre. Train sweet peas (*Lathyrus odoratus*) up canes during their short, merry season to reinforce the height of the perennials.

The middle storey

Strengthen the middle storey with clumps of different plants.

While a rose in front is appropriate, it must not be too strong for the tall, elegant perennials. Choose a shrub rose such as 'Penelope' that grows only a metre or so high. 'Penelope' flowers freely, and its flesh tones blend easily with most colours.

Among the middle-range plants around and in front of the rose, you might choose geums, which display a mound of shapely, rich green leaves all year round, and clumps of evergreen daylilies (*Hemerocallis*), with their paler, grasslike leaves. Consider also lavender species – English, French, Italian and dwarf forms in various lovely shades of blue-mauve, mauve, rich purple, heliotrope, pink and white – and *Santolina chamaecyparissus* (confusingly called cotton lavender, though no relation), with its silvery grey foliage and dainty, bright yellow flowers. Be careful of *Lavandula dentata* 'Allardi', which is a giant, summer-flowering purple lavender, if you are really after the blue-mauve, velvet-flowered French lavender (*L. dentata*). 'Allardi' has similar, though more deliciously pungent, leaves, but will break your heart with its thrusting stems so hard to cut back well.

Rosemary can also be used as a permanent structure; for some reason, although it can grow tall if you allow it to, it sits quite well on the edge of a path with lower flowers placed back from it. *Rosmarinus officinalis* is tall and straight, with pale flowers; 'Blue Lagoon' is more sprawling in form, with brilliant azure flowers in winter. There is also a prostrate rosemary (*R. prostratus*) with paler flowers, which will readily hang down a wall.

Marguerites (*Chrysanthemum frutescens*), pelargoniums and wallflowers (*Cheiranthus cheiri*) are cottage-garden stalwarts. A slender, silvery plant with yellow daisy flowers, which in its season becomes tall, is *Senecio cineraria*. It can be kept compact by being clipped back. The velvet groundsel (*S. petasitis*) has superb, sculptured leaves and yellow winter flowers. *Centaurea cineraria* has mauve thistle heads borne on long stems in early December. Pastel-shaded Michaelmas daisy (*Aster*) is a handy perennial; it tucks well out of the way until it is ready to send its bud-covered stems up for autumn flowering.

Medium to small plants

Winter roses (*Helleborus*), obedient plants (*Physostegia*), pinks (*Dianthus*), silver and purple sages and other *Salvia*, true geraniums, medium-height irises, lavender showers (*Thalictrum aquilegiifolium*), bleeding hearts (*Dicentra spectabilis*), chamomile (*Anthemis tinctoria*), primulas, campanulas, campions (*Silene*) and a host of others could inspire your choice here. Some are a little tall, but still suitable near the garden edge.

Edging plants

For the edges choose from the tiny spires of pink or blue veronicas (*Hebe spicata*), ajugas, candytufts (*Iberis*), creeping and upright thymes, sandwort (*Arenaria*), sea pinks (*Armeria maritima*) and small campanulas.

Bulbs

What a joy to be able to punctuate the patches of soil between an array of perennials with bulbs for all seasons. Remember tall-growing lilies (*Lilium*) for summer, planted well back; dainty dwarf agapanthus for permanent green clumps – right near the edge if you like – nerines for autumn and snowflakes (*Leucojum*) for winter, as well as all the spring surprise packages appearing from late winter on. The section on Bulbs in Chapter 3 will give you further inspiration.

Annuals

Whenever there is a gap in your pictures, think of annuals. Cosmos, which seeds and returns year after year, and tall cleome are wonders in late summer and autumn. Larkspurs (*Delphinium*) are tall, brilliant fillers and make fine cut flowers as well. Further to the front delicate, cheery Californian poppy (*Eschscholzia californica*), in orange or cream tonings, and granny's bonnet or columbines (*Aquilegia*) provide flowers from late winter on, in empty spots, and seed readily.

Violas are uncomplicated, being mostly of single colours: blue, apricot, mauve, yellow, cream or white. They flower through the winter as well as the summer months, depending on when they are planted. Pansies (*Viola* × *wittrockiana*) are irresistible front-liners; some are available now in subtle, rich tones as well as the stained-glass-window colours we know so well. Cheekiest of all the pansies are the Johnny jump-ups (*V. tricolor*), which seed all over the garden and flower as they choose. Long known as heartsease, they gave of their best for Elizabethan gardens as they give of their best for us today. Sweet Alice (*Alyssum*), a self-seeding edging plant, is now in a range of pastel shades. Lobelia, another charming edging plant in shades of blue, mauve and white, prefers more shelter and will only seed in moist soil.

Where three or four pretty plants are mixed together, chances are you have the start of your cottage garden.

A COURTYARD GARDEN

A courtyard is an enclosed garden. It may be enclosed by interior or external house walls – sometimes largely consisting of glass – garden walls, hedges and screens or a mixture of these. It must be designed to be viewed from close quarters: from the house, from gateways and from upstairs windows that overlook it.

In a courtyard a great deal has to happen in a small space. It is important to have a clear idea about how you want it to look and feel, taking each viewing point into account; you need also to take into account certain factors that pertain to small enclosed gardens.

ASPECT

Having four walls, a courtyard experiences a concentration of climatic conditions, though it will usually have a dominant aspect: for instance, if one of its walls is formed by a two-storey house the shade and heat of the wall will influence the whole area. Winter may be colder and more dank within the confines of a courtyard, and summer will be hotter there.

DRAINAGE AND WATER SUPPLY

In an enclosed area it is important that surface and soil water can escape. Check for downpipes, which run down to stormwater pipes. If the internal courtyard has no stormwater pipe running through its soil, the area will gather water. Proper drainage should always be included when a house is being built. Agricultural drains can be laid if the courtyard does have reasonable access to a stormwater outlet.

If the internal courtyard does not have a stormwater outlet but the house has wooden stumps, it may be possible to run drainage pipes under the house to a stormwater pipe. However, if the house has a slab foundation, the best solution is to dig a soak in much of the area, removing some of the soil and replacing it with porous scoria, which will absorb surplus moisture

A formal pond of brick and concrete in an entrance courtyard sets a stylish pace.

and help it to disperse gradually in the surrounding soil. This means a lot of digging. An alternative treatment is to dig a hollow and face it with mossy rocks or granite to make a dry, porous pond that from time to time collects water. Ferns, *Pratia pedunculata*, Chinese indigo (*Indigofera decora*), gardenias and other moisture lovers that can cope with the humidity that a small courtyard creates can be grown.

Paved external courtyards should have a drainage grid connected to a stormwater system.

Carrying water to an internal courtyard is hard work. As with an external courtyard, a tap from which can be run a small sprinkler system is most convenient; or the garden can be watered by hose or can.

DESIGN

Don't forget to make a sketch in your head or on paper of what you want before you begin work on your courtyard.

Practicalities

Make sure your design is practical. If access through the area is required, work out where the path should logically go. Utility items such as clotheslines and rubbish bins will probably need to be screened.

Scale

You can do practically anything in a courtyard as long as it is in scale. The tree you choose can be tall or quite small, but the surrounding items must then relate to it. If you want to use shrubs or middle-storey plants, they will need to sit comfortably under the tree's branches. If your tree is small, you may have to disgard the idea of shrubs and just site the tree, with its low-slung branches, among rocks and ground covers. If you must have a middle storey, you will have to choose a larger tree.

The same principle applies to the structural and decorative aspects of the courtyard, also. However, you may stretch the rule by, for instance, using a big sculpture close up to the main windows or sitting area, with low plants streaming off into the distance to achieve contrast. That is fine, but any unusual variations such as this should be consciously arrived at so that the effect looks controlled, not haphazard.

Tricks with texture, colour and shape

Small-leafed plants create an intricate texture, making a courtyard seem larger; large fan- and elephant-ear-shaped leaves bring everything closer to the eye. You can play tricks and get a pleasing contrast with the fine texture of the rest of the vegetation by planting a few large-leafed plants, such as bergenia, arum lilies, acanthus and fatsia, in the foreground. Even one close-up, broad-leafed clump adds to the interest of a space.

Remember that each colour has its own quality. Dark plum-coloured leaves are likely to leap forward rather than retreat among greens. Blue-green foliage is very comforting to the eye, though it lacks the life of yellow-green plants. Silvers and blue-grey tones at the back of a planting give depth to the garden, while in the foreground and middle ground they have the effect of making it seem larger.

Even a line of stepping stones can play a trick or two. Japanese landscapers discovered long ago that one or two irregular stones in a run of stepping stones makes the distance they cover seem shorter and the path more purposeful. Stepping stones placed close together behave like a solid path and can lose their special charm. A path leading away from the central area of the courtyard can be gradually tapered to create distance; stepping stones can be smaller as they lead to a gate, with the same result.

Design ideas

- Create an informal courtyard, using rocks, ferns and other softly growing plants, some stepping stones or a small pond, and perhaps a flowering cherry tree. Ferns do, however, need the shelter of walls or trees.
- Make a flowery, cottage-garden type of courtyard. Give the flower plots a definite outline by planting edging plants, and build up to tall plants in one area. In the tricky environment of a courtyard it's a challenge to find spots for shade-loving plants and spots for sun-loving ones. Watchfulness through the seasons is the way to success.
- Have as a focal point a beautiful tree or group of small trees – perhaps a gordonia, a group of Japanese maples (*Acer palmatum*) or a *Magnolia denudata* – chosen for their seasonal moods and individual shapes. Rocks, a minimal ground cover and some flagstones provide the setting.

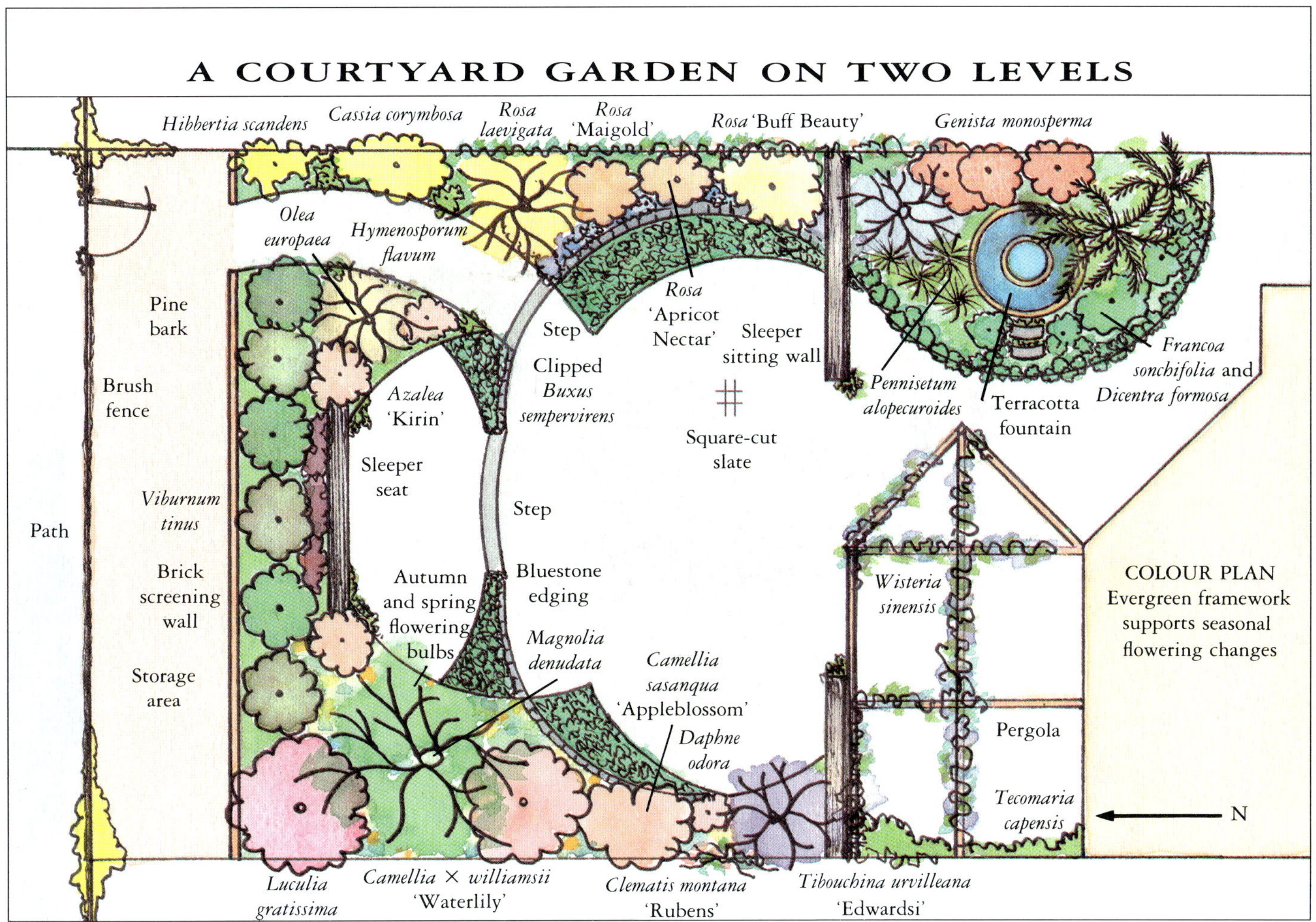

A COURTYARD GARDEN ON TWO LEVELS

As well as being enjoyable to be in, this courtyard is lovely to look down on from the upstairs windows.

- Choose an austere courtyard design, with for ornament just a fine modern sculpture, a piece of driftwood and a shallow pottery dish filled with water. Plant a patch or two of *Raoulia australis* at the base of the statue, if the courtyard is sunny, or mother of thousands (*Saxifraga stolonifera*), if it is mostly shady. Pave the surface of the courtyard, devising an innovative design in pebbles of different textures.
- Adapt one of the design concepts given in this book. Tropical, oriental and Italian gardens are suited to courtyards.
- Try a formal courtyard if your house lends itself to this style. There have been formal courtyard gardens for thousands of years. Perhaps have an axial ground plan, with a rectangular pond or a central path, or a wonderful knot garden, containing one or two intricate paths and a central ornament. Alternatively, divide your garden space into two or more compartments, perhaps edged with lavender (*Lavandula*) hedges and filled with flowers.
- Make leisure the keynote of your courtyard. Add outdoor furniture, sun umbrellas or canopies and perhaps a pergola to a large paved area. You will want some garden but it may need to be around the perimeter, with one or two shade-giving trees, such as a honey locust (*Gleditsia triacanthos*), golden rain tree (*Koelreuteria paniculata*) or a jacaranda, included. Choose three or four lovely pots, not too wide and about 75 centimetres high, to fill with flowering plants, and place them at key spots on your paved area.

A BALCONY GARDEN

Not everybody has a garden at ground level or only at ground level. If you live in an apartment you may have a balcony (or in older buildings a verandah, perhaps) that you can make into a garden.

There is nothing especially labour saving about a balcony garden. Establishing some interesting pot plants upstairs can mean transporting a seemingly endless procession of pots, potting mix, fertiliser, plants, watering cans, plastic sheeting and gardening implements. However, forethought and planning will help smooth the way.

A balcony should be seen as an intimate garden room. A large umbrella makes a shelter to be folded away on a perfect day.

PLANNING

'Know your site' has a familiar ring, but the principle applies to a balcony just as much as it does to a 1-hectare block of land. As always, you need to consider the aspect of your balcony. Note the areas that get shade, and at which times of the day and in which seasons, and any parts that receive full sun for quite a long time through the day. Observe the ways of the winds. If your balcony is a windfunnel, you may need to put up a trellis or screen for protection. Also check that your balcony can take the weight of your plants and objects, particularly if it is a cantilevered construction.

Think carefully before you put any plan into action, so that there is not too much toing and froing. Your small garden needs to be in proportion to its surroundings both inside and out. Pots and plants must be selected for their size and shape: not too bold and not too retiring and certainly chosen to give you something harmonious to glimpse through your adjoining windows.

It may be worth having a tap installed on your balcony if you have plumbing nearby. If you do, add a sprinkler system with an outlet in each pot and a manual timing device. Keep a hand fork and secateurs, a full watering can and a container of liquid manure ready for action. Having these things nearby encourages you to tend the garden in a few spare moments.

Growing plants hydroponically, that is without soil, means your containers will weigh much less, and your plants will largely care for themselves once you have added nutrients to the water. You can obtain the appropriate nutrients, the necessary equipment and information from hydroponic suppliers.

BEAUTIFUL – AND USEFUL

The architectural style of your building, the balustrade and the balcony's floor surface should have some bearing on your choice of ornaments and containers. If you have room for a small birdbath throw a flower or two into it when the birds aren't looking. A mixture of pots can look interesting – one or two terracotta ones and perhaps a couple with a deep blue or turquoise glaze. As a rule pots look best if they are of different heights and sizes. Do not have too many or they will have less impact. The section on Gardens in Containers in Chapter 6 provides further suggestions for pots and pot plants.

Your balcony can be made useful as well as beautiful. Add a chair or, if you have the space, a small table and a couple of chairs and you have an extra room. Grow culinary herbs in a suitable pot and tomatoes (*Lycopersicon lycopersicum*) if your balcony is sunny enough. Silverbeet (*Beta vulgaris* var. *cicla*) is quite easily grown.

PLANTS FOR BALCONY GARDENS

SMALL PLANTS

Begonia corallina
Brachyscome multifida (rock daisy)
Cheiranthus cheiri (wallflower)
Daphne odora
Fragaria (strawberry)
Gardenia florida
Heliotropium arborescens (cherry pie, heliotrope)
Indigofera decora (Chinese indigo)
Lavandula (lavender)
Liatris
Lippia citriodora (lemon-scented verbena)
Lobelia erinus (edging lobelia)
Pelargonium
Santolina chamaecyparissus (cotton lavender)
Sedum 'Autumn Joy' (stonecrop)
Thryptomene 'Paynei'
Tropaeolum (nasturtium)

LARGE PLANTS

Artemisia arborescens (wormwood)
Callistemon viminalis (weeping bottlebrush)
Callistemon viminalis 'Captain Cook'
Ceratostigma willmottianum
Choisya ternata (Mexican orange blossom)
Feijoa sellowiana
Fortunella japonica (cumquat)
Hebe (veronica)
Nerium oleander (oleander)
Olearia magniflora (splendid daisy bush)
Rosmarinus officinalis (rosemary)

OTHER HARDY PLANTS

Banksia marginata (silver banksia)
Grevillea banksii (Banks's grevillea)
Kunzea ambigua (tick bush, white kunzea)
Melaleuca incana (honey myrtle)
Westringia fruticosa (coast or native rosemary)

GARDENS FOR PEOPLE WITH SPECIAL NEEDS

Gardens and gardening are for everyone, irrespective of age or physical dexterity. If you are elderly or disabled you may like to design a garden to meet your needs and taking your limitations into account. If necessary seek help from a gardening friend or professional. The aims of the design are threefold: to provide access to all parts; to facilitate gardening; and to offer maximum enjoyment of the pleasures of a garden. Safety and convenience, as well as beauty, should always be paramount in any garden, of course.

ACCESS AND MOVEMENT

You will want to consider the following points, when you are designing the garden, to ensure free movement:

- paths should be wide enough for safe passage
- paths must not be slippery or rough
- paths should have some logic to them, and no sudden bends and twists
- adequate lighting must be provided at night
- driveways and carport facilities should be within sensible reach of the house
- seats with backs should be set at suitable intervals through the garden to provide resting spots
- ponds, protruding rockwork and trees with obstructive trunks and branches should not be included in a new garden, and their whereabouts should be thoroughly known in an existing one
- trees and shrubs should be kept pruned, particularly near paths, and no sharp stubs should be left protruding
- prickly plants are best left out of parts of the gardens near paths and lawns
- handrails can be installed on both sides of a stairway if necessary and a single rail placed along a curving path; ramps are often easier to use than steps, and they provide access for wheel chairs
- a wooden bridge – just a wide, raftlike structure, perhaps with a handrail – built across a low area that is rather muddy can provide a link with an otherwise inaccessible area.

A sheltered seat in a special place is important in any garden, whatever your special needs.

GARDEN TENDING

There comes a time when all of us have to modify our gardening habits, but it is quite possible to continue to enjoy the pleasures of gardening despite physical limitations.

Simple ergonomics suggests that a raised herb garden will save household cooks considerable effort, and clearly the idea could spill over to other sorts of gardens. When you are designing raised garden beds, make sure that they are set at a height that offers maximum arm comfort and flexibility.

The right tools, well maintained, can greatly contribute to garden happiness. Multi-purpose tools, such as those with interchangeable fittings, are particularly convenient. Long-handled secateurs controlled by the arm and hand may be easier to manage than finger–hand operated ones. Especially light or single-handed tools are available, and also light and efficient manual lawnmowers for small areas of grass. Specialist advice is obtainable from Horticultural Therapy Association branches in New South Wales, Victoria and Western Australia.

Grow plants that are not demanding, not too prone to disease and not too quick growing – the section on Gardens for Busy People in this chapter offers many ideas. Unfortunately a number of vegetables and some fruit need regular attention; however, herbs, rhubarb (*Rheum rhaponticum*), lettuces (*Lactuca sativa*), shallots (*Allium ascalonicum*), silverbeet (*Beta vulgaris* var. *cicla*) and beetroot are rewarding to grow because they don't require great care. If you are visually impaired use light stakes to identify plants that are difficult to distinguish by touch: set the stakes at different heights or attach markers, such as string.

Mulching to conserve moisture, suppress weeds and improve soil texture is valuable to any garden and saves considerable labour.

Some people consider lawn a low-maintenance garden component. To others its care is a constant nuisance or worry and turning some or all of it into a safe, paved sitting area may be quite a relief.

Hanging baskets can get in the way, so care should be taken to hang them where you will not bump into them. However, they need to be placed where you can tend them easily. Window-boxes and pots (see Chapter 6) should also be placed within comfortable reach. Because the containers are small and easy to get at, a great deal of effort can be concentrated in the one spot. Hydroponics, the method of growing plants in a soilless medium, with nutrients added, can also be confined to one place and is much less messy than the usual gardening methods.

Never lift excessive weights, whatever your age and agility. Use a hand trolley or a wheelbarrow to move heavy objects. Two buckets half full and well balanced, one on either side of you, are much easier to carry than one full bucket carried on one side.

ENJOYING THE GARDEN

Some of the greatest pleasures of a garden are available to everyone. Scented plants are one of the special joys, and never more so than if your sight is impaired. There are a host of plants with lovely perfumes. They range from small violets (*Viola odorata*), mignonette (*Reseda odorata*) and *Dianthus plumarius* 'Mrs Sinkins' to thyme (*Thymus*), lavenders (*Lavandula*), heliotrope (*Heliotropium arborescens*), pelargoniums, boronia, daphne, gardenias and roses to wisteria, jasmine, wintersweet (*Chimonanthus praecox*) and buddleias.

The touch of many of our plants is intriguing. Sticky wattles (*Acacia*) and bottlebrushes (*Callistemon*), ropy cypress and spiky pine, round, firm gumnuts and other seed cases, and velvety lamb's ears (*Stachys lanata*), peppermint pelargoniums and mosses all offer tactile pleasure.

Birds offer sudden musical delights for listeners and movement and life for onlookers. By planting even just a few native plants, such as banksias, callistemons, wattles (*Acacia*) and correas you will attract birds to your garden. The Chinese lantern bush (*Abutilon*) is another appealing plant for many birds. Have a partly hidden birdbath or a pond to attract them (and you) to the garden – there's usually something happening in or by water.

The sound of tumbling or splashing water itself is restful and evocative of the natural sounds of the countryside. Beside water is an ideal place to have a seat. A garden that is to be appreciated slowly needs sheltered spots or alcoves where seats and wheel chairs can be stationed.

GARDENS FOR BUSY PEOPLE

Sometimes you may not have the time to do as much work in your garden as you would like to. Other demands mount up and time goes by. There is something about a garden that makes it the first thing dropped when the pressure is on. However, a garden is forgiving, and when you eventually get out there and cut, tidy and sweep it will spring back with renewed vigour.

LABOUR-SAVING DESIGNS

If you are not able to put the time in, yet want a pleasant garden, you need a sensible design that provides a great deal of structural appeal without placing too many demands on the gardener. If keeping a lawn mown would be too difficult, have an attractive paved space instead. Perhaps include a pond. Ponds do not demand much care once they are set up with fish, snails and water plants, and they are restful and interesting to look at and into.

A busy person, like a beginner gardener, should not take on too much. If time is limited it is wise to work with a small range of plants and get to know their needs. Fill up your spaces with striking repetitious plantings. Patches of bulbs and petunias of a single colour, or sweeps of just two or three perennial plants, will have tremendous impact. A colour strategy always simplifies planting. Plan a green and white garden, or one of blue, cream and lime-green colours, or a combination of pinks and mauves. Make sure your colours work well together, though, for any mistake is magnified in mass plantings.

There are a few plants that cause very little work because they do not require cutting back, just the removal of dead wood every now and then. Camellias, particularly the japonicas, are good examples; also *Raphiolepis* × *delacourii*, *Nandina domestica*, the port wine magnolia (*Michelia figo*) and small conifers. As well, these plants are not prone to disease. Viburnums, melaleucas, guavas (*Psidium guajava*) and *Feijoa sellowiana* are low-maintenance plants, too. They only require cutting back if they are growing too large for their space. Tree ferns are excellent shade plants for busy people and are very restful to look at. Each one takes up a lot of space, and although you should keep the tired brown fronds properly clipped off at the trunk this is all the care they need if they receive reasonable water. Distribute cut-up pieces of the removed fronds beneath the tree ferns to make a forest floor for them.

OPPOSITE PAGE This front garden is eye-catching but simple. The generous space allocated to path, steps and massed plantings of tough, ground-covering plants makes for easy care as well as beauty.

Buy pots of annual plants in full flower to touch up the garden for special occasions. You will find petunias, impatiens, daisies, pansies, violas, marigolds, primulas and a host of other flowers in plastic pots ready to be slipped inside your decorative containers. By using containers to add instant glamour, you save a lot of fiddling about with seedlings and your seasonal transformations will take attention away from less orderly background plants.

Against a backdrop of easily maintained shrubs, such as a curved planting of camellias, place a sculpture. Its elegant or intriguing form will give focus to a rather blank space. And remember not all pots need plants: you can treat a pot as a sculpture.

Labour-saving tips

- Cover bare spots in your garden with a 4-centimetre layer of mulch. It will suppress weeds, conserve moisture in the ground and improve the soil texture. A luxuriant mat of low, spreading plants acts in the same way.
- Install a comprehensive sprinkler system. You can buy a kit and assemble the system yourself or pay someone to do it for you. A simple computerised timer can be used to initiate and control watering.
- Understand the basic tasks required in a garden. Mostly plants need pruning and feeding at set times each year and can then be left alone. Weeding is essential: do it whenever you see a weed so that it doesn't get out of hand.
- Build a set amount of gardening time – perhaps one and a half hours – into your weekly schedule if you're not the kind of person who is always dashing out for a few minutes in the garden.
- Have sharp, efficient and appropriate tools and store them conveniently close by.
- Above all, get to know your garden. Sometimes you can believe you have not got time for your garden just because you are really afraid or in awe of it. Try to get out there more, with coffee or a drink. Sit in the garden and walk round it, observing the plants and their settings. Try a little gardening on the spot. Look for insects attacking a plant so that you can take action right away. Gather up a weed or two as you pass and clip back an intruding creeper – you will hardly notice this type of gardening.

AN ORIENTAL GARDEN

Anyone who studies the origins of plants widely used in Australian gardens today will notice the rich collection of plants with Chinese origins: the peony (*Paeonia*), the gordonia, the luculia, the kolkwitzia, the abelia, the photinia, the cedrela, the Chinese weeping cypress (*Cupressus funebris*), the willow (*Salix*), the ginkgo, the Chinese elm (*Ulmus parvifolia*) and many bulbs, camellias, hibiscus and rose species – on goes the list.

Japan, too, has contributed many fine plants to the world's gardens, including the flowering quince (*Chaenomeles japonica*), the gold dust plant (*Aucuba japonica* 'Variegata'), golden-flowered *Kerria japonica*, the sacred bamboo (*Nandina domestica*), *Magnolia stellata* and, of course, the Japanese maple (*Acer pal-*

An oriental place has been created in a small courtyard. Blocks of stone lead from one door to another across a dry pond lined with granite slate pieces and chips.

matum). Plants such as the flowering cherry (*Prunus serrulata*) and *Spiraea cantoniensis* and *S. thunbergii* are native to both countries. In these countries, the primeval range of flora was preserved during the ravages of the Ice Ages, while in North America and Europe many species were destroyed. If plants of eastern Asian origin alone were used in a garden, it would be a garden indeed.

Records of gardens created in China go back to 2000 BC. Given the rich variety of native plants, the forests and plains must have abounded with beauty, so it is not surprising that the first made gardens were embellishments of nature – a bridge here and there over running water, and pathways, gates and buildings sited to catch the beauty of rocks and mountain slopes, trees and other plants. When gardens were needed where there were no natural mountains and lakes, artificial lakes were built and large, craggy rocks used to emulate mountains or the seashores. Flowering plants such as camellias, peonies, spiraeas, magnolias and plum and cherry trees became a decorative element to be arranged, at times quite elaborately. The reconstructed Chinese gardens that can be visited today reflect the extremely ornate style gradually developed, rather than the ancient gardens.

The use of craggy, vertical rocks in early Chinese gardens has always been highly meaningful. Stone 'mountains' are expressions of the inner force of mountains – a source of strength. For the Chinese, stones from mountains, rivers or lakes, unshaped and uncarved, represent creation. The Chinese, and the Japanese, have had such respect for natural rock that it is usually only lightly carved and used sparingly in statuary. Stories and travel adventures were often depicted through the symbolic materials of the gardens.

In the recreated gardens compositions of grouped rocks and a plant or two – a flowering plum or cherry tree, a magnolia, peonies or mondo grass (*Cophiopogon japonica*) – are often arranged to be viewed from a geometrical, often circular, window just as we might do today in a small internal courtyard. Dry stone gardens, also taken up by the Japanese, and elaborate pebble mosaic are another part of the Chinese heritage.

The Japanese absorbed the aims of early Chinese landscapers. They related readily to the lake-and-island concept, Japanese interpretations being influenced by their own magnificent coastlines and islands. From the seventh century onwards they produced gardens of great elegance, with some quite flowery and elaborate. Gradually, however, the Japanese love for the rustic and simple emerged, and gardens came closer to resembling nature: the rocks, for example, were set flatter than in the Chinese ornamental rockscapes. Naturalistic dry waterfalls were built from rock as early as the fourteenth century. The range of plants used in gardens became selective. Designers achieved impact and dignity by repetitive, naturalistic plantings of trees such as Japanese maples or birches or low shrubs such as azaleas or *Enkianthus* species. Sometimes a lake was filled with lotus plants, and clumps of weeping willows were set on the shore. The whole garden might be small or on quite a large scale.

LEARNING FROM ORIENTAL GARDENS

We can learn not only from the form and materials of oriental gardens, but also from their underlying concepts. Reflect on the underlying principle of the first Chinese gardens. Its enduring wisdom applies to all natural sites and settings whose resources can be developed to make a garden. If a site is bulldozed something lovely may be created, but it will never have the natural grace and integrity of the original setting. Perhaps the concept behind a bush retreat is not so different from that of the Chinese mountain-and-forest gardens of centuries ago.

In broad, open expanses of garden, paths of stone cut in regular shapes are laid. Even in smaller spaces such paving is quite suitable. Although the patterns used have a formal quality, they also have an appealing simplicity. Granite gravel is often laid between path edges of cut stone, particularly to cover large, open courtyards.

Small gardens are very tightly designed and so, like the larger gardens, they can often include water. Frequently there is a special building from which the moon can be viewed across the water, the perfume of nearby osmanthus enjoyed or birdsong heard. Then there are the small courtyard gardens, modelled on the tea garden, an especially lovely garden, sometimes viewed from within, which sets the atmosphere of serenity for the tea ceremony. With the tea garden goes the approach garden through which people pass before the tea ceremony, shedding their day-to-day concerns in readiness.

Take time to think of the differences of design and planting between a garden that you might have along a path, which is seen mainly in transit, and a garden to be viewed by people as they sit in a room. An approach garden must create an immediate impression, whether of intimacy, colourfulness, restfulness or neutral uniformity, but also draw attention to something beyond itself. A courtyard garden seen from within can be much more subtle for there will be more time in which to understand it. Give attention to the changing moods created by the sun's movements through the day and by the changes in plants and light through the seasons.

Japanese landscapers have long used weathered-looking rocks that suggest they have become exposed and mossy over centuries. Some, of course, are genuinely weathered, but others are arranged to appear so: they are partly buried in the earth, with their greatest visible width at their point of emergence. The principle employed is the basis of all good rockwork. It applies also to the placement of rocks in a pond, which may be supported by a base of bricks or stones beneath the water. And, as long ago as the fifteenth century, Zen Buddhist priests in Japan advocated the creative use of local materials, rather than the transportation of materials from remote areas at great cost – certainly good advice to this day.

The treatment of pathways in Japanese gardens also offers us a fresh approach. In the rustic parts of the garden anything more than stepping stones would seem out of harmony. Here the paths are rough, with somewhat irregular stepping stones almost buried, leaving only a low-set walking surface. Large and small stepping stones are combined to create interest. Beauty and concern for perspective are uppermost, although the paths are also designed to control the behaviour of those who pass through the garden. Trickily positioned rocks or awkward steps compel people to look down and take special care; when they arrive at a safer part they look up again, to see that the garden has changed in a spectacular way, giving them a surge of pleasure and surprise. Walking pace is also controlled by the distances between stepping stones. The further apart they are placed, the quicker people walk over them.

Depicting nature is one of gardening's finest arts, and the Japanese have cultivated it over the centuries. Once a picture is created, the gardeners work to maintain it in its perfect form by constantly clipping the trees and shrubs. Many Japanese gardens are grand natural scenes in miniature, and all components must remain in proportion. The round-topped azaleas, for example, are an echo of the forms of water-worn rocks and must be kept to scale. All the plants must continue in the same relationship and in harmony with added features: a stone lantern, stepping stones, a water dish. In any small garden vigilance in keeping plants to various sizes and maintaining a balance, season by season and year by year, is the key to success.

We can learn from the Japanese wonderful tricks of borrowing scenery from beyond the garden and of extending the garden into its surroundings. One technique is to plant a tree or a group of trees so that a mountain beyond becomes more than a view; the mountain's beauty is brought into the garden by its interplay with the foreground planting. Another trick is to position a window to frame a particularly lovely part of a general view beyond the garden or house.

Rocks, too, command respect and skill in handling. The Japanese always assess their individuality and use it to good effect. More than two rocks set together are arranged in odd-numbered groups of three, five or seven and to reveal the interesting features of each.

The oriental garden, in which the power of nature is revealed in forms at once simple and grand, is an approach quite different from that of many Western garden makers who display their skills by manipulating natural ingredients for decorative purposes. If you choose to work within the Japanese style, be careful to distinguish the beautiful from the flamboyant. Perhaps the art of restraint is the greatest legacy of Japanese gardens.

OPPOSITE PAGE This ancient place, the garden of the Saihō-ji or Moss Temple, at Kyōto, Japan, is a blend of natural beauty and nature understood.

AN ITALIAN GARDEN

For some, perhaps including yourself, an Italian garden conjures up an image of grape vines on frames, figs and olives, citrus, pomegranates and almonds. There are sandy paths, terracotta tiles and terracotta pots or urns, arranged in curves or lines rather than groups and full of scarlet pelargoniums. There are tall pencil cypresses, oleanders, lilacs and mock orange, roses and irises, marguerites and rosemary, carnations and lavenders. If the garden is in northern Italy, there are poplars; if to the south, more olives and the Aleppo pine. In every garden there are vegetables, herbs growing like weeds, poppies and cornflowers running wild and sometimes a wisteria draped over a rough-hewn pergola. The sun bakes the ground hard in summer, the rain softens it again come wintertime.

LEFT You can feel the sun in this garden inspired by Italy: in the rough rendered house wall; the vines, lavenders and herbs; the paving and quaint brick sitting wall; the balconies; and the bright blue sky.

OPPOSITE PAGE Wall fountains like the old communal drinking ones of Italy add to the Mediterranean atmosphere of a warm garden.

The relaxed, colourful gardens of rural Italy give you the feeling of captured sunshine bringing out the flowers and ripening the fruit. They originally existed for the importance of the harvest more than for the beauty of plants, yet the secondary and incidental nature of their beauty is also their charm. Understanding this principle and the bright and earthy colours that reflect the Mediterranean region, you can create a rustic Italian garden in the similar light and warmth of Australia. Houses with high-pitched roofs, gables, rendered walls and pergolas particularly lend themselves to the style.

From such gardens, reflecting the abundance of rural Italy, your mind may ramble on through woodlands, wild with lilac, rock roses, broom and lavender and overhung by robinia and birch, to grand seventeenth-century landscaped gardens, with classical ornaments and formal pools, and thence to the strictly disciplined gardens of the Italian Renaissance villas and palaces.

The symmetrical Renaissance gardens, with their solid architectural features echoed in formal planting, can be quite small but are always impressive. Plants are clipped, often in topiary of amazing intricacy. Fountains splash at the centre of rectangular or circular pools or from a wall or a grotto at one end of a long pool.

Balustrades and colonnades, masonry arches and statues are just some of the decorative devices used in these gardens. Pots or urns, merely ornamental or planted with lemon trees or box, provide dramatic accents along walls or on terraces, perhaps by pools. The pots are of glazed or unglazed terracotta, carved stone or moulded cement.

Often vistas of the countryside beyond or further garden compartments are framed by the arches and colonnades or seen from terraces bounded by ornate balustrades. Sometimes a walk through such an Italian garden, particularly in Tuscany, ends in a secret garden full of flowers – a great joy to the households of the past.

CREATING A FORMAL ITALIAN GARDEN

Some of the formal elements of Italian Renaissance gardens can be incorporated in the gardens of contemporary houses, particularly those with a classical façade: a traditional wall fountain, for example, is an architectural element that will help create the style, and the trickle of water will bring life to what is a rather austere setting. The style is also well suited to modern lifestyles because, while regular clipping of shrubs is needed, only a limited variety of plants is included, making care straightforward.

The most frequently used plants are the cypresses *Cupressus sempervirens* and *C. s.* 'Stricta', holly (*Ilex aquifolium*), Portugal laurel (*Prunus lusitanica*) and English box (*Buxus sempervirens*). In the secret garden bloom irises and carnations (*Dianthus*), lilac (*Syringa vulgaris*), mock orange (*Philadelphus coronarius*), wintersweet (*Chimonanthus praecox*), roses and wisteria.

Sometimes the planting style of formal Italian gardens is applied to other kinds of gardens, using atypical plants – repetition being the one principle upheld. Rows of lavender and 'Iceberg' roses have recently appeared in many gardens in Australia. The challenge now is to think of less usual but equally lovely plants.

In the Renaissance gardens of Italy, noble statues were frequently set among clipped hedges. In the recreated Renaissance garden of La Pietra, in Florence, Italy, a rose-clad pergola is a graceful embellishment.

A GARDENER'S CALENDAR

Australian gardeners must often contend with a wide range of elements, but the reward, in the form of beauty, leisure, food and flowers, is boundless.

Wherever you live, this month-by-month guide is intended to help you understand what is happening in your garden throughout the year. It suggests how you can get the best from each month by appreciating the weather it brings and becoming aware of the plants that require attention or make a particular contribution at that time. It will also, we hope, help you to get greater enjoyment out of the simple tasks of growing, caring and harvesting. We believe that you as a gardener should enjoy managing your garden – given the effort required to make a garden to suit your needs, this is only fair. The main aim should be productiveness and beauty through sound design, wise plant selection and good nurturing. So, whatever you grow, from azaleas to zucchini, you should grow them well – in an attractive, workable setting that also provides a place in which you can sometimes just sit and enjoy the fruits of your labours.

The calendar deals with all aspects of gardening: each month offers ideas for plantings and tips on moisture control, rose and lawn care, pests and diseases, pruning, feeding and garden planning. For more detail on specific activities, refer to the earlier chapters, especially Chapters 3, 4 and 6.

In the calendar Australia has generally been treated as one large garden to which certain basic principles of good gardening apply. However, in recognition of the widely divergent environmental conditions of gardens throughout the continent, we have divided Australia into three climatic regions:

- cool
- temperate and semi-arid
- tropical and sub-tropical.

These are, of course, broad categories within which there are many combinations of temperature, rainfall and frost. As well, local factors, such as aspect, altitude, nearness to the sea and microclimatic features, will determine the conditions experienced in any garden. For each region, therefore, we indicate where activities and conditions differ from the norm in any particular month.

THE COOL REGION

The cool region runs from Queensland down the Great Dividing Range, through New South Wales to Victoria, taking in Canberra and the Blue Mountains. The region extends across southern Victoria, through Melbourne, to Mt Gambier in South Australia and covers all of Tasmania. On the whole the zone is associated with warm to hot summers and cool to cold, wet winters, with frosts and snow in some parts. Further north, the rain is likely to be more evenly distributed through the year.

THE TEMPERATE AND SEMI-ARID REGION

The temperate and semi-arid region covers the coast of New South Wales from Coffs Harbour, through Sydney, down to the Victorian border. It also extends across the centre of Australia, including Alice Springs, and covers nearly all South Australia (including Adelaide), the southern part of Western Australia (including Perth), inland New South Wales and northern Victoria. Summer temperatures are higher and more frosts are likely in inland areas than along the coast. Rainfall in the north is fairly well distributed throughout the year but gradually lessens inland. In the interior, temperatures can be extremely high in summer, with warm to hot winters and variable, though mostly sparse, rain throughout the year. Further south, there is a pattern of less rain in summer, the rain being mainly distributed in winter.

THE TROPICAL AND SUB-TROPICAL REGION

The tropical and sub-tropical region covers most of Queensland, running down the east coast through Brisbane to Coffs Harbour in New South Wales. It also covers the Northern Territory and the northern part of Western Australia. Throughout the year temperatures are mostly hot to very hot. Most rain is received during that part of the year known as the wet season, from November through to March. Much less rain is received in the remaining months, called the dry season, but temperatures remain high. In subtropical parts the rain may be less concentrated and temperatures lower, but tropical conditions prevail. The change from 'summer' to 'winter' is gradual and autumn and spring are noticeably lacking because there is no truly dormant season.

In all regions, some plants adapt and others do not. Some appear to thrive, but go under during climatic extremes. Some plants that are perennials in temperate areas, such as fuchsias, marguerites and pelargoniums, need to be treated as annuals in cold areas (cuttings can be propagated for next year). In the tropics they are likely to get fungal diseases including rust, mildew and leaf rot. In semi-arid parts the dry air can suit them to some extent, but if there is insufficient water they will succumb.

At the beginning of each month we present a selection of plants featuring (whether for their flowers, leaves or berries) around the country. A plant may grow in one climatic region or occur more widely: for each region we have named one or two trees, shrubs and climbing plants that are noticeably at their best at this time. In many cases, as with Chinese lantern (*Abutilon*) and cherry pie (*Heliotropum arborescens*), flowering may extend for more than a month, even into another season, according to the zone. The climatic regions are not given in the case of annuals, perennials and bulbs, as often with these plants it is a case of trial and error according to your particular site or aspect.

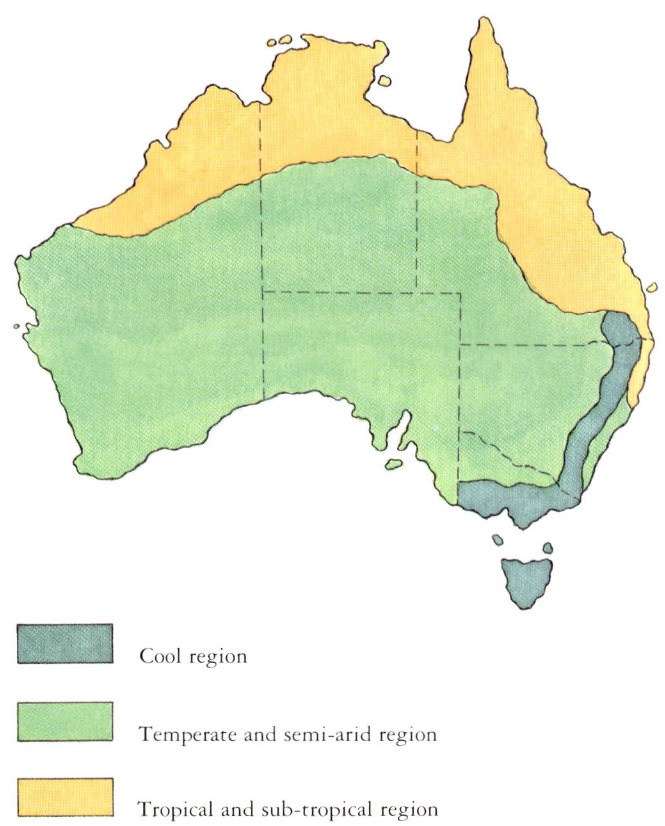

LEFT Australia, for the purposes of the calendar, has been divided into three broad climatic regions.

RIGHT For the best results, the individual needs of plants – in this case for a warm, dry position – must be met.

JANUARY

In January the weather varies tremendously across the continent. In the north the wet season produces heavy rain and humidity, while inland and further south conditions range from mild to extreme dryness. In many areas water may be at a premium. For some people, concern about the threat of bushfires and making their properties safe dominates outdoor activities. Others are enjoying a summer break away from home. If you are at home this is a good time to enjoy the shade and leisure offered by your garden and to plan some garden projects, for now or for later in the year.

SOME PLANTS FEATURING NOW

TREES

Cool: *Calodendrum capense* (Cape chestnut), *Clethra arborea* (lily of the valley tree).
Temperate: *Acacia elata* (cedar wattle), *Lagerstroemia indica* (crêpe myrtle).
Semi-arid: *Brachychiton populneo-acerifolius* (kurrajong), *Eucalyptus leucoxylon* var. *macrocarpa* (pink-flowered yellow gum).
Tropical and sub-tropical: *Delonix regia* (royal poinciana), *Cassia fistula* (golden shower tree).

SHRUBS

Cool: *Abelia × grandiflora*, *Abutilon* (Chinese lantern).
Temperate: *Buddleja davidii* (butterfly bush), *Hibiscus*.
Semi-arid: *Nerium oleander* (oleander), *Russelia juncea* (coral plant).
Tropical and sub-tropical: *Crotalaria agatifolia* (bird flower), *Murraya exotica* (orange jessamine).

CLIMBING PLANTS

Cool: Climbing roses, *Solanum jasminoides* (potato vine).
Temperate: *Hibbertia scandens* (snake vine), *Mandevilla laxa* (Chilean jasmine).
Tropical and sub-tropical: *Allemanda cathartica* (golden allemander), *Solandra maxima* (cup of gold).

ANNUALS AND PERENNIALS

Alyssum maritimum (sweet Alice), *Cleome spinosa* (spider flower), *Cosmos bipinnatus*, *Digitalis lutea*, *Francoa sonchifolia*, *Impatiens wallerana*, *Nicotiana* (tobacco plant), *Penstemon versicolor* (bearded tongue), *Phlox*, *Salvia* (flowering sage).

BULBS

Agapanthus (Nile lily), *Canna indica* (Indian shot), *Crinum flaccidum*, *C. moorei*, *Dahlia*, *Gladiolus*, *Gloriosa rothschildiana* (gloriosa lily), *Hemerocallis* (daylily), *Hymenocallis*, *Lilium*, including *L. longiflorum* (successful in the tropics) and *L. tigrinum* (tiger lily), and *Tulbaghia violacea* (wild garlic).

MOISTURE CONTROL

Check mulches and top up with compost or other organic matter after watering thoroughly. Where there is insufficient rain, deep watering and mulching are essential for most gardens to survive the heat. Compost breaks down more quickly during the hotter months, so try to make as much as you can to keep up mulch supplies on the garden – this is a busy time!

Remember that watering in the morning is preferable. Evening watering encourages fungal diseases and watering during the day is less effective owing to the greater rate of evaporation. Try not to over-water: as a guide to water requirements, feel the soil under the mulch, consider the weather and check your plants for signs of water stress. Plants such as hydrangeas and impatiens are less tolerant of dryness than many other plants and quickly wilt, thus reminding you of their needs. Fully grown fruit trees need plenty of moisture to sustain their crop, particularly during a heatwave. Afterwards, too, they should be thoroughly soaked to avoid stress to next year's developing fruit.

Where water is in short supply it is essential that plants chosen are fit for the job of surviving the prolonged dry heat and winds (see the section on A Garden Hot and Dry in Chapter 7). In very hot areas, water supply permitting, apply a fine misty spray during hot, windy days.

In the tropics it is necessary to take account of the extreme variations in conditions (from monsoons to dry periods) in managing garden moisture. Sometimes soils can become quite waterlogged with heavy rains, so check in case agricultural drains are needed. It is wise to plant in raised beds or retained areas, to assist drainage and to retain soil which might otherwise be washed away. Mulches and close planting can also help reduce soil loss. Leaching can cause nutrient deficiencies, so additional nutrients should be added as rains subside.

LAWN CARE

Let your lawn grow longer than you might in cooler months, to protect the roots and make it more difficult for weeds to become established. Water thoroughly to encourage roots to go deeper, and water only when the surface soil has really dried out. In areas where water is scarce, don't water at all.

This is a good time to spot the tall seed heads of paspalum above finer grasses, and it is worth the effort of removing this rampant weed with a two-pronged weeder.

PLANTING IDEAS

VEGETABLES

In all regions sow beans (except broad beans), beetroot, broccoli, Brussels sprouts (except in the tropics), cabbages, carrots, cauliflowers, kohlrabi, parsnips, radishes, silverbeet and sweetcorn. (It is useful to remember that radishes and carrots can be sown together: the radishes are pulled earlier and so help thin out the developing carrots.) In tropical and sub-tropical areas also sow artichokes, capsicums, eggplants, melons, peanuts, pumpkins, rhubarb, spinach, sweet potatoes and tomatoes. (Remember that beans, beetroot, lettuces, radishes, tomatoes and zucchini can be sown all year round in sub-tropical regions.) The herbs cress, coriander, dill and parsley can also be sown.

Seeds *or* seedlings may be planted for broccoli, Brussels sprouts, cauliflowers, celery, leeks, lettuces, silverbeet and zucchini. In all but cool areas plant bush squash, Chinese cabbage, cucumbers, spring onions and zucchini.

ANNUALS AND PERENNIALS

Seeds to sow include *Alcea rosea* (hollyhock), *Aquilegia* × *hybrida* (columbine), *Delphinium* (larkspur), *Digitalis purpurea* (foxglove), *Gypsophila*, *Linaria maroccana* (baby snapdragon), *Liriope* (candle flower), *Lobelia erinus*, *Myosotis* (forget-me-not), *Papaver nudicaule* (Iceland poppy) and *Primula* × *polyantha* (polyanthus).

Plant seedlings of *Delphinium*, *Dianthus* (carnation, pink), *Digitalis purpurea* and *Primula obconica*.

BULBS

For autumn plant *Amaryllis belladonna* (belladonna lily), *Brunsvigia*, *Clivia* (kaffir lily), *Crinum moorei*, *Cyclamen*, *Nerine* (spider lily), *Sternbergia lutea*, *Vallota speciosa* (Scarborough lily) and *Zephyranthes candida* (flower of the west wind).

These bulbs are not suited to the moist tropics. Clivias may do better in warmer districts and nerines in cooler parts.

ROSE GUIDE

Prune modern roses lightly, mainly to clear out dead and weak, twiggy growth, to strengthen plants for autumn flowering. Feed them with plenty of well-rotted animal manure (cow manure works well), a sprinkled handful of blood and bone and a teaspoon of potash, or a commercial rose food. Remember that every time you pick a rose you should cut it according to the pruning rules.

PLANT WATCH

Develop the habit of walking around your garden, looking at each plant to see if it is at risk from pests or disease. Try to pre-empt major problems by dealing with them early and conservatively (that is, without resorting to chemicals), if you can, for this will save you both work and disappointment. Keep a clean garden by always gathering up diseased material and putting it in the rubbish – pests breed and diseases thrive in hot, humid conditions.

This month be on the lookout for the following pests.

- Aphids, especially on roses. Remove with fingers or a soapy rag, or spray with pyrethrum.
- Black spot and other fungal diseases. Check your roses: remove infected leaves and put in the garbage. Spray with a fungicide.
- Fruit fly. This is a serious problem and any infested fruit must be destroyed. The most effective form of control is a powerful poison such as Lebacid, which should be used according to directions.
- Passionvine hoppers. Disturb with a jet of water from your hose. Remove quickly with a soapy rag at nightfall, when they are slower, or if necessary spray with pyrethrum.
- Pear and cherry slug. A dusting of lime over the leaves may repel them. Hose leaves after three days. Try to avoid using carbaryl spray.
- Possums. Feed them apples and other goodies to deter them from eating berries, buds and fruit.
- Scale. These insects often invade citrus, daphne, gardenia, lilly pilly, persimmon and pittosporum. Spray with white oil, which is also effective against sooty mould.
- Thrips. Prevalent during dry spells. Reduce numbers with repeated water jets from a hose.
- Whitefly. Disturb frequently by hosing, or spray with pyrethrum. They are hard to control without powerful chemical sprays, so generally continue to make their habitat uncomfortable.

PRUNING PROGRAMME

Remember to remove dead flower heads, using sharp secateurs, to stimulate growth and improve appearance.

- Berry fruit: prune back canes as they finish fruiting.
- Callistemons: remove dead heads after flowering, to encourage prettier, stronger bushes. With larger plants just remove as many heads as you can manage.
- Climbers: prune lightly to keep them in check, especially in the tropics.

JANUARY

- Fuchsias: shorten lank growth back to healthy shoots, to encourage flowering.
- Herbs: cut back leggy, dried-out plants so they will shoot again.
- Hibiscus: in tropical areas, prune for better winter flowers.
- Native plants: these will become more compact and vigorous with tip-pruning of slender, lank growth before they have a chance to develop a permanently leggy framework. You may do this two or three times during the growing season, as needed, but not when the plant is due to flower.
- Petunias: young plants will need cutting back a little. Try to remove dead heads as they appear.
- Strawberries: remove runners.
- Tomatoes: remove laterals.
- Trees and shrubs: cut back after flowering to encourage growth and good shape. Prune early-flowering fruit trees, such as plums, peaches and nectarines, to strengthen new growth.

FEEDING TIME

Stimulate flowers and vegetables with regular applications of weak liquid manure. Vegetables can bolt in the heat, prematurely running to seed if not fed well and watered regularly.

Give dahlias liquid manure, and mulch when flower buds appear. Give passionfruit dressings of blood and bone or complete fertiliser.

Penstemons are generously flowering perennials that love the sun.

OTHER JOBS

Last year's cyclamen plants can be repotted in good potting mix. Keep them moist if they are not yet shooting, then water them regularly when soil is dry.

Indoor pot plants can be aired outside and freshened in the rain, but bring them inside before it becomes too hot.

Shorten dahlia shoots back to two or three buds down the stem when the plants are 50 centimetres tall, to encourage bushy growth.

Divide congested clumps of iris and replant the best pieces. Leave the top of the rhizome exposed.

Do some weeding and general tidying. Weeds flourish in summer, reaching seedling stage rapidly: catch them before they spread, and remember that a thorough mulch will assist weed control. Remember to keep your garden clean to discourage pests and diseases.

BONUSES AND HARVESTS

Propagate semi-hardwood cuttings of azaleas, camellias, daphnes and rhododendrons. You can also take tip-cuttings of plants such as *Coleus* (painted nettle), fuchsias, impatiens and *Plectranthus*, *Hypoestes* and other soft succulents.

January is the peak month for harvesting stone fruits – try to beat the birds to them. In the tropics there may be lychees to pick. In the vegetable garden things move fast. Pick vegetables while they are young and tender, to increase production, particularly in the case of beans, peas, silverbeet and zucchini. Harvest English lavender (*Lavandula angustifolia*) this month and tie the flowers in bunches to hang and dry.

Find a shady seat somewhere and just sit for a while to enjoy your garden. Be sure to wear a hat outside.

PLANNING NOTES

Notice the effects of the sun throughout the day during the hotter months. Your sun and shade needs will vary according to where your garden is, and whether you are after a sunny sitting place or shelter from the fierce rays of the sun. Don't be afraid to lift the canopies of suitable trees to make shady sitting spots, or to cut back branches which keep the sun from you or garden areas that want more light. Consider planting new trees for shade, or placing upright or columnar trees where sunlight or vertical silhouettes are needed.

Check for boring spots in your garden and resolve to have improved your arid summer picture by this time next year.

FEBRUARY

In most parts of Australia, February is a trying month. Whatever the weather, it seems to go on too long: the humid tropical wet season, the grey, damp, humid days in some temperate areas and the often-severe dry heat of the south are among this month's climatic trials. It is a time when heat-resistant plants show their class.

SOME PLANTS FEATURING NOW

TREES

Cool: *Eucalyptus ficifolia* (Western Australian flowering gum), *Lagunaria patersonia* (pyramid tree).
Temperate: *Acacia schinoides* (frosty wattle), *Tamarix pentandra* (late tamarisk).
Semi-arid: *Cassia artemisiodes*, *Tamarix aphylla* (athel tree).
Tropical: *Buckinghamia celsissima* (ivory-curl tree), *Syzygium floribundum* (lilly pilly).

SHRUBS

Cool: *Calluna vulgaris* (Scotch heather), *Fuchsia*.
Temperate: *Cassia corymbosa*, *Clerodendrum ugandense* (blue butterfly bush).
Semi-arid: *Grevillea lavandulacea*, *Alyogyne huegelii* (lilac hibiscus).
Tropical: *Malvaviscus mollis* (wax mallow), *Plumeria rubra* (frangipani).

CLIMBING PLANTS

Cool: *Cobaea scandens* (cup-and-saucer vine), *Passiflora manicata* (scarlet passionflower).
Temperate: *Pandorea jasminoides* (bower of beauty), *Solanum seaforthianum* (Brazilian nightshade).
Tropical: *Petrea volubilis* (purple wreath), *Thunbergia grandiflora* (blue trumpet vine).

ANNUALS AND PERENNIALS

Last month's list still applies, with the addition of *Aster* (Easter and Michaelmas daisy), *Begonia*, *Eschscholzia californica* (Californian poppy), *Helichrysum* (everlasting), *Impatiens wallerana*, *Liriope* (candle flower), *Phlox*, *Physostegia* (obedient plant) and *Scaevola* (fan flower).

BULBS

Alpinia speciosa (shell ginger), *Amaryllis*, *Canna indica* (Indian shot), *Dahlia*, *Dietes bicolor*, *Hedychium coronarium* (white ginger plant), *Hemerocallis* (daylily), *Polianthes tuberosa* (tuberose).

Cosmos come in vibrant colours as well as pastel tonings.

FEBRUARY

MOISTURE CONTROL

Continue the moisture regime recommended for January. It is a good idea to check your sprinkler system to make sure water is getting to all your plants. Where plants have grown strongly, some adjustments may be necessary.

In hot weather plants in pots, window-boxes and baskets must have regular thorough soakings to keep them healthy. Sometimes it may be best to evacuate them to sheltered cooler spots. They can be brought out for special occasions and an occasional sun-bask.

Fruit trees need one or two good soakings this month, as do camellias, rhododendrons and azaleas. Try to wet both sides of their foliage.

LAWN CARE

Keep the lawn long to protect roots from the harsh sun and wind. In warm, moist conditions fungal diseases may attack lawns and are best handled by spraying with a fungicide. Dollar-spot fungus occurs as a small, brown, round patch of wet grass, which increases in size. This disease is encouraged, sadly enough, by good care – feeding and over-watering.

PLANTING IDEAS

VEGETABLES

In all gardens sow beetroot, broccoli, cabbages, Chinese cabbage, carrots, cauliflowers, lettuces, leeks, white onions, parsnips, radishes, silverbeet, spinach and turnips. Of the herbs, sow cress and parsley. In warm coastal districts sow dwarf beans till mid-March.

In all districts plant seedlings of broccoli, cabbage, celery, leeks, lettuces and silverbeet.

ANNUALS AND PERENNIALS

Sow *Alcea rosea* (hollyhock), *Alyssum maritimum* (sweet Alice), *Bellis perennis* (English daisy), *Campanula* (bell flower), *Centaurea cyanus* (cornflower), *Delphinium* (larkspur), *Linaria maroccana* (baby snapdragon), *Lobelia erinus*, *Nigella damascena* (love-in-a-mist) and *Senecio* × *hybridus* (cineraria).

In warmer areas plant seedlings of *Ageratum* (floss flower), *Phlox drummondii* (annual phlox) and *Tagetes* (marigold).

Beware of damping off (see this month's Plant Watch).

BULBS

In temperate and cool zones you can plant cyclamen for autumn and winter. Spring-flowering bulbs can also be planted, but there is no hurry as you have over two months for this job. Choose from *Babiana* (baboon flower), *Iris* (bearded and Dutch), *Ixia* (corn lily), *Lachenalia* (soldier boy), *Leucojum* (snowflake), *Muscari* (grape hyacinth), *Hyacinthoides* (bluebell) and *Sparaxis* (harlequin flower).

ROSE GUIDE

If January seemed too early to do so, lightly prune and feed your roses now. You are really pruning to encourage them to flower in autumn, and of course this applies more to modern roses.

Check for aphids and try to remove them physically, perhaps with a damp tissue. Otherwise spray quite frequently with pyrethrum to keep them at bay. If mildew and black spot are severe, spray with a fungicide. Always remove the affected leaves and gather any diseased leaves that have fallen, to put in the rubbish. White scale can be wiped off with a soapy rag, scrubbed with a nailbrush and soapy water or sprayed with white oil. If your roses repeatedly get scale, they may be lacking food or sun.

PLANT WATCH

- Fungal diseases. These thrive in damp or humid weather, so remember to water in the morning, not at night. Sulphur dust can be sprinkled on diseased areas, but don't use on melons, cucumbers and other vine plants.

  To help prevent damping off of seedlings, do not water at night and dust seeds with a fungicide before sowing.
- Cabbage moth. Treat with derris dust, according to directions.
- Fruit fly. See January Plant Watch.
- Lemon scab. This scablike formation on fruit, leaves or twigs should be sprayed with white oil or a fungicide.
- Passionvine hoppers. Disturb with a strong jet of water, or spray with pyrethrum.
- Tomato wilt. This is a fungal disease: it is really better to pull up affected plants, but otherwise spray with Malathion.

PRUNING PROGRAMME

Flowers of all description should be dead-headed. This is barely pruning, but as with roses it should be done with respect for precious buds nestling between leaf and stem, and with a view to invigorating the bush, resulting in more flowers. It is always best done with sharp secateurs to avoid mishandling.

- Azaleas: can be neatened up, but this is the last month to do so without affecting their spring flowering.
- Fuchsias: shorten back to half their size in warm, frost-free districts to encourage spring flowers. In cooler areas, some tip-pruning will encourage autumn flowers.
- Gardenias: shoots should be shortened back after flowering to encourage compact vigorous growth.
- Hydrangeas: these are really best left until July or August, although you could dead-head now and remove a pair or two of sunburnt leaves near the top. This way their autumn foliage can be enjoyed and the leaves can fall naturally to form a mulch.
- Pelargoniums: cut back progressively as flowers die. Unhealthy or weak plants can be replaced now; find some healthy pieces to propagate.
- Shrubs and trees: abelias, cotoneasters and others may also have runaway summer shoots and branches in need of pruning. In tropical areas, stone-fruit trees can be pruned after harvest.
- Wisterias: long, waving growths should be shortened to keep the climber in check.

FEEDING TIME

Seedlings and other plants can be stimulated with liquid manure. Agapanthus will perform better if given a handful of blood and bone. Compost, cow manure and some liquid manure would be ideal now for fuchsias. Hibiscus need a good feed, perhaps cow manure and blood and bone or a complete fertiliser.

In tropical regions it is time to fertilise avocado, macadamia, mango, pawpaw and other heat-loving fruit trees.

OTHER JOBS

Vegetable beds should be prepared now for plantings in autumn. Put clean leaves in the compost, and infected or prickly leaves into the rubbish. Also thicken up mulches to last through the heat.

Clean up beds of annuals and perennials as they finish. Remember to leave the withering leaves of bulbs to die down as their job is to nourish next year's flowers.

On a windy or exposed site check stakes for plants such as dahlias and chrysanthemums.

Watsonias should be divided and replanted this month.

BONUSES AND HARVESTS

The last month of summer is the peak time for taking semi-hardwood cuttings. Azaleas, conifers, gardenias and lavenders are among some to try, and most native plants (including correas, grevilleas, thryptomenes and wattles) are not hard to strike. Try any other woody-stemmed plant that you can. Layer evergreen plants, including daphne, pieris and rhododendron.

There is much gathering to be done. Late-summer flower arrangements can have lots of daisies, everlastings and dry grasses. Lavender flowers and love-in-a-mist seed cases on long stems can be gathered to dry. Tie the lavender with ribbon, making fragrant sheaves to give away. The season for sun-ripened apples, figs, quinces and walnuts is well under way. Think of lovely ways to serve them at mealtime.

PLANNING NOTES

February will really test whether you have enough sitting spots. You may decide to make a simple seat of sleepers or other strong timber, or buy a ready-made seat or two to add to the pleasures of your garden.

February and March are great harvesting and propagating months, and if you haven't got a handy potting table or work bench for cleaning up the vegetables for indoors, you may decide to deal with this need soon.

Ornamental passionfruit (*Passiflora*) flower abundantly in warm spots in many parts of Australia.

MARCH

This is a month of transition in many parts of Australia. In tropical regions the wet may be easing or will do so soon, after which you can get into some serious gardening again. Weather can be turbulent and both stakes and long waving boughs may need to be checked. In southern temperate and cool regions the harsh late summer may have a last fling – don't count on cooler days until late March.

Whatever the weather, this is a time of planning and preparation – investment for spring returns. You need to work fast in the south over the next few weeks to get the benefits before the soil cools down.

SOME PLANTS FEATURING NOW

TREES

Cool: *Crataegus crus-galli* (cockspur thorn), *Erythrina crista-galli* (coral tree).
Temperate: *Acacia terminalis* (sunshine wattle), *Arbutus unedo* (strawberry tree).
Semi-arid: *Melia azederach* var. *australasica* (white cedar), *Pittosporum rhombifolium*.
Tropical and sub-tropical: *Backhousia anisata* (aniseed tree).

SHRUBS

Cool: *Begonia corallina* (coral begonia), *Plectranthus ecklonii* (blue spur flower).
Temperate: *Leonotis leonuris* (lion's ear), *Tibouchina urvilleana* (lasiandra).
Semi-arid: *Malvaviscus mollis* (wax mallow).
Tropical and sub-tropical: *Ixora*, *Cyphomandra betacea* (tamarillo).

CLIMBING PLANTS

Cool: *Ampelopsis brevipedunculata* (turquoise berry vine), *Passiflora caerulea* (blue passionflower).
Temperate: *Billardiera scandens* (common appleberry), *Hoya carnosa* (wax plant).
Tropical and sub-tropical: *Manettia bicolor* (Brazilian manettia), *Quisqualis indica* (Rangoon creeper).

ANNUALS AND PERENNIALS

Aconitum (monkshood), *Anemone japonica* (Japanese windflower), *Aster*, *Begonia*, *Chrysanthemum* hybrids, *Helianthus* (sunflower), *Impatiens wallerana*, *Liriope* (candle flower), *Physostegia* (obedient plant), *Rudbeckia* (cone flower) and *Tagetes* (marigold).

BULBS

Amaryllis belladonna (belladonna lily), *Colchicum*, *Eucomis comosa* (pineapple lily), *Hemerocallis* (daylily), *Iris foetidissima*, *Nerine* (spider lily), *Sternbergia lutea* and *Zephyranthes candida* (flower of the west wind).

MOISTURE CONTROL

With the change of season approaching, rainfall is likely to be uncertain, whether lessening in the north and much of Western Australia or increasing in southern regions. The message is to observe what is happening and take appropriate precautions. Check mulches, supplement diminishing natural water supplies or ease off because of autumn rains.

LAWN CARE

There is often less mowing to be done as cooler conditions reduce lawn growth, and you can cut lawns closer. March is a good top-dressing month, for there is enough warmth in the soil and air to induce growth. Keep a lookout for fungal disease in lawns in humid regions.

PLANTING IDEAS

VEGETABLES

In all regions sow beetroot, broccoli, cabbages, carrots, cauliflowers, leeks, onions, radishes, silverbeet, swedes and turnips. Herbs to be sown include chives, chervil, cress, dill, marjoram, mustard, parsley, sage and thyme.

Plant seedlings of broccoli, cabbages, cauliflowers, leeks and lettuces and offsets or seeds of shallot. Silverbeet can be planted, but in some cool districts it may be too late. Choose winter lettuce for cool districts. Vegetables will bolt to seed if planted at the wrong time. Avoid planting peas if frosts are likely at flowering time (in such areas it is best to sow in June), but they can be planted in temperate and tropical zones; try dwarf snap peas or rig up a frame for climbing types. In tropical areas plant beans, cucumbers, eggplants, Cape gooseberry, rhubarb and tomatoes.

ANNUALS AND PERENNIALS

Sow *Alyssum maritimum* (sweet Alice), *Antirrhinum majus* (snapdragon), *Bellis perennis* (English daisy), *Campanula* (bell flower), *Centaurea cyanus* (cornflower), *Clarkia amoenia* (godetia), *Delphinium* (larkspur), *Dianthus barbatus* (sweet William), *Eschscholzia californica* (Californian poppy), *Helichrysum* (everlasting), *Limonium* (statice), *Nemesia versicolor*, *Papaver nudicaule* (Iceland poppy), *Phlox*, *Primula malacoides*, *Reseda odorata* (mignonette), *Salpiglossis sinuata* (velvet flower), *Salvia* (flowering sage) and *Viola* (pansy and viola).

Sow seeds or plant seedlings of *Calendula officinalis* (pot marigold), *Cheiranthus cheiri* (wallflower), *Lathyrus odoratus* (sweet pea) and *Matthiola incana* (stock).

BULBS

Plant spring-flowering bulbs now or in April, or even in early May – later plantings generally produce later flowers. Remember when selecting your bulbs that you will get larger flowers from larger bulbs. *Fritillaria*, *Hyacinthus*, *Tulipa* and *Ranunculus* are best planted later, from mid-April to mid-May, except in very cold districts.

Bulbs to plant include *Anemone*, *Babiana* (baboon flower), *Crocus*, *Freesia*, *Hyacinthus* (hyacinth), *Hyacinthoides* (bluebell), *Ipheion uniflorum* (star flower), *Ixia* (corn lily), *Lachenalia* (soldier boy), *Leucojum* (snowflake), *Muscari* (grape hyacinth), *Narcissus* (daffodil and jonquil), *Ornithogalum*, *Tritonia* and *Sparaxia* (harlequin flower).

ROSE GUIDE

Keep roses thriving with a deep watering about every fourth day, or adjust their needs to local conditions. Do not water the foliage. Continue to dead-head, always pruning to strong outside shoots, and you should be repaid with extra blooms.

Continue to check for troublemakers such as aphids, black spot or white scale. You may also find leaf-rolling caterpillars: they and the affected leaves are best removed and squashed.

PLANT WATCH

- Aphids. Black aphids may be found on chrysanthemum shoots: remove by hand or spray with pyrethrum. Green or greyish aphids will appear on southern-grown hibiscus, which start to miss the sun. Spray with pyrethrum or ignore – the cold will soon disperse them and the plant will be semi-dormant until the strong sun returns in November.
- Cabbage moths. These may persist and derris dust should be used on all members of the cabbage family as a safeguard.
- Caterpillars. They sometimes have a late run on vegetables, grape vines, fuchsias and gardenias, or whatever they fancy. Look out here, too, for the leaf-rolling types: if they are too widespread for physical removal, pyrethrum is the safest spray to use.
- Fungal diseases still flourish in the hot and wet, and, further south, as the stamina of plants weakens with the waning sun. Water in the morning, not at night, and sprinkle with sulphur dust (except on vine plants such as melons or cucumbers).
- Lemon scab. Spray with white oil or a fungicide.
- Rust. This fungal disease may affect pelargoniums at this time of year. Cut the plants back or take healthy young cuttings and propagate them.
- Sawflies. Active particularly in temperate and tropical areas. They can affect such trees as paperbarks, cypress pines and tea trees, and the larvae can even affect construction timbers. Cut off and destroy infected parts, or spray with Malathion, to pre-empt serious damage.
- Snails. Families are out now – watch for hoards of tiny ones, often on shrubby leaves, and do not let them grow older.
- White cedar moth. This can prematurely defoliate white cedar trees (*Melia azedarach*) in autumn. To combat, spray with Malathion. But better still, tie a hessian band around the tree trunk to catch the larvae as they climb the trunk at night.

PRUNING PROGRAMME

Keep dead-heading to stimulate growth. Keep gardens tidy by picking up prunings, and reduce disease-harbouring places.

- Fuchsias and pelargoniums: can be pruned now.
- Lavender: dead-head French lavenders to the twin nodes below, to encourage side shoots to flower continuously through the year. English lavenders can be cut back now or next month to the strongest visible shoots (robust if possible) further down the stem, to keep bushes compact. Rangy *Lavandula dentata* 'Allardi' (Allard's lavender) must be cut back hard to healthy shoots after flowering to help stop the strong branches from eventually breaking up the bush.
- Marguerites: these need cutting back when there are more spent flowers than pretty ones, and when they are getting too big for their site. If there are plenty of flower buds, trim the spent flowers and non-budding stems. If there's not much doing, shape the bushes all over. In frost-prone areas don't be too hard on them from now on or frost can destroy them.
- Wisteria: bring any wispy shoots to heel. To keep your plant as you want, cut the shoots where they leave the branch. If you are not vigilant, wisteria is likely to cause damage to spoutings, roofs and other plants.

MARCH

Sunflowers (*Helianthus*), as their name suggests, are a cheery lot that delight in full sun.

FEEDING TIME

Blood and bone can be broadcast over beds you are preparing for annuals, perennials and vegetables. A dressing will also revitalise trees and shrubs. Potassium sulphate (potash) can also be used as a tonic at this time of year. Remember the golden rule when fertilising: always water the soil to be treated first, and water in well after application. Don't allow it to settle or splash onto leaves as leaf-cell damage can occur.

Leaching in sandy or light soils after summer's strict watering programmes and heavy temperate coastal and tropical rains means that soil nutrients should now be replenished. You may want to use a complete fertiliser for this, mixed with compost, but if there are no obvious imbalances blood and bone can supplement a well-made compost to do the job. Leached soils are invariably in need of textural improvement, so compost is almost essential to recondition them.

Azaleas, camellias and rhododendrons can be given a liquid fertiliser now, then no more until flowering has finished some time in winter or early spring, depending on the type.

OTHER JOBS

Preparing garden beds is a very important March job.

If you have planted sweet peas you may need a trellis or other support. Tripod plantings of just three or four seedlings look pretty. Also you must provide some sort of frame for your autumn–winter plantings of peas.

Watch for diseased plants when you are tidying up, and keep them out of the compost. A mass of weeds may appear in autumn, often bolting to seed. Try to remove them before they do this, and dig out perennial weeds before they toughen up for reshooting in spring.

BONUSES AND HARVESTS

Propagate softwood and semi-hardwood cuttings, including fuchsias, pelargoniums, hydrangeas, lavender and wallflowers. To keep up your mint supply strike some tip-pruned pieces in a pot.

March is a great harvesting month – sometimes from the gardens of friends. You can collect medlars, pears, quinces, figs, crab apples, strawberries, guavas, feijoas and pomegranates, and the tiny, delicious berries of *Myrtus ugnii*. You may find armfuls of decorative berries if you have a big garden in a moderately temperate, or cool, district. In cottage gardens there are usually some interesting dried seed cases to gather, too, including those of love-in-a-mist, columbine and obedient plant: shake the remaining seed out, or gather some for friends first. And it's fun to peel the old, dry coatings off the spent heads of honesty: keep the stems long, and use the pearly membranes indoors.

PLANNING NOTES

March is the peak time for planting spring bulbs, but April is not too late so do some quick thinking now that you've seen what is about in catalogues or nurseries. If you miss special lines, order early for next year and keep a note of where you want to use them. Remember that the majority of bulbs are very rewarding for little effort. Do not forget, when you are planning, that ixias really love a harsh, sunny spot.

Think about some lovely combinations for your winter and spring pots.

APRIL

This month, the efforts made in March to produce lovely spring gardens are consolidated in most parts of Australia. In temperate and cool regions the autumn season really starts to take form. In the tropics from now through to September is the main time for planting trees and shrubs.

SOME PLANTS FEATURING NOW

TREES
Cool: *Acacia retinodes* (wiralda), *Crataegus phaenopyrum* (Washington thorn).
Temperate: *Sapium sebiferum* (Chinese tallow-tree), *Diospyros kaki* (persimmon).
Semi-arid: *Acacia salicina* (willow wattle).
Tropical: *Koelreuteria paniculata* (golden rain tree), *Pittosporum undulatum* (sweet pittosporum).

SHRUBS
Cool: *Datura arborea* (angel's trumpet), *Erica* × *darleyensis*.
Temperate: *Euphorbia pulcherrima* (poinsettia), *Solanum rantonnetii* (Paraguay nightshade).
Semi-arid: *Berberis thunbergii* 'Atropurpurea', *Melaleuca lateritia* (robin redbreast bush).
Tropical: *Hibiscus tiliaceus* (coast cottonwood), *Melastoma denticulatum* (pink lasiandra).

CLIMBING PLANTS
Cool: *Parthenocissus tricuspidata* 'Lowii' (Boston ivy), *Passiflora antioquiensis*.
Temperate: *Mandevilla amabilis* 'Alice Du Pont', *Parthenocissus quinquefolia* (five-leafed Virginia creeper).
Tropical: *Tecoma* × *smithii*.

ANNUALS AND PERENNIALS
Aconitum (monkshood), *Alyssum maritimum* (sweet Alice), *Anemone japonica* (Japanese windflower), *Aster* (Easter and Michaelmas daisy), *Chrysanthemum* hybrids, *Dianthus barbatus* (sweet William), *Erigeron karvinskianus* (baby's tears), *Helianthus* (sunflower), *Physostegia* (obedient plant), *Rudbeckia* (cone flower), *Salvia* (flowering sage), *Tweedia caerula* (southern star) and *Viola* (pansy and viola).

BULBS
Canna indica (Indian shot), *Clivia* (kaffir lily), *Cyclamen*, *Dahlia*, *Hedychium gardnerianum* (yellow ginger lily), *Hemerocallis* (daylily), *Nerine* (spider lily), *Vallota speciosa* (Scarborough lily) and *Zephyranthes candida* (flower of the west wind).

MOISTURE CONTROL

In most areas this is a matter of adjusting watering according to local needs. Over-watering is a sure way to encourage fungal diseases including mildew and rust. Remember that most plants need less water than they did in hotter periods, and that less moisture is lost to evaporation. Some parts of southern gardens are noticeably receiving less sunlight as shadows lengthen at all times of the day. Too much water in protected spots can cause mildew on leaves.

LAWN CARE

Always be aware of the effect that mowing may be having on the lawn. If you create bare patches by cutting lower you are making clearings in which wandering weed seed could grow, so adjust the mower up a notch.

PLANTING IDEAS

This is a good time to plant, as roots have time to settle while the soil is still warm and can establish during winter for an early spring getaway. Plant trees, shrubs, climbing plants and ground covers as well as the plants listed below.

VEGETABLES
In all regions sow the same plants listed for March, plus broad beans. In tropical and sub-tropical regions you can also sow beans, capsicums, cucumbers, endives, marrows, pumpkins and zucchini.

The coast cottonwood (*Hibiscus tiliaceus*) is a fine Australian plant for a warm site.

APRIL

Growing a fine pumpkin or two, a long marrow and other members of the family is easy and the harvest is magnificent.

Plant seedlings also as for last month, again avoiding peas in cooler districts if frosts are likely at flowering time. In the temperate zone, artichoke offsets can be planted and celery and broccoli seedlings planted out. In warmer temperate areas and tropical regions garlic and shallot offsets can be planted out and potato tubers planted. In tropical and subtropical areas plant out eggplants and tomatoes.

ANNUALS AND PERENNIALS

Sow the annual plants you particularly like or have worked into a mental picture of your spring garden. Choose from last month's list.

Seedlings of *Papaver nudicaule* (Iceland poppy), *Primula malacoides*, *Senecio × hybridus* (cineraria) and *Viola* (pansy and viola) are particularly rewarding in late winter and early spring, or even later. Cineraria seedlings must be planted in a frost-protected site away from early morning sun.

BULBS

Here, too, use the list from last month, remembering that if your region is not subject to a very cold autumn you can leave *Fritillaria, Hyacinthus, Ranunculus* and *Tulipa* until late this month or early in May. Some gardeners like to chill their tulips in the vegetable drawer of the refrigerator for four to six weeks to simulate a cold autumn.

If you plant bulbs in pots for indoors wait until the buds are near to opening before bringing them inside.

ROSE GUIDE

Try to encourage roses to keep flowering by checking aphids, making sure that plants have sufficient moisture and mulch, removing any diseased leaves and pruning spent flower heads back to shoots. In this way you are getting maximum benefit from that summer prune and feed you gave them. However, don't try to force your plants to flower: you must know your roses. Some of them are by nature spring and summer flowering – they have been lovely, but their time is past.

If some of your roses have failed to perform as you had expected despite the fact that you fed them well, they may not be getting enough sun and you must consider transplanting them in their dormant time. Always give a new rose planted in winter two spring–summer seasons to prove itself.

Continue fungicide treatment if needed. White scale can be wiped or scrubbed off using soapy water, or sprayed with white oil.

PLANT WATCH

Green and black aphids, caterpillars (including leaf rollers), fungal disease, mildew, rust and scale may continue to cause problems in your garden. For treatment methods see Plant Watch for March. Bordeaux mixture combined with mineral oil can be sprayed on stone-fruit trees at leaf fall, to keep fungal diseases away during the dormant period.

- Brown rot. This is a fungus associated with stone fruit. It can be largely eliminated by gathering and burning any damaged fruit remaining on the branches.
- Leaf miner. This pest of citrus causes curling and silvery trails on foliage. Spray with Malathion.
- Petal blight. This is probably a new peril for the year, associated with the opening of azalea buds as they come into season. Damp conditions and hosing foliage from budding time through the flowering period will bring it on. Spray with a fungicide.

PRUNING PROGRAMME

April is more a time for planting than for pruning. Logical tidying should be the main form of cutting now – stay away from winter- and spring-flowering shrubs. Remember that far more damage in gardens is done by over-zealous pruning than too little.

- Cassias: will finish flowering this month and next, and branches can then be cut back up to 20 centimetres to a good shoot to keep bushes compact.
- Dahlias: can be cut back.
- Escallonias: can be shortened all over after autumn flowering.

FEEDING TIME

Fruit trees like an autumn feed of well-rotted manure and blood and bone. It is not too late to recharge your soil with nutrients after rains and summer watering, especially if it is sandy.

OTHER JOBS

There is plenty more to do in the garden this month.

Caring gardeners value the chance to give something back to the gardens that give them so much pleasure. It is a good idea to dig over the mulches and compost that have served your garden so well through the summer; add some blood and bone or complete fertiliser for extra goodness. When digging, don't go near the roots of shrubs, trees or any other plant, as root disturbance should be avoided where possible. Having reworked your mulch, add some more compost, straw or other organic material, particularly in cold areas where it is important to protect roses and other plants against frost. In many areas, compost-making receives a boost this month with barrowloads of leaves. Mix them in layers with other compost items for the most efficient results. If you have a mulching machine, the compost process can be speeded up by mulching the leaves before putting them in the bin.

It is time to divide the crowns of perennial plants including phlox, shasta daisies and bearded and Japanese irises, all of which may be dealt with now or in early May. Gladiolus corms are best lifted and stored for winter.

Your strawberry plants that have grown from runners should be separated and planted out where you want them, or given away.

Divide up clumps of polyanthus and perennial primula, discarding old, tired parts and setting out new rooted pieces with a ring of compost and cow manure around them – they are gross feeders and if you check for slugs and snails and put your plants in a warm, protected aspect they will repay you grandly.

BONUSES AND HARVESTS

Propagating opportunities continue. Carnation cuttings taken now should flower by December, while pelargoniums and marguerites will bloom even sooner. If you keep picking out the growing tips until spring, the cuttings will grow into fine bushy plants for summer. Coleus can be struck using tip-prunings: keep them in a warm, protected place or a glasshouse if you want new spring plants. Impatiens can be struck in the same way and requires the same protection. New banana palms can be started by planting out banana suckers. They can form an attractive clump and make a useful screen as well as providing fruit in a suitable climate.

For indoor decorations this month, leaves may matter more than flowers. There are the last few autumn-toned hydrangeas, bracken fern, rose hips and berries, a few dry grasses and some stems of wild blackberry. There are still grapes and luscious strawberry guavas to be picked, feijoas and pumpkins to be brought in.

PLANNING NOTES

As autumn gathers about you it is not hard to think of some more trees and shrubs for your garden, if there is room. Choose them when they're in autumn colour at the nursery, to ensure that you know what you are buying. Think too about those roses you need to order.

A smoke bush (*Cotinus coggygria*) is twined through a rustic sapling fence to display its autumn leaves to the full.

MAY

In this, the last month of autumn, signs of winter appear in temperate and cool regions. Further north and in the tropics there is a feeling of urgency about planning and planting for the pleasant months ahead.

SOME PLANTS FEATURING NOW

TREES

Cool: *Acmena smithii* (lilly pilly), *Prunus subhirtella* 'Autumnale'.
Temperate: *Crataegus pubescens* (Mexican hawthorn), *Fortunella japonica* (cumquat).
Semi-arid: *Eucalyptus erythrocorys* (illyarie), *E. forrestiana* (fuchsia gum).
Tropical and sub-tropical: *Acacia suaveolens* (sweet wattle), *Eucalyptus citriodora* (lemon-scented gum).

SHRUBS

Cool: *Camellia sasanqua*, *Luculia gratissima*.
Temperate: *Clerodendrum ugandense* (blue butterfly bush), *Dombeya natalensis* (Cape wedding-flower).
Semi-arid: *Banksia ornata* (desert banksia), *Duranta repens* (sky flower).
Tropical and sub-tropical: *Callistemon citrinus*.

CLIMBING PLANTS

Cool: *Eustrephus latifolius* (wombat berry), *Stauntonia hexaphylla* (Japanese staunton vine).
Temperate: *Podranea ricasoliana* (pink tecoma), *Kennedia prostrata* (running postman).
Tropical and sub-tropical: *Thunbergia gibsonii* (orange glory creeper).

ANNUALS AND PERENNIALS

Chrysanthemum hybrids, *Impatiens wallerana*, *Primula obconica*, *Tagetes* (marigolds) and *Viola odorata* (sweet violet).

BULBS

Canna indica (Indian shot), *Clivia* (kaffir lily), *Colchicum*, *Cyclamen*, *Dahlia imperialis* (tree dahlia) and *Iris unguicularis* (winter iris).

MOISTURE CONTROL

The advice given last month really holds for this month as the weather gets cooler. Most plants need less water now than in the warmer months, and less moisture is being lost by evaporation. It is a matter of adjusting your habits to changing conditions.

LAWN CARE

The advice for last month applies here: avoid cutting too low and allowing bare patches to develop that may harbour weed seed. Keep an eye out for fungal diseases, including dollar spot, which can be dealt with by spraying with a fungicide.

If you did not sow your lawn as planned in April do it now (wait until September in southern parts).

If you are planning to naturalise bulbs in cool regions you should stop mowing the area from the end of this month. You can still selectively clip grass if the untidiness bothers you.

PLANTING IDEAS

It is still a good time to plant trees, shrubs, climbing and ground-cover plants. May is the month to be active in tropical areas, particularly in the far north where a definite summer wet season is experienced. It is a good time to plant vegetable and ornamental gardens while the sun shines and there is not too much rain. In the tropics this is the latest time for putting in spring-flowering annuals.

VEGETABLES

In all regions sow parsnips, radishes and spinach; onions can be sown or transplanted out. In tropical and sub-tropical zones sow beans, beetroot, cabbages, carrots, Chinese cabbage, endives, kohlrabi, leeks, parsley, parsnips, peas, radishes, tomatoes and turnips. Broad beans can be sown in cool and temperate areas.

In the tropics, plantings include potato tubers, garlic cloves and shallot offsets as well as seedlings of cabbages, leeks, lettuces, silverbeet and tomatoes. Strawberries planted in the tropics this month can be harvested in twelve weeks (longer elsewhere). In cool areas plant out cabbages and leeks, and in both cool and temperate zones plant rhubarb crowns. In temperate zones plant artichoke offsets.

ANNUALS AND PERENNIALS

Amaranthus tricolor (Joseph's coat), *Coleus* × *hybridus*, *Cosmos bipinnatus*, *Linaria maroccana* (baby snapdragon), *Petunia* × *hybrida*, *Phlox drummondii*, *Salvia* (flowering sage) *Tagetes* (marigold) and *Zinnia elegans*. The flowers usually planted in October in southern gardens can be planted now in the semi-tropics.

In temperate areas, seeds of *Calendula officinalis* (pot marigold), *Iberis sempervirens* (candytuft), *Myosotis* (forget-me-not), *Nemophila* (baby blue-eyes), *Malcolmia maritima* (Virginian stock) and *Tropaeolum majus* (nasturtium) can be sown direct.

If you have a really sunny spot and you are running late, there is just time to plant seedlings of *Alyssum maritimum* (sweet Alice), *Antirrhinum majus* (snapdragon), *Bellis perennis* (English daisy), *Cheiranthus cheiri* (wallflower), *Delphinium* (larkspur), *Lathyrus odoratus* (sweet pea), *Lobelia erinus*, *Matthiola incana* (stock), *Primula malacoides*, *P.* × *polyantha* and *Senecio* × *hybridus* (cineraria).

BULBS

Continue to plant from the list of bulbs given in March. *Convallaria majalis* (lily of the valley) should be in early this month; *Anemone*, *Hyacinthus*, *Ranunculus* and *Tulipa* should be in by mid-May.

ROSE GUIDE

Continue to care for roses as outlined in April, although the bushes will be losing interest and vigour. Remove leaves infected with black spot and mildew-clad buds, and consign them to the rubbish. It is pruning time next month, although roses that are still flourishing can be pruned as late as July.

Check rose places and spaces in case you have or can make room for more plants next month, but avoid overcrowding.

PLANT WATCH

- Aphids. They must be dealt with as usual, although they will be less prevalent in the cooler months. You may spot them on the young growth of many plants.
- Snails. They must as usual be held in check. Look out for them among clivia leaves and flowers, and in other bulb clumps as well as among annual plants.
- Shot-hole disease. This blight of stone fruit and almonds can be recognised by a stickiness on fruit buds. It may be dealt with by spraying with Bordeaux mixture at leaf fall, as can brown rot (another disease of stone fruit), which is recognised by the occurrence of rotted fruit on the tree. These should be picked and destroyed.

PRUNING PROGRAMME

- Chrysanthemums: cut to ground level.
- Sweet peas: tip-prune for bushiness.

FEEDING TIME

Nerines and other autumn-flowering bulbs will benefit from a dressing of blood and bone. Keep stimulating seedlings with applications of weak liquid manure. In the tropics, it is important to fertilise ornamental plants at this time.

Make sure that fruit trees are fed, as outlined in April.

OTHER JOBS

Cut back any spent summer and autumn perennials. Liliums for summer will need mulching for protection and to hold moisture during the winter.

Dahlias can be lifted this month if you need their space. Just rest them out of the way somewhere for a week or two, then store them in a cool, dark place. Gladiolus corms can also be lifted and stored this month if you have not already done so.

Transplanting camellias and conifers – in fact practically anything – is safer in May and June than at other times, if care is taken. Always water a plant well before and after transplanting and have the new hole dug ready to receive it. Cut foliage back in proportion to size to reduce the shock and aid recovery.

Hydrangeas can be changed from pink to blue by regularly adding a blueing agent, starting this month. Otherwise they tend to colour according to the nature of their soil (see Soil Acidity and Alkalinity in Chapter 4).

Pea waste should be dug into the garden when the crop has finished. Rake up leaves and make a pile to feed into your compost, layer by layer. In May every three or four years it is worthwhile adding lime (according to directions) to vegetable gardens and lawns to keep the soil sweet and not too acidic.

BONUSES AND HARVESTS

Propagating opportunities continue. Take hardwood cuttings of deciduous plants.

Some lovely lichen-clad boughs can be found in many regions: use them as an evocative frame for an indoor arrangement, adding gleanings from your own garden or local area. You only need a few pieces, which may well be all you will find.

PLANNING NOTES

May can be largely about dreams: the plants you would like to grow, the paths you want to create, and how you hope things will look next spring and summer. But don't dream for too long – you are wasting precious planting time.

JUNE

In the south, June is for the most part a good time to stay indoors and read garden books, with some of your spare time spent obtaining and planting roses. But before you get too cosy read our notes for June and July to see what should be done outside. Meanwhile, to the north the dry season is a time of outdoor pleasure amid brilliant colour. Gardeners can enjoy a brisk growing season for a wide range of plants.

SOME PLANTS FEATURING NOW

TREES

Cool: *Sorbus aucuparia* (rowan tree), *Prunus mume* 'Alboplena' (double white Japanese apricot).
Temperate: *Prunus mume* 'Alphandii' (double pink Japanese apricot), *Acacia baileyana* (Cootamundra wattle).
Semi-arid: *Acacia calamifolia* (wallowa), *Eucalyptus caesia* (gungurru).
Tropical: *Acacia podalyriifolia* (Mount Morgan wattle), *Elaeocarpus grandis* (brush quandong).

SHRUBS

Cool: *Banksia ericifolia* (heath banksia), *Epacris impressa*.
Temperate: *Gordonia axillaris*, *Banksia spinulosa* (hairpin banksia).
Semi-arid: *Eremophila macdonnellii*, *Euryops abrotanifolius*.
Tropical and sub-tropical: *Galphimia glauca*.

CLIMBING PLANTS

Cool: *Solanum jasminoides* (potato vine).
Temperate: *Pyrostegia venusta* (orange trumpet creeper).
Tropical and sub-tropical: *Odontadenia grandiflora*.

ANNUALS AND PERENNIALS

Bergenia cordifolia (elephant's ear), *Dicentra formosa* (bleeding heart), *Helleborus* (Lenten or winter rose), *Primula malacoides* and *P.* × *polyantha* (polyanthus).

BULBS

Cyclamen, *Galanthus nivalis* (snowdrop), *Iris* (bearded and winter), *Leucojum aestivum* (snowflake) and *Narcissus* (daffodil and jonquil).

INDOOR PLANTS

During the winter months these assume a special importance owing to the dearth of cut flowers. Include *Begonia*, *Cyclamen*, *Primula obconica*, *Schlumbergera* and *Zygocactus* in your selection.

MOISTURE CONTROL

It is important to monitor the weather in all regions, as winter rains can be unpredictable and gardens may need supplementary watering. In addition, frost can have a drying effect if rain does not follow. In tropical regions rain can be sparse or variable during the dry season. Mulching therefore continues to be important in every garden – conserving water, protecting roots from frost and cold, and ultimately improving soil texture and thus the soil's ability to retain water and nutrients.

LAWN CARE

Tropical and temperate lawns are likely to be at their loveliest and easiest to manage. Take care not to over-water, which encourages the ever-lurking fungal diseases. Watch for bindii, with its small, ferny leaves, and remove. In areas of winter rain, lawns can be aerated with a hollow-tyne fork or a conventional garden fork to improve drainage. Less mowing is needed during this and the next two months, but don't neglect the edges or let your lawn become scruffy.

PLANTING IDEAS

Continue to plant as directed in April and May, with the addition of the bare-rooted deciduous plants that should be available in nurseries and ready for planting. Some supplies may not be available until July, but all winter months are suitable for planting deciduous stock. It is important that these plants do not dry out or suffer from exposure: keep them out of draughts and extreme cold, in a potting medium or damp sawdust, or just rough-heel them into the earth until you can attend to them. (Holding them in plastic for more than a day or two can cause sweating and deterioration). Also you should avoid planting out during extreme wind and cold.

In tropical regions citrus trees should be planted now to allow them to settle in before the wet season. Plant tropical fruit trees, such as *Musa* (banana), *Carica* (pawpaw), *Annona* (custard apple), *Persea* (avocado) and *Mangifera* (mango), all valued for their beauty and as windbreaks and screens as well as for their fruit. Sometimes they are more appealing planted as mixed clumps, arranged according to their needs and attributes, rather than in rows.

LEFT Brassica, such as cabbages and broccoli, are important winter crops.

ABOVE Many delicious varieties of potatoes can be grown by the home gardener.

VEGETABLES

In tropical areas sow beans, beetroot, cabbages, capsicums, carrots, chicory, chokoes, lettuces, snow peas, spring onions, parsnips, silverbeet, tomatoes, cress and herbs. In temperate and cool zones sow broad beans, beetroot, cabbages, onions, shallots, silverbeet and spinach. Peas can be sown if there is no risk of frost in eight weeks (flowering) time.

Seedlings of celery, marrow, zucchini, cucumber and pumpkin can be planted out in tropical gardens or in sheltered pots in semi-tropical areas. In tropical and temperate regions you can plant asparagus crowns and in temperate and cool zones plant artichokes.

In temperate areas rhubarb can be planted or divided; it is greedy, so feed often with cow manure and blood and bone. Strawberries can also be set out in a well-prepared bed and left for three years, apart from the removal of unruly runners and of newly formed crowns for planting elsewhere.

Berry bushes and brambles including blueberries, boysenberries, currants (black, red and white), gooseberries, loganberries and youngberries can be planted now if you have the space. You can grow them from rooted pieces or cuttings.

ANNUALS AND PERENNIALS

In temperate and cool gardens flowers to sow include *Alcea rosea* (hollyhock), *Campanula* (bell flower), *Clarkia amoena* (godetia), *Iberis sempervirens* (candytuft), *Linaria maroccana* (baby snapdragon), *Nigella damascena* (love-in-a-mist), *Reseda odorata* (mignonette), *Malcolmia maritima* (Virginian stock) and *Matthiola indica* (stock). In tropical gardens you can put in a wide range of annuals, drawing on the planting lists given in April and May.

BULBS

Lilium varieties can be planted this month in readiness for summer flowering. They are mostly for cool areas but may grow in temperate, humid coastal conditions. Suggestions include *L. auratum* (golden ray lily), *L. formosanum*, *L. longiflorum*, *L. regale* (regal lily), *L. speciosum* and *L. tigrinum* (tiger lily). Other bulbs for planting now include *Gladiolus*, *Hippeastrum*, *Iris* (Dutch and Japanese), *Nymphaea* (waterlily) and *Vallota speciosa* (Scarborough lily).

ROSE GUIDE

Select or collect new roses, remembering always to choose healthy plants.

The optimum pruning time varies with location and conditions. It is best to prune when the leaves have fallen or will fall when lightly touched. The last week in June is usually considered to be the beginning of pruning time.

Roses can be fed after pruning if you are using organic food. Commercial rose food or complete fertilisers are absorbed more directly and can be applied in late July or August.

JUNE

PLANT WATCH

- Aphids. May make occasional appearances on young tips during the colder months.
- Brown rot. The presence of this disease is indicated by rotten fruit, which is sometimes covered with a velvety fungus. The fruit must be removed and burnt.
- Caterpillars and grubs. They are still about, even on gum trees. Always check cabbage seedlings.
- Gall wasp. This pest causes swelling on the stems of citrus: cut out and burn the affected parts.
- Leaf miner. Identified by silvery trails on leaves, particularly those of cinerarias and nasturtiums. Try to deal conservatively with them by removing affected leaves and giving a good feed of liquid manure.
- Mildew and associated fungal diseases. These may persist during wet weather, particularly in temperate zones. Spray with a fungicide, but ask yourself whether some continuously affected plants may not be in the wrong position and should be replaced by more shade- and damp-tolerant types.
- Rust. This may occur on calendulas, pelargoniums, hollyhocks and snapdragons: spray with a fungicide.
- Slugs and snails. These often persist, however vigilant you are. Preferably remove by hand but if their numbers make this impossible use a commercial bait, with caution.

PRUNING PROGRAMME

June and July are the months for pruning summer- and autumn-flowering plants, but continue to leave spring-flowering varieties alone or you may have no flowers.

- Cannas, chrysanthemums and ginger lilies: cut back.
- Brambles and berries: shorten back lank growth and tie strong shoots onto frames. Shorten bush blueberries and currants to strong-looking outside shoots.
- Flowering shrubs: those in need of pruning now include abelia, Chinese lantern, shrimp plant, barberry, *Ceratostigma willmottianum*, oleander, plumbago and summer-flowering tamarisk. Leave the pruning of crêpe myrtle and hydrangea until July or August. Extremely frost-tender plants such as gardenias and hibiscus are best left until the fear of frost is past.
- Sweet peas: can be tip-pruned to make plants stronger and more compact.

FEEDING TIME

Plant growth generally slows down in the south during winter, so it is not necessary to feed until late winter or spring. However, liquid manure should be given to seedlings in all regions to keep them growing.

Newly planted or divided crowns of asparagus, rhubarb, strawberries and perennials can be mulched and given well-rotted animal manure and blood and bone.

Feed roses: see Rose Guide.

OTHER JOBS

To minimise further loss, frost-damaged plants should be left with the damaged parts intact until the threat of frost is past.

Lift dahlias now if you have not already done so. Perennials that flowered in summer and autumn can still be divided if they have been in for about three years or are looking untidy. Discard tired-looking plants.

Spoutings and drains should be checked after the autumn deluge of leaves. Compost the debris.

Weeds should be kept at bay around growing bulbs, annuals and vegetables.

Keep fuchsia and pelargonium cuttings growing nicely by tip-pruning and giving weak liquid manure every two to three weeks.

BONUSES AND HARVESTS

Propagate hardwood cuttings – long pieces of mature old wood – particularly from deciduous shrubs and trees. Try this with wintersweet, hydrangea, magnolia, roses, viburnum, weigela, tulip tree, willow, grapes and wisteria. You may get better results if you dip your cuttings in hormone rooting powder before planting.

PLANNING NOTES

You still have time left to plant deciduous trees and shrubs, but bear in mind the mature tree's demands on space, nutrients and water.

In the tropics you may be thinking of cool garden features – an airy gazebo planted with *Allemanda*, or a tranquil pond.

JULY

How you regard the month of July depends very much on where you are. Colourful warm coastal and tropical gardens are a reassuring sight to the expatriate southerners who gather there to escape their winter. Often too, further away from the coast, there are some frost-hardy treasures to be found among our native plants. Meanwhile, in cooler temperate areas people will be getting back into the garden after a brief dormant period – to prune and plant, to knock up a garden seat or potting bench, or to put a second tap at the gully trap.

SOME PLANTS FEATURING NOW

TREES

Cool: *Atherosperma moschatum* (black sassafras), *Elaeocarpus grandis* (blueberry ash).
Temperate: *Banksia marginata* (silver banksia).
Semi-arid: *Buddleja salviifolia* (winter buddleja), *Eucalyptus woodwardii*.
Tropical and sub-tropical: *Bauhinia blakeana*.

Many wattles (*Acacia*) come into flower in the winter months just when some colour is most needed.

SHRUBS

Cool: *Camellia japonica*, *Crassula lactea*.
Temperate: *Impatiens oliveri*, *Jacobinia carnea* (pink jacobinia).
Semi-arid: *Alyogyne huegelii* (lilac hibiscus), *Strelitzia reginae* (bird's-tongue flower).
Tropical and sub-tropical: *Grevillea banksii*.

CLIMBING PLANTS

Cool: *Gelsemium sempervirens* (Carolina jasmine).
Temperate: *Clerodendrum splendens*, *C. thomsonae* (bleeding-heart vine).
Tropical: *Lotus bertholetii* (scarlet lotus).

ANNUALS AND PERENNIALS

Bergenia cordifolia (elephant's ear), *Calendula officinalis* (pot marigold), *Chieranthus cheiri* (wallflower), *Dianella* (flax lily), *Helleborus* (Lenten or winter rose), *Papaver* (poppy), *Reseda odorata* (mignonette), *Viola* (pansy and viola) and *Viola odorata* (sweet violet).

BULBS

As for June: *Cyclamen*, *Galanthus nivalis* (snowdrop), *Iris germanica*, *I. unguicularis* (winter iris), *Leucojum aestivum* (snowflake) and *Narcissus* (daffodil and jonquil).

MOISTURE CONTROL

Continue as described for June. In the tropics weather may be dry and trees and shrubs may need one or two thorough soakings as well as careful watering and mulching of smaller plants.

LAWN CARE

Again, continue as for June. In warmer areas, broad-leafed weeds and bindii cause problems, so check them before they take hold.

PLANTING IDEAS

Continue to plant trees, shrubs, climbing plants, perennials and berry fruits.

VEGETABLES

In all gardens sow peas of all kinds. In cool and temperate zones sow broad beans and parsley. In all temperate zones sow capsicums and in warmer temperate areas sow beetroot, radishes and silverbeet. In tropical gardens sow dwarf and French beans, carrots, celery, eggplants, lettuces, radishes, squash, sweetcorn, pumpkins and zucchini.

JULY

There is a special beauty about *Narcissus* flowering beneath bare-branched trees while winter is still upon the land.

In all regions plant out cabbages and onions and plant potato tubers (or wait until next month if it seems too cold). In cool zones asparagus crowns can be planted now. Plant rhubarb in cool and temperate areas. In all temperate regions plant globe artichokes and shallot offsets, and plant out eggplants and leeks. In tropical and warmer temperate areas plant out tomato seedlings.

ANNUALS AND PERENNIALS

In cool and temperate zones continue to use the June list, as conditions are much the same this month. In tropical zones you may like to make more sowings, aiming for variety or just looking for two or three plants to mass with larger plants. You could choose from the following: *Ageratum* (floss flower), *Amaranthus tricolor* (Joseph's coat), *Antirrhinum majus* (snapdragon), *Arctotis hybrida* (aurora daisy), *Begonia semperflorens* (bedding begonia), *Centaurea cyanus* (cornflower), *Cleome spinosa* (spider flower), *Eschscholtzia californica* (Californian poppy), *Gerbera jamesonii*, *Limonium sinuatum* (statice), *Lunaria annua* (honesty), *Lupinus* (lupin), *Molucella laevis* (Molucca balm), *Petunia* × *hybrida* and *Zinnia elegans*. In temperate and sub-tropical areas scatter *Malcolmia maritima* (Virginian stock) direct in any bare patch for a spring reward.

In temperate and sub-tropical zones, particularly warmer places, use seedlings of *Alyssum maritimum* (sweet Alice), *Arctotis hybrida* (aurora daisy), *Calendula officinalis* (pot marigold), *Delphinium* (larkspur), *Dianthus* (carnation, pink), *Limonium sinensis* (statice) and *Lunaria annua* (honesty).

If your herb garden tends to disintegrate in winter try making a small plot for the cooler months in a sheltered, sunny spot. You should be able to grow chives, garlic, land cress, oregano, parsley, rosemary, winter savory, salad burnet and French sorrel, and mint in a pot.

BULBS

Agapanthus (Nile lily), *Eucomis comosa* (pineapple lily), *Gladiolus* × *colvillei*, *Hippeastrum*, *Lilium*, *Vallota speciosa* (Scarborough lily) and *Zantedeschia* (arum and calla lily).

ROSE GUIDE

In most areas this is the main month for pruning and feeding roses. If you have some early spring-flowering varieties you should certainly make a start so that they will be in good shape for blooming then. The evergreen *Rosa banksiae* 'Lutea' may need to be trimmed a little. If you cut it quite close to its support, a healthy plant will reward you with masses of tight flower clusters; if you let it arch freely it will look like a primrose-coloured waterfall.

Heavy pruning is now mainly reserved for modern hybrid bush roses. With climbing roses remove old, weak canes and twiggy growth and tie as many stems as possible horizontally. In tropical areas, after a major flush of flowers, a maintenance prune should be given and this pattern continued through the year, with accompanying feeding.

PLANT WATCH

The same cautions apply as for May and June.

- Aphids. This month you may find these on stock, which should be sprayed with pyrethrum.
- Borers. They may attack eucalypts and acacias as well as deciduous trees including ornamental prunus and fruit trees. Methylated spirits or Malathion may be successful; seek advice about stronger treatment if this does not succeed and the tree appears threatened.
- Cup moth. This may infest *Angophora*, *Tristaniopsis* and eucalypts. Spray with Malathion, and be careful of stinging spines on larvae.
- Leaf curl. This may affect prunus and stone-fruit trees, including peaches and nectarines, and must be treated with Bordeaux mixture just as colour shows in the opening flower buds. It is a matter of timing the treatment correctly for individual trees from now on through spring, to catch them as they are about to flower.
- Petal blight. This is of more concern as we move into the azalea season: it is produced by damp conditions during the budding and flowering phases. Spray with a fungicide.
- White scale and mites. Use dormant spraying oil on roses after pruning, and on affected fruit trees and vines.

PRUNING PROGRAMME

The June pruning programme applies in July also: when you do it depends on where your garden is and on how busy you are. Towards the end of the month is also the main pruning time for the following plants.

- Fuchsias: in frost-free areas can be shortened back to about two-thirds from the tip.
- Grape vines: should have dead and weak growths removed and strong shoots cut back to the last two or three healthy buds before permanent wood.
- Kiwi fruit or Chinese gooseberries: prune at the same time as grape vines.
- Stone and pome fruit (apples, pears and quinces): the trees are pruned to a size to suit the space and to produce a number of good-quality fruit rather than an excess number of inferior samples. Pears, nectarines and peaches are usually pruned harder than plums, apples, apricots or cherries, following established styles.
- Wisterias: shorten back unruly growth to firm stems and buds.

FEEDING TIME

This is the time to feed fruit trees and roses.

Bearded iris should be fed with bone meal or blood and bone, and polyanthus needs weak liquid manure every two to three weeks. Seedlings such as Iceland poppies, pansies and violas should be stimulated with liquid manure.

OTHER JOBS

Weeding is important. There are usually still plenty of weeds about in winter, but they do grow more slowly. If you can catch onion weed and oxalis this month you will forestall the formation of spring bulblets – a very worthwhile exercise. Do not disturb young seedlings as you weed.

Put down more compost when it is ready, to suppress weeds and keep the garden protected from the cold. In a bare patch of ground, dig compost through roughly and let it lie fallow.

BONUSES AND HARVESTS

It is not too late to take a few more hardwood cuttings. Remember that some plants are easy to strike at any time of the year, particularly pelargoniums, fuchsias, herbs and marguerites. Take soft *and* semi-hardwood cuttings if you are uncertain. In warmer areas, take cuttings of frangipani while they are dormant.

One of the special harvests of July is a bunch or two of daphne. It is a pity that so many of us do not think of having more than one bush: plan one day to plant a row along a little path, in acid soil, facing east.

PLANNING NOTES

In the south, resolve to pursue your study of lovely plants and effects for winter gardens. If you live in a hotter region plan to get the best from the wonderful plants that are available to you, by creating garden pictures in your mind's eye.

AUGUST

This is certainly one of the windiest months over much of Australia – ask any magnolia that tries to open its delicate flowers at this time of year. In the north it is a very pleasant time of year, and on still days almost everywhere it is good to be outside – if in some parts a little cool as spring tussles with the last of winter.

SOME PLANTS FEATURING NOW

TREES

Cool: *Prunus campanulata* (bell-flower cherry), *Magnolia denudata*.
Temperate: *Acacia melanoxylon* (blackwood), *Sophora tetraptera* (common kowhai).
Semi-arid: *Ceratonia siliqua* (carob tree), *Pittosporum phillyreoides* (weeping pittosporum).
Tropical and sub-tropical: *Bauhinia purpurea*, *Erythrina indica* (Indian coral tree).

SHRUBS

Cool: *Chaenomeles speciosa* (flowering quince), *Spiraea thunbergii*.
Temperate: *Boronia metastigma* (brown boronia), *Eriostemon myoporoides* (wax plant).
Semi-arid: *Cassia brewsteri* (cigar cassia), *Grevillea thelemanniana*.
Tropical and sub-tropical: *Grevillea pteridifolia*, *Pentas lanceolata*.

CLIMBING PLANTS

Cool: *Jasminum mesnyi* (primrose jasmine).
Temperate: *Hardenbergia violacea*.
Tropical and sub-tropical: *Beaumontia grandiflora* (Easter herald-trumpet), *Congea tomentosa*.

ANNUALS AND PERENNIALS

Aquilegia × *hybrida* (columbine), *Rhemannia elata* (Chinese foxglove), *Helleborus* (Lenten or winter rose), *Papaver nudicaule* (Iceland poppy), *Primula* × *polyantha* (polyanthus), *Saxifraga* and *Viola* (pansy and viola).

BULBS

Clivia (kaffir lily), *Freesia*, *Galanthus nivalis* (snowdrop), *Hyacinthus* (hyacinth), *Lachenalia* (soldier boy), *Leucojum aestivum* (snowflake), *Narcissus* (daffodil and jonquil) and *Tulipa* (tulip).

LAWN CARE

This is a good time to think about sowing new lawns. Couch varieties make hardy green lawns all year round in hot districts. In the south, however, the cold turns them brown in winter. You may decide to top-dress your lawn for spring, using some sandy loam, blood and bone, and good seed. Always remove unsightly weeds before top-dressing. In warmer areas, fertilise the lawn.

Bindii is a fern-leafed weed with barbed seeds, very painful to bare feet. Use a two-pronged weeder to remove these plants as they develop; if bindii has spread extensively, use a selective commercial spray. Moss in your lawn can be treated now, or you may decide to like it – in Japan a moss lawn would be preferred. But if you want to check it, first see if it is caused by bad drainage and correct this. Otherwise it can be treated by pouring 2 tablespoons of sulphate of iron in half a bucket of water over the moss, repeating the process one week later.

PLANTING IDEAS

Keep planting trees and shrubs as you need to, always watering them well and frequently for three months while they establish. Citrus trees do well planted this month.

VEGETABLES

In all regions onions can be sown now for early harvest as spring onions. In tropical regions sow as for June and July. Except in frosty areas cucumbers, marrows, melons, pumpkins and zucchini can be sown direct: cold will badly check them, though, so you may do better to wait a few more weeks to avoid trouble. In temperate areas also sow as for June and July, but tomatoes can be sown now if you move them to a sheltered place at night. In cool regions also sow as for June and July, leaving out broad beans but adding parsnips, swedes and turnips.

In all regions August is a good month for planting peas, and potatoes can be planted from sprouting tubers.

ANNUALS AND PERENNIALS

This is rather an in-between time in temperate and cool zones – too late for spring and too early for summer. It doesn't hurt to have a break from planting, but if you cannot bear empty spots put in seeds (or seedlings if you can find them) of *Alyssum maritimum* (sweet Alice), *Iberis* (candytuft), *Petunia* × *hybrida*, *Phlox drummondii* (annual phlox) and *Tagetes* (marigold). In the tropics you could choose from the May, June or July lists, although later plantings will have a shorter life. If you are growing perennial plants such as gerberas, hebes, perennial phlox or salvias they can save you having to plant lots of annuals, making a garden more restful on the eyes.

BULBS

July's planting ideas still apply, but you could think of planting for late summer either this month or next. Include *Amaryllis belladonna* (belladonna lily), *Eucomis comosa* (pineapple lily), *Nerine* (spider lily) and *Zephyranthes candida* (flower of the west wind). Also consider *Gloriosa rothschildiana* (gloriosa lily), a tropical variety that favours a dry summer and further south does best in a container.

ROSE GUIDE

Wherever you are, spring-flowering and recurrently flowering roses should be pruned by now and fed well. Even roses in cold and frosty gardens must be attended to before they burst into leaf, although their cycle runs a month or so later than those in warmer areas. Attend to the new roses planted in the last couple of months, shortening rough-ended stems to outgoing shoots.

Watch for aphids gathering in the lush shoots of new or established roses. Try as always to remove by hand, or use a pyrethrum spray.

PLANT WATCH

- Aphids. These may gather around tulip flowers. Use pyrethrum if you cannot remove them by hand.
- Fruit fly. This is a serious pest and in some areas control is compulsory. They become active in warmer months and infested fruit must be destroyed. Baits to trap the fly can be used, but a chemical spray is the only really effective control.
- Gall wasps. These are sometimes found on lemon trees: swelling on the stems indicates that the tunnelling larvae are present. Cut out these stems immediately you see them and put in the garbage, as they will hatch half-way through the month if not destroyed.
- Lemon scab. This fungal disease occurs particularly in coastal districts. It attacks around blossom time and petal fall, but is noticed more when scabby patches appear on fruit, twigs and leaves. It should not affect quality but can cause fruit to fall. Spray with Bordeaux mixture, adding white oil as a wetting agent.
- Petal blight. May affect azaleas: signs to look for are brownish drooped buds that previously flourished. When you see this, or if it was a problem last year, use a fungicide every two weeks through the flowering season. Spray the ground around the plant at the end of flowering, as organisms rest there through the non-flowering period.
- Slugs and snails. They can demolish new lilium shoots overnight. You may also catch them hiding away among clivia leaves or munching the flowers. Remove by hand if possible.

PRUNING PROGRAMME

Prune summer- and autumn-flowering shrubs, fuchsias, pelargoniums and hydrangeas, and trim autumn-flowering cassia. Remember not to prune spring-flowering shrubs until after flowering, whether they are deciduous or evergreen.

- Berry fruit: remove old canes of loganberries and tie down the new ones formed last season.
- Bougainvilleas: cut hard back to stimulate a new surge of growth and flowers.
- Camellias: remove bare and woody stems and branches, and shorten back leggy growth to encourage buds to shoot further back after flowering.
- Citrus: healthy trees do not need much pruning, just an occasional tidying or shaping of irregular branches. Sometimes there are dead twigs and branches to be taken out, and growth can be stimulated by shortening growths back

Clivia miniata in a sheltered spot will surprise you with its early spring blooms if you feed it well.

AUGUST

to healthy shoots. It is a good practice to look at them when they are fed in August, and prune as required; do this again in February during their summer feeding time.
- Crêpe myrtle: prune as lightly or as heavily as you like, to achieve a shrubby, rounded look or a free-spreading tree.
- Hibiscus: prune now or next month in cool gardens, depending on the threat of frosts. In warmer temperate and tropical gardens give an occasional prune during the year, when flowers are few, feeding with organic manure or a complete fertiliser.
- Hydrangeas: prune now if you have not already done so. Late pruning helps to reduce the risk of frost damage to young leaves.
- Maidenhair and other ferns: brown or shrivelled stems can safely be cut to ground level, over the entire plant if necessary. Dress with rotted leaf mould.
- Ornamental winter-flowering peaches: cut back to just above the lower buds of recently flowered shoots to encourage better flowering next year.
- Poinsettias: prune back to lower shoots after winter flowering.

FEEDING TIME

Fertilise bananas well. Also feed citrus, wetting the soil thoroughly first (and again after application) to avoid burning the tiny roots near the surface. Follow the manufacturer's instructions for application rates, according to the size of the tree. Citrus can also be fed with lots of well-rotted cow manure and blood and bone. They should be mulched with compost throughout the year, but always keep the trunk clear.

Do *not* attempt to feed azaleas or camellias until after they have finished flowering. Then give them well-rotted cow manure or blood and bone. Let pelargonium buds form now, and give a light dressing of complete plant food (a heaped teaspoon around a medium-sized plant) or some cow manure and wood ash. Polyanthus likes liquid manure every fortnight. Hibiscus in the tropics will relish a monthly feed of animal manure and compost or blood and bone.

Feed maidenhair and other ferns with a diluted soluble manure, using a very weak solution and applying this only when new growth is well under way.

OTHER JOBS

Pull off the spent flower heads of bulbs such as jonquils and daffodils to prevent seeding, but leave the leaves to wither and so nourish next year's embryo bulbs. Keep removing the buds of Iceland poppies until your plants have made lush leafy crown clumps. The roots must not be disturbed – just keep well mulched.

Divide and replant perennials and bulbs, including achilleas, helenium, bergamot, sunflowers, daylilies, red-hot poker, cannas and agapanthus. Nip tips out of wallflowers to force side shoots, thus increasing the number of flower heads and making the plant more lush. Cut back and divide crowded ferns to make new pots or for new spots in the ground. Dress with leaf mould.

Mulch strawberries liberally with fibrous matter such as straw, dry leaves, grass clippings and mulched twigs which have been heaped for a couple of weeks. Try to lift parts of the plant to mulch under them as well as in between.

If violets fail to flower they should be moved to a sunnier spot. Avoid nitrogenous fertiliser, as it can cause excessive leaf growth.

BONUSES AND HARVESTS

Begin to take softwood cuttings: marguerites, of course, and wallflowers and dianthus are also worthwhile. This will give you many plants to use around the garden. Strike poinsettia prunings for Christmas flowers.

Indulge yourself by picking a few branches (particularly the untidy ones) of flowering camellia to use indoors. Use florist's wire near the flower base to hold the flower head on to the top of the stem. Spray blooms with water daily, as camellias absorb water through their petals. Early blossoming branches of forsythia, spiraea, flowering quince, prunus and crab apple can be forced to flower by bringing some inside into the warmth. To ensure water intake continues, shorten stems a little each day. Hellebores can be disappointing as a cut flower, but you can trick them by floating their heads in a pottery bowl – just a few are exquisite. The flowers tend to hold better when the stamens have withered.

Buy a boronia for its fragrance.

PLANNING NOTES

There seems so much to do now, but don't overlook your garden planning. For instance, think about what you will do with your propagated plants – put them in pots, or in beds for a massed effect? And perhaps consider massing dianthus along the front path for a fragrant passage.

SEPTEMBER

In many areas September is a special month of gentle breezes and nectar-scented air. Sometimes plants you have forgotten about, or which normally never 'do' anything, suddenly take off; and in nature crowds of wildflowers suddenly appear, even the deserts coming to life.

SOME PLANTS FEATURING NOW

TREES

Cool: *Agonis flexuosa* (Western Australian weeping myrtle), *Elaeocarpus grandis* (brush quandong).
Temperate: *Davidia involucrata* (dove tree), *Prunus persica* (flowering peach).
Semi-arid: *Acacia pendula*, *Cercis siliquastrum* (Judas tree).
Tropical and sub-tropical: *Bauhinia variegata*, *Schotia brachypetala* (Hottentot bean).

SHRUBS

Cool: *Spiraea cantoniensis*, *Viburnum carlesii*.
Temperate: *Choisya ternata* (Mexican orange blossom), *Kolkwitzia amabilis* (Chinese beauty bush).
Semi-arid: *Lavatera assurgentiflora* (California tree mallow), *Jasminum lineare* (desert jasmine).
Tropical and sub-tropical: *Dendrobium bigibbum* (Cooktown orchid), *Odontonema strictum* (fire spike).

Gazanias are tough, vibrant small plants for full sun.

CLIMBING PLANTS

Cool: *Berberidopsis corallina* (coral Chile vine), *Clematis armandii*.
Temperate: *Clematis aristata* (Australian clematis, old man's beard), *Fuchsia procumbens* (trailing fuchsia).
Tropical and sub-tropical: *Bauhinia corymbosa* (climbing bauhinia), *Jasminum nitidum*.

ANNUALS AND PERENNIALS

Actinotis helianthi (flannel flower), *Antirrhinum majus* (snapdragon), *Aubrieta deltoidea* (rock cress), *Bellis perennis* (English daisy), *Campanula* (bell flower), *Centaurea cyanus* (cornflower), *Cheiranthus cheiri* (wallflower), *Gazania hybrida*, *Gerbera jamesonii*, *Gypsophila*, *Lobelia erinus*, *Matthiola incana* (stock), *Nemesia versicolor*, *Penstemon* (bearded tongue), *Primula hybrida*, *Papaver orientale* (oriental poppy), *Schizanthus* × *wisetonensis* (poor man's orchid) and *Vinca* (periwinkle).

BULBS

Anemone, *Babiana* (baboon flower), *Clivia* (kaffir lily), *Convallaria majalis* (lily of the valley), *Crocus*, *Freesia*, *Hyacinthus* (hyacinth), *Hyacinthoides* (bluebell), *Ipheion uniflorum* (star flower), *Iris* (bearded and Dutch), *Ixia* (corn lily), *Lachenalia* (soldier boy), *Narcissus* (daffodil and jonquil), *Ranunculus*, *Sparaxis* (harlequin flower), *Tulipa* (tulip) and *Watsonia*.

MOISTURE CONTROL

Gardens should be kept moist at this time. Many plants are directing their energy to growing, and drying out will check their development.

LAWN CARE

Fertilise lawns with sulphate of ammonia or a high-nitrogen lawn food. Apply evenly according to instructions, and water in well.

Top-dress by oversowing with lawn seed to improve lawns. Aerate lawns if compacted.

PLANTING IDEAS

In frost-free areas plant out all container-grown trees, shrubs and climbers, including azaleas, citrus, hibiscus, passionfruit, rhododendrons, wisterias and any native plants.

Climbing plants that can be grown from seed include *Aristolochia elegans* (Dutchman's pipe), *Cobaea scandens* (cup-and-saucer plant), *Cucurbita* (gourd), *Mina lobata* (crimson star glory) and *Thunbergia gibsonii* (black-eyed Susan).

SEPTEMBER

The sweet pea (*Lathyrus odoratus*) is as loved in today's gardens as it was in cottage gardens long ago.

VEGETABLES

In all areas sow capsicums, celery, peas, pumpkins, squash, tomatoes and zucchini. It is also a good time to plant potato tubers.

ANNUALS AND PERENNIALS

Ageratum houstonianum (dwarf ageratum), *Amaranthus tricolor* (Joseph's coat), *Aster*, *Cleome spinosa* (spider flower), *Cosmos bipinnatus, Dianthus* (carnation, pink), *Pelargonium* (geranium), *Phlox drummondii*, *Rudbeckia* (cone flower), *Salpiglossis sinuata* (velvet flower), *Salvia* (flowering sage), *Tagetes* (marigold), *Tropaeolum majus* (nasturtium), *Verbena* × *hybrida* and *Zinnia elegans*.

BULBS

Agapanthus (Nile lily), Allium, *Amaryllis belladonna* (belladonna lily), *Anemone blanda*, *Canna indica* (Indian shot), *Colchicum*, *Crinum flaccidum*, *C. moorei*, *Dahlia*, *Gladiolus*, *Gloriosa rothschildiana* (gloriosa lily), *Hemerocallis* (daylily), *Hippeastrum*, *Lilium*, *Lycoris*, *Nerine* (spider lily), *Sprekelia* (Jacobean lily), *Vallota speciosa* (Scarborough lily).

ROSE GUIDE

Watch for aphids on new shoots.

PLANT WATCH

- Aphids. They are likely to appear on spring growth. In particular black aphids may infest camellia and rhododendron shoots and lemon trees. Remove by hand or use a pyrethrum spray.
- Cabbage moth. Check not just on cabbages and other vegetables but on stocks and wallflowers as well. Derris dust should be used, according to directions.
- Petal blight. Spray affected azaleas with a fungicide.
- Snails and slugs. They will be about, as always. Look out for them particularly on clivias and other bulbs.
- Vine moth. This may be found on fruiting and ornamental grapes. Try to remove by hand, using a tissue, but if there are too many use Malathion spray.

PRUNING PROGRAMME

- Azaleas: cut any wayward branches and use them for indoors when they are flowering, which will help even-up the bush.
- Camellias: can be trimmed to shape after new growth appears.
- Diosma: clip back to lower shoots to keep the plant compact after flowering. Always cut to a visible shoot.
- Flowering quince: can be pruned after flowering.
- Fuchsias and pelargoniums: tip-prune to encourage bushy growth.
- Gardenias: prune lightly, in very warm districts.
- Hibiscus: prune once the danger of frost is past.
- Native mint: trim below the spent flowers.
- Passionfruit: lightly prune established vines.
- Plumbago: trim to tidy up.
- Poinsettias: prune hard after they have flowered.
- Wax mallow: particularly in inland gardens, prune to prevent legginess.

FEEDING TIME

Give compost to abelia and other summer-flowering shrubs and feed agapanthus with compost and cow manure. Bulbs that have finishing flowering could have a complete fertiliser, bone meal or liquid manure.

Camellias, azaleas and rhododendrons can be fed after flowering, with cow manure, compost, blood and bone, or azalea food. Fruit trees should be fed with a complete fertiliser. Gardenias can get yellow leaves from a magnesium deficiency: sprinkle 1 tablespoon of Epsom salts around the plant and water in.

Hibiscus and hydrangeas respond well to cow manure and blood and bone or a complete fertiliser. Spring-flowering annuals can be kept thriving with liquid manure. Summer-flowering shrubs will bloom better if given a complete fertiliser or blood and bone, well watered in.

In tropical regions some fruit trees (including avocado, banana, mango and pawpaw) are fed now. Feed again in November and January, or a little further apart, with a complete fertiliser in proportions to suit individual needs.

OTHER JOBS

Dig up chrysanthemums. Choose healthy pieces for propagation from cuttings, and discard the old crowns.

Divide gerbera if the clumps are crowded. Trim back the roots and cut back the leaves to a few centimetres above the leaf stalks (do this later in warmer districts). Leave crowns slightly above soil level, especially in heavy soils.

Repot container plants and house plants.

BONUSES AND HARVESTS

Spring is the time for softwood cuttings. Take poinsettia cuttings when pruning.

Look around your garden – there is always something to pick for gift posies and for indoors. Make some fragrant posies, or tussie-mussies, using whatever herbs you have in your garden with the addition of flowers such as Virginian stock, scented pelargoniums, heliotrope and colourful nasturtiums. Collect armfuls of lilac to perfume your house.

PLANNING NOTES

Check borders and beds for colour and perfume. Take a reference photograph of how they looked this spring and make a few notes for next year.

Snapdragons (*Antirrhinum*) and pansies (*Viola*) make a showy spring border, but pansies must be dead-headed to keep them flowering.

OCTOBER

Spring is at its peak in October. Nature seems to take over in everyone's garden, especially in south-eastern Australia where native flowers and the blossoms of introduced plants are out everywhere.

SOME PLANTS FEATURING NOW

TREES
Cool: *Paulownia tomentosa* (royal paulownia), *Prunus serrulata* 'Ukon' (Ukon cherry).
Temperate: *Acacia cognata* (bower wattle), *Virgilia divaricata*.
Tropical and sub-tropical: *Bombax ceiba* (silk cotton tree), *Spathodea campanulata* (South African tulip tree).

SHRUBS
Cool: *Syringa vulgaris* (lilac), *Viburnum opulus* 'Sterile' (snowball tree).
Temperate: *Hakea laurina* (pincushion hakea), *Philadelphus mexicanus* (Mexican mock orange).
Semi-arid: *Eremophila maculata* (spotted emu bush), *Strelitzia reginae* (bird's-tongue flower).
Tropical and sub-tropical: *Bauhinia hookeri*, *Ixora coccinea* (flame tree).

CLIMBING PLANTS
Cool: *Rosa* 'Lorraine Lee', *Lonicera hildebrandiana* (giant Burmese honeysuckle).
Temperate: *Comesperma volubile* (love creeper), *Billardiera ringens* (Chapman River creeper).
Tropical and sub-tropical: *Faradaya splendida*, *Hoya macgillivrayi*.

ANNUALS AND PERENNIALS
Antirrhinum majus (snapdragon), *Aquilegia* × *hybrida* (columbine), *Armeria* (thrift), *Aubrieta deltoidea* (rock cress), *Bellis perennis* (English daisy), *Campanula* (bell flower), *Centaurea cyanus* (cornflower), *Cheiranthus cheiri* (wallflower), *Delphinium* (larkspur), *Dianthus* (carnation, pink), *Papaver orientale* (oriental poppy) and *Viola* (pansy and viola).

BULBS
Anemone, *Babiana* (baboon flower), *Freesia*, *Hyacinthoides* (bluebell), *Ipheion uniflorum* (star flower), *Iris* (bearded and Dutch), *Ixia* (corn lily), *Lachenalia* (soldier boy), *Muscari* (grape hyacinth), *Ranunculus*, *Tulipa* (tulip) and *Zantedeschia* (arum and calla lily).

MOISTURE CONTROL

As in September, gardens should be kept moist as this is the growing season for many plants. Be sure to water on drying, windy days, especially fruit trees such as citrus.

LAWN CARE

Make sure lawns are well mown regularly to keep spring weeds down.

October is a good month for sowing and establishing new lawns. In the tropics, top-dress before the wet season arrives.

PLANTING IDEAS

All container-grown plants can be planted out now. Water well and stake if needed.

VEGETABLES
In all districts sow tomatoes, and basil, chervil, coriander and parsley.

You can plant a large range of vegetables including beans, beetroot, capsicums, cucumbers, eggplant, lettuces, marrows, pumpkins, radishes, snap peas, snow peas, sweetcorn and zucchini.

ANNUALS
Alyssum maritimum (sweet Alice), *Aster*, *Cleome spinosa* (spider flower), *Chrysanthemum*, *Dianthus* (carnation, pink), *Petunia* × *hybrida*, *Phlox*, *Salpiglossis sinuata* (velvet flower), *Salvia* (flowering sage), *Tagetes* (marigold), *Torenia fournieri* (wishbone flower), *Tropaeolum majus* (nasturtium) and *Zinnia elegans*.

BULBS
Canna indica (Indian shot), *Dahlia*, *Dianella* (flax lily), *Diplarrhena moraea*, *Eucomis comosa* (pineapple lily), *Gladiolus*, *Nerine* (spider lily), *Patersonia* (native iris), *Sprekelia formosissima* (Jacobean lily), *Vallota speciosa* (Scarborough lily), *Zephyranthes candida* (flower of the west wind).

ROSE GUIDE

Spring-flowering climbing roses, such as *Rosa banksiae* 'Lutea', *R.* 'Black Boy', *R.* 'Lorraine Lee' and *R. laevigata*, can be pruned after their spring flush. Remove very old canes, shorten lateral growth, and feed with cow manure and blood and bone. 'Black Boy' should flower again in summer, and 'Lorraine Lee' will flower intermittently throughout the year. Keep aphids at bay.

Always dead-head roses, pruning correctly as you go.

Perhaps the loveliest of all the poppies is *Papaver orientale*.

Remember that all rose debris is rubbish, not compost – with luck, the thrips on the dead flowers will be thrown out too. Watch for dieback: affected branches must be pruned off or the decay will continue.

PLANT WATCH

- Grey mould. This may appear on carnations, petunias and stocks. It is similar to petal blight and should be dealt with in the same way.
- Petal blight. This fungal disorder of azaleas and rhododendrons may need treating with a fungicide spray.
- Vine moth. The caterpillars may infect vines. Spray with Malathion only if physical removal is too arduous.
- Webbing caterpillar. Can be identified by a cluster or two of dead foliage and cobwebs in your tree or shrub. *Leptospermum* (tea tree) is particularly susceptible. Cut out widespread clusters and put them in the rubbish. Watch for further outbreaks: try to treat the disease conservatively, separating the infected lumps of web and dead foliage with a rag dipped in warm soapy water or cutting them out again. Use carbaryl dust or spray if all else fails.

PRUNING PROGRAMME

- Bottlebrush: cut spent flowers well back to healthy shoots.
- Cannas: in the tropics, cut back hard.
- Climbers: prune jasmine, wisteria and other enthusiastic spring-flowering climbers, to check vigorous growth after flowering.
- Diosma: cut off all spent flowers and then clip back branches to healthy growth.
- Fruit trees: spring-flowering peaches can be pruned after flowering, while flowering cherry or crab apple need only be shaped a little as required. Dwarf peaches need severe pruning after flowering: cut almost to the ground, which will produce flowers on long slender stems next year.
- Native plants: as a rule, prune lightly when they have finished flowering, to prevent legginess.
- Pelargoniums: cut back, and nip out the young shoots to encourage bushy growth all over.

FEEDING TIME

Directions for September still apply.

OTHER JOBS

Remove spent flower heads on all plants. Weed all garden areas conscientiously, wherever possible catching weeds in their infancy.

Make some hanging baskets to decorate pergolas. Plant pots for summer flowers.

BONUSES AND HARVESTS

Softwood and semi-hardwood cuttings can still be struck.

Spring is flower time. Gather lots of garden flowers and arrange them in containers inside baskets for a lovely and luxuriant effect. Remember that at this time of year the more you pick the more you will grow.

PLANNING NOTES

Look for more lovely spring-flowering plants. You are sure to find you 'need' them in your garden.

Check for overshadowing boughs in places where your garden really needs the sun. Look at your garden critically. There may be some way in which you can improve its shapes, or you may want to replant one or more areas.

If you have never done so before, consider regal pelargoniums for a spring display. They can be grown in pots or borders: use them in exposed places that might be too harsh for azaleas, as they can look similar. Cut them back and feed them a small amount of potash to encourage flowering.

NOVEMBER

This is a great time to be in gardens. In the north people are beginning to batten down the hatches at the prospect of the approaching wet season. Further south it is not usually too hot yet, and there is a great feeling of vitality conveyed by flowers, foliage and fragrance, insects, birds and bees.

SOME PLANTS FEATURING NOW

TREES

Cool: *Agonis flexuosa* (Western Australian weeping myrtle), *Catalpa bignonioides* (Indian bean tree).
Temperate: *Angophora costata* (apple myrtle), *Hymenosporum flavum* (native frangipani).
Semi-arid: *Brachychiton gregorii* (desert kurrajong).
Tropical and sub-tropical: *Acacia elata* (cedar wattle), *Calodendrum capense* (Cape chestnut).

SHRUBS

Cool: *Escallonia macrantha*, *Kalmia latifolia* (mountain laurel).
Temperate: *Brunfelsia calycina* (yesterday, today and tomorrow), *Philadelphus coronarius* (mock orange).
Semi-arid: *Cantua buxifolia* (flower of the Incas).
Tropical and sub-tropical: *Allemanda neriifolia*, *Calliandra haematocephala*.

CLIMBING PLANTS

Cool: *Billardiera bignoniacea* (orange bell climber), *Hydrangea petiolaris* (climbing hydrangea).
Temperate: *Kennedia nigricans* (black coral pea), *Rosa* (climbers and ramblers including 'Albertine' and 'Wedding Day').
Tropical and sub-tropical: *Doxantha unguis-cati* (cat's-claw creeper), *Jasminum grandiflorum*.

ANNUALS AND PERENNIALS

Ageratum (floss flower), *Antirrhinum majus* (snapdragon), *Alonsoa* (mask flower), *Brachyscome multifida* (rock daisy), *Cerastium tomentosum* (snow-in-summer), *Delphinium* (larkspur), *Dianthus* (carnation, pink), *Eschscholtzia californica* (Californian poppy), *Gaura lindheimeri*, *Gazania* × *hybrida*, *Gerbera jamesonii*, *Centranthus ruber* (red valerian), *Lobelia erinus*, *Nepeta* (catmint), *Petunia* × *hybrida*, *Phlox drummondii* (annual phlox), *Portulaca grandiflora* (sun plant), *Salvia* (flowering sage), *Tagetes* (marigold) and *Tropaeolum majus* (nasturtium).

BULBS

Agapanthus (Nile lily), *Canna indica* (Indian shot), *Dierama pulcherrimum* (fairy fishing rod), *Gladiolus*, *Hippeastrum*, *Iris*, *Lilium candidum* (Madonna lily), *Watsonia*, *Zantedeschia* (arum and calla lily).

MOISTURE CONTROL

Citrus trees need frequent soakings, but do not leave the soil constantly wet. On the other hand citrus (oranges in particular) can drop fruit if the soil dries out.

Mulching is important before summer arrives in earnest, to reduce water loss from evaporation, suppress weeds and ultimately improve soil texture to increase its moisture-holding capacity.

LAWN CARE

This is a good time in tropical areas to plant buffalo runners and sow couch. In either case the surface should be kept moist for two or three weeks afterwards.

Feed established lawns. Lawns can be top-dressed but this should only be done to fill in hollows or for regrowth under deciduous trees.

Leave clippings on the lawn to dry out for a few days before you rake them up for mulch. In very hot weather leave them on the grass as a light, protective mulch.

PLANTING IDEAS

This month plant bulbs, corms such as gladiolus, and a range of trees, shrubs, climbers and ground covers.

VEGETABLES

In all regions plant beans, cabbages, capsicums, carrots, Chinese cabbage, celery, cress, cucumbers, eggplants, leeks (except in tropical areas), lettuces, marrows, melons, okra, parsnips, potatoes, pumpkins, radishes, rhubarb, salsify, silverbeet, spring onions, squash, sweetcorn, tomatoes and zucchinis. Plant all herbs except parsley, and also plant Cape gooseberries.

Sweet-potato cuttings or seedlings can still be planted in tropical or temperate districts.

ANNUALS AND PERENNIALS

In all regions sow or plant out *Ageratum* (floss flower), *Amaranthus tricolor*, *Anigozanthos* (kangaroo paw), *Aster*, *Begonia semperflorens* (bedding begonia), *Capsicum annuum* (ornamental chilli), *Celosia* (cockscomb), *Chrysanthemum*, *Cleome* (spider flower), *Cosmos bipinnatus*, *Dahlia*, *Dianthus* (carnation, pink), *Eschscholtzia californica* (Californian poppy), *Gazania* × *hybrida*, *Gerbera jamesonii*, *Gomphrena globosa* (globe amaranth), *Gypsophila*, *Helianthus* (sunflower), *Impatiens wallerana*, *Pelargonium* (geranium), *Petunia* × *hybrida*, *Phlox*, *Portulaca* (sun plant), *Rudbeckia* (cone flower), *Salpiglossis sinuata* (velvet flower), *Salvia* (flowering sage),

Tagetes (marigold), *Torenia fournieri* (wishbone flower), *Tropaeolum majus* (nasturtium), *Verbena* and *Zinnia elegans*. Seedlings of dwarf *Ageratum*, *Petunia*, *Phlox*, dwarf marigold and *Torenia* planted out early this month should flower by Christmas.

Remember that in the tropics flowering times will be short owing to the heat and the approach of the wet season.

BULBS

Continue using the planting list given for October.

ROSE GUIDE

Many roses will be in full flower now. Check for aphids, and prune dead heads back to appropriate shoots. Prune early-flowering climbers and ramblers once they have finished flowering.

Check for vigorous shoots of suckers appearing below the trunk grafts on your roses, and remove them carefully.

In the tropics, give roses a complete fertiliser.

PLANT WATCH

- Bronze orange bug. In the tropics especially, this can cause serious damage to citrus. They are quite visible and should be picked off (though their offensive smell may discourage you) or sprayed with Malathion.
- Caterpillars. You may find them especially on the undersides of leaves. Remove, or spray with pyrethrum.
- Codlin moth. The larvae can be trapped with hessian or cardboard placed around the tree's trunk. If you feel spraying is necessary, use carbaryl with caution and follow instructions.
- Fruit fly. In some areas these must be controlled. Any infested fruit must be removed and destroyed. A chemical spray such as Lebacid is the most effective means of control.
- Lace bug. This affects azalea foliage in particular. It is best controlled by spraying Malathion regularly over the next few months.
- Pear and cherry slug. A dusting of lime over the leaves may repel them. Hose leaves after three days. Try to avoid carbaryl spray.
- Red spider mite. This causes mottling on the leaves of a wide range of plants: remove badly affected foliage and water the infested plants from above. Feed as directed.

PRUNING PROGRAMME

Prune spring-flowering shrubs, such as lilacs, mock orange, spiraeas and viburnums, as they finish blooming. Cut out old branches to make room for vigorous new wood.

- Chrysanthemums: shorten new growths when they reach about 12 centimetres, and then also cut back any side shoots stimulated as a result. This process should continue until late December.
- Jasmine: prune the soft new shoots back to curb the plant's ascent, and cut back as much of the previous year's growth as feasible to prevent the plant from becoming too bulky.
- Native plants: spent flower heads should be cut back to appropriate shoots.

FEEDING PROGRAMME

Ideally, all vegetables and annuals should have weak liquid manure every two to three weeks. Bananas should be fed with potash and passionfruit vines with blood and bone. Gerberas will appreciate a teaspoon of complete fertiliser, watered in well.

OTHER JOBS

Plant out dahlia tubers and insert stakes in readiness for later growth if shoots have not developed already.

The leaves of spring-flowering bulbs can be removed once they have withered. Tulips, bearded iris and other bulbs can be lifted now and stored in a cool dry place in mesh bags.

In the vegetable garden bend onion tops over when the bulbs are forming, to hasten maturity. Pinch out tomato laterals, leaving only those with clustered buds ready to form fruit. Tie to stakes as they grow.

Weed, weed, weed – before the weeds seed! Dig out bulbous perennial weeds and firmly rooted annuals.

BONUSES AND HARVESTS

Softwood and semi-hardwood cuttings can be taken from many native plants, house plants and succulents.

If you have roses, enjoy their flowers both out of doors and inside. Make pot-pourri from the petals.

PLANNING NOTES

Make a note of any of the roses out now that particularly impress you.

DECEMBER

The festive season makes many people even more garden-proud than usual and they make special efforts. More nature strips and lawns are mown this month than at any other time of the year. If you are planning to go away, don't forget your garden and its needs during your absence.

SOME PLANTS FEATURING NOW

TREES

Cool: *Dais cotinifolia* (pompon tree), *Grevillea robusta* (silky oak).
Temperate: *Eucalyptus sideroxylon* (red ironbark), *Magnolia grandiflora* (Bull Bay magnolia).
Semi-arid: *Eucalyptus microtheca* (coolibah), *E. torquata* (coral gum).
Tropical and sub-tropical: *Brachychiton acerifolius* (Illawarra flame tree), *Jacaranda mimosifolia*.

SHRUBS

Cool: *Hydrangea macrophylla*, *Metrosideros excelsa* (New Zealand Christmas tree).
Temperate: *Ceratopetalum gummiferum* (New South Wales Christmas bush), *Vitex lucens*.
Semi-arid: *Aloe arborescens* (tree aloe), *Punica granatum* (pomegranate).
Tropical and sub-tropical: *Caesalpinia gilliesii* (bird of paradise), *Gardenia florida*.

CLIMBING PLANTS

Cool: *Lonicera* (honeysuckle, woodbine), *Pandorea pandorana* (wonga vine).
Temperate: *Campsis grandiflora* (Chinese trumpet creeper), *Tecomaria*.
Tropical and sub-tropical: *Phaseolus caracalla* (snail creeper), *Stephanotis floribunda*.

ANNUALS AND PERENNIALS

Acanthus mollis (oyster plant), *Actinotus helianthi* (flannel flower), *Ageratum* (floss flower), *Alcea rosea* (hollyhock), *Antirrhinum majus* (snapdragon), *Aster*, *Calceolaria* (granny's purse), *Campanula* (bell flower), *Centaurea cyanus* (cornflower), *Cerastium tomentosum* (snow-in-summer), *Chrysanthemum* (marguerite, pyrethrum and shasta daisy), *Clarkia amoenia* (godetia), *Cleome spinosa* (spider flower), *Dianthus* (carnation, pink), *Erigeron karvinskianus* (baby's tears), *Gazania* × *hybrida*, *Iberis* (candytuft), *Linaria maroccana* (baby snapdragon), *Nepeta* (catmint), *Nymphaea* (waterlily), *Petunia* × *hybrida*, *Phlox*, *Rudbeckia* (cone flower), *Stokesia laevis* (Stoke's aster), *Tagetes* (marigold), *Torenia fournieri* (wishbone flower), *Verbena* and *Zinnia elegans*.

BULBS

Agapanthus (Nile lily), *Anigozanthos* (kangaroo paw), *Canna indica* (Indian shot), *Dahlia*, *Dierama pulcherrimum* (fairy fishing rod), *Dietes bicolor*, *Hemerocallis* (daylily), *Lilium* (including Christmas and regal lily).

Indian shot (*Canna indica*) is a versatile plant for hot or cool temperatures, coastal conditions, boggy places or even ponds.

MOISTURE CARE

Continue to water citrus to prevent harmful drying out.

Ferns in containers must remain moist. They and other smaller pots and baskets can be submerged in buckets or baths to wet them thoroughly. Palms and other plants grown largely for their foliage should not receive water continuously. Let the surface dry out between waterings, but when watering always water thoroughly.

Fuchsias can die out from lack of water during strong heat, so be sure to keep their soil moist.

Check and supplement mulches. Make sure that the deep waterings you give are able to penetrate the mulch: if this is not occurring, you may have to fork up the mulch to create passages through to the soil below.

LAWN CARE

Feed your lawn early in December for a good-looking Christmas carpet. Weeds can be removed with a two-pronged weeder, if you catch them early by checking the lawn regularly. Mowing reduces weeds in lawns by preventing seeding, but close mowing is harmful as it burns roots and can create bare patches in which weeds will establish more readily.

Lawns should be trained to withstand dryness: avoid light, frequent waterings and instead give deep soakings every four to seven days.

In the tropics, watch for early signs of lawn grubs and grass caterpillars.

PLANTING IDEAS

Trees, shrubs, climbers and perennials bought in pots can be planted out now if you have time to keep them well watered.

VEGETABLES

Sow as for November, although in cool districts it is too late for Cape gooseberries, capsicums, eggplants and tomatoes unless they are well-established seedlings planted in protected, sunny spots.

ANNUALS AND PERENNIALS

Semi-tropical and tropical areas are mainly too hot and wet for flower growing at this time of the year. In temperate and cool gardens, where water supply permits, you can sow seeds or plant seedlings of: *Ageratum*, *Alyssum maritimum* (sweet Alice), *Aster* (Easter or Michaelmas daisy), *Capsicum annuum* (ornamental chilli), *Cosmos bipinnatus*, *Celosia cristata* (cockscomb), *Chrysanthemum* hybrids, *Cleome spinosa* (spider flower), *Coleus*, *Cyclamen*, *Dahlia*, *Gazania* × *hybrida*, *Impatiens wallerana*, *Phlox drummondii* (annual phlox), *Portulaca grandiflora* (sun plant), *Tropaeolum majus* (nasturtium), *Torenia fournieri* (wishbone flower), *Verbena* and *Zinnia elegans*. Seedlings of *Celosia*, *Cosmos*, *Chrysanthemum*, *Dahlia*, *Pelargonium* (geranium), *Petunia* and *Salvia* (flowering sage) are preferable to seeds in all but warmer districts.

Spring-flowering perennials such as *Digitalis* (foxglove), *Alyssum saxatile* (golden alyssum), *Primula* × *polyantha* and *P. obconica* should be sown now.

BULBS

Suitable plantings this month include *Iris* (bearded), *Crinum moorei* and *Nerine* (spider lily).

The taste of bought sweetcorn can never compare with that of cobs straight from your vegetable garden in the summer months.

ROSE GUIDE

Roses may be in between flushes of flowers. Make sure to prune spent blooms.

Watch for aphids on new shoots. With the gathering heat thrips may also attack blooms: hose them away or spray regularly with pyrethrum. More than anything, a change of weather will do wonders.

PLANT WATCH

- Caterpillars. They may appear on vegetables and the growing tips of ornamentals, so keep checking and removing. Use pyrethrum if needed.
- Christmas beetles. Yes, they do really come around at Christmas. They are hard to kill once they are munching up your leaves, so it is much better to deal with them while they are still larvae – which look like small, white witchetty grubs.

DECEMBER

- Grasshoppers. Watch for them in warmer areas and follow local advice for control.
- Red spider mite. This can be deterred by frequent misting of foliage. Plants protected from the weather are most susceptible. Container plants (except large ones) can be inverted in soapy water, covering the ailing foliage completely.
- Whitefly. Attacks are frequent at this time of the year, particularly affecting beans, cucumbers, pumpkins, tomatoes and vine crops. Douse with your hose to encourage them to live elsewhere, and spray with pyrethrum (avoid stronger sprays, as these will destroy the larvae of the wasp that preys on whitefly).

PRUNING PROGRAMME

Dead-head all spent flowers. Make sure that you have completed the pruning of all your spring-flowering trees and shrubs, as outlined in November.

- Tomatoes: remove side shoots at the leaf joint, to encourage fruiting.

FEEDING TIME

Apply a weak solution of liquid fertiliser to vegetables and flowers every three weeks, or give side dressings of blood and bone or a complete fertiliser. Give agapanthus, fuchsias, hibiscus and hydrangeas a dressing of animal manure and all-purpose fertiliser.

Luscious berries, such as loganberries, are part of the Christmas festive season and summer holidays.

Azaleas, camellias, daphnes and rhododendrons should be fed (using blood and bone, cow manure or azalea food), watered and mulched. You are really bedding them down for the warmer months.

OTHER JOBS

Lift ranunculus and anemone corms now the leaves have withered.

Thin out vegetable seedlings as required. Stake tomatoes and continue to tie growing plants, pruning surplus laterals.

BONUSES AND HARVESTS

Take tip cuttings of azaleas and camellias from new growth, dipping the cuttings in a hormone powder for the best results. Daphne cuttings are best raised under glass – they can take a long time to strike, so don't give up.

In the north poinsettias can come inside for Christmas, perhaps as a table centrepiece with short stems of agapanthus and kangaroo paw in a low, wide dish. There may also be some stunning bottlebrush heads or scarlet hibiscus, which will be available further south, too. In cool districts, boughs of spruce and fir, variegated holly leaves and white hydrangeas give a Christmas feeling. Also look for some cut *Protea magnifica* (giant woolly beard), a really festive flower.

Try to pick your vegetables young, harvesting as fast as they grow. Pick some for your friends and arrange for someone to enjoy them if you are going away. In the tropics, it's mango time.

PLANNING NOTES

You might like to think about the past year in your garden – the efforts, the pleasures, the problems and the rewards. Do remember that some plants take time to establish. It is worth waiting two or three years for a reluctant but worthwhile plant to flourish.

Notice how the garden – that living, changing picture – has grown. Some plants will be starting to mature as you hoped they would, while others may have outworn their welcome; some may never have been meant to linger so long. Be sure to keep your mind on the overall scheme – the original dream tempered by time, the performance of individual plants and the happy chance occurrences that are so frequently part and parcel of a developing garden.

Think of a few small projects, new Plant Watch vigils and some special touches for next year – perhaps a couple of colour adjustments or a bird-attracting native plant.

FURTHER READING

Barrett, Margaret. *Gardening Through the Year*. Viking, Australia, 1986.

Beales, Peter. *Classic Roses*. Collins Harvill, London, 1985.

Brickell, Christopher. *The Royal Horticultural Society Gardeners' Encyclopedia of Plants and Flowers*. Dorling Kindersley, London, 1989.

Brunning's Home Gardener. Angus and Robertson, Sydney, 1979.

Edmanson, Jane. *Cheap and Easy Propagation*. Lothian, Melbourne, 1991.

Elliot, W. Rodger, and Jones, David L. *Encyclopedia of Australian Plants*. 4 vols. Lothian, Melbourne, 1990.

Griffiths, Trevor. *My World of Old Roses*, vol. 1. Nelson, Melbourne, 1986.

Hillier, Harold G. *Hillier's Manual of Trees and Shrubs*. Van Nostrand Reinhold, New York, 1981.

Hitchmough, James. *Garden Bulbs for Australia and New Zealand*. Viking O'Neil, Melbourne, 1989.

Jekyll, Gertrude. *Wall, Water and Woodland Gardens*. Antique Collectors' Club, England, 1982.

Jekyll, Gertrude. *Wood and Garden*. Antique Collectors' Club, England, 1983.

Johnson, Hugh. *The Principles of Gardening*. Mitchell Beazley, London, 1979.

Krempin, Jack. *Palms and Cycads*. Horwitz Grahame, Sydney, 1990.

Latreille, Anne. *The Natural Garden: Ellis Stones: His Life and Work*. Viking O'Neil, Melbourne, 1990.

Lord, Ernest E., and Willis, J. H. *Shrubs and Trees for Australian Gardens*. 5th edn. Lothian, Melbourne, 1984.

Oakman, Harry. *Tropical and Subtropical Gardening*. Jacaranda Press, Brisbane, 1981.

Perry, Frances. *The Water Garden*. Ward Lock, London, 1981.

Pizzetti, Ippolito, and Cocker, Henry. *Flowers: A Guide for Your Garden*. 2 vols. Abrams, New York, 1968.

Ratcliffe, Richard. *Australia's Master Gardener: Paul Sorenson and His Gardens*. Kangaroo Press, Sydney, 1990.

Ross, Deane. *The Ross Guide to Rose Growing*. Lothian, Melbourne, 1990.

Nicholson, Philippa (ed.). *Vita Sackville-West's Garden Book*. Michael Joseph, London, 1968.

Seale, Alan. *Gardening for Pleasure*. Harper and Row, Sydney, 1979.

Simpfendorfer, K. J. *An Introduction to Trees for South-Eastern Australia*. Inkata Press, Melbourne, 1975.

Stackhouse, Shirley. *Shirley Stackhouse's Gardening Year*. Angus and Robertson, Sydney, 1985.

Stones, Ellis. *Australian Garden Design*. Macmillan, Melbourne, 1971.

Thomas, Graham Stuart. *Perennial Garden Plants*. J. M. Dent and Sons, London, 1985.

Tolley, E., and Mead, C. *Herbs*. Sidgwick and Jackson, London, 1985.

Walling, Edna. *Gardens in Australia*. 3rd edn. Oxford University Press, Melbourne, 1946.

Walling, Edna, *The Edna Walling Book of Australian Garden Design*. Anne O'Donovan, Melbourne, 1980.

Williams, Keith A. W. *Native Plants of Queensland*. 2 vols. Keith A. W. Williams, Ipswich, 1979.

Wright, Michael. *The Complete Handbook of Garden Plants*. Rainbird, London, 1984.

Wrigley, John W., and Fagg, Murray. *Australian Native Plants*. William Collins, Sydney, 1979.

ACKNOWLEDGEMENTS

Our thanks go to Tony Fawcett, Editor in Chief of *Australian Home Beautiful* magazine, for his encouragement and interest in *The Australian Garden*, and also to the staff of the National Herbarium, Royal Botanic Gardens, Melbourne, and Maranoa Gardens, Balwyn, Victoria. We are grateful to Norma and Laurence Gedye who guided us through the world of water gardens. A special thanks for the assistance and support given by Elizabeth van Herk, Victor Stoller, Kathy Every and Bob Young; and also to Margaret Barrett and Gail Thomas. We would like to express our appreciation to Leonie Stott, who designed the book; Cathy Larsen for all the illustrations (with the exception of those on page 200, which were drawn by Lisa Berriman); Lorraine Ellis for hand colouring the garden designs; and our editor, Lesley Dunt, for her resolute care and concern for the book.

We wish to thank the following owners of private gardens photographed or illustrated in the book: Phillip Adams, formerly of Hawthorn, Victoria; Margaret and Bruce Appleton, East Malvern, Victoria; Stephanie Alexander and Dur-é Dara, Hawthorn East, Victoria; Flora Anderson, Wonga Park, Victoria; The Bentinck Private Hotel, Woodend, Victoria; Maryanne and Brian Birley, Canterbury, Victoria; Pam Barrand and Wolf Damschitz, Hawthorn East, Victoria; Joanna Barrett, Hawthorn, Victoria; Margaret and John Barrett, Arthurs Creek, Victoria; Nola and Herb Bennetto, Kew, Victoria; Geoffrey Bills, Kew, Victoria; Barbara and John Blanch, Hawthorn, Victoria; Mrs and Mr D. Burns, Bowral, New South Wales; Joan Cameron and Peter Cohn, Ivanhoe, Victoria; Clare Coney and Peter Nicholls, Surrey Hills, Victoria; Convent Gallery, Daylesford, Victoria; John Crisp, Canterbury, Victoria; Gwen and Doug Crocker, Auburn, Victoria; Helen Dunachie, Strathbogie, Victoria; Penny and Clive Dunn, Macedon, Victoria; Barbara and Peter Edmanson, Buronga, New South Wales; Penny, John and Claire Edmanson, Golgol, New South Wales; Mrs and Mr D. Ellerington, Brighton, Victoria; Gabrielle and John Endacott, Surrey Hills, Victoria; June Fullagar, Kew, Victoria; Norma and Laurence Gedye, Doncaster, Victoria; Ann and David Gordon, Irymple, Victoria; Paula and Michael Gorton, Canterbury, Victoria; Lauris Grant, Brunswick, Victoria; Sally Greaves and Peter Hyde, Alphington, Victoria; Trish and John Halfpenny, Yarrawonga, Victoria; Brian Hart, St Ives, New South Wales; Jane and Phillip Hemstritch, Middle Park, Victoria; Anthea Hill, Malvern, Victoria; Judy and Don Hill, Kew, Victoria; Carmel and Evan Hines, Carmelflora Fuchsia Nursery, Ballarat, Victoria; James Hitchmough, Malvern, Victoria; Meryl Hyde, Camberwell, Victoria; Alice Jeffery, Kew, Victoria; Beverley and John Joyce, Toorak, Victoria; Elwyn and Tony Kennedy, Hawthorn, Victoria; Sandy Kilpatrick, Richmond, Victoria; Rosamund and Ivo Krivanek, Camberwell, Victoria; Joan Law-Smith, Macedon, Victoria; Noreen and Jim McCarthy, Kooyong, Victoria; Maria and Michael McGarvie, Eaglemont, Victoria; Kris and Roger McGhee, Canterbury, Victoria; Carolyn and Rob Macafee, Hawthorn East, Victoria; Sandra and Geoffrey Masel, Hawthorn East, Victoria; Marilyn and Ivan Mayes, Toorak, Victoria; John Moran and the late Mary Moran, Toorak, Victoria; Morongo Girls' College, Geelong, Victoria; Lella and Con Nicolas, Hawthorn, Victoria; Geoffrey Nuske and the late Carol Nuske, Doreen, Victoria; Marion Page, Yarrawonga, Victoria; Lyndal and Jeremy Pascoe, Kew, Victoria; Andrea and Bruce Pulbrook, Hawthorn East, Victoria; Janet and Frank Pyke, Hawthorn East, Victoria; Nona Reid, Camberwell, Victoria; Maggie and Max Richards, Surrey Hills, Victoria; Sue and Philipp Schudmak, South Yarra, Victoria; Maree and Stan Schweitzer, Canterbury, Victoria; Jane Scully, Melbourne, Victoria; Nona and Cyril Seward, Kew, Victoria; Leslie van der Sluys, Fitzroy, Victoria; Victor Stoller, Woodend, Victoria; Paul Thompson, Melbourne, Victoria; Cecily and Ian Tulloch, Kew, Victoria; Rob Wallis and Win Janssen, Ferny Creek, Victoria; Lyn and David White, Kallista, Victoria; Beverley and Kelvin Whitford, Canterbury, Victoria; Heather and Roger Wood, Malvern, Victoria; the late Aileen Wren, Kew, Victoria; Kathy Wright, Brighton, Victoria; Mandy and Edward Yencken, Malvern, Victoria.

We would also like to thank the following photographers and magazines for permission to reproduce the photographs on the pages listed: Gary Chowanetz, Robin Gauld, Guy Lamothe and Tony Miller, *Australian Home Beautiful* magazine, pages vii, 1, 3, 4, 6, 7, 8, 10, 11, 12, 13 (above and left), 14, 15, 16, 18, 19, 20–21, 22, 23, 24, 25, 26, 27, 28, 29, 32, 34, 37, 39, 41, 43, 44, 45 (above), 46, 48, 50, 55, 58, 78, 81, 86, 100, 113, 124–25, 127, 134–35, 140, 141, 143, 150, 163, 169, 172, 173, 175, 176, 178, 180, 185, 191 (bottom), 192, 193, 194–95, 197, 199, 203, 207, 208, 210, 211, 216, 236, 240, 242–43, 248, 249, 251, 267, 274 and 276; Rick de Carteret, pages viii, 14, 115, 151 and 170–71; John Colwill, pages 153, 156, 157 (bottom), 159 and 160; Rodger Elliot, page 157 (top); Joy Harland, page 225; Ponch Hawkes, pages 230, 283 and 317; Neil Lorimer, page 183; John Patrick, front jacket photograph of Heide Park and Art Gallery, and pages 233 and 255; Picci Bank, *Gardening Australia* magazine, pages 232 and 270; Bruce Postle, pages 63, 70, 111, 114, 154 and 254; Fritz Prenzel and Australian Picture Library, jacket image of flowering gums; Ted Rotherham, pages 133, 188 and 280; Gail Thomas, pages 296, 301 and 318; and *Your Garden* magazine, page 219.

Lorrie Lawrence designed the gardens shown on pages viii, 1, 6, 10, 12, 13–14, 15, 16 (left), 22–26, 37, 40, 44–45, 46, 51, 88, 122, 170–71, 173, 181, 186, 191 (bottom), 197, 199, 208, 212–13, 217, 227, 228, 231, 242–43, 247, 269 and 276. A number of the owners we have acknowledged – some of whom are professional landscape designers – designed their own gardens. Other professional designers (where known) whose work appears in photographs in the book are: Paul Bangay, page 225; Robert Boyle, pages 27 and 267; Graeme Greenhalgh, page 255; Ellis Stones, page 127; and Edna Walling, page 185.

INDEX